Second Workshop on Abusive Language Online 2018

Brussels, Belgium
31 October 2018

ISBN: 978-1-5108-7419-0

EMNLP 2018

Second Workshop on Abusive Language Online

Proceedings of the Workshop, co-located with EMNLP 2018

October 31, 2018
Brussels, Belgium

Sponsors

Primary Sponsor

Platinum Sponsors

Gold Sponsors

Silver Sponsors

Bronze Sponsors

Order copies of this and other ACL proceedings from:

Association for Computational Linguistics (ACL)
209 N. Eighth Street
Stroudsburg, PA 18360
USA
Tel: +1-570-476-8006
Fax: +1-570-476-0860
acl@aclweb.org

Introduction

Interaction amongst users on social networking platforms can enable constructive and insightful conversations and civic participation; however, on many sites that encourage user interaction, verbal abuse has become commonplace. Abusive behavior such as cyberbullying, hate speech, and scapegoating can poison the social climates within online communities. The last few years have seen a surge in such abusive online behavior, leaving governments, social media platforms, and individuals struggling to deal with the consequences.

As a field that works directly with computational analysis of language, the NLP community is uniquely positioned to address the difficult problem of abusive language online; encouraging collaborative and innovate work in this area is the goal of this workshop. The first year of the workshop saw 14 papers presented in a day-long program including interdisciplinary panels and active discussion. In this second edition, we have aimed to build on the success of the first year, maintaining a focus on computationally detecting abusive language and encouraging interdisciplinary work. Reflecting the growing research focus on this topic, the number of submissions received more than doubled from 22 in last year's edition of the workshop to 48 this year.

The workshop will be broken into four sessions throughout the day. In the first session, we are delighted to have two invited speakers from beyond the NLP community joining us to share their unique perspectives and expertise:

Mikki Kendall

The Gamification of Hate

Mikki Kendall has written for The Washington Post, Boston Globe, Time, Ebony, Essence, and other online and print markets. Born and raised in Chicago, her books *Hood Feminism* and *Amazons, Abolitionists, and Activists: A Graphic History of Women's Fight For their Rights* will be published by Penguin Random House in 2019. Having experienced online harassment, she has worked on projects related to abusive online cultures for nearly a decade.

Maryant Fernández Pérez

The Damaging Effect of Privatised Law Enforcement in Tackling Illegal Content

Maryant Fernández Pérez is a Senior Policy Advisor at European Digital Rights (EDRi) and a lawyer admitted to the Madrid Bar association. She leads EDRi's work on surveillance and law enforcement, freedom of expression and intermediary liability, net neutrality, digital trade, transparency, internet governance and international engagement. Maryant is the author of several publications and has been a speaker at multiple conferences in Europe and around the world.

In the second session, a panel of experts both from within and outside of the NLP community will debate and frame the major issues facing the computational analysis of abusive language online, particularly as relevant to the morning's talks. This panel will be followed by a period for a discussion amongst all attendees.

The third session will be used for sharing the research results archived in these proceedings, presented as posters to encourage discussion. Finally, in the fourth session, the panelists, speakers, and participants will return to give feedback on what they've seen and heard, leading into a synthesizing discussion amongst all attendees facilitated by workshop organizer Jacqueline Wernimont. With this format we aim to open a space for synergies between the talks, panels, and discussions throughout the day and encourage interdisciplinary approaches to future work in the field.

The submissions to be presented at the workshop represent a compelling diversity of methods, topics, and approaches to the difficult problem of abusive language online, including embedding-based, adversarial, and neural models; the creation of new datasets from diverse sources such as WhatsApp and white supremacist forums; in-depth error analysis and classification interpretability analysis; and studies of languages beyond English such as Slovene, Croatian, and code-mixed Hindi and English. The workshop received 48 paper submissions, of which 21 were accepted, for an acceptance rate of 43%.

In organizing this workshop we collaborated with StackOverflow to curate a dataset of moderated comments, proposed as an unshared task. This dataset was ultimately utilized by one of the accepted papers and will hopefully encourage more work moving forward in close collaboration with industry partners. We have also reached an agreement with the journal First Monday to publish a special issue resulting from the joint proceedings of this workshop and the previous edition, wherein a subset of the papers will be nominated and the authors given an opportunity to expand them into full journal articles.

In closing, we wish to extend our sincere gratitude to our sponsors for their generous financial contributions and our reviewers for their time and expertise, without which this workshop would not have been possible.

- Zeerak, Jacque, Vinod, Darja, Ruihong, and Rob

Kathleen McKeown, Columbia University, United States of America
Mainack Mondal, Max Planck Institute for Software Systems, Germany
Hamdy Mubarak, Qatar Computing Research Institute, Qatar
Smruthi Mukund, A9.com Inc, United States of America
Kevin Munger, New York University, United States of America
Preslav Nakov, Qatar Computing Research Institute, Qatar
Chikashi Nobata, Apple, United States of America
Gustavo Paetzold, Federal University of Technology - Paraná, Brasil
John Pavlopoulos, StrainTek, Greece
Daniel Preoţiuc-Pietro, Bloomberg, United States of America
Michal Ptaszynski, University of Duisburg-Essen, Germany
Vladan Radosavljevic, OLX Group, Argentina
Georg Rehm, Deutsche Forschungszentrum für Künstliche Intelligenz, Germany
Björn Ross, University of Duisburg-Essen, Germany
Masoud Rouhizadeh, Stony Brook University & University of Pennsylvania, United States of America
Niloofar Safi Samghabadi, University of Houston, United States of America
Christina Sauper, Facebook, United States of America
Xanda Schofield, Cornell, United States of America
Caroline Sinders, Wikimedia Foundation, United States of America
Maite Taboada, Simon Fraser University, Canada
Dennis Yi Tenen, Columbia University, United States of America
Dimitrios Tsarapatsanis, University of Sheffield, United Kingdom
Ingmar Weber, Qatar Computing Research Institute, Qatar
Amanda Williams, University of Bristol, United Kingdom
Michael Wojatzki, University of Duisburg-Essen, Germany
Lilja Øvrelid, University of Oslo, Norway

Invited Speakers:

Mikki Kendall, Writer and Diversity Consultant
Maryant Fernandez Perez, Senior Policy Advisor of European Digital Rights

Table of Contents

Conference Program

Wednesday, October 31, 2018

9:00–9:15	***Opening Remarks***
9:15–10:00	*Invited Speaker* Mikki Kendall
10:00–10:45	*Invited Speaker* Maryant Fernandez Perez
10:45–11:15	***Break***
11:15–12:15	***Panel***
12:15–12:45	***Plenary Discussions***
12:45–14:00	***Lunch***
14:00–15:30	***Posters***
14:00–15:30	*Social contagion in ethnic abusive swearing during periods of increased terrorist activity* Christoph Spörlein
14:00–15:30	*Neural Character-based Composition Models for Abuse Detection* Pushkar Mishra, Helen Yannakoudakis and Ekaterina Shutova
14:00–15:30	*Hate Speech Dataset from a White Supremacy Forum* Ona de Gibert, Naiara Perez, Aitor García Pablos and Montse Cuadros
14:00–15:30	*A Review of Standard Text Classification Practices for Multi-label Toxicity Identification of Online Content* Isuru Gunasekara and Isar Nejadgholi

Neural Character-based Composition Models for Abuse Detection

Pushkar Mishra
Dept. of CS & Technology
University of Cambridge
United Kingdom
pm576@alumni.cam.ac.uk

Helen Yannakoudakis
The ALTA Institute
University of Cambridge
United Kingdom
hy260@cl.cam.ac.uk

Ekaterina Shutova
ILLC
University of Amsterdam
The Netherlands
e.shutova@uva.nl

Abstract

The advent of social media in recent years has fed into some highly undesirable phenomena such as proliferation of offensive language, hate speech, sexist remarks, etc. on the Internet. In light of this, there have been several efforts to automate the detection and moderation of such abusive content. However, deliberate obfuscation of words by users to evade detection poses a serious challenge to the effectiveness of these efforts. The current state of the art approaches to abusive language detection, based on recurrent neural networks, do not explicitly address this problem and resort to a generic OOV (out of vocabulary) embedding for unseen words. However, in using a single embedding for all unseen words we lose the ability to distinguish between obfuscated and non-obfuscated or rare words. In this paper, we address this problem by designing a model that can compose embeddings for unseen words. We experimentally demonstrate that our approach significantly advances the current state of the art in abuse detection on datasets from two different domains, namely Twitter and Wikipedia talk page.

1 Introduction

Pew Research Center has recently uncovered several disturbing trends in communications on the Internet. As per their report (Duggan, 2014), 40% of adult Internet users have personally experienced harassment online, and 60% have witnessed the use of offensive names and expletives. Expectedly, the majority (66%) of those who have personally faced harassment have had their most recent incident occur on a social networking website or app. While most of these websites and apps provide ways of flagging offensive and hateful content, only 8.8% of the victims have actually considered using such provisions.

Two conclusions can be drawn from these statistics: (i) *abuse* (a term we use henceforth to collectively refer to toxic language, hate speech, etc.) is prevalent in social media, and (ii) passive and/or manual techniques for curbing its propagation (such as flagging) are neither effective nor easily scalable (Pavlopoulos et al., 2017). Consequently, the efforts to automate the detection and moderation of such content have been gaining popularity (Waseem and Hovy, 2016; Wulczyn et al., 2017).

In their work, Nobata et al. (2016) describe the task of achieving effective automation as an inherently difficult one due to several ingrained complexities; a prominent one they highlight is the deliberate structural obfuscation of words (for example, *fcukk*, *w0m3n*, *banislam*, etc.) by users to evade detection. Simple spelling correction techniques and edit-distance procedures fail to provide information about such obfuscations because: (i) words may be excessively fudged (e.g., *a55h0le*, *n1gg3r*) or concatenated (e.g., *stupidbitch*, *feminismishate*), and (ii) they fail to take into account the fact that some character sequences like *musl* and *wom* are more frequent and more indicative of abuse than others (Waseem and Hovy, 2016).

Nobata et al. (2016) go on to show that simple character n-gram features prove to be highly promising for supervised classification approaches to abuse detection due to their robustness to spelling variations; however, they do not address obfuscations explicitly. Waseem and Hovy (2016) and Wulczyn et al. (2017) also use character n-grams to attain impressive results on their respective datasets. That said, the current state of the art methods do not exploit character-level information, but instead utilize recurrent neural network (RNN) models operating on word embeddings alone (Pavlopoulos et al., 2017; Badjatiya et al., 2017). Since the problem of deliberately

Proceedings of the Second Workshop on Abusive Language Online (ALW2), pages 1–10
Brussels, Belgium, October 31, 2018. ©2018 Association for Computational Linguistics

noisy input is not explicitly accounted for, these approaches resort to the use of a generic OOV (out of vocabulary) embedding for words not seen in the training phase. However, in using a single embedding for all unseen words, such approaches lose the ability to distinguish obfuscated words from non-obfuscated or rare ones. Recently, Mishra et al. (2018) and Qian et al. (2018), working with the same Twitter dataset as we do, reported that many of the misclassifications by their RNN-based methods happen due to intentional misspellings and/or rare words.

Our contributions are two-fold: first, we experimentally demonstrate that character n-gram features are complementary to the current state of the art RNN approaches to abusive language detection and can strengthen their performance. We then explicitly address the problem of deliberately noisy input by constructing a model that operates at the character level and learns to predict embeddings for unseen words. We show that the integration of this model with the character-enhanced RNN methods further advances the state of the art in abuse detection on three datasets from two different domains, namely Twitter and Wikipedia talk page. To the best of our knowledge, this is the first work to use character-based word composition models for abuse detection.

2   Related Work

Yin et al. (2009) were among the first ones to apply supervised learning to the task of abuse detection. They worked with a linear support vector machine trained on local (e.g., n-grams), contextual (e.g., similarity of a post to its neighboring posts), and sentiment-based (e.g., presence of expletives) features to recognize posts involving harassment.

Djuric et al. (2015) worked with comments taken from the Yahoo Finance portal and demonstrated that distributional representations of comments learned using the *paragraph2vec* framework (Le and Mikolov, 2014) can outperform simpler bag-of-words BOW features under supervised classification settings for hate speech detection. Nobata et al. (2016) improved upon the results of Djuric et al. by training their classifier on an amalgamation of features derived from four different categories: linguistic (e.g., count of insult words), syntactic (e.g. part-of-speech POS tags), distributional semantic (e.g., word and comment embeddings) and n-gram based (e.g., word bi-grams).

They noted that while the best results were obtained with all features combined, character n-grams had the highest impact on performance.

Waseem and Hovy (2016) utilized a logistic regression (LR) classifier to distinguish amongst racist, sexist, and clean tweets in a dataset of approximately $16k$ of them. They found that character n-grams coupled with gender information of users formed the optimal feature set for the task. On the other hand, geographic and word-length distribution features provided little to no improvement. Experimenting with the same dataset, Badjatiya et al. (2017) improved on their results by training a gradient-boosted decision tree (GBDT) classifier on averaged word embeddings learnt using a long short-term memory (LSTM) models initialized with random embeddings. Mishra et al. (2018) went on to incorporate community-based profiling features of users in their classification methods, which led to the state of the art performance on this dataset.

Waseem (2016) studied the influence of annotators' knowledge on the task of hate speech detection. For this, they sampled $7k$ tweets from the same corpus as Waseem and Hovy (2016) and recruited expert and amateur annotators to annotate the tweets as *racism*, *sexism*, *both* or *neither*. Combining this dataset with that of Waseem and Hovy (2016), Park et al. (2017) evaluated the efficacy of a 2-step classification process: they first used an LR classifier to separate abusive and non-abusive tweets, and then used another LR classifier to distinguish between the racist and sexist ones. They showed that this setup had comparable performance to a 1-step classification approach based on convolutional neural networks (CNNs) operating on word and character embeddings.

Wulczyn et al. (2017) created three different datasets of comments collected from the English Wikipedia Talk page: one was annotated for personal attacks, another for toxicity, and the third for aggression. They achieved their best results with a multi-layered perceptron classifier trained on character n-gram features. Working with the personal attack and toxicity datasets, Pavlopoulos et al. (2017) outperformed the methods of Wulczyn et al. by having a gated recurrent unit (GRU) to model the comments as dense low-dimensional representations, followed by an LR layer to classify the comments based on those representations.

Davidson et al. (2017) produced a dataset of

about $25k$ *racist*, *offensive* or *clean* tweets. They evaluated several multi-class classifiers with the aim of discerning clean tweets from racist and offensive tweets, while simultaneously being able to distinguish between the racist and offensive ones. Their best model was an LR classifier trained using TF–IDF and POS n-gram features coupled with features like count of hash tags and number of words.

3 Datasets

Following the proceedings of the 1st *Workshop on Abusive Language Online* (Waseem et al., 2017), we use three datasets from two different domains.

3.1 Twitter

Waseem and Hovy (2016) prepared a dataset of $16,914$ tweets from a corpus of approximately $136k$ tweets retrieved over a period of two months. They bootstrapped their collection process with a search for commonly used slurs and expletives related to religious, sexual, gender and ethnic minorities. After having manually annotated $16,914$ of the tweets as *racism*, *sexism* or *neither*, they asked an expert to review their annotations in order to mitigate against any biases. The inter-annotator agreement was reported at $\kappa = 0.84$, with further insight that 85% of all the disagreements occurred in the *sexism* class alone.

The authors released the dataset as a list of $16,907$ tweet IDs and their corresponding annotations. We could only retrieve $16,202$ of the tweets with python's *Tweepy* library since some of them have been deleted or their visibility has been limited. Of the ones retrieved, 1,939 (12%) are *racism*, 3,148 (19.4%) are *sexism*, and the remaining 11,115 (68.6%) are *neither*; the original dataset has a similar distribution, i.e., 11.7% *racism*, 20.0% *sexism*, and 68.3% *neither*.

3.2 Wikipedia talk page

Wulczyn et al. (2017) extracted approximately $63M$ talk page comments from a public dump of the full history of English Wikipedia released in January 2016. From this corpus, they randomly sampled comments to form three datasets on personal attack, toxicity and aggression, and engaged workers from *CrowdFlower* to annotate them. Noting that the datasets were highly skewed towards the non-abusive classes, the authors oversampled comments from banned users to attain a more uniform distribution.

In this work, we utilize the toxicity and personal attack datasets, henceforth referred to as W-TOX and W-ATT respectively. Each comment in both of these datasets was annotated by at least 10 workers. We use the majority annotation of each comment to resolve its gold label: if a comment is deemed toxic (alternatively, attacking) by more than half of the annotators, we label it as *abusive*; otherwise, as *non-abusive*. 13,590 (11.7%) of the 115,864 comments in W-ATT and 15,362 (9.6%) of the 159,686 comments in W-TOX are abusive. Wikipedia comments, with an average length of 25 tokens, are considerably longer than the tweets which have an average length of 8.

4 Methods

We experiment with ten different methods, eight of which have an RNN operating on word embeddings. Six of these eight also include character n-gram features, and four further integrate our word composition model. The remaining two comprise an RNN that works directly on character inputs.

Hidden-state (HS). As our first baseline, we adopt the "RNN" method of Pavlopoulos et al. (2017) since it produces state of the art results on the Wikipedia datasets. Given a text formed of a sequence $w_1, \ldots, w_n$ of words (represented by d-dimensional word embeddings), the method utilizes a 1-layer GRU to encode the words into hidden states $h_1, \ldots, h_n$. This is followed by an LR layer that classifies the text based on the last hidden state h_n. We modify the authors' original architecture in two minor ways: we extend the 1-layer GRU to a 2-layer GRU and use softmax as the activation in the LR layer instead of sigmoid.[1]

Following Pavlopoulos et al., we initialize the word embeddings to GLoVe vectors (Pennington et al., 2014). In all our methods, words not present in the GLoVe set are randomly initialized in the range ±0.05, indicating the lack of semantic information. By not mapping these words to a single random embedding, we mitigate against the errors that may arise due to their conflation (Madhyastha et al., 2015). A special OOV (out of vocabulary) token is also initialized in the same range. All the embeddings are updated during training, allowing for some of the randomly-initialized ones to get

---

[1] We also experimented with 1-layer GRU/LSTM and 1/2-layer bi-directional GRUs/LSTMs but the performance only worsened or showed no gains; using sigmoid instead of softmax did not have any noteworthy effects on the results either.

task-tuned (Kim, 2014); the ones that do not get tuned lie closely clustered around the OOV token to which unseen words in the test set are mapped.

Word-sum (WS). The "LSTM+GLoVe+GBDT" method of Badjatiya et al. (2017) constitutes our second baseline. The authors first employ an LSTM to task-tune GLoVe-initialized word embeddings by propagating error back from an LR layer. They then train a gradient-boosted decision tree (GBDT) classifier to classify texts based on the average of the constituent word embeddings.[2] We make two minor modifications to the original method: we utilize a 2-layer GRU[3] instead of the LSTM to tune the embeddings, and we train the GBDT classifier on the L_2-normalized sum of the embeddings instead of their average.[4]

Hidden-state + char n-grams (HS + CNG). Here we extend the *hidden-state* baseline: we train the 2-layer GRU architecture as before, but now concatenate its last hidden state h_n with L_2-normalized character n-gram counts to train a GBDT classifier.

Augmented hidden-state + char n-grams (AUGMENTED HS + CNG). In the above methods, unseen words in the test set are simply mapped to the OOV token since we do not have a way of obtaining any semantic information about them. However, this is undesirable since racial slurs and expletives are often deliberately fudged by users to prevent detection. In using a single embedding for all unseen words, we lose the ability to distinguish such obfuscations from other non-obfuscated or rare words. Taking inspiration from the effectiveness of character-level features in abuse detection, we address this issue by having a character-based word composition model that can compose embeddings for unseen words in the test set (Pinter et al., 2017). We then augment the *hidden-state + char n-grams* method with it.

Specifically, our model (Figure 1b) comprises a 2-layer bi-directional LSTM, followed by a hidden layer with *tanh* non-linearity and an output layer at the end. The model takes as input a sequence $c_1, \ldots, c_k$ of characters, represented as one-hot vectors, from a fixed vocabulary (i.e., lowercase English alphabet and digits) and outputs a d-dimensional embedding for the word '$c_1 \ldots c_k$'. Bi-directionality of the LSTM allows for the semantics of both the prefix and the suffix (last hidden forward and backward state) of the input word to be captured, which are then combined to form the hidden state for the input word. The model is trained by minimizing the mean squared error (MSE) between the embeddings that it produces and the task-tuned embeddings of words in the training set. This ensures that newly composed embeddings are endowed with characteristics from both the GLoVe space as well as the task-tuning process. While approaches like that of Bojanowski et al. (2017) can also compose embeddings for unseen words, they cannot endow the newly composed embeddings with characteristics from the task-tuning process; this may constitute a significant drawback (Kim, 2014).

During the training of our character-based word composition model, to emphasize frequent words, we feed a word as many times as it appears in the training corpus. We note that a 1-layer CNN with global max-pooling in place of the 2-layer LSTM provides comparable performance while requiring significantly less time to train. This is expected since words are not very long sequences, and the filters of the CNN are able to capture the different character n-grams within them.

Context hidden-state + char n-grams (CONTEXT HS + CNG). In the *augmented hidden-state + char n-grams* method, the word composition model infers semantics of unseen words solely on the basis of the characters in them. However, for many words, semantic inference and sense disambiguation require context, i.e., knowledge of character sequences in the vicinity. An example is the word *cnt* that has different meanings in the sentences *"I cnt undrstand this!"* and *"You feminist cnt!"*, i.e., *cannot* in the former and the sexist slur *cunt* in the latter. Yet another example is an obfuscation like *''You mot otherf uc ker!* where the expletive *motherfucker* cannot be properly inferred from any fragment without the knowledge of surrounding character sequences.

---

[2] In their work, the authors report that initializing embeddings randomly rather than with GLoVe yields state of the art performance on the Twitter dataset that we are using. However, we found the opposite when performing 10-fold stratified cross-validation (CV). A possible explanation of this lies in the authors' decision to not use stratification, which for such a highly imbalanced dataset can lead to unexpected outcomes (Forman and Scholz, 2010). Furthermore, the authors train their LSTM on the entire dataset including the test part without any early stopping criterion; this facilitates overfitting of the randomly-initialized embeddings.

[3] The deeper 2-layer GRU slightly improves performance.

[4] L_2-normalized sum ensures uniformity of range across the feature set in all our methods; GBDT, being a tree based model, is not affected by the choice of monotonic function.

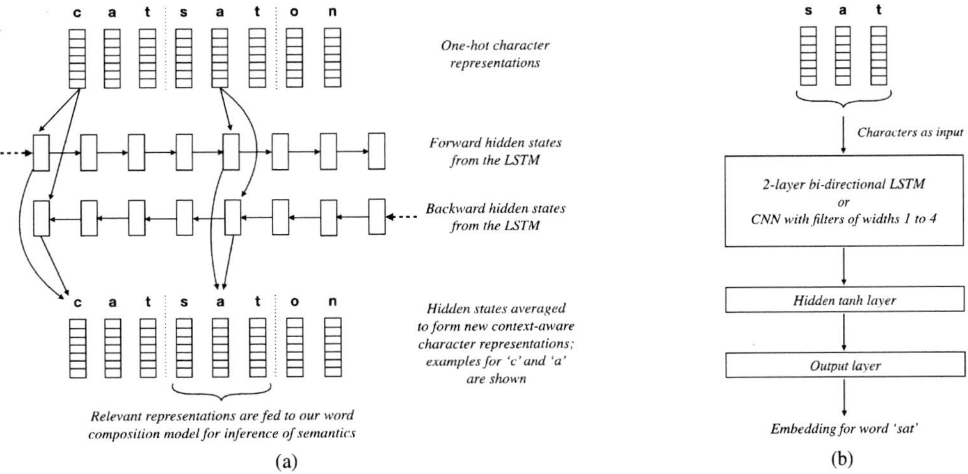

Figure 1: Context-aware approach to word composition. The figure on the left shows how the encoder extracts context-aware representations of characters in the phrase *"cat sat on"* from their one-hot representations. The dotted lines denote the space character ␣ which demarcates word boundaries. Semantics of an unseen word, e.g., *sat*, can then be inferred by our word composition model shown on the right.

To address this, we develop *context-aware representations* for characters as inputs to our character-based word composition model instead of one-hot representations.[5] We introduce an encoder architecture to produce the context-aware representations. Specifically, given a text formed of a sequence $w_1, \ldots, w_n$ of words, the encoder takes as input one-hot representations of the characters $c_1, \ldots, c_k$ within the concatenated sequence '$w_1␣ \ldots ␣w_n$', where ␣ denotes the space character. This input is passed through a bi-directional LSTM that produces hidden states $h_1, \ldots, h_k$, one for every character. Each hidden state, referred to as context-aware character representation, is the average of its designated forward and backward states; hence, it captures both the preceding as well as the following contexts of the character it corresponds to. Figure 1 illustrates how the context-aware representations are extracted and used for inference by our character-based word composition model. The model is trained in the same manner as done in the *augmented hidden-state + char n-grams* method, i.e., by minimizing the MSE between the embeddings that it produces and the task-tuned embeddings of words in the training set (initialized with GLoVe). However,

the inputs now are context-aware representations of characters instead of one-hot representations.

Word-sum + char n-grams (WS + CNG), Augmented word-sum + char n-grams (AUGMENTED WS + CNG), and Context word-sum + char n-grams (CONTEXT WS + CNG). These methods are identical to the *(context/ augmented) hidden-state + char n-grams* methods except that here we include the character n-grams and our character-based word composition model on top of the *word-sum* baseline.

Char hidden-state (CHAR HS) and Char word-sum (CHAR WS). In all the methods described up till now, the input to the core RNN is word embeddings. To gauge whether character-level inputs are themselves sufficient or not, we construct two methods based on the *character to word* (C2W) approach of Ling et al. (2015). For the *char hidden-state* method, the input is one-hot representations of characters from a fixed vocabulary. These representations are encoded into a sequence $w_1, \ldots, w_n$ of intermediate word embeddings by a 2-layer bi-directional LSTM. The word embeddings are then fed into a 2-layer GRU that transforms them into hidden states $h_1, \ldots, h_n$. Finally, as in the *hidden-state* baseline, an LR layer with softmax activation uses the last hidden state h_n to perform classification while propagating error backwards to train the network. The *char word-sum* method

---

[5]We also experimented with word-level context but did not get any significant improvements. We believe this is due to higher variance at word level than at the character level.

is similar except that once the network has been trained, we use the intermediate word embeddings produced by it to train a GBDT classifier in the same manner as done in the *word-sum* baseline.

5 Experiments and Results

5.1 Experimental setup

We normalize the input by lowercasing all words and removing stop words. For the GRU architecture, we use exactly the same hyper-parameters as Pavlopoulos et al. (2017),[6] i.e., 128 hidden units, Glorot initialization, cross-entropy loss, and Adam optimizer (Kingma and Ba, 2015). Badjatiya et al. (2017) also use the same settings except they have fewer hidden units. The LSTM in our character-based word composition model has 256 hidden units while that in our encoder has 64; the CNN has filters of widths varying from 1 to 4. The results we report are with an LSTM-based word composition model. In all the models, besides dropout regularization (Srivastava et al., 2014), we hold out a small part of the training set as validation data to prevent over-fitting. We use 300d embeddings and 1 to 5 character n-grams for Wikipedia and 200d embeddings and 1 to 4 character n-grams for Twitter. We implement the models in *Keras* (Chollet et al., 2015) with *Theano* back-end. We employ *Lightgbm* (Ke et al., 2017) as our GDBT classifier and tune its hyper-parameters using 5-fold grid search.

5.2 Twitter results

For the Twitter dataset, unlike previous research (Badjatiya et al., 2017; Park and Fung, 2017), we report the macro precision, recall, and F_1 averaged over 10 folds of stratified CV (Table 1). For a classification problem with N classes, macro precision (similarly, macro recall and macro F_1) is given by:

$$Macro\ P = \frac{1}{N}\sum_{i=1}^{N} P_i$$

where P_i denotes precision on class i. Macro metrics provide a better sense of effectiveness on the minority classes (Van Asch, 2013).

We observe that character n-grams (CNG) consistently enhance performance, while our augmented approach (AUGMENTED) further improves

upon the results obtained with character n-grams. All the improvements are statistically significant with $p < 0.05$ under 10-fold CV paired t-test.

As Ling et al. (2015) noted in their POS tagging experiments, we observe that the CHAR HS and CHAR WS methods perform worse than their counterparts that use pre-trained word embeddings, i.e., the HS and WS baselines respectively.

To further analyze the performance of our best methods (CONTEXT/AUGMENTED WS/HS + CNG), we also examine the results on the racism and sexism classes individually (Table 2). As before, we see that our approach consistently improves over the baselines, and the improvements are statistically significant under paired t-tests.

Method	P	R	F_1
HS	79.14	77.06	78.01
CHAR HS	79.48	69.00	72.36
HS + CNG[†]	80.36	**78.20**	79.19
AUGMENTED HS + CNG[†]	81.28	77.84	**79.37**
CONTEXT HS + CNG[†]	**81.39**	77.47	79.21
WS	80.78	72.83	75.93
CHAR WS	80.04	68.17	71.94
WS + CNG[†]	83.16	76.60	79.31
AUGMENTED WS + CNG[†]	**83.50**	**77.20**	**79.80**
CONTEXT WS + CNG[†]	83.44	77.06	79.67

Table 1: Results on the Twitter dataset. The methods we propose are denoted by [†]. Our best method (AUGMENTED WS + CNG) significantly outperforms all other methods.

Method	P	R	F_1
HS	74.15	72.46	73.24
AUGMENTED HS + CNG[†]	76.28	**72.72**	**74.40**
CONTEXT HS + CNG[†]	**76.61**	72.15	74.26
WS	76.43	67.77	71.78
AUGMENTED WS + CNG[†]	**78.17**	72.20	**75.01**
CONTEXT WS + CNG[†]	77.90	**72.26**	74.91

(a) Racism

Method	P	R	F_1
HS	76.04	68.84	72.24
AUGMENTED HS + CNG[†]	80.07	**69.28**	**74.26**
CONTEXT HS + CNG[†]	**80.29**	68.52	73.92
WS	81.75	57.37	67.38
AUGMENTED WS + CNG[†]	85.61	**65.91**	**74.44**
CONTEXT WS + CNG[†]	**85.80**	65.41	74.18

(b) Sexism

Table 2: The baselines (WS, HS) vs. our best approaches ([†]) on the racism and sexism classes.

Additionally, we note that the AUGMENTED WS + CNG method improves the F_1 score of the WS

+ CNG method from 74.12 to 75.01 for the racism class, and from 74.03 to 74.44 for the sexism class. The AUGMENTED HS + CNG method similarly improves the F_1 score of the HS + CNG method from 74.00 to 74.40 on the racism class while making no notable difference on the sexism class.

We see that the CONTEXT HS/WS + CNG methods do not perform as well as the AUGMENTED HS/WS + CNG methods. One reason for this is that the Twitter dataset is not able to expose the methods to enough contexts due to its small size. Moreover, because the collection of this dataset was bootstrapped with a search for certain commonly-used abusive words, many such words are shared across multiple tweets belonging to different classes. Given the above, context-aware character representations perhaps do not provide substantial distinctive information.

5.3 Wikipedia results

Following previous work (Pavlopoulos et al., 2017; Wulczyn et al., 2017), we conduct a standard 60:40 train–test split experiment on the two Wikipedia datasets. Specifically, from W-TOX, $95,692$ comments (10.0% abusive) are used for training and $63,994$ (9.1% abusive) for testing; from W-ATT, $70,000$ (11.8% abusive) are used for training and $45,854$ (11.7% abusive) for testing. Table 3 reports the macro F_1 scores. We do not report scores from the CHAR HS and CHAR WS methods since they showed poor preliminary results compared to the HS and WS baselines.

Method	W-TOX	W-ATT
HS	88.65	86.28
HS + CNG[†]	89.29	87.32
AUGMENTED HS + CNG[†]	89.31	87.33
CONTEXT HS + CNG[†]	**89.35**	**87.44**
WS	85.49	84.35
WS + CNG[†]	87.12	85.80
AUGMENTED WS + CNG[†]	87.02	85.75
CONTEXT WS + CNG[†]	**87.16**	**85.81**

Table 3: Macro F_1 scores on the two Wikipedia datasets. The current state of the art method for these datasets is HS. [†] denotes the methods we propose. Our best method (CONTEXT HS + CNG) outperforms all the other methods.

Mirroring the analysis carried out for the Twitter dataset, Table 4 further compares the performance of our best methods for Wikipedia (CONTEXT/AUGMENTED HS + CNG) with that of the state of the art baseline (HS) on specifically the abusive classes of W-TOX and W-ATT.

Method	P	R	F_1
HS	84.48	74.60	79.24
AUGMENTED HS + CNG[†]	**85.43**	76.02	80.45
CONTEXT HS + CNG[†]	85.42	**76.17**	**80.53**

(a) W-TOX

Method	P	R	F_1
HS	78.61	72.88	75.64
AUGMENTED HS + CNG[†]	81.23	74.06	77.48
CONTEXT HS + CNG[†]	**81.39**	**74.28**	**77.67**

(b) W-ATT

Table 4: The current state of the art baseline (HS) vs. our best methods ([†]) on the abusive classes of W-TOX and W-ATT.

We observe that the augmented approach substantially improves over the state of the art baseline. Unlike in the case of Twitter, our context-aware setup for word composition is now able to further enhance performance courtesy of the larger size of the datasets which increases the availability of contexts. All improvements are significant ($p < 0.05$) under paired t-tests. We note, however, that the gains we get here with the word composition model are relatively small compared to those we get for Twitter. This difference can be explained by the fact that: (i) Wikipedia comments are less noisy than the tweets and contain fewer obfuscations, and (ii) the Wikipedia datasets, being much larger, expose the methods to more words during training, hence reducing the likelihood of unseen words being important to the semantics of the comments they belong to (Kim et al., 2016).

Like Pavlopoulos et al. (2017), we see that the methods that involve summation of word embeddings (WS) perform significantly worse on the Wikipedia datasets compared to those that use hidden state (HS); however, their performance is comparable or even superior on the Twitter dataset. This contrast is best explained by the observation of Nobata et al. (2016) that taking average or sum of word embeddings compromises contextual and word order information. While this is beneficial in the case of tweets which are short and loosely-structured, it leads to poor performance of the WS and WS + CNG methods on the Wikipedia datasets, with the addition of the word composition model (CONTEXT/AUGMENTED WS + CNG) providing little to no improvements.

Abusive sample	Predicted class		
	WS	**WS + CNG**	**AUGMENTED WS + CNG**
@mention I love how the Islamofascists recruit 14 and 15 year old jihadis and then talk about minors in reference to 17 year olds.	*neither*	*racism*	*racism*
@mention @mention @mention As a certified inmate of the Islamasylum, you don't have the ability to judge.	*neither*	*racism*	*racism*
@mention "I'll be ready in 5 minutes" from a girl usually means "I'll be ready in 20+ minutes." #notsexist #knownfromexperience	*neither*	*sexism*	*sexism*
RT @mention: #isis #muslim #Islamophobia? I think the word you're searching for is #Islamorealism http://t.co/NyihT8Bqyu http://t.c...	*neither*	*neither*	*racism*
@mention @mention And looking at your page, I can see that you are in the business of photoshopping images, Islamist cocksucker.	*neither*	*neither*	*racism*
I think Kat is on the wrong show. #mkr is for people who can cook. #stupidbitch #hopeyouareeliminated	*neither*	*neither*	*sexism*
@mention because w0m3n are a5sh0les #feminismishate	*neither*	*neither*	*sexism*

Table 5: Improved classification upon the addition of character n-grams (CNG) and our word composition model (AUGMENTED). Names of users have been replaced with *mention* for anonymity.

6 Discussion

To investigate the extent to which obfuscated words can be a problem, we extract a number of statistics. Specifically, we notice that out of the approximately $16k$ unique tokens present in the Twitter dataset, there are about $5.2k$ tokens that we cannot find in the English dictionary.[7] Around 600 of these $5.2k$ tokens are present in the racist tweets, $1.6k$ in the sexist tweets, and the rest in tweets that are neither. Examples from the racist tweets include *fuckbag, ezidiz, islamofascists, islamistheproblem, islamasylum* and *isisaremuslims*, while those from the sexist tweets include *c*nt, bbbbitch, feminismisawful*, and *stupidbitch*. Given that the racist and sexist tweets come from a small number of unique users, 5 and 527 respectively, we believe that the presence of obfuscated words would be even more pronounced if tweets were procured from more unique users.

In the case of the Wikipedia datasets, around $15k$ unique tokens in the abusive comments of both W-TOX and W-ATT are not attested in the English dictionary. Examples of such tokens from W-TOX include *fuggin, n*gga, fuycker*, and *1d10t*; and from W-ATT include *f**king, beeeitch, musulmans*, and *motherfucken*. In comparison to the tweets, the Wikipedia comments use more "standard" language. This is validated by the fact that only 14% of the tokens present in W-TOX and W-ATT are absent from the English dictionary as opposed to 32% of the tokens in the Twitter dataset even though the Wikipedia ones are almost ten times larger.

Across the three datasets, we note that the addition of character n-gram features enhances the performance of RNN-based methods, corroborating the previous findings that they capture complementary structural and lexical information of words. The inclusion of our character-based word composition model yields state of the art results on all the datasets, demonstrating the benefits of inferring the semantics of unseen words. Table 5 shows some abusive samples from Twitter that are misclassified by the WS baseline method but are correctly classified upon the addition of character n-grams (WS + CNG) and the further addition of our character-based word composition model (AUGMENTED WS + CNG).

Many of the abusive tweets that remain misclassified by the AUGMENTED WS + CNG method are those that are part of some abusive discourse (e.g., *@Mich_McConnell Just "her body" right?*) or contain URLs to abusive content (e.g., *@salmonfarmer1: Logic in the world of Islam http://t.co/6nALv2HPc3*).

In the case of the Wikipedia datasets, there are abusive examples like *smyou have a message re your last change, go fuckyourself!!!* and *F-uc-k you, a-ss-hole Motherf–ucker!* that are misclassified by the state of the art HS baseline and the HS + CNG method but correctly classified by our best method for the datasets, i.e., CONTEXT HS + CNG.

---

[7] We use the US English spell-checking utility provided by the *PyEnchant* library of python.

Word	Similar words in training set
women	*girls, woman, females, chicks, ladies*
w0m3n[†]	*woman, women, girls, ladies, chicks*
cunt	*twat, prick, faggot, slut, asshole*
a5sh0les[†]	*assholes, stupid, cunts, twats, faggots*
stupidbitch[†]	*idiotic, stupid, dumb, ugly, women*
jihad	*islam, muslims, sharia, terrorist, jihadi*
jihaaadi[†]	*terrorists, islamist, jihadists, muslims*
terroristislam[†]	*terrorists, muslims, attacks, extremists*
fuckyouass[†]	*fuck, shit, fucking, damn, hell*

Table 6: Words in the training set that exhibit high cosine similarity to the given word. The ones marked with [†] are not seen during training; embeddings for them are composed using our word composition model.

To ascertain the effectiveness of our task-tuning process for embeddings, we conducted a qualitative analysis, validating that semantically similar words cluster together in the embedding space. Analogously, we assessed the merits of our word composition model by verifying the neighbors of embeddings formed by it for obfuscated words not seen during training. Table 6 provides some examples. We see that our model correctly infers the semantics of obfuscated words, even in cases where obfuscation is by concatenation of words.

7 Conclusions

In this paper, we considered the problem of obfuscated words in the field of automated abuse detection. Working with three datasets from two different domains, namely Twitter and Wikipedia talk page, we first comprehensively replicated the previous state of the art RNN methods for the datasets. We then showed that character n-grams capture complementary information, and hence, are able to enhance the performance of the RNNs. Finally, we constructed a character-based word composition model in order to infer semantics for unseen words and further extended it with context-aware character representations. The integration of our composition model with the enhanced RNN methods yielded the best results on all three datasets. We have experimentally demonstrated that our approach to modeling obfuscated words significantly advances the state of the art in abuse detection. In the future, we wish to explore its efficacy in tasks such as grammatical error detection and correction. We will make our models and logs of experiments publicly available at `https://github.com/pushkarmishra/AbuseDetection`.

Acknowledgements

Special thanks to the anonymous reviewers for their valuable comments and suggestions.

References

Pinkesh Badjatiya, Shashank Gupta, Manish Gupta, and Vasudeva Varma. 2017. Deep learning for hate speech detection in tweets. In *Proceedings of the 26th International Conference on World Wide Web Companion*, WWW '17 Companion, pages 759–760, Republic and Canton of Geneva, Switzerland. International World Wide Web Conferences Steering Committee.

Piotr Bojanowski, Edouard Grave, Armand Joulin, and Tomas Mikolov. 2017. Enriching word vectors with subword information. *Transactions of the Association for Computational Linguistics*, 5:135–146.

François Chollet et al. 2015. Keras.

Thomas Davidson, Dana Warmsley, Michael Macy, and Ingmar Weber. 2017. Automated hate speech detection and the problem of offensive language. In *Proceedings of the 11th International AAAI Conference on Web and Social Media*, ICWSM '17.

Nemanja Djuric, Jing Zhou, Robin Morris, Mihajlo Grbovic, Vladan Radosavljevic, and Narayan Bhamidipati. 2015. Hate speech detection with comment embeddings. In *Proceedings of the 24th International Conference on World Wide Web*, WWW '15 Companion, pages 29–30, New York, NY, USA. ACM.

Maeve Duggan. 2014. Online harassment.

George Forman and Martin Scholz. 2010. Apples-to-apples in cross-validation studies: Pitfalls in classifier performance measurement. *SIGKDD Explor. Newsl.*, 12(1):49–57.

Guolin Ke, Qi Meng, Thomas Finley, Taifeng Wang, Wei Chen, Weidong Ma, Qiwei Ye, and Tie-Yan Liu. 2017. Lightgbm: A highly efficient gradient boosting decision tree. In I. Guyon, U. V. Luxburg, S. Bengio, H. Wallach, R. Fergus, S. Vishwanathan, and R. Garnett, editors, *Advances in Neural Information Processing Systems 30*, pages 3149–3157. Curran Associates, Inc.

Yoon Kim. 2014. Convolutional neural networks for sentence classification. In *Proceedings of the 2014 Conference on Empirical Methods in Natural Language Processing (EMNLP)*, pages 1746–1751. Association for Computational Linguistics.

Yoon Kim, Yacine Jernite, David Sontag, and Alexander M. Rush. 2016. Character-aware neural language models. In *Proceedings of the Thirtieth AAAI Conference on Artificial Intelligence*, AAAI'16, pages 2741–2749. AAAI Press.

Diederik P. Kingma and Jimmy Ba. 2015. Adam: A method for stochastic optimization. In *Proceedings of the 3rd International Conference on Learning Representations*, ICLR '15.

Quoc Le and Tomas Mikolov. 2014. Distributed representations of sentences and documents. In *Proceedings of the 31st International Conference on International Conference on Machine Learning*, ICML '14.

Wang Ling, Chris Dyer, Alan W Black, Isabel Trancoso, Ramon Fermandez, Silvio Amir, Luis Marujo, and Tiago Luis. 2015. Finding function in form: Compositional character models for open vocabulary word representation. In *Proceedings of the 2015 Conference on Empirical Methods in Natural Language Processing*, pages 1520–1530. Association for Computational Linguistics.

Pranava Swaroop Madhyastha, Mohit Bansal, Kevin Gimpel, and Karen Livescu. 2015. Mapping unseen words to task-trained embedding spaces. *CoRR*, abs/1510.02387.

Pushkar Mishra, Marco Del Tredici, Helen Yannakoudakis, and Ekaterina Shutova. 2018. Author profiling for abuse detection. In *Proceedings of the 27th International Conference on Computational Linguistics*, pages 1088–1098. Association for Computational Linguistics.

Chikashi Nobata, Joel Tetreault, Achint Thomas, Yashar Mehdad, and Yi Chang. 2016. Abusive language detection in online user content. In *Proceedings of the 25th International Conference on World Wide Web*, WWW '16, pages 145–153, Republic and Canton of Geneva, Switzerland. International World Wide Web Conferences Steering Committee.

Ji Ho Park and Pascale Fung. 2017. One-step and two-step classification for abusive language detection on twitter. In *Proceedings of the First Workshop on Abusive Language Online*, pages 41–45. Association for Computational Linguistics.

John Pavlopoulos, Prodromos Malakasiotis, and Ion Androutsopoulos. 2017. Deep learning for user comment moderation. In *Proceedings of the First Workshop on Abusive Language Online*, pages 25–35. Association for Computational Linguistics.

Jeffrey Pennington, Richard Socher, and Christopher D. Manning. 2014. Glove: Global vectors for word representation. In *Empirical Methods in Natural Language Processing (EMNLP)*, pages 1532–1543.

Yuval Pinter, Robert Guthrie, and Jacob Eisenstein. 2017. Mimicking word embeddings using subword rnns. In *Proceedings of the 2017 Conference on Empirical Methods in Natural Language Processing*, pages 102–112. Association for Computational Linguistics.

J. Qian, M. ElSherief, E. Belding, and W. Wang. 2018. Leveraging intra-user and inter-user representation learning for automated hate speech detection. *NAACL HLT, New Orleans, LA, June 2018.*, page *to appear*.

Nitish Srivastava, Geoffrey Hinton, Alex Krizhevsky, Ilya Sutskever, and Ruslan Salakhutdinov. 2014. Dropout: A simple way to prevent neural networks from overfitting. *Journal of Machine Learning Research*, 15:1929–1958.

Vincent Van Asch. 2013. Macro-and micro-averaged evaluation measures [[basic draft]]. *Computational Linguistics & Psycholinguistics, University of Antwerp, Belgium.*

Zeerak Waseem. 2016. Are you a racist or am I seeing things? annotator influence on hate speech detection on twitter. In *Proceedings of the First Workshop on NLP and Computational Social Science*, pages 138–142. Association for Computational Linguistics.

Zeerak Waseem, Wendy Hui Kyong Chung, Dirk Hovy, and Joel Tetreault. 2017. Proceedings of the first workshop on abusive language online. In *Proceedings of the First Workshop on Abusive Language Online*. Association for Computational Linguistics.

Zeerak Waseem and Dirk Hovy. 2016. Hateful symbols or hateful people? predictive features for hate speech detection on twitter. In *Proceedings of the NAACL Student Research Workshop*, pages 88–93, San Diego, California. Association for Computational Linguistics.

Ellery Wulczyn, Nithum Thain, and Lucas Dixon. 2017. Ex machina: Personal attacks seen at scale. In *Proceedings of the 26th International Conference on World Wide Web*, WWW '17, pages 1391–1399, Republic and Canton of Geneva, Switzerland. International World Wide Web Conferences Steering Committee.

Dawei Yin, Brian D. Davison, Zhenzhen Xue, Liangjie Hong, April Kontostathis, and Lynne Edwards. 2009. Detection of harassment on web 2.0. In *Processings of the Content Analysis in the WEB 2.0*, 2:1-7.

Hate Speech Dataset from a White Supremacy Forum

Ona de Gibert   **Naiara Perez**   **Aitor García-Pablos**   **Montse Cuadros**

HSLT Group at Vicomtech, Donostia/San Sebastián, Spain

{odegibert,nperez,agarciap,mcuadros}@vicomtech.org

Abstract

Hate speech is commonly defined as any communication that disparages a target group of people based on some characteristic such as race, colour, ethnicity, gender, sexual orientation, nationality, religion, or other characteristic. Due to the massive rise of user-generated web content on social media, the amount of hate speech is also steadily increasing. Over the past years, interest in online hate speech detection and, particularly, the automation of this task has continuously grown, along with the societal impact of the phenomenon. This paper describes a hate speech dataset composed of thousands of sentences manually labelled as containing hate speech or not. The sentences have been extracted from Stormfront, a white supremacist forum. A custom annotation tool has been developed to carry out the manual labelling task which, among other things, allows the annotators to choose whether to read the context of a sentence before labelling it. The paper also provides a thoughtful qualitative and quantitative study of the resulting dataset and several baseline experiments with different classification models. The dataset is publicly available.

1 Introduction

The rapid growth of content in social networks such as Facebook, Twitter and blogs, makes it impossible to monitor what is being said. The increase of cyberbullying and cyberterrorism, and the use of hate on the Internet, make the identification of hate in the web an essential ingredient for anti-bullying policies of social media, as Facebook's CEO Mark Zuckerberg recently acknowledged[1]. This paper releases a new dataset of hate speech to further investigate the problem.

Although there is no universal definition for *hate speech*, the most accepted definition is provided by Nockleby (2000): "any communication that disparages a target group of people based on some characteristic such as race, colour, ethnicity, gender, sexual orientation, nationality, religion, or other characteristic". Consider the following[2]:

(1)   "God bless them all, to hell with the blacks"

This sentence clearly contains hate speech against a target group because of their skin colour. However, the identification of hate speech is often not so straightforward. Besides defining hate speech as a verbal abuse directed to a group of people because of specific characteristics, other definitions of hate speech in previous studies care to include the speaker's determination to inflect harm (Davidson et al., 2017).

In all, there seems to be a pattern shared by most of the literature consulted (Nockleby, 2000; Djuric et al., 2015; Gitari et al., 2015; Nobata et al., 2016; Silva et al., 2016; Davidson et al., 2017), which would define hate speech as *a)* a deliberate attack, *b)* directed towards a specific group of people, and *c)* motivated by actual or perceived aspects that form the group's identity.

This paper presents the first public dataset of hate speech annotated on Internet forum posts in English at sentence-level. The dataset is publicly available in GitHub[3]. The source forum is Stormfront[4], the largest online community of white nationalists, characterised by pseudo-rational discussions of race (Meddaugh and Kay, 2009), which include different degrees of offensiveness. Stormfront is known as the first hate website (Schafer, 2002).

---

[1]https://www.washingtonpost.com/news/the-switch/wp/2018/04/10/transcript-of-mark-zuckerbergs-senate-hearing/

[2]The examples in this work may contain offensive language. They have been taken from actual web data and by no means reflect the authors' opinion.

[3]https://github.com/aitor-garcia-p/hate-speech-dataset

[4]www.stormfront.org

Proceedings of the Second Workshop on Abusive Language Online (ALW2), pages 11–20
Brussels, Belgium, October 31, 2018. ©2018 Association for Computational Linguistics

The rest of the paper is structured as follows: Section 2 describes the related work and contextualises the work presented in the paper; Section 3 introduces the task of generating a manually labelled hate speech dataset; this includes the design of the annotation guidelines, the resulting criteria, the inter-annotator agreement and a quantitative description of the resulting dataset; next, Section 4 presents several baseline experiments with different classification models using the labelled data; finally, Section 5 provides a brief discussion about the difficulties and nuances of hate speech detection, and Section 6 summarises the conclusions and future work.

2 Related Work

Research on hate speech has increased in the last years. The conducted studies are diverse and work on different datasets; there is no official corpus for the task, so usually authors collect and label their own data. For this reason, there exist few publicly available resources for hate speech detection.

Hatebase[5] is the an online repository of structured, multilingual, usage-based hate speech. Its vocabulary is classified into eight categories: archaic, class, disability, ethnicity, gender, nationality, religion, and sexual orientation. Some studies make use of Hatebase to build a classifier for hate speech (Davidson et al., 2017; Serra et al., 2017; Nobata et al., 2016). However, Saleem et al. (2016) prove that keyword-based approaches succeed at identifying the topic but fail to distinguish hateful sentences from clean ones, as the same vocabulary is shared by the hateful and target community, although with different intentions.

Kaggle's Toxic Comment Classification Challenge dataset[6] consists of 150k Wikipedia comments annotated for toxic behaviour. Waseem and Hovy (2016) published a collection of 16k tweets classified into racist, sexist or neither. Sharma et al. (2018) collected a set of 9k tweets containing harmful speech and they manually annotated them based on their degree of hateful intent. They describe three different classes of hate speech. The definition on which this paper is based overlaps mostly with their Class I, described as speech *a)* that incites violent actions, *b)* directed at a particular group, and *c)* with the intention of convey-

ing hurting sentiments.

Google and Jigsaw developed a tool called Perspective[7] that measures the "toxicity" of comments. The tool is published as an API and gives a toxicity score between 0 and 100 using a machine learning model. Such model has been trained on thousands of comments manually labelled by a team of people[8]; to our knowledge, the resulting dataset is not publicly available.

The detection of hate speech has been tackled in three main different ways. Some studies focus on subtypes of hate speech. This is the case of Warner and Hirschberg (2012), who focus on the identification of anti-Semitic posts versus any other form of hate speech. Also in this line, Kwok and Wang (2013) target anti-black hate speech. Badjatiya et al. (2017); Gambäck and Sikdar (2017) study the detection of racist and sexist tweets using deep learning.

Other proposals focus on the annotation of hate speech as opposed to texts containing derogatory or offensive language (Davidson et al., 2017; Malmasi and Zampieri, 2017, 2018; Watanabe et al., 2018). They build multi-class classifiers with the categories "hate", "offensive", and "clean".

Finally, some studies focus on the annotation of hate speech versus clean comments that do not contain hate speech (Nobata et al., 2016; Burnap and Williams, 2015; Djuric et al., 2015). Gitari et al. (2015) follow this approach but further classify the hateful comments into two categories: "weak" and "strong" hate. Del Vigna et al. (2017) conduct a similar study for Italian.

In all, experts conclude that annotation of hate speech is a difficult task, mainly because of the data annotation process. Waseem (2016) conducted a study on the influence of annotator knowledge of hate speech on classifiers for hate speech. Ross et al. (2016) also studied the reliability of hate speech annotations and acknowledge the importance of having detailed instructions for the annotation of hate speech available.

This paper aims to tackle the inherent subjectivity and difficulty of labelling hate speech by following strict guidelines. The approach presented in this paper follows (Nobata et al., 2016; Burnap and Williams, 2015; Djuric et al., 2015) (i.e., "hateful" versus "clean"). Furthermore, the annotation has been performed at sentence level as op-

---

[5]https://www.hatebase.org/
[6]https://www.kaggle.com/c/jigsaw-toxic-comment-classification-challenge/data
[7]https://www.perspectiveapi.com
[8]https://www.nytimes.com/2017/02/23/technology/google-jigsaw-monitor-toxic-online-comments.html

posed to full-comment annotation, with the possibility to access the original complete post for each sentence. To our knowledge, this is the first work that releases a manually labelled hate speech dataset annotated at sentence level in English posts from a white supremacy forum.

3 Hate Speech Dataset

This paper presents the first dataset of textual hate speech annotated at sentence-level. Sentence-level annotation allows to work with the minimum unit containing hate speech and reduce noise introduced by other sentences that are clean.

A total number of 10,568 sentences have been extracted from Stormfront and classified as conveying hate speech or not, and into two other auxiliary classes, as per the guidelines described in Section 3.2. In addition, the following information is also given for each sentence: a post identifier and the sentence's position in the post, a user identifier, a sub-forum identifier[9]. This information makes it possible re-build the conversations these sentences belong to. Furthermore, the number of previous posts the annotator had to read before making a decision over the category of the sentence is also given.

3.1 Data extraction and processing

The content was extracted from Stormfront using web-scraping techniques and was dumped into a database arranged by sub-forums and conversation threads (Figea et al., 2016). The extracted forum content was published between 2002 and 2017. The process of preparing the candidate content to be annotated was the following:

1. A subset of 22 sub-forums covering diverse topics and nationalities was random-sampled to gather individual posts uniformly distributed among sub-forums and users.
2. The sampled posts were filtered using an automatic language detector[10] to discard non-English texts.
3. The resulting posts were segmented into sentences with ixa-pipes (Agerri et al., 2014).
4. The sentences were grouped forming batches of 500 complete posts ($\sim$ 1,000 sentences per batch).

---

[9]All the identifiers provided are fake placeholders that facilitate understanding relations between sentences, Stormfront users, etc., but do not point back to the original source.

[10]https://github.com/shuyo/language-detection/blob/wiki/ProjectHome.md

The manual annotation task was divided into batches to control the process. During the annotation of the first two batches, the annotation procedure and guidelines were progressively refined and adapted. In total, 10,568 sentences contained in 10 batches have been manually annotated.

A post-processing step was performed to filter excessively long or short sentences. The cleansing process removed sentences shorter than 3 words or longer than 50 words. In total, 652 sentences were discarded, which represent 6.17% of the original dataset. The resulting dataset (henceforth referred to as the "clean" dataset) is the one described in Section 3.4 and used for experimentation in Section 4. The release of the dataset will contain both the raw sentences without any post-processing and the clean version, both annotated.

3.2 Annotation guidelines

Schmidt and Wiegand (2017) acknowledge that the procedure for hate speech annotation is fairly vague in previous studies, which translates into low agreement scores. In this study, all the annotators together created and discussed the guidelines to ensure all participants had the same understanding of hate speech. The final guidelines consider 4 types of sentences:

3.2.1 HATE

Sentences in this category contain hate speech. Hate speech is a

a) deliberate attack
b) directed towards a specific group of people
c) motivated by aspects of the group's identity.

The three premises must be true for a sentence to be categorized as HATE. Consider the following examples:

(2) "Poor white kids being forced to treat apes and parasites as their equals."

(3) "Islam is a false religion however unlike some other false religions it is crude and appeals to crude people such as arabs."

In (2), the speaker uses "apes" and "parasites" to refer to children of dark skin and implies they are not equal to "white kids". That is, it is an attack to the group composed of children of dark skin based on an identifying characteristic, namely, their skin colour. Thus, all the premises are true and (2) is a valid example of HATE. Example (3) brands all people of Arab origin as crude. That is, it attacks the group composed of Arab people based on their origin. Thus, all the premises are true and (3) is a valid example of HATE.

3.2.2 NOHATE

This label is used to categorise sentences that do not convey hate speech per the established definition. Consider the following examples:

(4) "Where can I find NS speeches and music, also historical, in mp3 format for free download on the net."

(5) "I know of Chris Rock and subsequently have hated him for a long time."

Example (4) mentions National Socialism ("NS"), but the user is just interested in documentation about it. Therefore, the sentence itself is not an attack, i.e., premise a) is not true, despite the sound assumption that the speaker forms part of a hating community. Thus, (4) is not a valid instance of HATE. Example (5) is directed towards an individual; thus, premise b) is false and the sentence is not a valid example of HATE, despite the sound assumption that the attack towards the individual is based on his skin colour.

Finally, it must be emphasized that the presence of pejorative language in a sentence cannot systematically be considered sufficient evidence to confirm the existence of hate speech. The use of "fag" in the following sentence:

(6) "Two black fag's holding hands."

cannot be said to be a deliberate attack, taken without any more context, despite it likely being offensive. Therefore, it cannot be considered HATE.

3.2.3 RELATION

When (6) (repeated as (7.1)) is read in context:

(7.1) "Two black fag's holding hands."
(7.2) "That's Great!"
(7.3) "That's 2 blacks won't be having kids."

it clearly conveys hate speech. The author is celebrating that two people belonging to the black minority will not be having children, which is a deliberate attack on a group of people based on an identifying characteristic. The annotation at sentence-level fails to discern that there exists hate speech in this example. The label RELATION is for specific cases such as this, where the sentences in a post do not contain hate speech on their own, but the combination of several sentences does. Consider another example:

(8.1) "Probably the most disgusting thing I've seen in the last year."
(8.2) "She looks like she has some African blood in her, or maybe it's just the makeup."
(8.3) "This is just so wrong."

Each sentence in isolation does not convey hate speech: in (8.1) and (8.3), a negative attitude is perceived, but it is unknown whether it is targeted towards a group of people; in (8.2), there is no hint of an attack, not even of a negative attitude. However, the three sentences together suggest that having "African blood" makes a situation (whatever "this" refers to) disgusting, which constitutes hate speech according to the definition proposed.

The label RELATION is given separately to all the sentences that need each other to be understood as hate speech. That is, consecutive sentences with this label convey hate speech but depend on each other to be correctly interpreted.

3.2.4 SKIP

Sentences that are not written in English or that do not contain information as to be classified into HATE or NOHATE are given this label.

(9) "Myndighetene vurderer n om de skal f permanent oppholdstillatelse."

(10) "YouTube - Broadcast Yourself."

Example (9) is in Norwegian and (10) is irrelevant both for HATE and NOHATE.

3.3 Annotation procedure

In order to develop the annotation guidelines, a draft was first written based on previous similar work. Three of the authors annotated a 1,144-sentence batch of the dataset following the draft, containing only the categories HATE, NOHATE and SKIP. Then, they discussed the annotations and modified the draft accordingly, which resulted in the guidelines presented in the previous section, including the RELATION category. Finally, a different batch of 1,018 sentences was annotated by the same three authors adhering to the new guidelines in order to calculate the inter-annotator agreement.

Table 1 shows the agreements obtained in terms of the average percent agreement (avg %), average Cohen's kappa coefficient (Cohen, 1960)

($avg\ k$), and Fleiss' kappa coefficient (Fleiss, 1971) (*fleiss*). The number of annotated sentences (# sent) and the number of categories to label (# cat) are also given for each batch. The results are in line with similar works (Nobata et al., 2016; Warner and Hirschberg, 2012).

	# sent	# cat	$avg\ \%$	$avg\ k$	*fleiss*
1	1,144	3	91.03	0.614	0.607
2	1,018	4	90.97	0.627	0.632

Table 1: Inter-annotator agreements on batches 1 and 2

All the annotation work was carried out using a web-based tool developed by the authors for this purpose. The tool displays all the sentences belonging to the same post at the same time, giving the annotator a better understanding of the post's author's intention. If the complete post is deemed insufficient by the annotator to categorize a sentence, the tool can show previous posts to which the problematic post is answering, on demand, up to the first post in the thread and its title. This consumption of context is registered automatically by the tool for further treatment of the collected data.

As stated by other studies, context appears to be of great importance when annotating hate speech (Watanabe et al., 2018). Schmidt and Wiegand (2017) acknowledge that whether a message contains hate speech or not can depend solely on the context, and thus encourage the inclusion of extra-linguistic features for annotation of hate speech. Moreover, Sharma et al. (2018) claim that context is essential to understand the speaker's intention.

3.4 Dataset statistics

This section provides a quantitative description and statistical analysis of the clean dataset published. Table 2 shows the distribution of the sentences over categories. The dataset is unbalanced as there exist many more sentences not conveying hate speech than 'hateful'' ones.

Table 3 refers to the subset of sentences that have required reading additional context (i.e. previous comments to the one being annotated) to make an informed decision by the human annotators. The category HATE is the one that requires more context, usually due to the use of slang unknown to the annotator or because the annotator needed to find out the actual target of an offensive mention.

Assigned label	# sent	%
HATE	1,119	11.29
NOHATE	8,537	86.09
RELATION	168	1.69
SKIP	92	0.93
total	9,916	100.00

Table 2: Distribution of sentences over categories in the clean dataset

	Context used	No context used
HATE	22.70	77.30
NOHATE	8.00	92.00

Table 3: Percentage of sentences for which the human annotators asked for additional context

The remaining of the section focuses only on the subset of the dataset composed of the categories HATE and NOHATE, which are the core of this work. Table 4 shows the size of said subset, along with the average sentence length for each class, their word counts and their vocabulary sizes.

	HATE	NOHATE
sentences	1,119	8,537
sentence length	20.39 ± 9.46	15.15 ± 9.16
word count	24,867	144,353
vocabulary	4,148	13,154

Table 4: Size of the categories HATE and NOHATE in the clean dataset

Regarding the distribution of sentences over Stormfront accounts, the dataset is balanced as there is no account that contributes notably more than any other: the average percentage of sentences is of 0.50 ± 0.42 per account, the total amount of accounts in the dataset being 2,723. The sub-forums that contain more HATE belong to the category of news, discussion of views, politics, philosophy, as well as to specific countries (i.e., Ireland, Britain, and Canada). In contrast, the sub-forums that contain more NOHATE sentences are about education and homeschooling, gatherings, and youth issues.

In order to obtain a more qualitative insight of the dataset, a HATE score (HS) has been calculated based on the Pointwise Mutual Information (PMI) value for each word towards the categories HATE and NOHATE. PMI allows calculating the correlation of each word with respect to each category. The difference of the PMI value of a word w and the category HATE and the PMI of the same word w and the category NOHATE results in the HATE score of w, as shown in Formula 1.

$$\text{HS}(w) = PMI(w, \text{HATE}) - PMI(w, \text{NOHATE}) \quad (1)$$

Intuitively, this score is a simple way of capturing whether the presence of a word in a HATE context occurs significantly more often than in a NO-HATE context. Table 5 shows the 15 most and least hateful words: the more positive a HATE score, the more hateful a word, and vice versa.

	HS		HS
ape	6.81	pm	-3.38
scum	6.25	group	-3.34
savages	5.73	week	-3.13
filthy	5.73	idea	-2.70
mud	5.31	thread	-2.68
homosexuals	5.31	german	-2.67
filth	5.19	videos	-2.67
apes	5.05	night	-2.63
beasts	5.05	happy	-2.63
homosexual	5.05	join	-2.63
threat	5.05	pictures	-2.60
monkey	5.05	eyes	-2.54
libtard	5.05	french	-2.52
coon	5.05	information	-2.44
niglet	4.73	band	-2.44

Table 5: Most (positive HS) and least (negative HS) hateful words

The results show that the most hateful words are derogatory or refer to targeted groups of hate speech. On the other hand, the least hateful words are neutral in this regard and belong to the semantic fields of Internet, or temporal expressions, among others. This shows that the vocabulary is discernible by category, which in turn suggests that the annotation and guidelines are sound.

Performing the same calculation with bi-grams yields expressions such as "gene pool", "race traitor", and "white guilt" for the most hateful category, which appear to be concepts related to race issues. The less hateful terms are expressions such as "white power", "white nationalism" and "pro white", which clearly state the right-wing extremist politics of the forum users.

Finally, the dataset has been contrasted against the English vocabulary in Hatebase. 9.28% of HATE vocabulary overlaps with Hatebase, a higher percentage than for NOHATE vocabulary, of which 6.57% of the words can be found in Hatebase. In Table 6, the distribution of HATE vocabulary is shown over Hatebase's 8 categories. Although some percentages are not high, all 8 categories are present in the corpus. Most of the HATE words from the dataset belong to ethnicity, followed by gender. This is in agreement with Silva et al. (2016), who conducted a study to analyse the targets of hate in social networks and showed that hate based on race was the most common.

category	%	examples
archaic	2.46	div, wigger
ethnicity	41.63	coon, paki
nationality	7.03	guinea, leprechaun
religion	1.34	holohoax, prod
gender	36.05	bird, dyke
sexual orientation	2.34	fag, queer
disability	2.01	mongol, retarded
social class	7.14	slag, trash
total	100.00	

Table 6: Distribution of HATE vocabulary over Hatebase categories

4 Experiments

In order to further inspect the resulting dataset and to check the validity of the annotations (i.e. whether the two annotated classes are separable based solely on the text of the labelled instances) a set of baseline experiments have been conducted. These experiments do not exploit any external resource such as lexicons, heuristics or rules. The experiments just use the provided dataset and well-known approaches from the literature to provide a baseline for further research and improvement in the future.

4.1 Experimental setting

The experiments are based on a balanced subset of labelled sentences. All the sentences labelled as HATE have been collected, and an equivalent number of NOHATE sentences have been randomly sampled, summing up 2k labelled sentences. From this amount, the 80% has been used for training and the remaining 20% for testing.

The evaluated algorithms are the following:

- Support Vector Machines (SVM) (Hearst et al., 1998) over Bag-of-Words vectors. Word-count-based vectors have been computed and fed into a Python Scikit-learn LinearSVM[11] classifier to separate HATE and NOHATE instances.
- Convolutional Neural Networks (CNN), as described in (Kim, 2014). The implementation is a simplified version using a single input channel of randomly initialized word embeddings[12].
- Recurrent Neural Networks with Long Short-term Memories (LSTM) (Hochreiter and Schmidhuber, 1997). A LSTM layer of size 128 over word embeddings of size 300.

All the hyperparameters are left to the usual values reported in the literature (Greff et al., 2017). No hyperparameter tuning has been performed. A more comprehensive experimentation and research has been left for future work.

4.2 Results

The baseline experiments include a majority class baseline showing the balance between the two classes in the test set. The results are given in terms of accuracy for HATEand NOHATE individually, and the overall accuracy, calculated according to the equations 2, 3 and 4, where TP are the true positives and FP are the false positives.

$$Acc_{\text{HATE}} = \frac{TP_{\text{HATE}}}{TP_{\text{HATE}} + FP_{\text{HATE}}} \qquad (2)$$

$$Acc_{\text{NOHATE}} = \frac{TP_{\text{NOHATE}}}{TP_{\text{NOHATE}} + FP_{\text{NOHATE}}} \qquad (3)$$

$$Acc_{\text{ALL}} = \frac{TP_{\text{ALL}}}{TP_{\text{ALL}} + FP_{\text{ALL}}} \qquad (4)$$

We show the accuracy for the both complementary classes instead of the precision-recall of a single class to highlight the performance of the classifiers for the both classes individually. Table 7 shows the results of using only sentences that did *not* require additional context to be labelled, while Table 8 shows the results of including those sentences that required additional context. Not surprisingly, the results are lower when including sentences that required additional context. If a human annotator required additional information to

make a decision, it is to expect that an automatic classifier would not have enough information or would have a harder time making a correct prediction. The results also show that NOHATE sentences are more accurately classified than HATE sentences. Overall, the LSTM-based classifier obtains better results, but even the simple SVM using bag-of-words vectors is capable of discriminating the classes reasonably well.

	Acc_{HATE}	Acc_{NOHATE}	Acc_{ALL}
Majority	n/a	n/a	0.50
SVM	0.72	0.76	0.74
CNN	0.54	0.86	0.70
LSTM	0.76	0.80	0.78

Table 7: Results excluding sentences that required additional context for manual annotation

	Acc_{HATE}	Acc_{NOHATE}	Acc_{ALL}
Majority	n/a	n/a	0.50
SVM	0.69	0.73	0.71
CNN	0.55	0.79	0.66
LSTM	0.71	0.75	0.73

Table 8: Results including sentences that required additional context for manual annotation

4.3 Error Analysis

In order to get a deeper understanding of the performance of the classifiers trained, a manual inspection has been performed on a set of erroneously classified sentences. Two main types of errors have been identified:

Type I errors Sentences manually annotated as HATE but classified as NOHATE by the system, usually due to a lack of context or to a lack of the necessary world knowledge to understand the meaning of the sentence:

(11) "Indeed, now they just need to feed themselves, educate themselves, police themselves ad nauseum...'

(12) "If you search around you can probably find "hoax of the 20th century" for free on the net."

In (11), it is not clear without additional context who "themselves" are. It actually refers to people of African origin. In its original context, the author

[11]http://scikit-learn.org/stable/modules/svm.html
[12]https://github.com/dennybritz/cnn-text-classification-tf

was implying that they are not able to feed, police nor educate themselves. This would make the sentence an example of hate speech, but it could also be a harmless comment given the appropriate context. In (12), the lack of world knowledge about what the Holocaust is, or what naming it "hoax" implies –i.e., denying its existence–, would make it difficult to understand the sentence as an act of hate speech.

Type II errors Sentences manually labelled as NOHATE and automatically classified as HATE, usually due to the use of common offensive vocabulary with non-hateful intent:

(13) "I dont like reporting people but the last thing I will do is tolerate some stupid pig who claims Hungarians are Tartars."

(14) "More black-on-white crime: YouTube - Black Students Attack White Man For Eating Dinner With Black"

In (13), the user accuses and insults a particular individual. Example (14) is providing information on a reported crime. Although vocabulary of targeted groups is used in both cases (i.e., "Hungarians", "Tartars", "black"), the sentences do not contain HATE.

5 Discussion

There are several aspects of the introduced dataset, and hate speech annotation in general, that deserve a special remark and discussion.

First, the source of the content used to obtain the resulting dataset is on its own a source of offensive language. Being Stormfront a white supremacists' forum, almost every single comment contains some sort of intrinsic racism and other hints of hate. However, not every expression that contains a racist cue can be directly taken as hate speech. This is a truly subjective debate related to topics such as free speech, tolerance and civics. That is one of the main reasons why this paper carefully describes the annotation criteria for what here counts as hate speech and what not. In any case, despite the efforts to make the annotation guidelines as clear, rational and comprehensive as possible, the annotation process has been admittedly demanding and far from straightforward.

In fact, the annotation guidelines were crafted in several steps, first paying attention to what the literature points about hate speech annotation. After a first round of manual labelling, inconsistencies among the human annotators were discussed and the guidelines and examples were adapted. From those debates we extract some conclusions and pose several open questions. The first annotation criteria (hate speech being a *deliberate attack*) still lacks robustness and a proper definition, becoming ambiguous and subject to different interpretations. A more precise definition of what an *attack* is and what it is not would be necessary: Can an objective fact that however undermines the honour of a group of people be considered an attack? Is the mere use of certain vocabulary (e.g. "nigger") automatically considered an attack? With regard to the second annotation criteria (hate speech being *directed towards a specific group of people*), it was controversial among the human annotators as well. Sentences were found that attacked individuals and mentioned the targets' skin colour or religion, political trends, and so on. Some annotators interpreted these as indirect attacks towards the collectivity of people that share the mentioned characteristics.

Another relevant point is the fact that the annotation granularity is sentence level. Most, if not all, of the existing datasets label full comments. A comment might be part of a more elaborated discourse, and not every part may convey hate. It is arguable whether a comment containing a single hate-sentence can be considered "hateful" or not. The dataset released provides the full set of sentences per comment with their annotations, so each can decide how to work with it.

In addition, and related to the last point, one of the labels included for the manual labelling is RELATION. This label is meant to be used when two or more sentences need each other to be understood as hate speech, usually because one is a premise and the following is the (hateful) conclusion. This label has been seldom used.

Finally, a very important issue to consider is the need of additional context to label a sentence (i.e., the rest of the conversation or the title of the forum-thread). It can happen to human annotators and, of course, to automatic classifiers, as confirmed in the error analysis (Section 4.3). Studying context dependency to perform the labelling, it has been observed that annotators learn to distinguish hate speech more easily over time, requiring less and less context to make the annotations (see Figure 1).

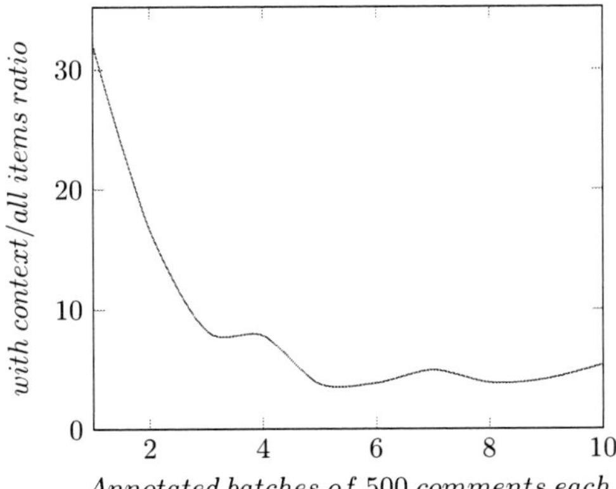

Figure 1: Percentage of comments per batch that required additional context to be manually labelled. The amount of context needed by a human annotator decreases over time.

6 Conclusions and Future Work

This paper describes a manually labelled hate speech dataset obtained from Stormfront, a white supremacist online forum.

The resulting dataset consists of ∼10k sentences labelled as conveying hate speech or not. Since the definition of hate speech has many subtleties, this work includes a detailed explanation of the manual annotation criteria and guidelines. Furthermore, several aspects of the resulting dataset have been studied, such as the necessity of additional context by the annotators to make a decision, or the distribution of the vocabulary used in the examples labelled as hate speech. In addition, several baseline experiments have been conducted using automatic classifiers, with a focus on examples that are difficult for automatic classifiers, such as those that required additional context or world knowledge. The resulting dataset is publicly available.

This dataset provides a good starting point for discussion and further research. As future work, it would be interesting to study how to include world knowledge and/or the context of an online conversation (i.e. previous and following messages, forum thread title, and so on) in order to obtain more robust hate speech automatic classifiers. Future studies could also explore how sentences labelled as RELATION affect classification, as this sentences have not been included in the experiments presented. In addition, more studies should be performed to characterize the content of the dataset in depth, regarding timelines, user behaviour and hate speech targets, for instance. Finally, since the proportion of HATE/NOHATE examples tends to be unbalanced, a more sophisticated manually labelling system with active learning paradigms would greatly benefit future labelling efforts.

7 Acknowledgements

This work has been supported by the European Commission under the project ASGARD (700381, H2020-FCT-2015). We thank the Hatebase team, in particular Hatebase developer Timothy Quinn, for providing Hatebase's English vocabulary dump to conduct this study. Finally, we would like to thank the reviewers of the paper for their thorough work and valuable suggestions.

References

R. Agerri, J. Bermudez, and G. Rigau. 2014. IXA pipeline: Efficient and Ready to Use Multilingual NLP tools. In *Proceedings of the Ninth International Conference on Language Resources and Evaluation (LREC'14)*, pages 3823–3828.

P. Badjatiya, S. Gupta, M. Gupta, and V. Varma. 2017. Deep Learning for Hate Speech Detection in Tweets. In *Proceedings of the 26th International Conference on World Wide Web (WWW 2017)*, pages 759–760.

P. Burnap and M. L. Williams. 2015. Cyber hate speech on twitter: An application of machine classification and statistical modeling for policy and decision making. *Policy & Internet*, 7(2):223–242.

J. Cohen. 1960. A Coefficient of Agreement for Nominal Scales. *Educational and Psychological Measurement*, 20(1):37–46.

T. Davidson, D. Warmsley, M. Macy, and I. Weber. 2017. Automated Hate Speech Detection and the Problem of Offensive Language. *Proceedings of the Eleventh International AAAI Conference on Web and Social Media (ICWSM 2017)*, pages 512–515.

F. Del Vigna, A. Cimino, F. Dell'Orletta, M. Petrocchi, and M. Tesconi. 2017. Hate me, hate me not: Hate speech detection on Facebook. In *Proceedings of the First Italian Conference on Cybersecurity (ITASEC17)*, pages 86–95.

N. Djuric, J. Zhou, R. Morris, M. Grbovic, V. Radosavljevic, and N. Bhamidipati. 2015. Hate Speech Detection with Comment Embeddings. pages 29–30.

L. Figea, L. Kaati, and R. Scrivens. 2016. Measuring online affects in a white supremacy forum. *IEEE International Conference on Intelligence and Security Informatics: Cybersecurity and Big Data, ISI 2016*, pages 85–90.

J. L. Fleiss. 1971. Measuring nominal scale agreement among many raters. *Psychological Bulletin*, 76(5):378.

B. Gambäck and U. K. Sikdar. 2017. Using convolutional neural networks to classify hate-speech. In *Proceedings of the First Workshop on Abusive Language Online (ALW1)*, pages 85–90.

N. D. Gitari, Z. Zuping, H. Damien, and J. Long. 2015. A Lexicon-based Approach for Hate Speech Detection. *International Journal of Multimedia and Ubiquitous Engineering*, 10(4):215–230.

K. Greff, R. K Srivastava, J. Koutník, B. R. Steunebrink, and J. Schmidhuber. 2017. LSTM: A Search Space Odyssey. *IEEE Transactions on Neural Networks and Learning Systems*, 28(10):2222–2232.

M. A. Hearst, S. T. Dumais, E. Osuna, J. Platt, and B. Scholkopf. 1998. Support vector machines. *IEEE Intelligent Systems and their Applications*, 13(4):18–28.

S. Hochreiter and J. Schmidhuber. 1997. Long Short-term Memory. *Neural Computation*, 9(8):1735–1780.

Y. Kim. 2014. Convolutional Neural Networks for Sentence Classification. In *Proceedings of the 2014 Conference on Empirical Methods in Natural Language Processing (EMNLP 2014)*, pages 1746–1751.

I. Kwok and Y. Wang. 2013. Locate the Hate: Detecting Tweets against Blacks. *Proceedings of the Twenty-Seventh AAAI Conference on Artificial Intelligence (AAAI-13)*, pages 1621–1622.

S. Malmasi and M. Zampieri. 2017. Detecting Hate Speech in Social Media. In *Proceedings of the International Conference Recent Advances in Natural Language Processing (RANLP 2017)*, pages 467–472.

S. Malmasi and M. Zampieri. 2018. Challenges in discriminating profanity from hate speech. *Journal of Experimental & Theoretical Artificial Intelligence*, 30(2):187–202.

P. M. Meddaugh and J. Kay. 2009. Hate Speech or "Reasonable Racism?" The Other in Stormfront. *Journal of Mass Media Ethics*, 24(4):251–268.

C. Nobata, J. Tetreault, A. Thomas, Y. Mehdad, and Y. Chang. 2016. Abusive Language Detection in Online User Content. In *Proceedings of the 25th International Conference on World Wide Web (WWW 2016)*, pages 145–153.

J. T. Nockleby. 2000. Hate speech. *Encyclopedia of the American Constitution*, 3:1277–79.

B. Ross, M. Rist, G. Carbonell, B. Cabrera, N. Kurowsky, and M. Wojatzki. 2016. Measuring the reliability of hate speech annotations: The case of the european refugee crisis. In *Proceedings of NLP4CMC III: 3rd Workshop on Natural Language Processing for Computer-Mediated Communication*, volume 17, pages 6–9.

H. M. Saleem, K. P. Dillon, S. Benesch, and D. Ruths. 2016. A Web of Hate: Tackling Hateful Speech in Online Social Spaces. In *Proceedings of the First Workshop on Text Analytics for Cybersecurity and Online Safety (TA-COS 2016)*.

Joseph A Schafer. 2002. Spinning the web of hate: Web-based hate propagation by extremist organizations. *Journal of Criminal Justice and Popular Culture*, 9(2):69–88.

A. Schmidt and M. Wiegand. 2017. A Survey on Hate Speech Detection using Natural Language Processing. In *Proceedings of the Fifth International Workshop on Natural Language Processing for Social Media (SocialNLP 2017)*, pages 1–10.

J. Serra, I. Leontiadis, D. Spathis, J. Blackburn, G. Stringhini, and A. Vakali. 2017. Class-based prediction errors to detect hate speech with out-of-vocabulary words. In *Abusive Language Workshop*, volume 1. Abusive Language Workshop.

S. Sharma, S. Agrawal, and M. Shrivastava. 2018. Degree based Classification of Harmful Speech using Twitter Data. *arXiv:1806.04197*.

L. Silva, M. Mondal, D. Correa, F. Benevenuto, and I. Weber. 2016. Analyzing the Targets of Hate in Online Social Media. In *Proceedings of the Tenth International AAAI Conference on Web and Social Media (ICWSM 2016)*, pages 687–690.

W. Warner and J. Hirschberg. 2012. Detecting Hate Speech on the World Wide Web. In *Proceedings of the Second Workshop on Language in Social Media (LSM 2012)*, pages 19–26.

Z. Waseem. 2016. Are You a Racist or Am I Seeing Things? Annotator Influence on Hate Speech Detection on Twitter. pages 138–142.

Z. Waseem and D. Hovy. 2016. Hateful Symbols or Hateful People? Predictive Features for Hate Speech Detection on Twitter. In *Proceedings of the NAACL Student Research Workshop (NAACL SRW 2018)*, pages 88–93.

H. Watanabe, M. Bouazizi, and T. Ohtsuki. 2018. Hate Speech on Twitter: A Pragmatic Approach to Collect Hateful and Offensive Expressions and Perform Hate Speech Detection. *IEEE Access*, 6:13825–13835.

A Review of Standard Text Classification Practices for Multi-label Toxicity Identification of Online Content

Isuru Gunasekara
IMRSV Data Labs
Ottawa, Canada
isuru@imrsv.ai

Isar Nejadgholi
IMRSV Data Labs
Ottawa, Canada
isar@imrsv.ai

Abstract

Language toxicity identification presents a gray area in the ethical debate surrounding freedom of speech and censorship. Today's social media landscape is littered with unfiltered content that can be anywhere from slightly abusive to hate inducing. In response, we focused on training a multi-label classifier to detect both the type and level of toxicity in online content. This content is typically colloquial and conversational in style. Its classification therefore requires huge amounts of annotated data due to its variability and inconsistency. We compare standard methods of text classification in this task. A conventional one-vs-rest SVM classifier with character and word level frequency-based representation of text reaches 0.9763 ROC AUC score. We demonstrated that leveraging more advanced technologies such as word embeddings, recurrent neural networks, attention mechanism, stacking of classifiers and semi-supervised training can improve the ROC AUC score of classification to 0.9862. We suggest that in order to choose the right model one has to consider the accuracy of models as well as inference complexity based on the application.

1 Introduction

While the sheer volume of online content presents a major challenge in information management, we are equally plagued by our current inability to effectively monitor its contents. In particular, social media platforms are ridden with verbal abuse, giving way to an increasingly unsafe and highly offensive online environment. With the threat of sanctions and user turnover, governments and social media platforms currently have huge incentives to create systems that accurately detect and remove abusive content.

When considering possible solutions, the binary classification of online data, as simply toxic and non-toxic content, can be very problematic. Even with very low error rates of misclassification, the removal of said flagged conversations can impact a user's reputation or freedom of speech. Developing classifiers that can flag the type and likelihood of toxic content is a far better approach. It empowers users and online platforms to control their content based on provided metrics and calculated thresholds.

While a multi-label classifier would yield a more powerful application, it's also a considerably more challenging natural language processing problem. Online conversational text contains shortenings, abbreviations, spelling mistakes, and ever evolving slang. Huge annotated datasets are needed so that the models can learn all this variability across communities and online platforms (Chandrasekharan et al., 2017). Furthermore, building a representative and high volume annotated dataset of social media contents for multiple types of toxicity can be exhaustive. It is a subjective, disturbing and time consuming task. Critical consideration of the relationships between different subtasks is needed to label this data (Waseem et al., 2017). Additionally, the annotated datasets will always be unbalanced since some types of toxic content are much more prevalent than others.

Some of the back-end approaches to this task have been well researched. Hand-authoring syntactic rules can be leveraged to detect offensive content and identify potential offensive users on social media (Chen et al., 2012). Also, morphological, syntactic and user behavior level features have been shown to be useful in learning abusive behavior

Proceedings of the Second Workshop on Abusive Language Online (ALW2), pages 21–25
Brussels, Belgium, October 31, 2018. ©2018 Association for Computational Linguistics

(Papegnies et al., 2017; Buckels et al., 2014; Yin et al., 2009; Chen et al., 2012). Conventional machine learning classifiers such as SVM classifiers (Nobata et al., 2016) and linear regressions models (Davidson et al., 2017; Xiang et al., 2012) have also been used to effectively detect abusive online language. Deep learning models with word embeddings as text representations are state-of-the-art text classification solutions that show effectiveness in many tasks such as sentiment analysis and the detection of hate speech (Gambäck and Sikdar, 2017). Although all these methods are well studied and established, it is not always clear what the best choice for a specific task is due to the trade-off between acquired success rate of the classification model and the complexities of its deployment and inference.

In our work, we used the Wikimedia Toxicity dataset to investigate how various methods of designing a standard text classifier can impact the classification success rate as well as its inference cost. This dataset was published and used for a Kaggle competition. In the context of the competition, it is a common practice to train multiple large size models and ensemble them to get the highest results, tailored for the competition test set. Here, however, we only looked at standard classification models that are suitable to be deployed and used for inference in real-time. For text representations, we looked at frequency-based methods and multiple word embeddings. For classification models, we considered neural network models that can learn sentence representation using recurrent neural networks and attention layers. We also investigated stacking classifiers and used them to automatically label the unannotated part of the dataset to be added to the training set. This paper highlights how we compared various standard methods to help identify what the best practices for this application are.

The paper is organized as follows. In Section 2, we describe the dataset, annotation, cleaning and augmentation steps that we applied. In Section 3, we review some of the commonly used text representation methods and look at how representation of text can impact the classification results. In Section 4, we compare neural network models that are effective in learning long sequences. In Section 5, we investigate how stacking two classifiers can improve results. In Section 6, we investigate the impact of using automatically labeled datasets to

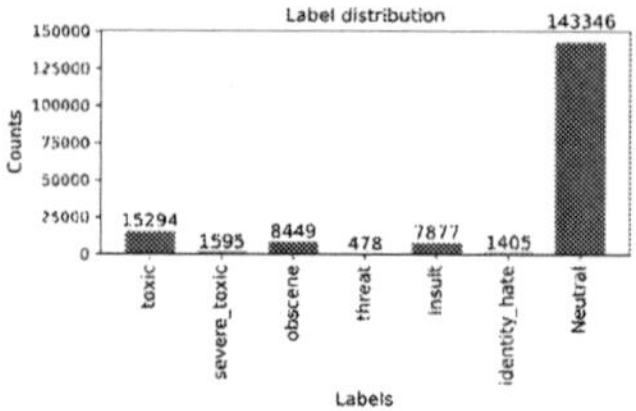

(a) counts of classes in annotated dataset

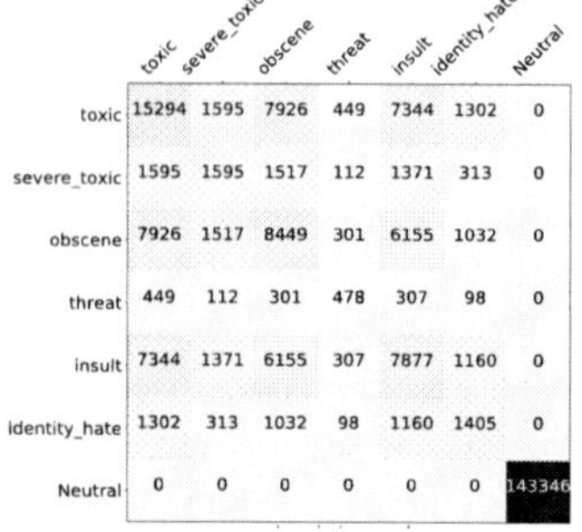

(b) overlap between class pairs

Figure 1: The counts and overlap of classes in training dataset

further train the classifiers and Section 7 discusses our findings.

2 Dataset

In this work, we used Wikimedias Toxicity Data Set (Wulczyn et al., 2016b,a). This dataset is also available on Figshare https://figshare.com/articles/ Wikipedia_Detox_Data/4054689 as the Wikipedia Human Annotations of Toxicity on Talk Pages and contains about 215K annotated examples from Wikipedia Talk pages. The dataset has been annotated by Kaggle based on asking 5000 crowd-workers to rate Wikipedia comments according to their toxicity (which they evaluated based on how likely they were to make others leave the conversation). The labels include seven types: neutral, toxic, severe toxic, obscene, threat, insult and identity hate. This dataset was published in two parts namely train and test set. The train set has 159571 annotated comments while the test set includes about 160k entries. However, only 63978 of test comments are identified as valid and annotated, which are used here as test set. There are more than 24 million words in this dataset yet the vocabulary size is only 495147. This is a very unbalanced dataset and a sample can get more than one label. Figure 1 shows the count of multiple labels in the train set as well as the training labels' overlaps. For all the experiments the AUC score is calculated which is the area under the curve (true positive rate vs the false positive rate) is calculated for the test set as the evaluation metric.

All classes except for the non-toxic examples are augmented through translation to French, Dutch and Spanish before translating back to English. Using this method, we get slightly different sentences and the label is preserved. Punctuation was removed and a set of very common word variations (including abbreviations) on social media were found and replaced by the original word. This cleaning reduced the vocabulary from 495147 to 434161.

3   Text Representation

We investigated word tf-idf and character tf-idf as frequency-based text representations and compared them with representing text using average of word embeddings. For these experiments stop words are removed from text. Character level tf-idf is calculated for character n-grams where $n = 1, \ldots, 6$. Word level tf-idf is calculated for word n-grams where $n = 1, 2, 3$. A fastText skip-gram model (Bojanowski et al., 2016) is trained to obtain 50D word embedding vectors for character level n-gram features where $n = 1, \ldots, 6$ and word n-gram features where $n = 1, 2, 3$. We also used pre-trained word embeddings, including Glove (Pennington et al., 2014) and 300D fastText vectors. In order to evaluate the impact of text representation, we trained seven one-vs-rest SVM classifiers to predict the labels independently. Table 1 shows the results obtained from our experiments. Our results show that word level tf-idf fails to achieve accurate classification when the data is informal and conversational. However, if character level tf-idf is added to the representations, results will improve drastically. Training a specialized word embedding is not shown to be effective in our experiments. The low volume of the training set can be attributed to this observation. Pre-trained fastText is shown to slightly outperform Glove since it can assign vectors to every word while Glove discards the OOV words. Based on these results we chose to represent the text with pre-trained fastText embedding for the rest of the experiments.

Table 1: Comparison of different text representation methods in training one-vs-rest SVM classifiers

Representation	AUC
word tfidf	0.5423
char and word tfidf	0.9763
Average of 50D trained fasttext	0.8765
Average of Glove	0.9725
Average of 300D Pretrained fasttext	0.9782

4   Neural Network Classification Models

While word embeddings are a semantic representation of words, bidirectional neural networks are the technology known for generating a semantic representation for a given sequence of words. Bidirectional recurrent neural networks learn the meaning of a sentence not only from the individual words but by processing the dependencies of the surrounding words through forward and backward connections. Both bi-LSTM (Chen et al., 2016) and bi-GRU (Chung et al., 2015) architectures are shown to perform well in sentence representation. LSTM and GRU layers have a proficient learning ability for long text, because they can control how much information should be received in the current step, how much should be forgotten, and how much information should be passed back.

Attention layers (Parikh et al., 2016; Felbo et al., 2017) are mechanisms suitable for converting sequence representations, which are usually in the form of matrices, to a vector representation that is tailored for the desired classification tasks. We investigated the impact of leveraging these technologies by training and testing of two neural network structures shown in Figures 2a and b. Pre-trained fasttext embeddings are used and stop words are not removed, since we want the LSTM and attention layer learn the complete sequences. The neural network shown in Figure 2a which contains two layers of biLSTM to encode the information of sequences achieves 0.9842 and the one shown in Figure 2b which uses attention mechanism to combine the context information from embedding layer and the sequence information from each biLSTM layer to get a summary vector of the sentence, reaches 0.9844 in AUC.

5   Stacking of Classifiers

Stacking of classifiers is a standard way of increasing the accuracy of a classification task by combining the predictions of multiple classifiers to-

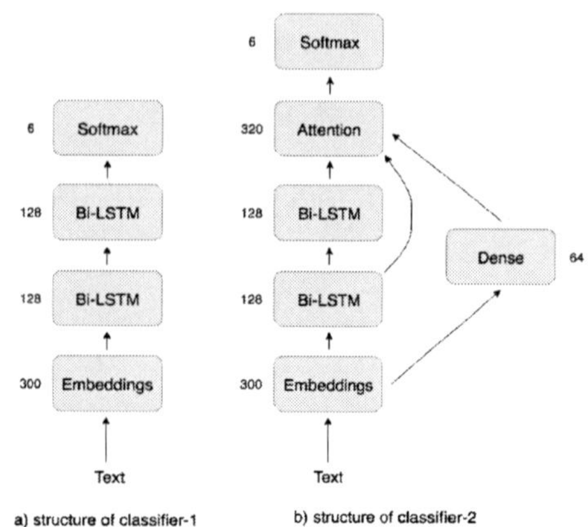

Figure 2: Structure of neural network classifiers trained and tested in this work

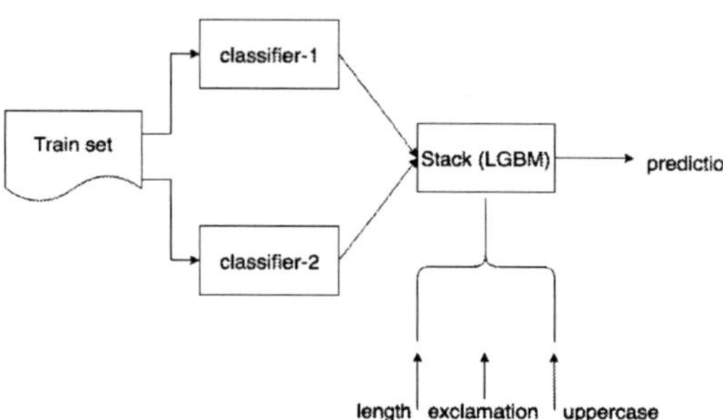

Figure 3: A schematic of applied stacking method

gether (Merz, 1999). In this method, a supervisor model is trained and learns how to combine the predictions of different types of models that differ in their variance, bias and capability of dealing with noise (Sluban and Lavrač, 2015). Figure 3 describes the stacking method applied in this work. We used a Light Gradient Boosting Machine (LGBM) stacking model which is a gradient boosting library implemented by Microsoft (Ke et al., 2017). LGBM is an implementation of fast gradient boosting on decision trees. Given a set of features, this classifier learns a linear combination of the predictions of preliminary classifiers to predict the label. The output of softmax layer from both classifiers (probabilities predicted for 6 classes) is fed to the LGBM. Also, the length of the text, frequency of exclamation marks and frequency of capital letters are considered as LGBM features. The LGBM classifier reached a 0.9847 score.

Table 2: comparison of different classification models

classifier	training	AUC
classifier-1	supervised	0.9842
classifier-2	supervised	0.9844
LGBM	supervised	0.9847
classifier-1	semi-supervised	0.9860
classifier-2	semi-supervised	0.9862

6 Semi-supervised Training

In this section, we investigate the impact of pseudo-labeling as a semi-supervised training method (Lee, 2013). Simply put, we split the test dataset into 10 folds. We then trained the two classifiers described in Section 4, in a supervised fashion, with both training set and 9 folds of test set. For test set, pseudo-labels are used which are the predictions calculated by the best classifier (the LGBM model) as if they were true labels. The trained classifier is tested on the 10th fold and the experiment is repeated for all 10 folds. This method has shown to be equivalent to entropy regularization (Grandvalet and Bengio, 2005) and makes up for dissimilarities of distributions between test and train dataset. Semi-supervised training of classifier-1 and classifier-2 improves the AUC score to 0.9860 and 0.9862 respectively.

7 Conclusion

Our investigation reveals that in the domain of conversational text, choosing the right text representation is crucial. Comparisons between multiple standard text representation techniques show that character-level representations outperform word-level representations in case of conversational text. Even with conventional SVM one-vs-rest classifiers, drastic improvement can be achieved when the text representation includes character level tfidf instead of only word level tfidf vectors (Table 1). We also showed that using various state-of-the-art classification techniques including sequence modeling neural network models, attention mechanisms and stacking of classifiers can slightly improve the AUC score of classification. Moreover, we demonstrated that further training of models through automatic labeling of unannotated datasets can improve the success rate of the classifier (Table 2). However, significance of these improvements depends on the application, inference cost and complexity and the amount of data that has to be processed during inference. Our research gave life to a language toxicity identification tool, which will be presented alongside this paper.

References

Piotr Bojanowski, Edouard Grave, Armand Joulin, and Tomas Mikolov. 2016. Enriching word vectors with subword information. *arXiv preprint arXiv:1607.04606*.

Erin E Buckels, Paul D Trapnell, and Delroy L Paulhus. 2014. Trolls just want to have fun. *Personality and individual Differences*, 67:97–102.

Eshwar Chandrasekharan, Mattia Samory, Anirudh Srinivasan, and Eric Gilbert. 2017. The bag of communities: Identifying abusive behavior online with preexisting internet data. In *Proceedings of the 2017 CHI Conference on Human Factors in Computing Systems*, pages 3175–3187. ACM.

Qian Chen, Xiaodan Zhu, Zhenhua Ling, Si Wei, and Hui Jiang. 2016. Enhancing and combining sequential and tree lstm for natural language inference. *arXiv preprint arXiv:1609.06038*.

Ying Chen, Yilu Zhou, Sencun Zhu, and Heng Xu. 2012. Detecting offensive language in social media to protect adolescent online safety. In *Privacy, Security, Risk and Trust (PASSAT), 2012 International Conference on and 2012 International Confernece on Social Computing (SocialCom)*, pages 71–80. IEEE.

Junyoung Chung, Caglar Gulcehre, Kyunghyun Cho, and Yoshua Bengio. 2015. Gated feedback recurrent neural networks. In *International Conference on Machine Learning*, pages 2067–2075.

Thomas Davidson, Dana Warmsley, Michael Macy, and Ingmar Weber. 2017. Automated hate speech detection and the problem of offensive language. *arXiv preprint arXiv:1703.04009*.

Bjarke Felbo, Alan Mislove, Anders Søgaard, Iyad Rahwan, and Sune Lehmann. 2017. Using millions of emoji occurrences to learn any-domain representations for detecting sentiment, emotion and sarcasm. *arXiv preprint arXiv:1708.00524*.

Björn Gambäck and Utpal Kumar Sikdar. 2017. Using convolutional neural networks to classify hate-speech. In *Proceedings of the First Workshop on Abusive Language Online*, pages 85–90.

Yves Grandvalet and Yoshua Bengio. 2005. Semi-supervised learning by entropy minimization. In *Advances in neural information processing systems*, pages 529–536.

Guolin Ke, Qi Meng, Thomas Finley, Taifeng Wang, Wei Chen, Weidong Ma, Qiwei Ye, and Tie-Yan Liu. 2017. Lightgbm: A highly efficient gradient boosting decision tree. In *Advances in Neural Information Processing Systems*, pages 3146–3154.

Dong-Hyun Lee. 2013. Pseudo-label: The simple and efficient semi-supervised learning method for deep neural networks. In *Workshop on Challenges in Representation Learning, ICML*, volume 3, page 2.

Christopher J Merz. 1999. Using correspondence analysis to combine classifiers. *Machine Learning*, 36(1-2):33–58.

Chikashi Nobata, Joel Tetreault, Achint Thomas, Yashar Mehdad, and Yi Chang. 2016. Abusive language detection in online user content. In *Proceedings of the 25th international conference on world wide web*, pages 145–153. International World Wide Web Conferences Steering Committee.

Etienne Papegnies, Vincent Labatut, Richard Dufour, and Georges Linares. 2017. Impact of content features for automatic online abuse detection. *arXiv preprint arXiv:1704.03289*.

Ankur P Parikh, Oscar Täckström, Dipanjan Das, and Jakob Uszkoreit. 2016. A decomposable attention model for natural language inference. *arXiv preprint arXiv:1606.01933*.

Jeffrey Pennington, Richard Socher, and Christopher Manning. 2014. Glove: Global vectors for word representation. In *Proceedings of the 2014 conference on empirical methods in natural language processing (EMNLP)*, pages 1532–1543.

Borut Sluban and Nada Lavrač. 2015. Relating ensemble diversity and performance: A study in class noise detection. *Neurocomputing*, 160:120–131.

Zeerak Waseem, Thomas Davidson, Dana Warmsley, and Ingmar Weber. 2017. Understanding abuse: a typology of abusive language detection subtasks. *arXiv preprint arXiv:1705.09899*.

Ellery Wulczyn, Nithum Thain, and Lucas Dixon. 2016a. Ex machina: Personal attacks seen at scale. *CoRR*, abs/1610.08914.

Ellery Wulczyn, Nithum Thain, and Lucas Dixon. 2016b. Wikipedia detox. *figshare*.

Guang Xiang, Bin Fan, Ling Wang, Jason Hong, and Carolyn Rose. 2012. Detecting offensive tweets via topical feature discovery over a large scale twitter corpus. In *Proceedings of the 21st ACM international conference on Information and knowledge management*, pages 1980–1984. ACM.

Dawei Yin, Zhenzhen Xue, Liangjie Hong, Brian D Davison, April Kontostathis, and Lynne Edwards. 2009. Detection of harassment on web 2. *Proceedings of the Content Analysis in the WEB*, 2:1–7.

Predictive Embeddings for Hate Speech Detection on Twitter

Rohan Kshirsagar[1] Tyrus Cukuvac[1] Kathleen McKeown[1] Susan McGregor[2]
[1]Department of Computer Science at Columbia University
[2]School of Journalism at Columbia University
`rmk2161@columbia.edu thc2125@columbia.edu`
`kathy@cs.columbia.edu sem2196@columbia.edu`

Abstract

We present a neural-network based approach to classifying online hate speech in general, as well as racist and sexist speech in particular. Using pre-trained word embeddings and max/mean pooling from simple, fully-connected transformations of these embeddings, we are able to predict the occurrence of hate speech on three commonly used publicly available datasets. Our models match or outperform state of the art F1 performance on all three datasets using significantly fewer parameters and minimal feature preprocessing compared to previous methods.

1 Introduction

The increasing popularity of social media platforms like Twitter for both personal and political communication (Lapowsky, 2017) has seen a well-acknowledged rise in the presence of toxic and abusive speech on these platforms (Hillard, 2018; Drum, 2017). Although the terms of services on these platforms typically forbid hateful and harassing speech, enforcing these rules has proved challenging, as identifying hate speech speech at scale is still a largely unsolved problem in the NLP community. Waseem and Hovy (2016), for example, identify many ambiguities in classifying abusive communications, and highlight the difficulty of clearly defining the parameters of such speech. This problem is compounded by the fact that identifying abusive or harassing speech is a challenge for humans as well as automated systems.

Despite the lack of consensus around what constitutes abusive speech, *some* definition of hate speech must be used to build automated systems to address it. We rely on Davidson et al. (2017)'s definition of hate speech, specifically: "language that is used to express hatred towards a targeted

group or is intended to be derogatory, to humiliate, or to insult the members of the group."

In this paper, we present a neural classification system that uses minimal preprocessing to take advantage of a modified Simple Word Embeddings-based Model (Shen et al., 2018) to predict the occurrence of hate speech. Our classifier features:

- A simple deep learning approach with few parameters enabling quick and robust training

- Significantly better performance than two other state of the art methods on publicly available datasets

- An interpretable approach facilitating analysis of results

In the following sections, we discuss related work on hate speech classification, followed by a description of the datasets, methods and results of our study.

2 Related Work

Many efforts have been made to classify hate speech using data scraped from online message forums and popular social media sites such as Twitter and Facebook. Waseem and Hovy (2016) applied a logistic regression model that used one- to four-character n-grams for classification of tweets labeled as racist, sexist or neither. Davidson et al. (2017) experimented in classification of hateful as well as offensive but not hateful tweets. They applied a logistic regression classifier with L2 regularization using word level n-grams and various part-of-speech, sentiment, and tweet-level metadata features.

Additional projects have built upon the data sets created by Waseem and/or Davidson. For example, Park and Fung (2017) used a neural network

Proceedings of the Second Workshop on Abusive Language Online (ALW2), pages 26–32
Brussels, Belgium, October 31, 2018. ©2018 Association for Computational Linguistics

approach with two binary classifiers: one to predict the presence abusive speech more generally, and another to discern the form of abusive speech.

Zhang et al. (2018), meanwhile, used pretrained word2vec embeddings, which were then fed into a convolutional neural network (CNN) with max pooling to produce input vectors for a Gated Recurrent Unit (GRU) neural network. Other researchers have experimented with using metadata features from tweets. Founta et al. (2018) built a classifier composed of two separate neural networks, one for the text and the other for metadata of the Twitter user, that were trained jointly in interleaved fashion. Both networks used in combination - and especially when trained using transfer learning - achieved higher F1 scores than either neural network classifier alone.

In contrast to the methods described above, our approach relies on a simple word embedding (SWEM)-based architecture (Shen et al., 2018), reducing the number of required parameters and length of training required, while still yielding improved performance and resilience across related classification tasks. Moreover, our network is able to learn flexible vector representations that demonstrate associations among words typically used in hateful communication. Finally, while metadata-based augmentation is intriguing, here we sought to develop an approach that would function well even in cases where such additional data was missing due to the deletion, suspension, or deactivation of accounts.

3   Data

In this paper, we use three data sets from the literature to train and evaluate our own classifier. Although all address the category of hateful speech, they used different strategies of labeling the collected data. Table 1 shows the characteristics of the datasets.

Data collected by Waseem and Hovy (2016), which we term the **Sexist/Racist (SR)** data set[1], was collected using an initial Twitter search followed by analysis and filtering by the authors and their team who identified 17 common phrases, hashtags, and users that were indicative of abusive speech. Davidson et al. (2017) collected the **HATE dataset** by searching for tweets using a lexicon provided by *Hatebase.org*. The final data

---

[1]Some Tweet IDs/users have been deleted since the creation, so the total number may differ from the original

Dataset	Labels and Counts		Total
SR	Sexist Racist 3086 1924	Neither 10,898	**15,908**
HATE	Hate Speech Not Hate Speech 1430	23,353	**24,783**
HAR	Harassment Non Harassing 5,285	15,075	**20,360**

Table 1: Dataset Characteristics

set we used, which we call **HAR**, was collected by Golbeck et al. (2017); we removed all retweets reducing the dataset to 20,000 tweets. Tweets were labeled as "Harrassing" or "Non-Harrassing"; hate speech was not explicitly labeled, but treated as an unlabeled subset of the broader "Harrassing" category(Golbeck et al., 2017).

4   Transformed Word Embedding Model (TWEM)

Our training set consists of N examples $\{X^i, Y^i\}_{i=1}^N$ where the input X^i is a sequence of tokens $w_1, w_2, ..., w_T$, and the output Y^i is the numerical class for the hate speech class. Each input instance represents a Twitter post and thus, is not limited to a single sentence.

We modify the SWEM-concat (Shen et al., 2018) architecture to allow better handling of infrequent and unknown words and to capture non-linear word combinations.

4.1   Word Embeddings

Each token in the input is mapped to an embedding. We used the 300 dimensional embeddings for all our experiments, so each word w_t is mapped to $x_t \in \mathbb{R}^{300}$. We denote the full embedded sequence as $x_{1:T}$. We then transform each word embedding by applying 300 dimensional 1-layer Multi Layer Perceptron (MLP) W_t with a Rectified Liner Unit (ReLU) activation to form an updated embedding space $z_{1:T}$. We find this better handles unseen or rare tokens in our training data by projecting the pretrained embedding into a space that the encoder can understand.

4.2   Pooling

We make use of two pooling methods on the updated embedding space $z_{1:T}$. We employ a max pooling operation on $z_{1:T}$ to capture salient word features from our input; this representation is denoted as m. This forces words that are highly indicative of hate speech to higher positive values within the updated embedding space. We also average the embeddings $z_{1:T}$ to capture the overall meaning of the sentence, denoted as a, which provides a strong conditional factor in conjunction with the max pooling output. This also helps regularize gradient updates from the max pooling operation.

4.3 Output

We concatenate a and m to form a document representation d and feed the representation into a 50 node 2 layer MLP followed by ReLU Activation to allow for increased nonlinear representation learning. This representation forms the preterminal layer and is passed to a fully connected softmax layer whose output is the probability distribution over labels.

5 Experimental Setup

We tokenize the data using Spacy (Honnibal and Johnson, 2015). We use 300 Dimensional Glove Common Crawl Embeddings (840B Token) (Pennington et al., 2014) and fine tune them for the task. We experimented extensively with preprocessing variants and our results showed better performance without lemmatization and lowercasing (see supplement for details). We pad each input to 50 words. We train using RMSprop with a learning rate of .001 and a batch size of 512. We add dropout with a drop rate of 0.1 in the final layer to reduce overfitting (Srivastava et al., 2014), batch size, and input length empirically through random hyperparameter search.

All of our results are produced from 10-fold cross validation to allow comparison with previous results. We trained a logistic regression baseline model (line 1 in Table 2) using character ngrams and word unigrams using TF*IDF weighting (Salton and Buckley, 1987), to provide a baseline since HAR has no reported results. For the SR and HATE datasets, the authors reported their trained best logistic regression model's[2] results on their respective datasets.

---

[2]Features described in Related Works section

[3]SR: Sexist/Racist (Waseem and Hovy, 2016), HATE: Hate (Davidson et al., 2017) HAR: Harassment (Golbeck et al., 2017)

Method	SR	HATE	HAR
LR(Char-gram + Unigram)	0.79	0.85	0.68
LR(Waseem and Hovy, 2016)	0.74	-	-
LR (Davidson et al., 2017)	-	0.90	-
CNN (Park and Fung, 2017)	0.83	-	-
GRU Text (Founta et al., 2018)	0.83	0.89	-
GRU Text + Metadata	**0.87**	0.89	-
TWEM (Ours)	0.86	**0.924**	**0.71**

Table 2: F1 Results[3]

6 Results and Discussion

The approach we have developed establishes a new state of the art for classifying hate speech, outperforming previous results by as much as 12 F1 points. Table 2 illustrates the robustness of our method, which often outperform previous results, measured by weighted F1. [4]

Using the Approximate Randomization (AR) Test (Riezler and Maxwell, 2005), we perform significance testing using a 75/25 train and test split

to compare against (Waseem and Hovy, 2016) and (Davidson et al., 2017), whose models we reimplemented. We found 0.001 significance compared to both methods. We also include in-depth precision and recall results for all three datasets in the supplement.

Our results indicate better performance than several more complex approaches, including Davidson et al. (2017)'s best model (which used word and part-of-speech ngrams, sentiment, readability, text, and Twitter specific features), Park and Fung (2017) (which used two fold classification and a hybrid of word and character CNNs, using approximately twice the parameters we use excluding the word embeddings) and even recent work by Founta et al. (2018), (whose best model relies on GRUs, metadata including popularity, network reciprocity, and subscribed lists).

On the SR dataset, we outperform Founta et al. (2018)'s text based model by 3 F1 points, while just falling short of the Text + Metadata Interleaved Training model. While we appreciate the potential added value of metadata, we believe a tweet-only classifier has merits because retrieving features from the social graph is not always

---

[4]This was used in previous work, as confirmed by checking with authors

tractable in production settings. Excluding the embedding weights, our model requires 100k parameters , while Founta et al. (2018) requires 250k parameters.

6.1 Error Analysis

False negatives[5]
Many of the false negatives we see are specific references to characters in the TV show "My Kitchen Rules", rather than something about women in general. Such examples may be innocuous in isolation but could potentially be sexist or racist in context. While this may be a limitation of considering only the content of the tweet, it could also be a mislabel.

> Debra are now my most hated team on #mkr after least night's ep. Snakes in the grass those two.

Along these lines, we also see correct predictions of innocuous speech, but find data mislabeled as hate speech:

> @LoveAndLonging ...how is that example "sexism"?

> @amberhasalamb ...in what way?

Another case our classifier misses is problematic speech within a hashtag:

> :D @nkrause11 Dudes who go to culinary school: #why #findawife #notsexist :)

This limitation could be potentially improved through the use of character convolutions or subword tokenization.

False Positives
In certain cases, our model seems to be learning user names instead of semantic content:

> RT @GrantLeeStone: @MT8_9 I don't even know what that is, or where it's from. Was that supposed to be funny? It wasn't.

Since the bulk of our model's weights are in the embedding and embedding-transformation matrices, we cluster the SR vocabulary using these transformed embeddings to clarify our intuitions about the model (8). We elaborate on our clustering approach in the supplement. We see that

---

[5]Focused on the SR Dataset (Waseem and Hovy, 2016)

the model learned general semantic groupings of words associated with hate speech as well as specific idiosyncrasies related to the dataset itself (e.g. *katieandnikki*)

Cluster	Tokens
Geopolitical and religious references around Islam and the Middle East	bomb, mobs, jewish, kidnapped, airstrikes, secularization, ghettoes, islamic, burnt, murderous, penal, traitor, intelligence, molesting, cannibalism
Strong epithets and adjectives associated with harassment and hatespeech	liberals, argumentative, dehumanize, gendered, stereotype, sociopath,bigot, repressed, judgmental, heinous, misandry, shameless, depravity, scumbag,
Miscellaneous	turnt, pedophelia, fricken, exfoliated, sociolinguistic, proph, cissexism, guna, lyked, mobbing, capsicums, orajel, bitchslapped, venturebeat, hairflip, mongodb, intersectional, agender
Sexist related epithets and hashtags	malnourished, katieandnikki, chevapi, dumbslut, mansplainers, crazybitch, horrendousness, justhonest, bile, womenaretoohardtoanimate,
Sexist, sexual, and pornographic terms	actress, feminism, skank, breasts, redhead, anime, bra, twat, chick, sluts, trollop, teenage, pantyhose, pussies, dyke, blonds,

Table 3: Projected Embedding Cluster Analysis from SR Dataset

7 Conclusion

Despite minimal tuning of hyper-parameters, fewer weight parameters, minimal text preprocessing, and no additional metadata, the model performs remarkably well on standard hate speech datasets. Our clustering analysis adds interpretability enabling inspection of results.

Our results indicate that the majority of recent deep learning models in hate speech may rely on word embeddings for the bulk of predictive power and the addition of sequence-based parameters provide minimal utility. Sequence based approaches are typically important when phenomena such as negation, co-reference, and context-dependent phrases are salient in the text and thus, we suspect these cases are in the minority for publicly available datasets. We think it would be valuable to study the occurrence of such linguistic phenomena in existing datasets and construct new datasets that have a better representation of subtle forms of hate speech. In the future, we plan to investigate character based representations, using character CNNs and highway layers (Kim et al., 2016) along with word embeddings to allow robust representations for sparse words such as hashtags.

References

Thomas Davidson, Dana Warmsley, Michael Macy, and Ingmar Weber. 2017. Automated hate speech detection and the problem of offensive language. *arXiv preprint arXiv:1703.04009*.

Kevin Drum. 2017. Twitter Is a Cesspool, But It's Our Cesspool. *Mother Jones*.

Antigoni-Maria Founta, Despoina Chatzakou, Nicolas Kourtellis, Jeremy Blackburn, Athena Vakali, and Ilias Leontiadis. 2018. A unified deep learning architecture for abuse detection. *arXiv preprint arXiv:1802.00385*.

Jennifer Golbeck, Zahra Ashktorab, Rashad O Banjo, Alexandra Berlinger, Siddharth Bhagwan, Cody Buntain, Paul Cheakalos, Alicia A Geller, Quint Gergory, Rajesh Kumar Gnanasekaran, et al. 2017. A large labeled corpus for online harassment research. In *Proceedings of the 2017 ACM on Web Science Conference*, pages 229–233. ACM.

Graham Hillard. 2018. Stop Complaining about Twitter — Just Leave It. *National Review*.

Matthew Honnibal and Mark Johnson. 2015. An improved non-monotonic transition system for dependency parsing. In *Proceedings of the 2015 Conference on Empirical Methods in Natural Language Processing*, pages 1373–1378, Lisbon, Portugal. Association for Computational Linguistics.

Ian T Jolliffe. 1986. Principal component analysis and factor analysis. In *Principal component analysis*, pages 115–128. Springer.

Yoon Kim, Yacine Jernite, David Sontag, and Alexander M Rush. 2016. Character-aware neural language models. In *AAAI*, pages 2741–2749.

Issie Lapowsky. 2017. Trump faces lawsuit over his Twitter blocking habits. *Wired*.

Ji Ho Park and Pascale Fung. 2017. One-step and two-step classification for abusive language detection on twitter. *CoRR*, abs/1706.01206.

F. Pedregosa, G. Varoquaux, A. Gramfort, V. Michel, B. Thirion, O. Grisel, M. Blondel, P. Prettenhofer, R. Weiss, V. Dubourg, J. Vanderplas, A. Passos, D. Cournapeau, M. Brucher, M. Perrot, and E. Duchesnay. 2011. Scikit-learn: Machine learning in Python. *Journal of Machine Learning Research*, 12:2825–2830.

Jeffrey Pennington, Richard Socher, and Christopher D. Manning. 2014. Glove: Global vectors for word representation. In *Empirical Methods in Natural Language Processing (EMNLP)*, pages 1532–1543.

Stefan Riezler and John T Maxwell. 2005. On some pitfalls in automatic evaluation and significance testing for mt. In *Proceedings of the ACL workshop on intrinsic and extrinsic evaluation measures for machine translation and/or summarization*, pages 57–64.

Gerard Salton and Chris Buckley. 1987. Term weighting approaches in automatic text retrieval. Technical report, Cornell University.

Dinghan Shen, Guoyin Wang, Wenlin Wang, Martin Renqiang Min, Qinliang Su, Yizhe Zhang, Ricardo Henao, and Lawrence Carin. 2018. On the use of word embeddings alone to represent natural language sequences.

Nitish Srivastava, Geoffrey Hinton, Alex Krizhevsky, Ilya Sutskever, and Ruslan Salakhutdinov. 2014. Dropout: A simple way to prevent neural networks from overfitting. *The Journal of Machine Learning Research*, 15(1):1929–1958.

Zeerak Waseem and Dirk Hovy. 2016. Hateful symbols or hateful people? predictive features for hate speech detection on twitter. In *Proceedings of the NAACL student research workshop*, pages 88–93.

Z. Zhang, D. Robinson, and J. Tepper. 2018. Detecting hate speech on twitter using a convolution-gru based deep neural network. © 2018 Springer Verlag.

A Supplemental Material

We experimented with several different preprocessing variants and were surprised to find that reducing preprocessing improved the performance on the task for all of our tasks. We go through each preprocessing variant with an example and then describe our analysis to compare and evaluate each of them.

A.1 Preprocessing

Original text

> RT @AGuyNamed_Nick Now, I'm not sexist in any way shape or form but I think women are better at gift wrapping. It's the XX chromosome thing

Tokenize (Basic Tokenize: Keeps case and words intact with limited sanitizing)

> RT @AGuyNamed_Nick Now , I 'm not sexist in any way shape or form but I think women are better at gift wrapping . It 's the XX chromosome thing

Tokenize Lowercase: Lowercase the basic tokenize scheme

> rt @aguynamed_nick now , i 'm not sexist in any way shape or form but i think women are better at gift wrapping . it 's the xx chromosome thing

Token Replace: Replaces entities and user names with placeholder)

> ENT USER now , I 'm not sexist in any way shape or form but I think women are better at gift wrapping . It 's the xx chromosome thing

Token Replace Lowercase: Lowercase the Token Replace Scheme

> ENT USER now , i 'm not sexist in any way shape or form but i think women are better at gift wrapping . it 's the xx chromosome thing

We did analysis on a validation set across multiple datasets to find that the "Tokenize" scheme was by far the best. We believe that keeping the case in tact provides useful information about the user. For example, saying something in all CAPS is a useful signal that the model can take advantage of.

Preprocessing Scheme	Avg. Validation Loss
Token Replace Lowercase	0.47
Token Replace	0.46
Tokenize	0.32
Tokenize Lowercase	0.40

Table 4: Average Validation Loss for each Preprocessing Scheme

A.2 In-Depth Results

	Waseem 2016			Ours		
	P	R	F1	P	R	F1
none	0.76	0.98	0.86	0.88	0.93	**0.90**
sexism	0.95	0.38	0.54	0.79	0.74	**0.76**
racism	0.85	0.30	0.44	0.86	0.72	**0.78**
			0.74			**0.86**

Table 5: SR Results

	Davidson 2017			Ours		
	P	R	F1	P	R	F1
none	0.82	0.95	0.88	0.89	0.94	**0.91**
offensive	0.96	0.91	0.93	0.95	0.96	**0.96**
hate	0.44	0.61	**0.51**	0.61	0.41	0.49
			0.90			**0.924**

Table 6: HATE Results

Method	Prec	Rec	F1	Avg F1
Ours	0.713	0.206	**0.319**	**0.711**
LR Baseline	0.820	0.095	0.170	0.669

Table 7: HAR Results

A.3 Embedding Analysis

Since our method was a simple word embedding based model, we explored the learned embedding space to analyze results. For this analysis, we only use the max pooling part of our architecture to help analyze the learned embedding space because it encourages salient words to increase their values to be selected. We projected the original pretrained embeddings to the learned space using the time distributed MLP. We summed the embedding dimensions for each word and sorted by the sum in descending order to find the 1000 most salient word embeddings from our vocabulary. We then ran PCA (Jolliffe, 1986) to reduce the dimensionality of the projected embeddings from 300 dimensions to 75 dimensions. This captured about 60% of the variance. Finally, we ran K means clustering for $k = 5$ clusters to organize the most salient embeddings in the projected space.

The learned clusters from the SR vocabulary were very illuminating (see Table 8); they gave insights to how hate speech surfaced in the datasets. One clear grouping we found is the misogynistic and pornographic group, which contained words like *breasts*, *blonds*, and *skank*. Two other clusters had references to geopolitical and religious issues in the Middle East and disparaging and resentful epithets that could be seen as having an intellectual tone. This hints towards the subtle pedagogic forms of hate speech that surface.

We ran silhouette analysis (Pedregosa et al., 2011) on the learned clusters to find that the clusters from the learned representations had a 35% higher silhouette coefficient using the projected embeddings compared to the clusters created from the original pre-trained embeddings. This reinforces the claim that our training process pushed hate-speech related words together, and words from other clusters further away, thus, structuring the embedding space effectively for detecting hate speech.

Cluster	Tokens
Geopolitical and religious references around Islam and the Middle East	bomb, mobs, jewish, kidnapped, airstrikes, secularization, ghettoes, islamic, burnt, murderous, penal, traitor, intelligence, molesting, cannibalism
Strong epithets and adjectives associated with harassment and hatespeech	liberals, argumentative, dehumanize, gendered, stereotype, sociopath,bigot, repressed, judgmental, heinous, misandry, shameless, depravity, scumbag,
Miscellaneous	turnt, pedophelia, fricken, exfoliated, sociolinguistic, proph, cissexism, guna, lyked, mobbing, capsicums, orajel, bitchslapped, venturebeat, hairflip, mongodb, intersectional, agender
Sexist related epithets and hashtags	malnourished, katieandnikki, chevapi, dumbslut, mansplainers, crazybitch, horrendousness, justhonest, bile, womenaretoohardtoanimate,
Sexist, sexual, and pornographic terms	actress, feminism, skank, breasts, redhead, anime, bra, twat, chick, sluts, trollop, teenage, pantyhose, pussies, dyke, blonds,

Table 8: Projected Embedding Cluster Analysis from SR Dataset

Challenges for Toxic Comment Classification:
An In-Depth Error Analysis

Betty van Aken[1], Julian Risch[2], Ralf Krestel[2], and Alexander Löser[1]

[1]Beuth University of Applied Sciences, Germany
{`bvanaken, aloeser`}@beuth-hochschule.de
[2]Hasso Plattner Institute, University of Potsdam, Germany
`firstname.lastname@hpi.de`

Abstract

Toxic comment classification has become an active research field with many recently proposed approaches. However, while these approaches address some of the task's challenges others still remain unsolved and directions for further research are needed. To this end, we compare different deep learning and shallow approaches on a new, large comment dataset and propose an ensemble that outperforms all individual models. Further, we validate our findings on a second dataset. The results of the ensemble enable us to perform an extensive error analysis, which reveals open challenges for state-of-the-art methods and directions towards pending future research. These challenges include missing paradigmatic context and inconsistent dataset labels.

1 Introduction

Keeping online conversations constructive and inclusive is a crucial task for platform providers. Automatic classification of toxic comments, such as hate speech, threats, and insults, can help in keeping discussions fruitful. In addition, new regulations in certain European countries have been established enforcing to delete illegal content in less than 72 hours.[1]

Active research on the topic deals with common challenges of natural language processing, such as long-range dependencies or misspelled and idiosyncratic words. Proposed solutions include bidirectional recurrent neural networks with attention (Pavlopoulos et al., 2017) and the use of pretrained word embeddings (Badjatiya et al., 2017). However, many classifiers suffer from insufficient variance in methods and training data and therefore often tend to fail on the long tail of real world data (Zhang and Luo, 2018). For future research, it is essential to know which challenges

are already addressed by state-of-the-art classifiers and for which challenges current solutions are still error-prone.

We take two datasets into account to investigate these errors: comments on Wikipedia talk pages presented by Google Jigsaw during Kaggle's Toxic Comment Classification Challenge[2] and a Twitter Dataset by Davidson et al. (2017). These sets include common difficulties in datasets for the task: They are labeled based on different definitions; they include diverse language from user comments and Tweets; and they present a multi-class and a multi-label classification task respectively.

On these datasets we propose an ensemble of state-of-the-art classifiers. By analysing false negatives and false positives of the ensemble we get insights about open challenges that all of the approaches share. Therefore, our main contributions are:

1) We are the first to apply and compare a range of strong classifiers to a new public multi-label dataset of more than 200,000 user comments. Each classifier, such as Logistic Regression, bidirectional RNN and CNN, is meant to tackle specific challenges for text classification. We apply the same classifiers to a dataset of Tweets to validate our results on a different domain.

2) We apply two different pretrained word embeddings for the domain of user comments and Tweets to compensate errors such as idiosyncratic and misspelled words.

3) We compare the classifiers' predictions and show that they make different errors as measured by Pearson correlation coefficients and F1-measures. Based on this, we create an ensemble that improves macro-averaged F1-measure especially on sparse classes and data with high variance.

---

[1]`https://www.bbc.com/news/technology-42510868`

[2]`https://www.kaggle.com/c/jigsaw-toxic-comment-classification-challenge`

Proceedings of the Second Workshop on Abusive Language Online (ALW2), pages 33–42
Brussels, Belgium, October 31, 2018. ©2018 Association for Computational Linguistics

4) We perform a detailed error analysis on results of the ensemble. The analysis points to common errors of all current approaches. We propose directions for future work based on these unsolved challenges.

2   Related Work

Task definitions. Toxic comment classification is not clearly distinguishable from its related tasks. Besides looking at toxicity of online comments (Wulczyn et al., 2017; Georgakopoulos et al., 2018), related research includes the investigation of hate speech (Badjatiya et al., 2017; Burnap and Williams, 2016; Davidson et al., 2017; Gambäck and Sikdar, 2017; Njagi et al., 2015; Schmidt and Wiegand, 2017; Vigna et al., 2017; Warner and Hirschberg, 2012), online harassment (Yin and Davison, 2009; Golbeck et al., 2017), abusive language (Mehdad and Tetreault, 2016; Park and Fung, 2017), cyberbullying (Dadvar et al., 2013; Dinakar et al., 2012; Hee et al., 2015; Zhong et al., 2016) and offensive language (Chen et al., 2012; Xiang et al., 2012). Each field uses different definitions for their classification, still similar methods can often be applied to different tasks. In our work we focus on toxic comment detection and show that the same method can effectively be applied to a hate speech detection task.

Multi-class approaches. Besides traditional binary classification tasks, related work considers different aspects of toxic language, such as "racism" (Greevy and Smeaton, 2004; Waseem, 2016; Kwok and Wang, 2013) and "sexism" (Waseem and Hovy, 2016; Jha and Mamidi, 2017), or the severity of toxicity (Davidson et al., 2017; Sharma et al., 2018). These tasks are framed as multi-class problems, where each sample is labeled with exactly one class out of a set of multiple classes. The great majority of related research considers only multi-class problems. This is remarkable, considering that in real-world scenarios toxic comment classification can often be seen as a multi-label problem, with user comments fulfilling different predefined criteria at the same time. We therefore investigate both a multi-label dataset containing six different forms of toxic language and a multi-class dataset containing three mutually exclusive classes of toxic language.

Shallow classification and neural networks. Toxic comment identification is a supervised classification task and approached by either methods including manual feature engineering (Burnap and Williams, 2015; Mehdad and Tetreault, 2016; Waseem, 2016; Davidson et al., 2017; Nobata et al., 2016; Kennedy et al., 2017; Samghabadi et al., 2017; Robinson et al., 2018) or the use of (deep) neural networks (Ptaszynski et al., 2017; Pavlopoulos et al., 2017; Badjatiya et al., 2017; Vigna et al., 2017; Park and Fung, 2017; Gambäck and Sikdar, 2017). While in the first case manually selected features are combined into input vectors and directly used for classification, neural network approaches are supposed to automatically learn abstract features above these input features. Neural network approaches appear to be more effective for learning (Zhang and Luo, 2018), while feature-based approaches preserve some sort of explainability. We focus in this paper on baselines using deep neural networks (e.g. CNN and Bi-LSTM) and shallow learners, such as Logistic Regression approaches on word n-grams and character n-grams.

Ensemble learning. Burnap and Williams (2015) studied advantages of ensembles of different classifiers. They combined results from three feature-based classifiers. Further the combination of results from Logistic Regression and a Neural Network has been studied (Gao and Huang, 2017; Risch and Krestel, 2018). Zimmerman et al. (2018) investigated ensembling models with different hyper-parameters. To our knowledge, the approach presented in this paper, combining both various model architectures and different word embeddings for toxic comment classification, has not been investigated so far.

3   Datasets and Tasks

The task of toxic comment classification lacks a consistently labeled standard dataset for comparative evaluation (Schmidt and Wiegand, 2017). While there are a number of annotated public datasets in adjacent fields, such as hate speech (Ross et al., 2016; Gao and Huang, 2017), racism/sexism (Waseem, 2016; Waseem and Hovy, 2016) or harassment (Golbeck et al., 2017) detection, most of them follow different definitions for labeling and therefore often constitute different problems.

Class	# of occurrences
Clean	201,081
Toxic	21,384
Obscene	12,140
Insult	11,304
Identity Hate	2,117
Severe Toxic	1,962
Threat	689

Table 1: Class distribution of Wikipedia dataset. The distribution shows a strong class imbalance.

Class	# of occurrences
Offensive	19,190
Clean	4,163
Hate	1,430

Table 2: Class distribution of Twitter dataset. The majority class of the dataset consists of offensive Tweets.

3.1 Wikipedia Talk Pages dataset

We analyse a dataset published by Google Jigsaw in December 2017 over the course of the 'Toxic Comment Classification Challenge' on Kaggle. It includes 223,549 annotated user comments collected from Wikipedia talk pages and is the largest publicly available for the task. These comments were annotated by human raters with the six labels 'toxic', 'severe toxic, 'insult', 'threat', 'obscene' and 'identity hate'. Comments can be associated with multiple classes at once, which frames the task as a multi-label classification problem. Jigsaw has not published official definitions for the six classes. But they do state that they defined a toxic comment as "a rude, disrespectful, or unreasonable comment that is likely to make you leave a discussion".[3]

The dataset features an unbalanced class distribution, shown in Table 1. 201,081 samples fall under the majority 'clear' class matching none of the six categories, whereas 22,468 samples belong to at least one of the other classes. While the 'toxic' class includes 9.6% of the samples, only 0.3% are labeled as 'threat', marking the smallest class.

Comments were collected from the English Wikipedia and are mostly written in English with some outliers, e.g., in Arabic, Chinese or German language. The domain covered is not

strictly locatable, due to various article topics being discussed. Still it is possible to apply a simple categorization of comments as follows:[4]

1) 'community-related':

> Example: *"If you continue to vandalize Wikipedia, you will be blocked from editing."*

2) 'article-related':

> Example: *"Dark Jedi Miraluka from the Mid-Rim world of Katarr, Visas Marr is the lone surviving member of her species."*

3) 'off-topic':

> Example: *"== I hate how my life goes today == Just kill me now."*

3.2 Twitter dataset

Additionally we investigate a dataset introduced by Davidson et al. (2017). It contains 24,783 Tweets fetched using the Twitter API and annotated by CrowdFlower workers with the labels 'hate speech', 'offensive but not hate speech' and 'neither offensive nor hate speech'. Table 2 shows the class distribution. We observe a strong bias towards the offensive class making up 77.4% of the comments caused by sampling tweets by seed keywords from Hatebase.org. We choose this dataset to show that our method is also applicable to multi-class problems and works with Tweets, which usually have a different structure than other online user comments due to character limitation.

3.3 Common Challenges

We observe three common challenges for Natural Language Processing in both datasets:

Out-of-vocabulary words. A common problem for the task is the occurrence of words that are not present in the training data. These words include slang or misspellings, but also intentionally obfuscated content.

Long-Range Dependencies. The toxicity of a comment often depends on expressions made in early parts of the comment. This is especially problematic for longer comments ($>$50 words) where the influence of earlier parts on the result can vanish.

---

[3]http://www.perspectiveapi.com/

[4]Disclaimer: This paper contains examples that may be considered profane, vulgar, or offensive. These contents do not reflect the views of the authors and exclusively serve to explain linguistic research challenges.

Multi-word phrases. We see many occurrences of multi-word phrases in both datasets. Our algorithms can detect their toxicity only if they can recognize multiple words as a single (typical) hateful phrase.

4 Methods and Ensemble

In this section we study baseline methods for the above mentioned common challenges. Further, we propose our ensemble learning architecture. Its goal is to minimize errors by detecting optimal methods for a given comment.

4.1 Logistic Regression

The Logistic Regression (LR) algorithm is widely used for binary classification tasks. Unlike deep learning models, it requires manual feature engineering. Contrary to Deep Learning methods, LR permits obtaining insights about the model, such as observed coefficients. Research from Waseem and Hovy (2016) shows that word and character n-grams belong to one of the most indicative features for the task of hate speech detection. For this reason we investigate the use of word and character n-grams for LR models.

4.2 Recurrent Neural Networks

Recurrent Neural Networks (RNNs) interpret a document as a sequence of words or character n-grams. We use four different RNN approaches: An LSTM (Long-Short-Term-Memory Network), a bidirectional LSTM, a bidirectional GRU (Gated Recurrent Unit) architecture and a bidirectional GRU with an additional attention layer.

LSTM. Our LSTM model takes a sequence of words as input. An embedding layer transforms one-hot-encoded words to dense vector representations and a spatial dropout, which randomly masks 10% of the input words, makes the network more robust. To process the sequence of word embeddings, we use an LSTM layer with 128 units, followed by a dropout of 10%. Finally, a dense layer with a sigmoid activation makes the prediction for the multi-label classification and a dense layer with softmax activation makes the prediction for the multi-class classification.

Bidirectional LSTM and GRU. Bidirectional RNNs can compensate certain errors on long range dependencies. In contrast to the standard LSTM model, the bidirectional LSTM model uses two LSTM layers that process the input sequence in opposite directions. Thereby, the input sequence is processed with correct and reverse order of words. The outputs of these two layers are averaged. Similarly, we use a bidirectional GRU model, which consists of two stacked GRU layers. We use layers with 64 units. All other parts of the neural network are inherited from our standard LSTM model. As a result, this network can recognize signals on longer sentences where neurons representing words further apart from each other in the LSTM sequence will 'fire' more likely together.

Bidirectional GRU with Attention Layer. Gao and Huang (2017) phrase that "attention mechanisms are suitable for identifying specific small regions indicating hatefulness in long comments". In order to detect these small regions in our comments, we add an attention layer to our bidirectional GRU-based network following the work of Yang et al. (2016).

4.3 Convolutional Neural Networks

Convolutional Neural Networks (CNNs) are recently becoming more popular for text classification tasks. By intuition they can detect specific combinations of features, while RNNs can extract orderly information (Zhang and Luo, 2018). On character level, CNNs can deal with obfuscation of words. For our model we choose an architecture comparable to the approach of Kim (2014).

4.4 (Sub-)Word Embeddings

Using word embeddings trained on very large corpora can be helpful in order to capture information that is missing from the training data (Zhang and Luo, 2018). Therefore we apply Glove word embeddings trained on a large Twitter corpus by Pennington et al. (2014). In addition, we use sub-word embeddings as introduced by Bojanowski et al. (2017) within the FastText tool. The approach considers substrings of a word to infer its embedding. This is important for learning representations for misspelled, obfuscated or abbreviated words which are often present in online comments. We train FastText embeddings on 95 million comments on Wikipedia user talk pages and article talk pages.[5] We apply the skip-gram method with a context window size of 5 and train for 5 epochs.

---

[5] `https://figshare.com/articles/`
`Wikipedia_Talk_Corpus/4264973`

Model	Wikipedia				Twitter			
	P	R	F1	AUC	P	R	F1	AUC
CNN (FastText)	.73	.86	.776	.981	.73	.83	.775	.948
CNN (Glove)	.70	.85	.748	.979	.72	.82	.769	.945
LSTM (FastText)	.71	.85	.752	.978	.73	.83	.778	.955
LSTM (Glove)	**.74**	.84	.777	.980	.74	.82	.781	.953
Bidirectional LSTM (FastText)	.71	.86	.755	.979	.72	.84	.775	.954
Bidirectional LSTM (Glove)	**.74**	.84	.777	.981	.73	**.85**	.783	.953
Bidirectional GRU (FastText)	.72	.86	.765	.981	.72	.83	.773	.955
Bidirectional GRU (Glove)	.73	.85	.772	.981	.76	.81	.784	.955
Bidirectional GRU Attention (FastText)	**.74**	**.87**	**.783**	**.983**	.74	.83	**.791**	**.958**
Bidirectional GRU Attention (Glove)	.73	**.87**	.779	**.983**	**.77**	.82	**.790**	.952
Logistic Regression (char-ngrams)	**.74**	.84	.776	.975	.73	.81	.764	.937
Logistic Regression (word-ngrams)	.70	.83	.747	.962	.71	.80	.746	.933
Ensemble	**.74**	**.88**	**.791**	**.983**	.76	.83	**.793**	.953

Table 3: Comparison of precision, recall, F1-measure, and ROC AUC on two datasets. The results show that the ensemble outperforms the individual classifiers in F1-measure. The strongest individual classifier on both datasets is a bidirectional GRU network with attention layer.

4.5 Ensemble Learning

Each classification method varies in its predictive power and may conduct specific errors. For example, GRUs or LSTMs may miss long range dependencies for very long sentences with 50 or more words but are powerful in capturing phrases and complex context information. Bi-LSTMs and attention based networks can compensate these errors to a certain extent. Subword Embeddings can model even misspelled or obfuscated words.

Therefore, we propose an ensemble deciding which of the single classifiers is most powerful on a specific kind of comment. The ensemble observes features in comments, weights and learns an optimal classifier selection for a given feature combination. For achieving this functionality, we observe the set of out-of-fold predictions from the various approaches and train an ensemble with gradient boosting decision trees. We perform 5-fold cross-validation and average final predictions on the test set across the five trained models.

5 Experimental Study

Our hypothesis is that the ensemble learns to choose an optimal combination of classifiers based on a set of comment features. Because the classifiers have different strengths and weaknesses, we expect the ensemble to outperform each individual classifier. Based on results from previous experiments mentioned in Section 2 we expect that the state-of-the-art models have a comparable performance and none outperforms the others significantly. This is important because otherwise the ensemble learner constantly prioritizes the outperforming classifier. We expect our ensemble to perform well on both online comments and Tweets despite their differing language characteristics such as comment length and use of slang words.

5.1 Setup

To evaluate our hypotheses, we use the following setup: We compare six methods from Section 4. For the neural network approaches we apply two different word embeddings each and for LR we use character and word n-grams as features.

We need binary predictions to calculate precision, recall and the resulting F1-measure. To translate the continuous sigmoid output for the multi-label task (Wikipedia dataset) into binary labels we estimate appropriate threshold values per class. For this purpose we perform a parameter search for the threshold to optimize the F1-measure using the whole training set as validation. In case of the multi-class task (Twitter dataset) the softmax layer makes the parameter search needless, because we can simply take the label with the highest value as the predicted one.

We choose the macro-average F1 measure since it is more indicative than the micro-average F1 for strongly unbalanced datasets (Zhang and Luo, 2018). For the multi-label classification we measure macro-precision and -recall for each class separately and average their results to get the F1-measure per classifier. The Area under the Receiver Operating Curve (ROC AUC) gives us a measurement of classifier performance without the need for a specific threshold. We add it to provide additional comparability of the results.

5.2 Correlation Analysis

Total accuracy of the ensemble can only improve when models with comparable accuracy produce uncorrelated predictions. We therefore measure the correlation of the predictions of different classifiers. We look at a set of combinations, such as shallow learner combined with a neural net, and inspect their potential for improving the overall prediction. For measuring the disparity of two models we use the Pearson correlation coefficient. The results are shown in Table 4.

5.3 Experimental Results

As shown in Table 3 our ensemble outperforms the strongest individual method on the Wikipedia dataset by approximately one percent F1-measure. We see that the difference in F1-measure between the best individual classifier and the ensemble is higher on the Wikipedia dataset as on the Twitter dataset. This finding is accompanied by the results in Table 4 which show that most classifier combinations present a high correlation on the Twitter dataset and are therefore less effective on the ensemble. An explanation for this effect is that the text sequences within the Twitter set show less variance than the ones in the Wikipedia dataset. This can be reasoned from 1) their sampling strategy based on a list of terms, 2) the smaller size of the dataset and 3) less disparity within the three defined classes than in the six from the Wikipedia dataset. With less variant data one selected classifier for a type of text can be sufficient.

As the results in Table 4 show, ensembling is especially effective on the sparse classes "threat" (Wikipedia) and "hate" (Twitter). The predictions for these two classes have the weakest correlation. This can be exploited when dealing with strongly imbalanced datasets, as often the case in toxic comment classification and related tasks. Table 4 gives us indicators for useful combinations of classifiers. Combining our shallow learner approach with Neural Networks is highly effective. Contrary

Class	F1		Pearson
	Different word embeddings		
	GRU+G	GRU+FT	
W avg.	.78	.78	.95
W threat	.70	.69	.92
T avg.	.79	.79	.96
T hate	.53	.54	.94
	CNN+G	CNN+FT	
W avg.	.75	.78	.91
W threat	**.67**	**.73**	**.82**
T avg.	.77	.78	.94
T hate	.49	.53	.90
	Different NN architectures		
	CNN	BiGRU Att	
W avg.	**.78**	**.78**	**.85**
W threat	**.73**	**.71**	**.65**
T avg.	.78	.79	.96
T hate	.50	.49	.93
	Shallow learner and NN		
	CNN	LR char	
W avg.	**.78**	**.78**	**.86**
W threat	**.73**	**.74**	**.78**
T avg.	.78	.76	.92
T hate	**.50**	**.51**	**.86**
	BiGRU Att	LR char	
W avg.	**.78**	**.78**	**.84**
W threat	**.71**	**.74**	**.67**
T avg.	.79	.76	.92
T hate	.49	.51	.88
	Character- and word-ngrams		
	LR word	LR char	
W avg.	**.75**	**.78**	**.83**
W threat	**.70**	**.74**	**.69**
T avg.	.75	.77	.94
T hate	.50	.51	.91

Table 4: F1-measures and Pearson correlations of different combinations of classifiers. When the pearson score is low and F1 is similar, an ensemble performs best. We see that this appears mostly on the Wikipedia dataset and on the respective minority classes 'threat' and 'hate'. 'W': Wikipedia dataset; 'T': Twitter dataset; 'G': Glove embeddings; 'FT': FastText embeddings; 'avg.': Averaged

to that we see that the different word embeddings used do not lead to strongly differing predictions. Another finding is that word and character n-grams learned by our Logistic Regression classifier produce strongly uncorrelated predictions that can be combined for increasing accuracy.

6 Detailed Error Analysis

The ensemble of state-of-the-art classifiers still fails to reach F1-measures higher than 0.8. To find out the remaining problems we perform an extensive error analysis on the result of the ensemble.

We analyse common error classes of our ensemble based on research from Zhang and Luo (2018); Zhang et al. (2018); Qian et al. (2018); Davidson et al. (2017); Schmidt and Wiegand (2017); Nobata et al. (2016). Moreover, we add additional error classes we encountered during our manual analysis. To address deficits in both precision and recall we inspect false negative and false positive classifications. We focus on error classes with the highest frequency in the observed samples. The occurrence of an error class within a comment is taken to be binary (occurs in comment or not).

We present the results on class 'toxic' of the Wikipedia dataset and class 'hate' of the Twitter dataset. Both classes are of high significance for the task of user comment moderation. Our ensemble results in 1794 false negatives and 1581 false positives for the Wikipedia dataset. We choose 200 random samples out of each set as representatives. For the smaller Twitter dataset we get 55 false negatives and 58 false positives, we perform our analysis on all of these samples.

6.1 Error Classes of False Negatives

Doubtful labels. We observe a high number of comments for which we question the original label when taking the respective class definition into account. A common occurrence is actual toxic or hateful content that is cited by the comment's author. Another pattern is the use of potentially toxic words within an explanation or self reproach.

> Example: *"No matter how upset you may be there is never a reason to refer to another editor as 'an idiot' "*

We find that 23% of sampled comments in the false negatives of the Wikipedia dataset do not fulfill the toxic definition in our view. Taking the hate speech definition of the authors into account, we question 9% of the Twitter dataset samples. For the remaining error classes we only include the comments with undoubtful labels.

Toxicity without swear words. Davidson et al. (2017) phrase the problem that hate speech may not contain hate or swear words at all.

> Example: *"she looks like a horse"*

50% of Wikipedia dataset samples have no common hate or swear word in them. This makes it the largest error class for the Wikipedia dataset and shows that our classifiers often fail when there are no obvious hateful words present. We observe this in 18% of hate speech comments from the Twitter dataset. It is important to notice that the frequency of swear words is naturally higher within this dataset, because of its sampling method with hateful words as seeds. In many cases the problem is a lack of paradigmatic context. Hence, an important research topic for future work is investigating improved semantic embeddings, which can better distinguish different paradigmatic contexts.

Rhetorical questions. It is common practice to wrap toxic statements online within rhetorical or suggestive questions as pointed out by Schmidt and Wiegand (2017).

> Example: *"have you no brain?!?!"*

21% of Wikipedia dataset samples and 10% of Twitter dataset samples contain a rhetorical or suggestive question. Again paradigmatic context can help to identify this kind of comments. An additional signal is the existence of question words and question marks.

Metaphors and comparisons. Subtle metaphors and comparisons often require understanding of implications of language or additional world knowledge. Zhang and Luo (2018) and Schmidt and Wiegand (2017) report on this common error class.

> Example: *"Who are you a sockpuppet for?"*

We only see this problem in the Wikipedia dataset samples with 16% of false negatives impacted.

Idiosyncratic and rare words. Errors caused by rare or unknown words are reported by Nobata et al. (2016); Zhang and Luo (2018); Qian et al. (2018). From our observation they include misspellings, neologisms, obfuscations, abbreviations and slang words. Even though some of these words appear in the embedding, their frequency may be too low to correctly detect their meaning on our word embeddings.

> Example: *"fucc nicca yu pose to be pullin up"*

We find rare or unknown words in 30% of examined false negatives from the Wikipedia dataset and in 43% of Twitter dataset samples. This also reflects the common language on Twitter with many slang words, abbreviations and mis-spellings. One option to circumvent this problem is to train word embeddings on larger corpora with even more variant language.

Sarcasm and irony. Nobata et al. (2016) and Qian et al. (2018) report the problem of sarcasm for hate speech detection. As sarcasm and irony detection is a hard task itself, it also increases difficulty of toxic comment classification, because the texts usually state the opposite of what is really meant.

> Example: *"hope you're proud of yourself. Another milestone in idiocy."*

Sarcasm or irony appears in 11% of Wikipedia dataset samples, but in none of the Twitter dataset samples.

6.2 Error Classes of False Positives

Doubtful labels. We find that 53% of false positive samples from the Wikipedia dataset actually fall under the definition of toxic in our view, even though they are labeled as non-toxic. Most of them contain strong hateful expressions or spam. We identify 10% of the Twitter dataset samples to have questionable labels.

> Example: *"IF YOU LOOK THIS UP UR A DUMB RUSSIAN"*

The analysis show that doubtful labels belong to one of the main reasons for a false classification on the Wikipedia dataset, especially for the false positives. The results emphasize the importance of taking labeler agreement into account when building up a dataset to train machine learning models. It also shows the need for clear defini-tions especially for classes with high variance like toxicity. Besides that, a deficient selection of annotators can amplify such problems as Waseem et al. (2018) point out.

Usage of swear words in false positives. Clas-sifiers often learn that swear words are strong indicators for toxicity in comments. This can be problematic when non-toxic comments contain such terms. Zhang and Luo (2018) describe this problem as dealing with non distinctive features.

> Example: *"Oh, I feel like such an asshole now. Sorry, bud."*

60% of false positive Wikipedia dataset samples and 77% of Twitter dataset samples contain swear words. In this case, the paradigmatic context is not correctly distinguished by the embedding. Hence, the classifier considered signals for the trigger word (a swear word) stronger, than other signals from the context, here a first person statement addressing the author himself.

Quotations or references. We add this error class because we observe many cases of ref-erences to toxic or hateful language in actual non-hateful comments.

> Example: *"I deleted the Jews are dumb comment."*

In the Wikipedia dataset samples this appears in 17% and in the Twitter dataset in 8% of com-ments. Again the classifier could not recognize the additional paradigmatic context referring to typical actions in a forum, here explicitly expressed with words 'I deleted the...' and '...comment'.

Idiosyncratic and rare words. Such words (as described in Section 6) in non-toxic or non-hateful comments cause problems when the classifier misinterprets their meaning or when they are slang that is often used in toxic language.

> Example: *"WTF man. Dan Whyte is Scottish"*

8% of Wikipedia dataset samples include rare words. In the Twitter dataset sample the fre-quency is higher with 17%, but also influenced by common Twitter language.

7 Conclusion

In this work we presented multiple approaches for toxic comment classification. We showed that the approaches make different errors and can be combined into an ensemble with improved F1-measure. The ensemble especially outperforms when there is high variance within the data and on classes with few examples. Some combinations such as shallow learners with deep neural net-works are especially effective. Our error analysis on results of the ensemble identified difficult sub-tasks of toxic comment classification. We find that a large source of errors is the lack of consistent quality of labels. Additionally most of the un-solved challenges occur due to missing training data with highly idiosyncratic or rare vocabulary. Finally, we suggest further research in represent-ing world knowledge with embeddings to improve distinction between paradigmatic contexts.

Acknowledgement

Our work is funded by the European Unions Horizon 2020 research and innovation programme under grant agreement No. 732328 (FashionBrain) and by the German Federal Ministry of Education and Research (BMBF) under grant agreement No. 01UG1735BX (NOHATE).

References

Pinkesh Badjatiya, Shashank Gupta, Manish Gupta, and Vasudeva Varma. 2017. Deep learning for hate speech detection in tweets. In *WWW*.

Piotr Bojanowski, Edouard Grave, Armand Joulin, and Tomas Mikolov. 2017. Enriching word vectors with subword information. *TACL*, 5:135–146.

Pete Burnap and Matthew L. Williams. 2015. Cyber hate speech on twitter : An application of machine classification and statistical modeling for policy and decision making. volume 7, pages 223–242.

Pete Burnap and Matthew L. Williams. 2016. Us and them: identifying cyber hate on twitter across multiple protected characteristics. *EPJ Data Science*, 5:1–15.

Ying Chen, Yilu Zhou, Sencun Zhu, and Heng Xu. 2012. Detecting offensive language in social media to protect adolescent online safety. *SOCIALCOM-PASSAT*, pages 71–80.

Maral Dadvar, Dolf Trieschnigg, Roeland Ordelman, and Franciska de Jong. 2013. Improving cyberbullying detection with user context. In *ECIR*.

Thomas Davidson, Dana Warmsley, Michael W. Macy, and Ingmar Weber. 2017. Automated hate speech detection and the problem of offensive language. In *ICWSM*.

Karthik Dinakar, Birago Jones, Catherine Havasi, Henry Lieberman, and Rosalind W. Picard. 2012. Common sense reasoning for detection, prevention, and mitigation of cyberbullying. *TiiS*, 2:18:1–18:30.

Björn Gambäck and Utpal Kumar Sikdar. 2017. Using convolutional neural networks to classify hate-speech. In *ALW1@ACL*.

Lei Gao and Ruihong Huang. 2017. Detecting online hate speech using context aware models. In *RANLP*.

Spiros V. Georgakopoulos, Sotiris K. Tasoulis, Aristidis G. Vrahatis, and Vassilis P. Plagianakos. 2018. Convolutional neural networks for toxic comment classification. In *SETN*.

Jennifer Golbeck, Zahra Ashktorab, Rashad O. Banjo, Alexandra Berlinger, Siddharth Bhagwan, Cody Buntain, Paul Cheakalos, Alicia A. Geller, Quint Gergory, Rajesh Kumar Gnanasekaran, Raja Rajan Gunasekaran, Kelly M. Hoffman, Jenny Hottle, Vichita Jienjitlert, Shivika Khare, Ryan Lau, Marianna J. Martindale, Shalmali Naik, Heather L. Nixon, Piyush Ramachandran, Kristine M. Rogers, Lisa Rogers, Meghna Sardana Sarin, Gaurav Shahane, Jayanee Thanki, Priyanka Vengataraman, Zijian Wan, and Derek Michael Wu. 2017. A large labeled corpus for online harassment research. In *WebSci*.

Edel Greevy and Alan F. Smeaton. 2004. Classifying racist texts using a support vector machine. In *SIGIR*.

Cynthia Van Hee, Els Lefever, Ben Verhoeven, Julie Mennes, Bart Desmet, Guy De Pauw, Walter Daelemans, and Véronique Hoste. 2015. Detection and fine-grained classification of cyberbullying events. In *RANLP*.

Akshita Jha and Radhika Mamidi. 2017. When does a compliment become sexist? analysis and classification of ambivalent sexism using twitter data. In *NLP+CSS@ACL*.

George W. Kennedy, Andrew W. McCollough, Edward Dixon, A. M. Parra Bastidas, J. Mark Ryan, and Chris Loo. 2017. Hack harassment : Technology solutions to combat online harassment. In *ALW1@ACL*.

Yoon Kim. 2014. Convolutional neural networks for sentence classification. In *EMNLP*.

Irene Kwok and Yuzhou Wang. 2013. Locate the hate: Detecting tweets against blacks. In *AAAI*.

Yashar Mehdad and Joel R. Tetreault. 2016. Do characters abuse more than words? In *SIGDIAL*.

Dennis Njagi, Z Zuping, Damien Hanyurwimfura, and Jun Long. 2015. A lexicon-based approach for hate speech detection. In *International Journal of Multimedia and Ubiquitous Engineering*, volume 10, pages 215–230.

Chikashi Nobata, Joel R. Tetreault, Achint Oommen Thomas, Yashar Mehdad, and Yi Chang. 2016. Abusive language detection in online user content. In *WWW*.

Ji Ho Park and Pascale Fung. 2017. One-step and two-step classification for abusive language detection on twitter. *CoRR*, abs/1706.01206.

John Pavlopoulos, Prodromos Malakasiotis, and Ion Androutsopoulos. 2017. Deeper attention to abusive user content moderation. In *EMNLP*.

Jeffrey Pennington, Richard Socher, and Christopher D. Manning. 2014. Glove: Global vectors for word representation. In *EMNLP*.

Michal Ptaszynski, Juuso Kalevi Kristian Eronen, and Fumito Masui. 2017. Learning deep on cyberbullying is always better than brute force. In *IJCAI*.

Jing Qian, Mai ElSherief, Elizabeth M. Belding-Royer, and William Yang Wang. 2018. Leveraging intrauser and inter-user representation learning for automated hate speech detection. In *NAACL-HLT*.

Julian Risch and Ralf Krestel. 2018. Aggression identification using deep learning and data augmentation. In *TRAC-1@COLING*, pages 150–158.

David Robinson, Ziqi Zhang, and Jonathan Tepper. 2018. Hate speech detection on twitter: Feature engineering v.s. feature selection. In *ESWC*.

Björn Ross, Michael Rist, Guillermo Carbonell, Benjamin Cabrera, Nils Kurowsky, and Michael Wojatzki. 2016. Measuring the reliability of hate speech annotations: The case of the european refugee crisis. *CoRR*, abs/1701.08118.

Niloofar Safi Samghabadi, Suraj Maharjan, Alan Sprague, Raquel Diaz-Sprague, and Thamar Solorio. 2017. Detecting nastiness in social media. In *ALW1@ACL*.

Anna Schmidt and Michael Wiegand. 2017. A survey on hate speech detection using natural language processing. In *SocialNLP@EACL*.

Sanjana Sharma, Saksham Agrawal, and Manish Shrivastava. 2018. Degree based classification of harmful speech using twitter data. *CoRR*, abs/1806.04197.

Fabio Del Vigna, Andrea Cimino, Felice Dell'Orletta, Marinella Petrocchi, and Maurizio Tesconi. 2017. Hate me, hate me not: Hate speech detection on facebook. In *ITASEC*.

W. Lloyd Warner and Julia Hirschberg. 2012. Detecting hate speech on the world wide web. In *LSM@ACL*.

Zeerak Waseem. 2016. Are you a racist or am i seeing things? annotator influence on hate speech detection on twitter. In *NLP+CSS@EMNLP*.

Zeerak Waseem and Dirk Hovy. 2016. Hateful symbols or hateful people? predictive features for hate speech detection on twitter. In *SRW@NAACL-HLT*.

Zeerak Waseem, James Thorne, and Joachim Bingel. 2018. Bridging the gaps: Multi task learning for domain transfer of hate speech detection. *Online Harassment*, pages 29–55.

Ellery Wulczyn, Nithum Thain, and Lucas Dixon. 2017. Ex machina: Personal attacks seen at scale. In *WWW*.

Guang Xiang, Bin Fan, Ling Wang, Jason I. Hong, and Carolyn Penstein Rosé. 2012. Detecting offensive tweets via topical feature discovery over a large scale twitter corpus. In *CIKM*.

Zichao Yang, Diyi Yang, Chris Dyer, Xiaodong He, Alex Smola, and Eduard Hovy. 2016. Hierarchical attention networks for document classification. In *NAACL-HLT*.

Dawei Yin and Brian D. Davison. 2009. Detection of harassment on web 2 . 0. In *CAW2.0@WWW*.

Ziqi Zhang and Lei Luo. 2018. Hate speech detection: A solved problem? the challenging case of long tail on twitter. *CoRR*, abs/1803.03662.

Ziqi Zhang, David Robinson, and Jonathan A. Tepper. 2018. Detecting hate speech on twitter using a convolution-gru based deep neural network. In *ESWC*.

Haoti Zhong, Hao Li, Anna Cinzia Squicciarini, Sarah Michele Rajtmajer, Christopher Griffin, David J. Miller, and Cornelia Caragea. 2016. Content-driven detection of cyberbullying on the instagram social network. In *IJCAI*.

Steven Zimmerman, Udo Kruschwitz, and Chris Fox. 2018. Improving hate speech detection with deep learning ensembles. In *LREC*.

Aggression Detection on Social Media Text Using Deep Neural Networks

Vinay Singh, Aman Varshney, Syed S. Akhtar, Deepanshu Vijay, Manish Shrivastava
Language Technologies Research Centre (LTRC)
International Institute of Information Technology Hyderabad, Telangana, India
{vinay.singh, aman.varshney, syed.akhtar, deepanshu.vijay}@research.iiit.ac.in
m.shrivastava@iiit.ac.in

Abstract

In the past few years, bully and aggressive posts on social media have grown significantly, causing serious consequences for victims/users of all demographics. Majority of the work in this field has been done for English only. In this paper, we introduce a deep learning based classification system for Facebook posts and comments of Hindi-English Code-Mixed text to detect the aggressive behaviour of/towards users. Our work focuses on text from users majorly in the Indian Subcontinent. The dataset that we used for our models is provided by **TRAC-1**[1] in their shared task. Our classification model assigns each Facebook post/comment to one of the three predefined categories: "Overtly Aggressive", "Covertly Aggressive" and "Non-Aggressive". We experimented with 6 classification models and our CNN model on a 10 K-fold cross-validation gave the best result with the prediction accuracy of 73.2%.

1 Introduction

It is observed that multilingual speakers often switch back and forth between languages when speaking or writing, mostly in informal settings. This language interchange involves complexing grammar, and the terms "code-switching" and "code-mixing" are used to describe it (Lipski, 1978). Code-mixing refers to the use of linguistic units from different languages in a single utterance or sentence, whereas code-switching refers to the co-occurrence of speech extracts belonging to two different grammatical systems (Gumperz, 1982). As both phenomena are frequently observed on social media platforms in similar contexts, we have considered the Code-Mixing scenario for our work.

Following is an instance from the dataset used:

T1 : *"Post tabah krne se kuch nhi hoga 2 k badale 200 ko maro"*

Translation: *"No point in destroying the Post, kill 200 in return for your 2 dead."*

Due to the massive rise of user-generated web content, in particular on social media networks, the amount of hate, aggressive, bully text is also steadily increasing. It has been estimated that there has been an increase of approximately 25% in the number of tweets per minutes and 22% increase in the number of Facebook posts per minute in the last 3 years. It is estimated that approximately 500 million tweets are sent per day, 4.3 billion Facebook messages are posted and more than 200 million emails are sent each day, and approximately 2 million new blog posts are created daily over the web [2]. Over the past years, interest in online hate/aggression/bullying detection and particularly the automatization of this task has continuously grown, along with the societal impact of the phenomenon (Ring, 2013). Natural language processing methods focusing specifically on this phenomenon are required since basic word filters do not provide a sufficient remedy. What is considered as an aggressive text might be influenced by aspects such as the domain of an utterance, its discourse context, as well as context consisting of co-occurring media objects (e.g. images, videos, audio), the exact time of posting and world events at this moment, identity of author and targeted recipient.

Hence, we can say that aggression and bullying by/against an individual can be performed in several ways beyond just using obvious abusive

---

[1] https://sites.google.com/view/trac1/shared-task?authuser=0

[2] https://www.gwava.com/blog/internet-data-created-daily

Proceedings of the Second Workshop on Abusive Language Online (ALW2), pages 43–50
Brussels, Belgium, October 31, 2018. ©2018 Association for Computational Linguistics

language (Vandebosch and Van Cleemput, 2008) (Sugandhi et al., 2015) – e.g., via constant sarcasm, trolling, etc. This can have deep effects on one's mental as well as social health and status (Phillips, 2015).

The structure of this paper is as follows. In Section 2, we review related research in the area of hate/aggression/bullying detection in social media texts. In Section 3, we describe the process of dataset creation which is a work of (Kumar et al., 2018). In Section 4, we discuss the pre-processing and data statistics. In Section 5, we summarize our classification systems and the construction of the feature vectors. In Section 6, we present the results of experiments conducted using various features and classification models along with CNN. In the last section, we conclude our paper, followed by future work and references.

2   Background and Related work

There have been several studies on computational methods to detect abusive/aggressive language published on social media in the last few years (Razavi et al., 2010) (Watanabe et al., 2018). The first thing to observe is that majority of the work in this domain has been done in English (Del Bosque and Garza, 2014) and a few more languages (Alfina et al.), (Mubarak et al., 2017), (Tarasova, 2016), but we know that social media abuse, bullying or aggression is independent of demography or language. With the advancement of new language keypads and social media websites supporting many new languages brings with itself the negative side of social media to those languages too. Hence, there is a need to address this problem and many others (Singh et al., 2018) for low resourced languages or say informal languages. (Bali et al., 2014) performed analysis of data from Facebook posts generated by English-Hindi bilingual users. Analysis depicted that significant amount of code-mixing was present in the posts. (Vyas et al., 2014) formalized the problem, created a POS tag annotated Hindi-English code-mixed corpus and reported the challenges and problems in the Hindi-English code-mixed text. They also performed experiments on language identification, transliteration, normalization and POS tagging of the dataset. (Sharma et al., 2016) addressed the problem of shallow parsing of Hindi-English code-mixed social media text and developed a system for Hindi-English code-mixed

Script	No. of posts/comments
Roman	10,000
Devnagari	2,000
Total	12,000

Table 1: Text statistics in corpus

Tag	Count
CAG	4869
NAG	2275
OAG	4856

Table 2: Tags and their Count in Corpus

text that can identify the language of the words, normalize them to their standard forms, assign them their POS tag and segment into chunks.

3   Dataset

We used the Hindi-English code-mixed dataset (Kumar et al., 2018) published as a shared task for 1st Workshop on Trolling, aggression and Cyberbullying (**TRAC-1**) [3] . The data was crawled from public Facebook Pages and Twitter. The data was mainly collected from the pages/issues that are expected to be discussed more among the Indians (and in Hindi) for the reason of the presence of Code-Mixed text.

While collecting data from Facebook more than 40 pages were identified and crawled. It included pages of the below-mentioned types:

- News websites/organizations like NDTV, ABP News, Zee News, etc.

- Web-based forums/portals like Firstost, The Logical Indian, etc.

- Political Parties/groups like INC, BJP, etc.

- Students' organisations/groups like SFI, JNUSU, AISA, etc.

- Support and opposition groups built around incidents in last 2 years in Indian Universities of higher education like Rohith Vemula's suicide in HCU, February 9, 2016, incident in JNU, etc.

For Twitter, the data was collected using some of the popular hashtags around such contentious themes as "beef ban", "India vs. Pakistan cricket

---

[3]https://sites.google.com/view/trac1/shared-task?authuser=0

match", "election results", "opinions on movies", etc. During collection, the data was not sampled on the basis of language and so it included data from English, Hindi as well as some other Indian languages. In the later stages, the data belonging to other languages was removed leaving only Hindi, English and Hindi-English Code-Mixed data.

The collected dataset was labelled into three classes naming:

Covertly-Aggressive (CAG): It refers to texts which are an indirect attack against the victim and is often packaged as (insincere) polite expressions (through the use of conventionalized polite structures), In general, a lot of cases of satire, rhetorical questions, etc. An example is given below -

T2 : *"Harish Om kya anti-national ko bail mil sakti hai? ? ?"*

Translation: *"Harish Om can an anti-national get bail?"*

Overtly-Aggressive (OAG): This refers to the texts in which aggression is overtly expressed either through the use of specific kind of lexical items or lexical features which is considered aggressive and/or certain syntactic structures. An example is given below -

T1 : *"Agar inke bas ki nahi hai toh Hume bhej do border"*

Translation: *"If they can't handle it, then send us to border"*

Non-Aggressive (NAG): It refers to texts which are not lying in the above two categories. An example is given below -

T1 : *"Waise bandhu jet lag se bachne ke liye Raat ko 10 baje ke baad so jao"*

Translation: *"By the way brother, sleep after 10 o'clock at night to avoid jet lag"*

3.1 Aggression and Abuse

Abuses and aggression are often correlated but neither entails the other. In cases of certain prag-

Tag	Average post length
CAG	28.10
NAG	27.40
OAG	27.63

Table 3: Average post length of different class text

Tag	Average word length
CAG	4.24
NAG	4.77
OAG	4.24

Table 4: Average word length in different class text

matic practices like 'banter' and 'jocular mockery', abusive constructions are used for establishing inter-personal relationships and increasing solidarity. So these instances cannot be labelled as aggressive. Moreover, In this dataset, both use of aggression and abuse is present in the text.

However, both aggression and abuse do co-occur in a lot of cases and a lot of times we are probably more concerned with (actual) abuses (and not the banter/teasing) than aggression itself. As such, we may consider abuse/curse as one aspect of aggression (even though not strictly a subtype of aggression). However, a more in-depth analysis is needed to discover the relationship between the two.

4 Pre-processing and Data Statistics

4.1 Data Statistics

The format of data provided was the "post/comment ID", "post/comment", "Tag". Where **ID** refers to users who posted the content, **post/comment** refers to the actual text content of the post/comment which we need to process to develop our features on, and **Tags** are the three class labels. It (the data) contained posts/comments both in Roman scripts as well as Devanagari scripts. Table 1 shows the statistics of the data distribution in Roman and Devanagari scripts. Table 2 shows the count of tags in the corpus.

4.2 Pre-Processing

The pre-processing step is done after extracting our useful features from the text as many elements get removed in pre-process step as they are not important for textual feature creation as well helps to keep the dimension of our feature vector small and

Tag	Precision	Recall	F1-score
CAG	0.51	0.72	0.60
NAG	0.98	0.13	0.23
OAG	0.60	0.60	0.60
avg / total	0.64	0.56	0.53

Table 5: Multi-modal Naive Bayes Model

Tag	Precision	Recall	F1-score
CAG	0.49	0.50	0.50
NAG	0.44	0.42	0.43
OAG	0.53	0.53	0.53
avg / total	0.50	0.50	0.50

Table 6: Decision Tree Model

dense. Below mentioned are the steps we did on our text for pre-processing:

- Transliterated Devnagari text to Roman using the system by (Bhat et al., 2014).

- Removed stop words.

- Removed Punctuation.

- Replaced multiple spaces (" ") or "." to a single one.

- Removed URLs.

- Removed emoticon Uni-codes and other unknown Uni-codes from text.

- Removed phone numbers ("+91-...").

5   System architecture and Features

5.1   Convolutional Neural Network

In this section, we outline the Convolutional Neural Networks (Fukushima, 1988) for classification and also provide the process description for text classification in particular. Convolutional Neural Networks are multistage trainable Neural Networks architectures developed for classification tasks (LeCun et al., 1998). Each of these stages, consist the types of layers described below (Georgakopoulos and Plagianakos, 2017):

- **Convolutional Layers:** These are major components of the CNN. A convolutional layer consists of a number of kernel matrices that perform convolution on their input and produce an output matrix of features where a bias value is added. The learning procedures aim to train the kernel weights and biases as shared neuron connection weights.

- **Pooling Layers:** These are the integral components of the CNN. The purpose of a pooling layer is to perform dimensionality reduction of the input feature images. Pooling layers make a sub-sampling to the output of the convolutional layer matrices combing neighbouring elements. The most common pooling function is the max-pooling function, which takes the maximum value of the local neighbourhoods.

- **Embedding Layer:** It is a special component of the CNN for text classification problems. The purpose of an embedding layer is to transform the text inputs into a suitable form for the CNN. Here, each word of a text document is transformed into a dense vector of fixed size.

- **Fully-Connected Layer:** It is a classic Feed-Forward Neural Network (FNN) hidden layer. It can be interpreted as a special case of the convolutional layer with kernel size 1x1. This type of layer belongs to the class of trainable layer weights and it is used in the final stages of CNN.

The training of CNN relies on the Back-Propagation (BP) training algorithm (LeCun et al., 1998). The requirements of the BP algorithm is a vector with input patterns x and a vector with targets y, respectively. The input x_i is associated with the output o_i. Each output is compared to its corresponding desirable target and their difference provides the training error. Our goal is to find weights that minimize the cost function

$$E_w = \frac{1}{n} \sum_{p=1}^{P} \sum_{j=1}^{N_L} (o_{j,p}^L - y_{j,p})^2$$

where P is the number of patterns, $o_{j,p}^L$ is the output of jth neuron that belongs to L^{th} layer, N_L is the number of neurons in output of Lth layer, $y_{j,p}$ is the desirable target of jth neuron of pattern p. To minimize the cost function E_w, a pseudo-stochastic version of SGD algorithm, also called mini-batch Stochastic Gradient Descent (mSGD), is usually utilized (Bottou, 1998).

5.2   LSTMs

As mentioned in (Lample et al., 2016) Recurrent neural networks (RNN) are a family of neural networks that operate on sequential data. They take

Tag	Precision	Recall	F1-score
CAG	0.54	0.68	0.60
NAG	0.70	0.31	0.43
OAG	0.60	0.59	0.59
Avg / total	0.59	0.57	0.56

Table 7: SVM Model with L2 penalty

Tag	Precision	Recall	F1-score
CAG	0.54	0.51	0.51
NAG	0.74	0.79	0.75
OAG	0.52	0.53	0.52
avg / total	0.41	0.42	0.39

Table 8: MLP model

Tag	Precision	Recall	F1-score
CAG	0.63	0.62	0.63
NAG	0.83	0.83	0.83
OAG	0.69	0.69	0.69
avg / total	0.58	0.57	0.58

Table 9: LSTM model

an input sequence of vectors $(x_1, x_2, \ldots, x_n)$ and return another sequence $(h_1, h_2, \ldots, h_n)$ that represents some information about the sequence at every step of the input. In theory, RNNs can learn long dependencies but in practice, they fail to do so and tend to be biased towards the most recent input in the sequence (Bengio et al., 1994). Long Short Term Memory networks or "LSTMs" are a special kind of RNN, capable of learning long-term dependencies. Here with our data where posts/comments are not very long in the size LSTMs can provide us with a better result as keeping previous contexts is one of the specialities of LSTM networks. LSTM networks were first introduced by (Hochreiter and Schmidhuber, 1997) and they were refined and popularized by many other authors. They work well with a large variety of problems especially the one consisting of sequence and are now widely used. They do so using several gates that control the proportion of the input to give to the memory cell, and the proportion from the previous state to forget. These network has been used in the past for tasks similar to our task like hate speech detection (Badjatiya et al., 2017), bullying detection (Agrawal and Awekar, 2018), Abusive language detection (Chu et al., 2016), etc on social media text. Hence, we experiment out data with LSTM model and compare the results as to how good our CNN model works as compares to LSTMs.

5.3 Features

- **Text Based:** In this stretch, we look into the presence of hashtags, uppercase text (indication of intense emotional state or 'shout-ing'), number of emoticons (emoticons and exclamation marks can be associated with more aggressive forms of online communication (Clarke and Grieve, 2017)), presence and repetition of punctuation, URLs, phone numbers, etc. The median value for URLs for "bully", "spam", "aggressive", and normal users is 1, 1, 0.9, and 0.6, respectively. The maximum number of URLs between users also varies: for the bully and aggressive users it is 1.17 and 2 respectively, while for spam and normal users it is 2.38 and 1.38. Thus, normal users tend to post fewer URLs than others. Also aggressive and bully users have a propensity to use more hashtags within their tweets, as they try to disseminate their attacking message to more individuals or groups (Chatzakou et al., 2017).

- **Abusive or Aggressive words:** We observe that the text with tags as aggressive either Covertly or Overly contains Abusive and Aggressive language usage which can be used as one of the important features to identify the aggressive posts/comments. It's not always though that the aggressive text contains these words but it's a feature which gives some certainty for the presence of Aggressive nature of the text (Chatzakou et al., 2017).

- **Numerical features:** It is observed that the average length of post/comment for aggressive texts is, in general, greater as compared to non-aggressive posts. It is also observed that the average size of words in the aggressive texts are smaller as compared to Non-aggressive posts which deny the findings of (Nobata et al., 2016). The stats for the average length of post/comment and that of words in these three class are shown in Table 3 and 4.

While creating the sentence vectors with the use of vocabulary from out dataset (top 4000 words) we removed sentences which had sizes

Tag	Precision	Recall	F1-score
CAG	0.63	0.63	0.63
NAG	0.83	0.85	0.84
OAG	0.69	0.68	0.69
avg / total	0.57	0.59	0.58

Table 10: CNN model

Model	Accuracy
Multimodal NB	0.56
Decision Tree	0.49
SVM	0.57
MLP	0.42
LSTM	0.58
CNN	0.73

Table 12: Test Accuracy of different models

greater than 400, which is a good threshold looking at the average size of a sentence which is 28. After removing the sentence having size more than 400 we are left with 11,617 sentences and our dimensionality reduced to 11617x400 from 11634x5000 as there were few sentences of 5000 length (noise in social media text). This reduction in dimensionality helps our training model to run faster without affecting the results/learning much.

Tag	Count
CAG	974
NAG	466
OAG	960
Total	2400

Table 11: Support Test instances for each Tags

List of all features that we used for our systems are as follows:

- Sentence vector after pre-processing.
- Count of abusive/aggressive/offensive words.
- Number of tokens.
- Size of post/comment.
- Presence of URLs.
- Presence of phone numbers.
- Presence of hash-tags.
- Number of single letters.
- Average length of words.
- Number of words with uppercase characters.
- Number of Punctuation.

We experimented with the different set of features for the CNN model which we have discussed in Section 6 and a report for which can be seen in Table 13.

6 Experiments

This section presents the experiments we performed with different combinations of features and models. The models on which we ran experiments are:

- Multimodal Naive Bayes
- Decision Tree
- Support Vector Machine (SVM)
- Multi layer Perceptrons (MLPs)
- Long-short Term Memory (LSTM) Networks
- Convolutional Neural Networks (CNNs)

For experiments on the first three models, we used only the text as features and used library feature extraction method which turns our text content into numerical features with bag-of-words strategy, ignoring the relative positions of words. The classification report for these three models has been shown in Table 5, 6, 7 respectively with their accuracy as shown in Table 12. The support for each tag during the experiments on our models shown in Table 5, 6 and 7 have the same numbers of data per tag which is shown in Table 11.

We then experimented with the three above mentioned neural networks and their classification report is shown in Tables 8, 9 and 10.

In order to determine the effect of each feature and parameter of different models, we performed several experiments with some and all feature at a time simultaneously changing the values of the parameters as well. We arrived at the provided values of parameters and hyper-parameters after fine empirical tuning.

7 Results and Observations

The classification report of all the models is shown in Tables 5, 6, 7, 8, 9, 10. From the experiments above we can conclude that CNN works best for our case classifying posts 73.2% of the times to

Feature Eliminated	Accuracy
None	72.8
Size of post	72.4
Avg. length of words	72.6
Single letters/chars count	**73.0**
Number of Tokens	72.2
Presence of URL	**73.2**
Presence of Phone-number	72.9
Total Uppercase words	72.5
Presence of hash-tags	72.3
Number of punctuation's	**73.1**
Aggressive words	72.2
All except sent vector	**73.2**

Table 13: Impact Of Each Feature Calculated By Eliminating One at A Time for CNN Model.

the correct class. The best classification accuracy of all the models is shown in Table 12.

One observation to keep in mind is that the nature of data that we used in our work also makes this classification task difficult to generalize (Davidson et al., 2017), this is because of the presence of noisy text in social media data.

8 Conclusion and Future work

In this paper, we experimented with machine learning as well as deep learning classification models for classifying social media Hindi-English Code-Mixed sentences as aggressive or not. We cannot always rely on neural networks to perform better than simple machine learning algorithms (eg. SVM performs better than MLP). CNN worked best with an accuracy of 73.2% and the best f1-score of 0.58. To make our predictions and models results more significant, we would like to choose a greater variety of social media text that could be considered as offensive/aggressive/hate speech. In addition, many of the posts were from the same thread i.e not much diverse. This has advantages and disadvantages. One advantage may be that this makes the system more fine-tuned: if two people are discussing the same topic, what differentiates one as using "aggressive/hate speech" versus one who is not? But on the other hand, many of the posts were similar in meaning and did not add much to our model to learn. In future, we would like to create a larger, more representative dataset of social media post/comments, perhaps those flagged as offensive by users/annotators as well as covering more diverse and general topic discussions on social media. We also plan to explore some more features from a different variety of texts and experiment them with the deep learning methodologies available in natural language processing. The processed dataset as well as the system models are made available online [4].

References

Sweta Agrawal and Amit Awekar. 2018. Deep learning for detecting cyberbullying across multiple social media platforms. In *European Conference on Information Retrieval*, pages 141–153. Springer.

Ika Alfina, Rio Mulia, Mohamad Ivan Fanany, and Yudo Ekanata. Hate speech detection in the indonesian language: A dataset and preliminary study.

Pinkesh Badjatiya, Shashank Gupta, Manish Gupta, and Vasudeva Varma. 2017. Deep learning for hate speech detection in tweets. In *Proceedings of the 26th International Conference on World Wide Web Companion*, pages 759–760. International World Wide Web Conferences Steering Committee.

Kalika Bali, Jatin Sharma, Monojit Choudhury, and Yogarshi Vyas. 2014. " i am borrowing ya mixing?" an analysis of english-hindi code mixing in facebook. In *Proceedings of the First Workshop on Computational Approaches to Code Switching*, pages 116–126.

Yoshua Bengio, Patrice Simard, and Paolo Frasconi. 1994. Learning long-term dependencies with gradient descent is difficult. *IEEE transactions on neural networks*, 5(2):157–166.

Irshad Ahmad Bhat, Vandan Mujadia, Aniruddha Tammewar, Riyaz Ahmad Bhat, and Manish Shrivastava. 2014. Iiit-h system submission for fire2014 shared task on transliterated search. In *Proceedings of the Forum for Information Retrieval Evaluation*, pages 48–53. ACM.

Léon Bottou. 1998. Online learning and stochastic approximations. *On-line learning in neural networks*, 17(9):142.

Despoina Chatzakou, Nicolas Kourtellis, Jeremy Blackburn, Emiliano De Cristofaro, Gianluca Stringhini, and Athena Vakali. 2017. Mean birds: Detecting aggression and bullying on twitter. In *Proceedings of the 2017 ACM on web science conference*, pages 13–22. ACM.

Theodora Chu, Kylie Jue, and Max Wang. 2016. Comment abuse classification with deep learning. *Von https://web. stanford. edu/class/cs224n/reports/2762092. pdf abgerufen.*

---

[4] https://github.com/SilentFlame/AggressionDetection

Isobelle Clarke and Jack Grieve. 2017. Dimensions of abusive language on twitter. In *Proceedings of the First Workshop on Abusive Language Online*, pages 1–10.

Thomas Davidson, Dana Warmsley, Michael Macy, and Ingmar Weber. 2017. Automated hate speech detection and the problem of offensive language. *arXiv preprint arXiv:1703.04009*.

Laura P Del Bosque and Sara Elena Garza. 2014. Aggressive text detection for cyberbullying. In *Mexican International Conference on Artificial Intelligence*, pages 221–232. Springer.

Kunihiko Fukushima. 1988. Neocognitron: A hierarchical neural network capable of visual pattern recognition. *Neural networks*, 1(2):119–130.

Spiros V Georgakopoulos and Vassilis P Plagianakos. 2017. A novel adaptive learning rate algorithm for convolutional neural network training. In *International Conference on Engineering Applications of Neural Networks*, pages 327–336. Springer.

John J Gumperz. 1982. *Discourse strategies*, volume 1. Cambridge University Press.

Sepp Hochreiter and Jürgen Schmidhuber. 1997. Long short-term memory. *Neural computation*, 9(8):1735–1780.

Ritesh Kumar, Aishwarya N Reganti, Akshit Bhatia, and Tushar Maheshwari. 2018. Aggression-annotated corpus of hindi-english code-mixed data. *arXiv preprint arXiv:1803.09402*.

Guillaume Lample, Miguel Ballesteros, Sandeep Subramanian, Kazuya Kawakami, and Chris Dyer. 2016. Neural architectures for named entity recognition. *arXiv preprint arXiv:1603.01360*.

Yann LeCun, Léon Bottou, Yoshua Bengio, and Patrick Haffner. 1998. Gradient-based learning applied to document recognition. *Proceedings of the IEEE*, 86(11):2278–2324.

John Lipski. 1978. Code-switching and the problem of bilingual competence. *Aspects of bilingualism*, 250:264.

Hamdy Mubarak, Kareem Darwish, and Walid Magdy. 2017. Abusive language detection on arabic social media. In *Proceedings of the First Workshop on Abusive Language Online*, pages 52–56.

Chikashi Nobata, Joel Tetreault, Achint Thomas, Yashar Mehdad, and Yi Chang. 2016. Abusive language detection in online user content. In *Proceedings of the 25th international conference on world wide web*, pages 145–153. International World Wide Web Conferences Steering Committee.

Whitney Phillips. 2015. *This is why we can't have nice things: Mapping the relationship between online trolling and mainstream culture*. Mit Press.

Amir H Razavi, Diana Inkpen, Sasha Uritsky, and Stan Matwin. 2010. Offensive language detection using multi-level classification. In *Canadian Conference on Artificial Intelligence*, pages 16–27. Springer.

Caitlin Elizabeth Ring. 2013. Hate speech in social media: An exploration of the problem and its proposed solutions.

Arnav Sharma, Sakshi Gupta, Raveesh Motlani, Piyush Bansal, Manish Srivastava, Radhika Mamidi, and Dipti M Sharma. 2016. Shallow parsing pipeline for hindi-english code-mixed social media text. *arXiv preprint arXiv:1604.03136*.

Vinay Singh, Deepanshu Vijay, Syed Sarfaraz Akhtar, and Manish Shrivastava. 2018. Named entity recognition for hindi-english code-mixed social media text. In *Proceedings of the Seventh Named Entities Workshop*, pages 27–35.

Rekha Sugandhi, Anurag Pande, Siddhant Chawla, Abhishek Agrawal, and Husen Bhagat. 2015. Methods for detection of cyberbullying: A survey. In *Intelligent Systems Design and Applications (ISDA), 2015 15th International Conference on*, pages 173–177. IEEE.

Natalya Tarasova. 2016. Classification of hate tweets and their reasons using svm.

Heidi Vandebosch and Katrien Van Cleemput. 2008. Defining cyberbullying: A qualitative research into the perceptions of youngsters. *CyberPsychology & Behavior*, 11(4):499–503.

Yogarshi Vyas, Spandana Gella, Jatin Sharma, Kalika Bali, and Monojit Choudhury. 2014. Pos tagging of english-hindi code-mixed social media content. In *Proceedings of the 2014 Conference on Empirical Methods in Natural Language Processing (EMNLP)*, pages 974–979.

Hajime Watanabe, Mondher Bouazizi, and Tomoaki Ohtsuki. 2018. Hate speech on twitter: A pragmatic approach to collect hateful and offensive expressions and perform hate speech detection. *IEEE Access*, 6:13825–13835.

Creating a WhatsApp Dataset to Study Pre-teen Cyberbullying

Rachele Sprugnoli[1], Stefano Menini[1], Sara Tonelli[1], Filippo Oncini[1,2], Enrico Maria Piras[1,3]
[1]Fondazione Bruno Kessler, Via Sommarive 18, Trento, Italy
[2]Department of Sociology and Social Research, University of Trento, Via Giuseppe Verdi 26, Trento
[3]School of Medicine and Surgery, University of Verona, Piazzale L. A. Scuro 10, Verona, Italy
{sprugnoli;menini;satonelli;piras}@fbk.eu
filippo.oncini@unitn.it

Abstract

Although WhatsApp is used by teenagers as one major channel of cyberbullying, such interactions remain invisible due to the app privacy policies that do not allow ex-post data collection. Indeed, most of the information on these phenomena rely on surveys regarding self-reported data.

In order to overcome this limitation, we describe in this paper the activities that led to the creation of a WhatsApp dataset to study cyberbullying among Italian students aged 12-13. We present not only the collected chats with annotations about user role and type of offense, but also the living lab created in a collaboration between researchers and schools to monitor and analyse cyberbullying. Finally, we discuss some open issues, dealing with ethical, operational and epistemic aspects.

1 Introduction

Due to the profound changes in ICT technologies over the last decades, teenagers communication has been subjected to a major shift. According to the last report by the Italian Statistical Institute (ISTAT, 2014) in Italy 82.6% of children aged 11-17 use the mobile phone every day and 56.9% access the web on a daily basis. Despite being of fundamental importance for teenagers' social life, the use of these new technologies paved the way to undesirable side effects, among which the digitalisation of traditional forms of harassment. We refer to these form of harassment as "cyberbullying". Should we adopt a narrow definition, cyberbullying refers only to actions repeated over time with the aim to hurt someone. By definition, cyberbullying is in fact 'an aggressive, intentional act carried out by a group or individual, using electronic forms of contact, repeatedly and over time against a victim who cannot easily defend him or herself' (Smith et al., 2008). In

everyday life, however, the notion of cyberbullying indicates each episode of online activity aimed at offending, menacing, harassing or stalking another person. The latter definition of cyberbullying is the one currently adopted in most of the research conducted on this phenomenon and in the present work. The phenomenon has been recognised as a ubiquitous public health issue, as the literature clearly highlights negative consequences for teenagers: studies show that victims are more likely to suffer from psychosocial difficulties, affective disorders and lower school performance (Tokunaga, 2010). Since the difference between cyberbullying and traditional forms of bullying lies in the intentional use of electronic forms of contact against the designed victim, data on verbal harassment and cyberbullying stances are particularly useful to analyse the phenomenon. However, due to the private nature of these verbal exchanges, very few datasets are available for the computational analysis of language. It should be noted that the possibilities offered by social networking platform to share privately content among users combined with the increasing digital literacy of teenagers has the paradoxical effect to hinder the possibility to scrutinize and study the actual cyberbullying activities. For instance, although WhatsApp is used by teenagers as one major channel of cyberbullying (Aizenkot and Kashy-Rosenbaum, 2018), their interactions remain invisible due to the privacy policies that impede ex-post data collection. Most of the information on these phenomena, though, relies on surveys regarding self-reported data. Yet, specifically for this reason, the possibility to study how cyberbullying interactions and offenses emerge through instant messaging app conversations is crucial to fight and prevent digital harassment.

In this light, this paper presents an innovative corpus of data on cyberbullying interaction gath-

Proceedings of the Second Workshop on Abusive Language Online (ALW2), pages 51–59
Brussels, Belgium, October 31, 2018. ©2018 Association for Computational Linguistics

ered through a WhatsApp experimentation with lower secondary school students. After outlining the CREEP project[1] (CybeRbullying EffEcts Prevention) during which the activities were carried out, and the living lab approach that led to the creation of the corpus, we present the provisional results of the computational analysis.

In the discussion, we address the main ethical concerns raised by the experimentation and we discuss the implications of such a methodology as a tool for both research and cyberbullying prevention programs. Annotated data, in a standoff XML format, and annotation guidelines are available online[2].

NOTE: This paper contains examples of language which may be offensive to some readers. They do not represent the views of the authors.

2 Related Work

In this Section we provide an overview of datasets created to study cyberbullying, highlighting the differences with respect to our Whatsapp corpus.

The sources used to build cyberbullying datasets are several and cover many different websites and social networks. However, the main differences are not in the source of the data but in the granularity and detail of the annotations. Reynolds et al. (2011) propose a dataset of questions and answers from Formspring.me, a website with a high amount of cyberbullying content. It consists of 12,851 posts annotated for the presence of cyberbullying and severity. Another resource developed by Bayzick et al. (2011) consists of conversation transcripts (thread-style) extracted from MySpace.com. The conversations are divided into groups of 10 posts and annotated for presence and typology of cyberbullying (e.g. denigration or harassment, flaming, trolling). Other studies cover more popular social networks such as Instagram and Twitter. For example, the dataset collected from Instagram by Hosseinmardi et al. (2015), consists of 2,218 media sessions (groups of 15+ messages associated to a media such as a video or a photo), with a single annotation for each media session indicating the presence of cyberagressive behavior. The work by Sui (2015) is instead on Twitter data, presenting a corpus of 7,321 tweets

manually annotated for the presence of cyberbullying. In this dataset, other than cyberbullying, the authors provide different layers of associated information, for example the role of the writer, the typology of attack and the emotion. The aforementioned works have two main differences with respect to the data presented in this paper. First, each annotation refers to an entire message (or a group of messages) and not to specific expressions and portions of text. Second, the categories used for the annotation are more generic than the ones adopted in our guidelines.

A more detailed investigation on the cyberbullying dynamics can be found in Van Hee et al. (2015b,a) presenting the work carried out within the project AMiCA[3], which aims at monitoring web resources and automatically tracing harmful content in Dutch. The authors propose a detailed analysis of cyberbullying on a dataset of 85,485 posts collected from Ask.fm and manually annotated following a fine-grained annotation scheme that covers roles, typology of harassment and level of harmfulness. This scheme has been recently applied also to English data (Van Hee et al., 2018). This approach is different from the previous ones since its annotations are not necessarily related to entire messages but can be limited to shorter strings (e.g., single words or short sequences of words). We found this approach the more suitable for our data, allowing us to obtain a detailed view of pre-teens use of offensive language and of the strategies involved in a group with ongoing cyberbullying. The details on how we use the guidelines from the AMiCA project (Van Hee et al., 2015c) as the starting point to define our annotation scheme can be found in Section 5.

Another important difference between our corpus and the datasets previously discussed is the source of our data. Indeed, among the many available instant messaging and social media platforms, WhatsApp is not much investigated because it is private, thus an explicit donation from the chat participants is required to collect data (Verheijen and Stoop, 2016). Although in the last few years WhatsApp corpora have been released in several languages including Italian (see for example the multilingual corpus built in the context of the "What's up, Switzerland?" project[4] (Ue-

---

[1] http://creep-project.eu/
[2] http://dh.fbk.eu/technologies/ whatsapp-dataset

[3] https://www.lt3.ugent.be/projects/ amica
[4] https://www.whatsup-switzerland.ch/ index.php/en/

berwasser and Stark, 2017), these corpora have been collected with the goal to investigate specific linguistic traits such as code-switching, or to study whether the informal language used in the chats affects the writing skills of students (Dorantes et al., 2018; Verheijen and Spooren, 2017). With respect to the aforementioned works focused on the analysis of linguistic phenomena in WhatsApp, our aim is to study a social phenomenon, that is cyberbullying, by analysing how it is linguistically encoded in WhatsApp messages. Even if the relation between cyberbullying and WhatsApp is strong, no annotated corpus of WhatsApp chats has been released so far. Therefore, our corpus represents a novel resource, useful to study in particular cyberbullying in classmates' groups (Aizenkot and Kashy-Rosenbaum, 2018).

3   Project Description

The corpus presented in this paper is part of the CybeRbullying EffEcts Prevention activities (CREEP), a larger project based in Italy and supported by EIT Digital[5], for the monitoring of cyberbullying and the assistance of students and teachers. The project goals are *i)* to develop advanced technologies for the early detection of cyberbullying stances through the monitoring of social media and *ii)* to create a virtual coaching system for communicating preventive advice and personalised messages to adolescents at risk of cyberbullying aggressions. To this purpose, one of the means to reach the objectives is the realisation of a living lab, namely an in vivo research methodology aimed at co-creating innovation through the involvement of aware users in a real-life setting (Dell'Era and Landoni, 2014). This approach permits to tackle the cyberbullying phenomenon within the social media platform from a user-centric perspective, thereby favouring the co-creation of prevention strategies whilst avoiding top-down planning. When applied to the school context, the living-lab approach presents a three-fold advantage. Researchers gain ecological validity by studying the phenomenon with target users through a role-play experiment. Teenagers can actively engage in the participatory design without being used as passive research subjects. Schools can count on a supplementary tool for raising awareness on cyberbullying and give pupils additional means to understand the phenomenon first-

hand.

The creation of the corpus required the involvement of students in a role-playing simulation of cyberbullying and has so far involved three lower secondary schools' classes of teenagers aged 12-13 from 2 different schools based in Trento, in the North-East of Italy. The experimentation itself, described in the next section, was embedded in a larger process that required four to five meetings, one per week, involving every time two social scientists, two computational linguists and at least two teachers for the class. The content of the meetings is briefly described below:

1. **Lecturing on cyberbullying**. Researchers introduce the theme of cyberbullying and elicit personal experiences and students' opinions.

2. **Pilot annotation of online interactions**. Students in pairs annotate semantically six online threads gathered from Instagram and Twitter. They discuss the hate speech categories that will be then annotated also in the WhatsApp interactions.

3. **Introducing the experimentation**. Researchers present the experimentation, both the practicalities and the rules of the role-playing.

4. **Participatory analysis**. Researchers present the preliminary analysis of the experimentation and elicit students interpretations of the data gathered.

5. **Feedback to teachers and parents** (optional but recommended). Researchers present the whole project to parents of students involved and teachers, discussing results and future activities.

The relevance and implications of this approach are presented in Section 6.

4   WhatsApp Experimentation

The choice of WhatsApp is based on two main considerations: first, the application is one of the most preferred and used messaging applications (Fiadino et al., 2014). In 2015, almost 60% of Italian teens aged 12-17 used the app (Save the Children, 2014). In fact, in each class involved in the living lab, around 70% of the children already had an active WhatsApp account on their

---

[5]https://www.eitdigital.eu/

Scenario	Type of addressed problem
Your shy male classmate has a great passion for classical dance. Usually he does not talk much, but today he has decided to invite the class to watch him for his ballet show.	Gendered division of sport practices
Your classmate is very good at school, but does not have many friends, due to his/her haughty and 'teacher's pet' attitude. Few days ago, s/he realised that his/her classmates brought cigarettes to school and snitched on them with the teacher. Now they will be met with a three days suspension, and they risk to fail the year.	Interference in others' businesses
Your classmate is very good at school, and everyone think s/he is an overachiever. S/He studies a lot and s/he never goes out. S/He does not speak much with his/her classmates, that from time to time tease him/her for his/her unsocial life. Things have slightly changed recently: your classmates mum convinced teachers to increase the homework for all the students. A heedless teacher revealed the request to the class, and now some students are very angry at him/her.	Lack of independence, parental intromission.
Your shy classmate is good in all subjects but in gymnastics. For this reason, his/her classmates often tease on him/her when s/he exercises. Recently, the class has found out a video on the social network Musical.ly, where s/he dances gracelessly, on a 90s song that no one has never heard before.	Web virality

Table 1: Scenarios adopted in our experimentation.

personal smartphones. Only a minority (around 5 or 6 teens) used their parents' smartphones to be able to participate. Second, the app provides all the functionalities of social networking services, and Whatsapp classmates' groups are identified by other studies as contexts of cyberbullying perpetration (Aizenkot and Kashy-Rosenbaum, 2018). Overall, a total number of 70 students participated in the experimentation.

After receiving the necessary authorisation from the school director, the school board, and teenagers' parents, the researchers presented the experimentation to the participants, conceived as a role-play. In each class, two WhatsApp groups with around 10 teens were created. Teachers were part of the groups and could assist to the conversation, but they never actively participated to the chat. In each group, one researcher played for the whole time the role of the victim. Students were instead given the following roles: cyberbully (2 students), cyberbully assistants (3-4 students), and victim assistants (3-4 students). Teachers divided the classes and assigned the roles to pupils, so to take into account previous class dynamics and childrens personalities. Each role-play lasted for 3 days, after which pupils changed roles within the same chat; students were allowed to participate in the chat only after the school hours, and could be excluded for a short time in case of misbehaviour. Teachers and researchers used dedicated mobile phones provided by the project, not their private ones. Each chat started with the following basic rules:

- Offenses must target only the designated victim (the researcher)

- Bad words are allowed, but do not exaggerate

- Do your best to play your role and try to interact in a realistic way

- Stick to the roles previously defined

- Do not hesitate to quit the chat if you feel offended

- Use the chat only after school hours

Moreover, in order to trigger the conversation, several scenarios, previously discussed and agreed by the students, opened the role-play. The scenarios, reported in Table 1, aim to address different types of problematics that teenagers can encounter, from the gendered division of sport practices to the embarrassment caused by a viral video. At the end of the experimentation, a two-hour meeting with each class was organised to reflect with students and teachers on the content of the conversation, and to discuss some of the taken-for-granted aspects of cyberbullying and raise awareness on teenagers. During this occasion, students could reflect on the experience, highlight with researchers and teachers the most problematic interactions, and point out the benefits and drawbacks of the methodology.

Three middle-school classes were involved in this experimentation. Since WhatsApp groups are closed and not accessible from the outside, a preliminary agreement was signed involving students' parents, teachers and headmasters to allow the activity. The threads were then saved in anonymous form and manually annotated by two expert linguists. The original names were not completely removed, but they were replaced by fictitious names, so that it was still possible to track all the messages exchanged by the same person.

5 Corpus Description

The corpus of Whatsapp chats is made of 14,600 tokens divided in 10 chats. All the chats have been annotated by two annotators using the CAT web-based tool (Bartalesi Lenzi et al., 2012) following the same guidelines.

Our guidelines are an adaptation to Italian of the "Guidelines for the Fine-Grained Analysis of Cyberbullying" developed for English by the Language and Translation Technology Team of Ghent University (Van Hee et al., 2015c). Following these guidelines, the annotator should identify all the harmful expressions in a conversation and, for each of it, he/she should annotate: (i) the cyberbullying role of the message's author; (ii) the cyberbullying type of the expression; (iii) the presence of sarcasm in the expression; (iv) whether the expression containing insults is not really offensive but a joke. The guidelines identifies four cyberbullying roles: Harasser (person who initiates the harassment), Victim (person who is harassed), Bystander-defender (person who helps the victim and discourages the harasser), Bystander-assistant (person who takes part in the actions of the harasser). As for the type of cyberbullying expressions, we distinguish between different classes of insults, discrimination, sexual talk and aggressive statements: Threat or blackmail, General Insult, Body Shame, Sexism, Racism, Curse or Exclusion, Insult Attacking Relatives, Harmless Sexual Talk, Defamation, Sexual Harassment, Defense, Encouragement to the Harassment, and Other. Each message in the chat can contain more than one expression to be annotated with a different associated type thus making the annotation fine-grained. For example the message *fai schifo, ciccione!* / *you suck, fat guy* is made of two harmful expressions e.g. [*fai schifo,*]General_Insult [*ciccione!*]Body Shame.

With respect to the original guidelines by Van Hee et al. (2015c), we added a new type of insult called Body Shame to cover expressions that criticize someone based on the shape, size, or appearance of his/her body. We did this addition because body shaming has become an important societal issue that according to existing literature has a strong impact on the cybervictimization of teens and pre-treens (Frisén et al., 2014; Berne et al., 2014). We have also changed the original type Encouragement to the Harasser into Encouragement to the Harassment, so to include all the incitements between the bully and his/her assistants. We indeed noticed that the exhortations to continue the persecution and the expressions of approval for insults and acts of intimidation do not have a single direction (that is, from the assistants to the bully) but all the people taking part in the harassment encourage each other.

We calculated the inter annotator agreement between our annotators on one of the chats, made of 1,000 tokens and belonging to the scenario about the video posted on musical.ly. Results are shown in Table 2 in terms of Dice coefficient (Dice, 1945) for the extension of the annotated expression and in terms of accuracy for the attributes associated to each message. Since that the roles where pre-defined, we did not measure the agreement on the assignment of the cyberbullying roles. Results are satisfactory given that the agreement is equal or above 0.8 both for the extension and the attributes. These scores are

Extension		Attributes		
Dice coefficient		Accuracy		
exact match	partial match	type	sarcasm	non-offensive
0. 80	0.88	0.87	1	1

Table 2: Results of Inter Annotator Agreement

TYPES		ROLES	
Defense	381 (31.7%)	Bystander_assistant	358 (29.8%)
General_Insult	313 (26.0%)	Harasser	343 (28.5%)
Curse_or_Exclusion	200 (16.6%)	Bystander_defender	334 (27.7%)
Threat_or_Blackmail	81 (6.7%)	Victim	168 (14.0%)
Encouragement_to_the_Harassment	63 (5.2%)		
Body Shame	45 (3.7%)	OFFENSIVE	
Discrimination-Sexism	45 (3.7%)	non-offensive	0
Attacking_relatives	28 (2.3%)		
Other	24 (2%)	SARCASM	
Defamation	23 (1.9%)	sarcasm	27 (2.2%)
TOTAL	**1203**		

Table 3: Annotated data on WhatsApp data

higher than those reported for the annotation made using the guidelines to which we were inspired (Van Hee et al., 2015b). This difference could be explained by the fact that our annotators were directly involved in the creation of our guidelines.

Table 3 reports statistics about the annotated data in the WhatsApp chats. We identified a total of 1,203 cyberbullying expressions, corresponding to almost 6,000 tokens: this means that the phenomenon we are investigating covers 41.1% of the whole corpus. Roles are quite balanced in the chats with many interactions among all the participants. Expressions of type Defense written by the victim or bystander defenders are the most numerous (31.7%): they include expressions in support of the victim specifying his/her positive characteristics (e.g., *secondo me è bravo! / I think he's good!*) but also showing disapproval and indignation (e.g., *lasciatelo stare! / leave him alone!*). Undesirable sexual talk (type Sexual_harassment) and expressions of discrimination that are based on the victim's race, skin color, ethnicity, nationality, or religion are never found in the WhatsApp corpus. Besides, all rude remarks and bad words are offensive in the context in which they are used (i.e., the non-offensive tag is never used). The defenders of the victim often fight back responding to attacks with insults (e.g., *le sfigate siete voi / you are the losers*) and threats (*e.g. Se non la*

smetti la vedrai con tutti noi / If you do not stop you will see it with all of us). These types of expressions correspond to the 37.1% of the annotations with the role Bystander-defender. Almost all the expressions in the category Curse_or_Exclusion (96%) are aimed at detaching the counterpart from social relations with expressions such as *chiudi il becco / shut up, nessuno ti vuole / nobody wants you, cambia classe / change class*. The strong majority of insults of type Attacking_relatives, corresponding to 82.1%, are addressed to the mother (e.g., *Tua madre fa schifo quanto te / Your mother sucks as much as you do*) whereas the others are attacks to sisters, brothers and friends in general. Different scenarios bring out different types of cyberbullying expressions and thus different types of insults. For example, the scenario about the ballet has a high presence of expressions with a sexist nature, starting from the idea that ballet is an activity only for girls, e.g. *Balli anche te così da gay? / Do you dance so gay too?*). The scenario related to the video on musical.ly has attracted many comments on the appearance of the victim and, as a consequence, we have high occurrence of insults of type Body_Shame. Typically, these insults contain references to animals stressing the heaviness of the victim, for example *Dimagrisci elefante / lose weight, you elephant, Sembra un bisonte quando corre! / He*

6 Discussion

The use of a simulation to create the corpus described in the previous sections raises a number of issues. A detailed and thorough exploration of such issues is beyond the scope of the present paper and it would require a paper in its own right. Nonetheless, in this last section we discuss some of the issues faced with no pretense of exhaustiveness, distinguishing between operational, ethical and epistemic issues. As we shall see, though, there are considerable overlaps among these categories.

6.1 Operational Issues

First and foremost, the creation of a WhatsApp corpus has required several accompanying measures. The effort required to gather the corpus is only a fraction of the overall effort needed to set up the living lab. Participation of schools was ensured by making data gathering only a part of a larger set of activities aimed at paving the way for experimentation (lecture, annotation) and providing teachers and parents, our internal stakeholders, with results to be further used for educational purposes (feedback). All these activities required to invest extra-time. At the same time, though, the prolonged involvement and exchanges with students and teachers allowed us to build a trust meant to ensure a smooth participation to the role-playing and avoid that researchers are perceived as judgmental.

A second issue, partially related to the former, is the need of a consistent engagement of researchers in the creation of the corpus. The experimentation, far from having a predictable behaviour, needed to be monitored to ensure that participants would adhere to the rules (i.e. not insulting each other) or stop interacting. This required making several decisions (e.g. sending private messages to remind the rules to specific students) to avoid the failure of the role-playing. Borderline cases were frequent and each required choices to be made on the fly. As a rule, researchers adopted a flexible approach towards rule-breaking, deeming that an excessive intervention would have broken the 'suspension of disbelief' of the role-playing.

On a separate note, the unfolding of the research process required to make some decisions regarding conflicting needs. For instance, the students without a smartphone were excluded from the role-playing experimentation. We evaluated the possibility to provide a smartphone to these students to avoid their exclusion from the activities of the rest of the classmates. The option was ruled out preferring realism over participation.

6.2 Ethical Issues

The ethical issues were a main concern since the drafting of the study design. The study has been co-designed with the schools involved and parents' informed consent was gathered beforehand. The role-playing methodology was adopted, among other considerations, as it did not require gathering sensitive information regarding minors. Students were assigned a role and they were asked to play it considering a fictional (even if realistic) scenario, so no information regarding lived experiences was collected.

Beside these formal considerations, ethics has been a central concern of the research team throughout the process and it was addressed by-design as far as possible. As briefly mentioned in the Project description (see Section 3), the role-playing activity was part of a larger set up. The purpose was to ensure a framing of the experimentation and its possible outcomes in a broader perspective, allowing students to play different roles. Therefore, the introductory lecture in class addressed the issue of cyberbullying adopting a distal perspective (cyberbullying as a topic). The annotation phase required students to be exposed to the raw material of cyberbullying in all its unpleasantness but filtering their perception by adopting the perspective of researchers (cyberbullying as an object of study). The role-playing was performed after each student had already been familiarized with cyberbullying. The role-playing allowed a protected space to experiment cyberbullying, avoiding students to impersonate the bullied (victims were always impersonated by researchers) and experiencing different roles (cyberbullying as a lived experience from multiple perspectives: bully, support to the bully, support to the victim). The participatory analysis allowed students to retrospectively frame and provide meaning to the lived experience in a protected environment (cyberbullying as a prop for reflectivity). The whole process was designed to allow the honest and realistic outburst during the role-playing but framing it with accompanying measures aimed at avoiding/minimizing the negative effects of harsh interactions during the role-playing. The presence and vigilance of two researchers and a teacher in each phase of the process ensured a failsafe mechanism to prevent the derangement of the experiment and its containment.

6.3 Epistemic Issues

At last, we shall address the issue of validity of the corpus created with the experimentation. Can the corpus be considered a substitute for a set of actual interactions or should it be considered just as the result of a playful experience with little (if any) resemblance to reality? The lack of a WhatsApp corpus of non-simulated cyberbullying activities does not allow for a comparison to assess the plausibility of the cyberbullying interactions gathered. Evaluating the realisticness of such interactions is both the main challenge and the key to replicate and extend the methodology adopted to other domains. While a clear-cut methodology to perform such evaluation was not developed for the case at hand, we tentatively assessed the plausibility of the corpus indirectly.

Since we could not assess the verisimilitude of the outcome (i.e. corpus) we collected information to evaluate the credibility of the process. We focused on three dimensions:

- observer effect, to estimate the self-censorship implied in being watched by adults;

- evolution of the interaction, to estimate the resemblance to actual online harassing;

- engagement in the interaction, to understand the constant awareness of being involved in a simulated activity.

The classes did not seem too worried about being under observation. Both classes had already experienced cyberbullying issues in the past years and teachers were informed by the students about it. In those occasions, to the surprise of the teachers, students voluntarily showed them the text to request their help, despite the presence of vulgar content. Moreover, during the experimentation, researchers had to remind several students to behave themselves and remember the basic rules of roleplaying. As for the evolution of the interaction, students declared that the experimentation mirrored a 'normal' heated conversation on

WhatsApp, with violent but short-lived outbursts regarding a single issue. About the engagement in the interaction, the participatory analysis revealed that some participants were forgetful of the text they sent, as if they got carried away by the role playing. While we are aware that a only a thorough methodology could respond to the question of the validity of the corpus gathered through the role playing, these preliminary findings suggest that the spirit of the game may lead participants to act with in a way that resembles real life.

7 Conclusions

In this work, we present and release a WhatsApp dataset in Italian created through a role-play by three classes of students aged 12-13. The data, which are freely available, have been anonymized and annotated according to user role and type of insult. Given the difficulty to retrieve WhatsApp data, since their chats are only accessible to the group members, we believe that datasets of this kind can give a better insight into the language used by pre-teens and teens in closed communities and into the dynamics of cyberbullying. The work has also highlighted the importance of creating a living lab with a setting suitable for experimentation and educational activities. Nevertheless, several open issues must be taken into account, from ethical issues related to exposing pre-teens to offensive language, to the problem of data realisticness when using a role-play environment.

Acknowledgments

Part of this work was funded by the CREEP project (http://creep-project.eu/), a Digital Wellbeing Activity supported by EIT Digital in 2018. This research was also supported by the HATEMETER project (http://hatemeter.eu/) within the EU Rights, Equality and Citizenship Programme 2014-2020. In addition, the authors want to thank all the students and teachers who participated in the experimentation.

References

Dana Aizenkot and Gabriela Kashy-Rosenbaum. 2018. Cyberbullying in whatsapp classmates groups: Evaluation of an intervention program implemented in israeli elementary and middle schools. *New Media & Society*, page 1461444818782702.

Valentina Bartalesi Lenzi, Giovanni Moretti, and Rachele Sprugnoli. 2012. Cat: the celct annotation tool. In *In Proceedings of LREC 2012*, pages 333–338.

Jennifer Bayzick, April Kontostathis, and Lynne Edwards. 2011. Detecting the presence of cyberbullying using computer software. In *3rd Annual ACM Web Science Conference (WebSci 11)*, pages 1–2.

Sofia Berne, Ann Frisén, and Johanna Kling. 2014. Appearance-related cyberbullying: A qualitative investigation of characteristics, content, reasons, and effects. *Body image*, 11(4):527–533.

Claudio Dell'Era and Paolo Landoni. 2014. Living lab: A methodology between user-centred design and participatory design. *Creativity and Innovation Management*, 23(2):137–154.

Lee R Dice. 1945. Measures of the amount of ecologic association between species. *Ecology*, 26(3):297–302.

Alejandro Dorantes, Gerardo Sierra, Tlauhlia Yamín Donohue Pérez, Gemma Bel-Enguix, and Mónica Jasso Rosales. 2018. Sociolinguistic corpus of whatsapp chats in spanish among college students. In *Proceedings of the Sixth International Workshop on Natural Language Processing for Social Media*, pages 1–6.

Pierdomenico Fiadino, Mirko Schiavone, and Pedro Casas. 2014. Vivisecting Whatsapp Through Large-scale Measurements in Mobile Networks. *SIGCOMM Comput. Commun. Rev.*, 44(4):133–134.

Ann Frisén, Sofia Berne, and Carolina Lunde. 2014. Cybervictimization and body esteem: Experiences of swedish children and adolescents. *European Journal of Developmental Psychology*, 11(3):331–343.

Homa Hosseinmardi, Sabrina Arredondo Mattson, Rahat Ibn Rafiq, Richard Han, Qin Lv, and Shivakant Mishr. 2015. Prediction of cyberbullying incidents on the Instagram social network. *arXiv preprint arXiv:1508.06257*.

ISTAT. 2014. Il Bullismo in Italia: Comportamenti offensivi tra i giovanissimi. `https://www.istat.it/it/files/2015/12/Bullismo.pdf`. [Online; accessed 26-July-2018].

Kelly Reynolds, April Kontostathis, and Lynne Edwards. 2011. Using machine learning to detect cyberbullying. In *Machine learning and applications and workshops (ICMLA), 2011 10th International Conference on*, volume 2, pages 241–244. IEEE.

Save the Children. 2014. I nativi digitali. Conoscono davvero il loro ambiente? . `https://www.savethechildren.it/blog-notizie/i-minori-e-internet-italia-infografica`. [Online; accessed 25-July-2018].

Peter K. Smith, Jess Mahdavi, Manuel Carvalho, Sonja Fisher, Shanette Russell, and Neil Tippett. 2008. Cyberbullying: its nature and impact in secondary school pupils. *Journal of Child Psychology and Psychiatry*, 49(4):376–385.

Junming Sui. 2015. *Understanding and fighting bullying with machine learning*. Ph.D. thesis, Ph. D. dissertation, The Univ. of Wisconsin-Madison, WI, USA.

Robert S. Tokunaga. 2010. Following you home from school: A critical review and synthesis of research on cyberbullying victimization. *Computers in Human Behavior*, 26(3):277 – 287.

Simone Ueberwasser and Elisabeth Stark. 2017. Whats up, switzerland? a corpus-based research project in a multilingual country. *Linguistik online*, 84(5).

Cynthia Van Hee, Gilles Jacobs, Chris Emmery, Bart Desmet, Els Lefever, Ben Verhoeven, Guy De Pauw, Walter Daelemans, and Véronique Hoste. 2018. Automatic detection of cyberbullying in social media text. *arXiv preprint arXiv:1801.05617*.

Cynthia Van Hee, Els Lefever, Ben Verhoeven, Julie Mennes, Bart Desmet, Guy De Pauw, Walter Daelemans, and Véronique Hoste. 2015a. Automatic detection and prevention of cyberbullying. In *International Conference on Human and Social Analytics (HUSO 2015)*, pages 13–18. IARIA.

Cynthia Van Hee, Els Lefever, Ben Verhoeven, Julie Mennes, Bart Desmet, Guy De Pauw, Walter Daelemans, and Véronique Hoste. 2015b. Detection and fine-grained classification of cyberbullying events. In *International Conference Recent Advances in Natural Language Processing (RANLP)*, pages 672–680.

Cynthia Van Hee, Ben Verhoeven, Els Lefever, Guy De Pauw, Véronique Hoste, and Walter Daelemans. 2015c. Guidelines for the fine-grained analysis of cyberbullying. Technical report, Language and Translation Technology Team, Ghent University.

AJP Verheijen and WPMS Spooren. 2017. The impact of whatsapp on dutch youths school writing. In *Proceedings of the 5th Conference on CMC and Social Media Corpora for the Humanities (cmccorpora17)*. Bolzano: Eurac Research.

Lieke Verheijen and Wessel Stoop. 2016. Collecting facebook posts and whatsapp chats. In *International Conference on Text, Speech, and Dialogue*, pages 249–258. Springer.

Improving Moderation of Online Discussions via Interpretable Neural Models

Andrej Švec[1], Matúš Pikuliak[2], Marián Šimko[2], Mária Bieliková[2]
Slovak University of Technology in Bratislava, Bratislava, Slovakia
Faculty of Informatics and Information Technologies
[1]andy.swec@gmail.com
[2]{matus.pikuliak,marian.simko,maria.bielikova}@stuba.sk

Abstract

Growing amount of comments make online discussions difficult to moderate by human moderators only. Antisocial behavior is a common occurrence that often discourages other users from participating in discussion. We propose a neural network based method that partially automates the moderation process. It consists of two steps. First, we detect inappropriate comments for moderators to see. Second, we highlight inappropriate parts within these comments to make the moderation faster. We evaluated our method on data from a major Slovak news discussion platform.

1 Introduction

Keeping the discussion on a website civil is important for user satisfaction as well as for legal reasons (European court of human rights, 2015). Manually moderating all the comments might be too time consuming. Larger news and discussion websites receive hundreds of comments per minute which might require huge moderator teams. In addition it is easy to overlook inappropriate comments due to human error. Automated solutions are being developed to reduce moderation time requirements and to mitigate the error rate.

In this work we propose a neural network based method to speed up the moderation process. First, we use trained classifier to automatically detect inappropriate comments. Second, a subset of words is selected with a method by (Lei et al., 2016) based on reinforcement learning. These selected words should form a rationale why a comment was classified as inappropriate by our model. Selected words are then highlighted for moderators so they can quickly focus on problematic parts of comments. We also managed to evaluate our solution on a major dataset (millions of comments) and in real world conditions at an important Slovak news discussion platform.

2 Related work

Inappropriate comments detection. There are various approaches to detection of inappropriate comments in online discussions (Schmidt and Wiegand, 2017). The most common approach is to detect inappropriate texts through machine learning. Features used include bag of words (Burnap and Williams, 2016), lexicons (Gitari et al., 2015), linguistic, syntactic and sentiment features (Nobata et al., 2016), Latent Dirichlet Allocation features (Zhong et al., 2016) or comment embeddings (Djuric et al., 2015). Deep learning was also considered to tackle this issue (Badjatiya et al., 2017; Mehdad and Tetreault, 2016).

Apart from detecting inappropriate texts, multiple works focus on detecting users that should be banned (Cheng et al., 2015) by analyzing their posts and their activity in general (Adler et al., 2011; Ribeiro et al., 2018a), their relationships with other users (Ribeiro et al., 2018b) and the reaction of other users (Cheng et al., 2014) or moderators (Cheng et al., 2015) towards them.

Interpreting neural models. Interpretability of machine learning models is common requirement when deploying the models to production. In our case moderators would like to know why was the comment marked as inappropriate.

Most of the works deal with interpretability of computer vision models (Zeiler and Fergus, 2014), but progress in interpretable text processing was also made. Several works try to analyze the dynamics of what is happening inside the neural network. Karpathy et al. (2015); Aubakirova and Bansal (2016) focus on memory cells activations. Li et al. (2016a) compute how much individual input units contribute to the final decision. Other techniques rely on attention mechanisms (Yang et al., 2016), contextual decomposition (Murdoch et al., 2018), representa-

60

Proceedings of the Second Workshop on Abusive Language Online (ALW2), pages 60–65
Brussels, Belgium, October 31, 2018. ©2018 Association for Computational Linguistics

tion erasure (Li et al., 2016b) or relevance propagation (Arras et al., 2017). Our work uses the method by Lei et al. (2016), which selects coherent subset of words responsible for neural network decision. The authors use this model to explain multi-aspect sentiment analysis over beer reviews and information retrieval over CQA system.

In the domain of detecting antisocial behavior Pavlopoulos et al. (2017) used attention mechanism to interpret existing model. Their work is the most relevant to ours, but we use other datasets as well as other, more explicit, technique for model interpretation.

3 Interpretable Neural Moderation

We propose a method to speed up the moderation process of online discussions. It consists of two steps:

1. We detect inappropriate comments. This is a binary classification problem. Comments are sorted by model confidence and shown to the moderators. In effect after this initial filtering moderators work mostly with inappropriate comments which improves their efficiency.

2. We highlight critical parts of inappropriate comments to convince moderators that selected comments are indeed harmful. The moderators can then focus on these highlighted parts instead of reading the whole comment.

3.1 Step 1: Inappropriate comments detection

We approach inappropriate comments detection as a binary classification problem. Each comment is either appropriate or inappropriate. We use recurrent neural network that takes sequence of word embeddings as input. The final output is then used to predict the probability of comment being inappropriate. We use RCNN recurrent cells (Barzilay et al., 2016) instead of more commonly used LSTM cells as they proved to be faster to train with practically identical results. This part of our method is trained in supervised fashion using Adam optimization algorithm.

3.2 Step 2: Inappropriate parts highlighting

Our method implements (Lei et al., 2016). It can learn to select the words responsible for a decision of a neural network called *rationale* without the need for word level annotations in the data.

The model processes comment word embeddings x and generates two outputs: binary flags z representing selection of individual words into rationale which is marked (z, x) and y being probability distribution over classes appropriate / inappropriate. The model is composed of two modules: generator *gen* and classifier *clas* called also encoder in the original work.

Generator *gen*. The role of generator is to select words that are responsible for a comment being in/appropriate. On its output layer it generates probabilities of selection for each word $p(z|x)$. A well trained model assigns high probability scores to words that should form the rationale and low scores to the rest. In the final step these probabilities are used to sample binary selections z. The sampling layer is called Z-layer.

Due to sampling in Z-layer *gen* graph becomes non-differentiable. To overcome this issue the method uses reinforcement learning method called policy gradients (Williams, 1992) to train the generator.

Classifier *clas*. *clas* is a softmax classifier that tries to determine whether a comment is inappropriate or not by processing only words from rationale (z, x).

Joint learning. In order to learn to highlight inappropriate words from inappropriate comments we need *gen* and *clas* to cooperate. *gen* selects words and *clas* provides feedback on the quality of selected words. The feedback is based on the assumption that the words are selected correctly if *clas* is able to classify comment correctly based on the rationale (z, x) and vice versa.

Furthermore, there are some conditions on the rationale: it must to be short and meaningful (the selected words must be near each other) what is achieved by adding regularization controlled by hyperparameters λ_1 (which forces the rationales to have fewer words) and λ_2 (which forces the selected words to be in a row). The following loss function expresses these conditions:

$$loss(x, z, y') = \|clas(z, x) - y'\|_2^2$$

$$+ \lambda_1 \|z\| + \lambda_2 \sum_{t=1}^{K-1} |z_t - z_{t+1}| \quad (1)$$

where x is original comment text, z contains binary flags representing non/selection of each word in x, (z, x) contains actual words selected to rationale, y' is correct output and K is the length of x and also z respectively.

From the loss function we can see that the training is based on a simple assumption that rationale is a subset of words that *clas* classifies correctly. If it is not classified correctly then the rationale is probably incorrect. This way we can learn to generate rationales without need to have word level annotations. We would like to make the point that training to generate these rationales is not done to improve the classification performance. It uses only the exact same data the classifier from Step 1 uses. Its only effect is to generate interpretable rationales behind the decisions classifier takes.

4 Experiments and Results

4.1 Dataset

We used a proprietary dataset of more than 20 million comments from a major Slovak news discussion platform. Over the years a team of moderators was considering reported comments and removing the inappropriate ones while also selecting a reason(s) from prepared list of possible discussion code violations. In this work we consider only those that were flagged because of following reasons: insults, racism, profanity or spam. The rest of the comments are considered appropriate. We split the dataset in train, validation and test set where validation and test set both were balanced to contain 10,000 appropriate and 10,000 inappropriate comments. Rest of the dataset forms the training set. Test and validation sets were sampled from the most recent months. During the training we balance it on batch level by supersampling inappropriate comments.

Highlights test set. We did not have any annotations on rationales in the dataset. We created a test set by manually selecting words that should form the rationales in randomly picked 100 comments. This way we created a test set containing 3,600 annotated words.

Word embeddings. We trained our own fast-Text embeddings (Bojanowski et al., 2017) on our dataset. These take into account character level information and are therefore suitable for inflected languages (such as Slovak) and online discussions where lots of grammatical and typing errors occur.

4.2 Inappropriate comments detection

We performed a hyperparameter grid search with our method. We experimented with different recurrent cells (RCNN and LSTM), depth (2, 3), hidden size (200, 300, 500), bi-directional RNN and in the case of RCNN also with cell order (2, 4). We also trained several non-neural methods for comparison. Results from this experiment are marked in Table 1. We measure accuracy as well as average precision (AP). The best results were achieved by bi-directional 2-layer RCNN with hidden size 300 and order 2. Deep neural network models outperform feature based models by almost 10% of accuracy. RCNN achieves results similar to LSTM but with approximately 8.5 times less parameters.

The results here might be significantly affected by noisy data. During the years many inappropriate comments went unnoticed and many appropriate comments were blocked if they were in inappropriate threads. Qualitative interviews we carried out with moderators indicate that our accuracy might be a bit higher.

We observed that model was the most confident about insulting and offensive comments. Thanks to sub-word based word embeddings the model can find profanities even when some characters within are replaced with numbers (e.g. *1nsult* instead of insult) or there are arbitrary characters inserted into the word (e.g. *i..n...s..u..l..t* instead of *insult*.

To better understand the impact of this classifier we plotted its results using ROC curve in Figure 1. Here we can see how many comments a moderator needs to read to find certain percentile of inappropriate ones. E.g. when looking for 80% of inappropriate comments, only 20% of reviewed comments will be falsely flagged by the model.

4.3 Highlighting inappropriate parts

gen and *clas* are implemented as recurrent neural networks with RCNN cells. *gen* is a bi-directional 2-layer RCNN with hidden size equal 200 and order equal 2. Z-layer is realized as unidirectional RNN with hidden size equal 30. *clas* is an unidirectional 2-layer RCNN with hidden size equal 200 and order equal 2. For regularization hyperparameters we found values $\lambda_1 \in [5 \times 10^{-4}, 3 \times 10^{-3}]$ and $\lambda_2 \in [2\lambda_1, 4\lambda_1]$ to perform well.

We observed a significant instability during the training caused by formulation of our loss func-

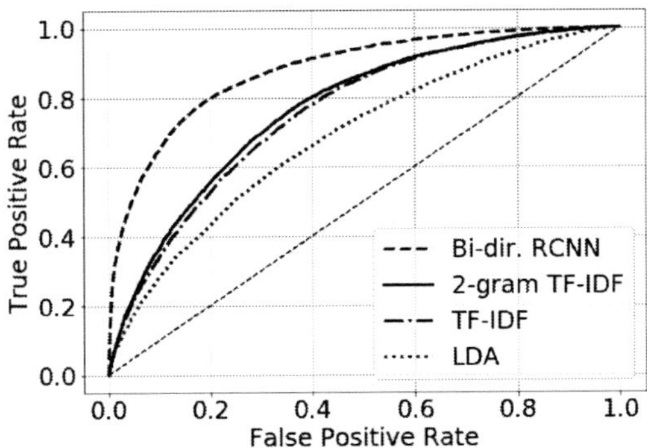

Figure 1: Receiver operating characteristic (ROC) of different models. We plot only one neural based solution as they almost completely overlap.

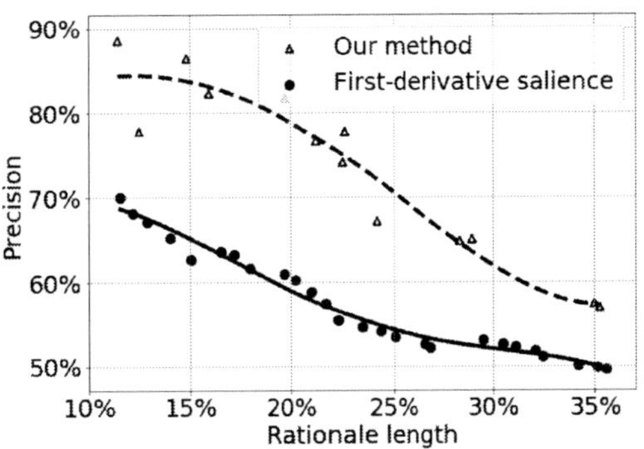

Figure 2: Test set performance of models highlighting inappropriate parts in comments.

Model	# params	% acc	AUC
LDA (75 topics)	-	63.2	0.684
LSA (300 topics)	-	66.2	-
TF-IDF	-	68.8	0.754
2-gram TF-IDF	-	70.1	0.766
Unidir. RCNN	0.6M	79.0	0.870
Unidir. LSTM	3.3M	78.9	0.872
Bi-dir. RCNN	**1.7M**	**79.4**	**0.872**
Bi-dir. LSTM	**14.6M**	**79.4**	**0.875**

Table 1: Comparison of test set performance of multiple classification models. Baseline models (first four) use various text representations that are classified by boosted decision trees (1,000 trees) (Freund and Schapire, 1995).

tion. The model would often converge to a state where it would pick all the words or no words at all. Especially the cases when the model started to pick all the words proved to be impossible to overcome. In such cases we restarted the training from a different seed what increased the probability of a model converging successfully by a factor of five.

We evaluated following metrics of our models:

- *Precision* – how many of selected words were actually part of golden inappropriate data. Correct selection of words is a prerequisite for saving moderators' time. Recall is not very important as we do not need to select all the inappropriate parts. One part is usually enough for the moderators to block a comment.

- *Rationale length* – the proportion of words selected into rationale. It is important to mea-

sure this metric as we want our model to only pick a handful of strongly predictive words.

We compare our proposed model with the model based on first-derivative saliency (Li et al., 2016a). The comparison of models is shown in Figure 2. We can see that with length reduction the precision grows as expected. Our best models achieve a precision of nearly 90% while selecting 10–15% of words. We consider this to be very good result. Our method outperforms the saliency based one and also produces less scattered rationales. By this we mean that the average length of a segment of subsequently selected words is 2.5 for our method, but only 1.5 for saliency-based method. Instead of picking individual words our model tries to pick longer segments.

5 Conclusion

Moderating online discussions is time consuming error-prone activity. Major discussion platforms have millions of users so they need huge teams of moderators. We propose a method to speed up this process and make it more reliable. The novelty of our approach is in the application of a model interpretation method in this domain.

Instead of simply marking the comment as inappropriate, our method highlights the words that made the model think so. This is significant help for moderators as they can now read only small part of comment instead of its whole text. We believe that our method can significantly speed up the moderation process and user study is underway to confirm this hypothesis.

We evaluated our model on dataset from a major Slovak news discussion platform with more than

20 million comments. Results are encouraging as we were able to obtain good results on inappropriate comments detection task. We also obtained good results (nearly 90% precision) when highlighting inappropriate parts of these comments.

In the future we plan to improve the evaluation of highlighting. Instead of measuring the global precision, we plan to analyze how well it performs with various types of inappropriateness, such as racism, insults or spam. We are also looking into the possibility of incorporating additional data into our algorithm – other comments from the same thread, article for which the comments are created or even user profiles. These could help us improve our results or even detect the possibility of antisocial behavior before it even happens.

Acknowledgments

This work was partially supported by the Slovak Research and Development Agency under the contracts No. APVV-17-0267 - Automated Recognition of Antisocial Behaviour in Online Communities and No. APVV-15-0508 - Human Information Behavior in the Digital Space. The authors would like to thank for financial contribution from the Scientific Grant Agency of the Slovak Republic, grant No. VG 1/0646/15.

References

B Thomas Adler, Luca De Alfaro, Santiago M Mola-Velasco, Paolo Rosso, and Andrew G West. 2011. Wikipedia vandalism detection: Combining natural language, metadata, and reputation features. In *International Conference on Intelligent Text Processing and Computational Linguistics*, pages 277–288. Springer.

Leila Arras, Franziska Horn, Grégoire Montavon, Klaus-Robert Müller, and Wojciech Samek. 2017. "what is relevant in a text document?": An interpretable machine learning approach. *PLOS ONE*, 12(8):1–23.

Malika Aubakirova and Mohit Bansal. 2016. Interpreting neural networks to improve politeness comprehension. In *Proceedings of the 2016 Conference on Empirical Methods in Natural Language Processing*, pages 2035–2041. Association for Computational Linguistics.

Pinkesh Badjatiya, Shashank Gupta, Manish Gupta, and Vasudeva Varma. 2017. Deep learning for hate speech detection in tweets. In *Proceedings of the 26th International Conference on World Wide Web Companion*, pages 759–760. International World Wide Web Conferences Steering Committee.

Tao Lei Hrishikesh Joshi Regina Barzilay, Tommi Jaakkola, Katerina Tymoshenko, and Alessandro Moschitti Lluıs Marquez. 2016. Semi-supervised question retrieval with gated convolutions. In *Proceedings of NAACL-HLT*, pages 1279–1289.

Piotr Bojanowski, Edouard Grave, Armand Joulin, and Tomas Mikolov. 2017. Enriching word vectors with subword information. *Transactions of the Association of Computational Linguistics*, 5(1):135–146.

Pete Burnap and Matthew L Williams. 2016. Us and them: identifying cyber hate on twitter across multiple protected characteristics. *EPJ Data Science*, 5(1):11.

Justin Cheng, Cristian Danescu-Niculescu-Mizil, and Jure Leskovec. 2014. How community feedback shapes user behavior. In *Eighth International AAAI Conference on Weblogs and Social Media*.

Justin Cheng, Cristian Danescu-Niculescu-Mizil, and Jure Leskovec. 2015. Antisocial behavior in online discussion communities. In *Ninth International AAAI Conference on Web and Social Media*.

Nemanja Djuric, Jing Zhou, Robin Morris, Mihajlo Grbovic, Vladan Radosavljevic, and Narayan Bhamidipati. 2015. Hate speech detection with comment embeddings. In *Proceedings of the 24th international conference on world wide web*, pages 29–30. ACM.

European court of human rights. 2015. Case of Delfi as v. Estonia. https://hudoc.echr.coe.int/eng#{"itemid":["001-155105"]}. [Online; accessed February 23th, 2018].

Yoav Freund and Robert E Schapire. 1995. A desicion-theoretic generalization of on-line learning and an application to boosting. In *European conference on computational learning theory*, pages 23–37. Springer.

Njagi Dennis Gitari, Zhang Zuping, Hanyurwimfura Damien, and Jun Long. 2015. A lexicon-based approach for hate speech detection. *International Journal of Multimedia and Ubiquitous Engineering*, 10(4):215–230.

Andrej Karpathy, Justin Johnson, and Li Fei-Fei. 2015. Visualizing and understanding recurrent networks. *arXiv preprint arXiv:1506.02078*.

Tao Lei, Regina Barzilay, and Tommi Jaakkola. 2016. Rationalizing neural predictions. In *Proceedings of the 2016 Conference on Empirical Methods in Natural Language Processing*, pages 107–117.

Jiwei Li, Xinlei Chen, Eduard Hovy, and Dan Jurafsky. 2016a. Visualizing and understanding neural models in nlp. In *Proceedings of NAACL-HLT*, pages 681–691.

Jiwei Li, Will Monroe, and Dan Jurafsky. 2016b. Understanding neural networks through representation erasure. *CoRR*, abs/1612.08220.

Yashar Mehdad and Joel Tetreault. 2016. Do characters abuse more than words? In *Proceedings of the 17th Annual Meeting of the Special Interest Group on Discourse and Dialogue*, pages 299–303.

W. James Murdoch, Peter J. Liu, and Bin Yu. 2018. Beyond word importance: Contextual decomposition to extract interactions from lstms. In *Proceedings of International Conference on Learning Representations (ICLR)*.

Chikashi Nobata, Joel Tetreault, Achint Thomas, Yashar Mehdad, and Yi Chang. 2016. Abusive language detection in online user content. In *Proceedings of the 25th international conference on world wide web*, pages 145–153. International World Wide Web Conferences Steering Committee.

John Pavlopoulos, Prodromos Malakasiotis, and Ion Androutsopoulos. 2017. Deeper attention to abusive user content moderation. In *Proceedings of the 2017 Conference on Empirical Methods in Natural Language Processing*, pages 1125–1135. Association for Computational Linguistics.

Manoel Horta Ribeiro, Pedro H Calais, Yuri A Santos, Virgílio AF Almeida, and Wagner Meira Jr. 2018a. Characterizing and detecting hateful users on twitter. *arXiv preprint arXiv:1803.08977*.

Manoel Horta Ribeiro, Pedro H Calais, Yuri A Santos, Virgílio AF Almeida, and Wagner Meira Jr. 2018b. "like sheep among wolves": Characterizing hateful users on twitter.

Anna Schmidt and Michael Wiegand. 2017. A survey on hate speech detection using natural language processing. In *Proceedings of the Fifth International Workshop on Natural Language Processing for Social Media*, pages 1–10.

Ronald J Williams. 1992. Simple statistical gradient-following algorithms for connectionist reinforcement learning. In *Reinforcement Learning*, pages 5–32. Springer.

Zichao Yang, Diyi Yang, Chris Dyer, Xiaodong He, Alexander J. Smola, and Eduard H. Hovy. 2016. Hierarchical attention networks for document classification. In *NAACL HLT 2016, The 2016 Conference of the North American Chapter of the Association for Computational Linguistics: Human Language Technologies, San Diego California, USA, June 12-17, 2016*, pages 1480–1489.

Matthew D. Zeiler and Rob Fergus. 2014. Visualizing and understanding convolutional networks. In *Computer Vision - ECCV 2014 - 13th European Conference, Zurich, Switzerland, September 6-12, 2014, Proceedings, Part I*, pages 818–833.

Haoti Zhong, Hao Li, Anna Squicciarini, Sarah Rajtmajer, Christopher Griffin, David Miller, and Cornelia Caragea. 2016. Content-driven detection of cyberbullying on the instagram social network. In *Proceedings of the Twenty-Fifth International Joint Conference on Artificial Intelligence*, pages 3952–3958. AAAI Press.

Aggressive language in an online hacking forum

Andrew Caines, Sergio Pastrana, Alice Hutchings & Paula Buttery
Department of Computer Science & Technology
University of Cambridge
Cambridge, U.K.
apc38@cam.ac.uk, sp849@cam.ac.uk,
alice.hutchings@cl.cam.ac.uk, paula.buttery@cl.cam.ac.uk

Abstract

We probe the heterogeneity in levels of abusive language in different sections of the Internet, using an annotated corpus of Wikipedia page edit comments to train a binary classifier for abuse detection. Our test data come from the CrimeBB Corpus of hacking-related forum posts and we find that (a) forum interactions are rarely abusive, (b) the abusive language which does exist tends to be relatively mild compared to that found in the Wikipedia comments domain, and tends to involve aggressive posturing rather than hate speech or threats of violence. We observe that the purpose of conversations in online forums tend to be more constructive and informative than those in Wikipedia page edit comments which are geared more towards adversarial interactions, and that this may explain the lower levels of abuse found in our forum data than in Wikipedia comments. Further work remains to be done to compare these results with other inter-domain classification experiments, and to understand the impact of aggressive language in forum conversations.

1 Introduction

The automatic identification of abusive language online[1] is of growing interest and concerns have proliferated about aggressive Internet behaviours commonly known as 'trolling'. From an applications perspective, the accurate detection of vitriolic language is one of the clearest examples of natural language processing for social good, assuming data has been collected ethically and stored legally, and that any intervention is left to the appropriate authorities (Kennedy et al., 2017; Kumar et al., 2018). Meanwhile from a theoretical

point of view, there are many outstanding linguistic and sociological research questions surrounding Internet aggression and how it manifests itself in writing (Pieschl et al., 2015; Waseem et al., 2017).

The question we address here is whether online abusive language is of one type or whether there is discernible variation in the level of abuse found in different subsections of the Internet. We do not claim to have the final answer to this nebulous question, but instead we have addressed one small part of the whole: is the level of abuse found in one Internet domain – namely discussions about English Wikipedia page edits – similar to that found in another domain, that of an online hacking forum?

We show that the type of abusive language occurring in the latter is more closely aligned with the milder levels of abuse of those found in Wikipedia discussions, and consider why this might be. We observe that the online hacking forum tends to contain texts aimed at helping or informing other users, whereas the Wikipedia conversations are inherently more adversarial since they relate to recent page edits and disputes arising. Where abusive language is found in the online hacking forum, it tends to involve profane name-calling, insults and heated disputes, rather than hate speech or threats of violence – those which have tended to be the more prominent causes for public concern.

Note here that we make a distinction between *aggressive* and *offensive* language: the former often involves the latter, but not always so. Offensive language – identifiable word tokens such as swearwords and the like – may offend but is not always used aggressively; sometimes it is used in a jocular fashion, for example. Aggressive language, which more often than not is built on the composition of many words, involves a hostile stance from

---

[1]Note that this paper quotes texts which many will find offensive and/or upsetting. Please contact the authors if you would prefer to read the article with all quotations removed.

Proceedings of the Second Workshop on Abusive Language Online (ALW2), pages 66–74
Brussels, Belgium, October 31, 2018. ©2018 Association for Computational Linguistics

one speaker or writer to another. It is this which might seem to be abusive and which we seek to automatically detect and better understand.

We also distinguish aggressive language from *hate speech* – that which might be characterised as prejudicial diatribes to provoke action, perhaps violent, against a group or groups – and from *cyberbullying* – that which involves a sustained period of persecution against an individual or individuals. Certainly the distinctions are fuzzy at the edges, but these might be thought of as the canonical definitions of these abuse types. We are dealing with what we deem to be one-off instances of aggression in online communities, though if these were shown to be prejudicial against a group, or sustained against an individual, then the instances start to move into hate speech or cyberbullying behaviours.

In both Wikipedia edits and the online hacking forum, abusive comments are infrequent in the community as a whole and the general objective of gaining reputation in the domain dis-incentivises aggressive behaviour. Nevertheless we show that aggressive language which does occur may be detected fairly well by training on the Wikipedia edits corpus – the advantage being that it has been multiply and widely annotated – and setting the threshold for a binary aggression classifier at a fairly moderate level relative to the worst types of abuse found in Wikipedia comments. Future work remains to be done to more broadly characterise intra-community behaviour in different subsections of the Internet.

2   Related work

Offensive language serves many purposes in everyday discourse: from deliberate effect in humour to self-directed profanity to toxic or abusive intent. We are not concerned here with humorous uses of offensive language or with general profanity. Instead we are interested in toxic and abusive behaviour, specifically online harassment involving abusive language, aggression and personal attacks. There has been work on other forms of abusive behaviour, such as hate speech (Warner and Hirschberg, 2012; Kwok and Wang, 2013; Ribeiro et al., 2018) and cyberbullying (Xu et al., 2013; Pieschl et al., 2015), and we put these aside for now as challenging, distinct topics (though with the fuzzy edges described above).

In terms of online harassment, previous work has centred around definitions, automatic detection, and dataset creation – for example the Hate Speech Twitter Annotations and Wikipedia Comments Corpus (Waseem and Hovy, 2016; Wulczyn et al., 2017). Most work has been conducted on English data, with some extensions to other languages (e.g. Arabic (Mubarak et al., 2017), Slovene (Fišer et al., 2017)).

Automated detection approaches have drawn on classic document classification methods for spam detection and sentiment analysis, and tend to use lexical and syntactic features (Nobata et al., 2016; Li et al., 2017; Bourgonje et al., 2018). Machine learning techniques range from logistic regression (Cheng et al., 2015) to support vector machines (Yin et al., 2009) to neural networks (Gambäck and Sikdar, 2017). Our aim here is not especially to push the boundaries on detection techniques – though naturally we wish our classifier to perform fairly well – but rather we are interested in how to make use of existing labelled training data when predicting personal attacks in other corpora.

In case any persuasion is needed that improved understanding, detection and action on abusive language are desirable, there is evidence that experience of online harassment leads to decreased online participation and is connected with oppression, violence and suicide (Dinakar et al., 2011; Sood et al., 2012; Wulczyn et al., 2017). Of course there may be reasons to be concerned about the perpetrator's wellbeing along with that of the victims (Cheng et al., 2017).

3   Training & test corpora

We have an inter-corpus experimental design, in which a document classifier is trained on one dataset and tested on other datasets. Our training data come from the Wikipedia Comments Corpus (WikiComments) (Wulczyn et al., 2017), which contains 115,864 discussion posts extracted from an English Wikipedia dump, judged as personal attacks or harassment by crowdworkers. Ten judgements were collected for each post; hence we have an *attack score* from zero to ten for every post[2], and we assume that the higher the attack score the greater the linguistic aggression shown in writing.

This assumption may be challenged, as we accept that there are many reasons why a text may not be unanimously judged to be an attack or ha-

---

[2]Note that the original authors scaled the attack score between 0 and 1, whereas we re-scale the scores from 0 to 10.

rassment – properties of the text such as poor grammar which obfuscates meaning, use of slang insults which are not universally known, or sarcastic phrasing which is not interpreted as an attack by all annotators. On the other hand, properties of the annotator, such as fatigue or inattention, inexperience with English or the terminology used, or idiosyncratic linguistic thresholds for attacks and harassment, could all play a part in judgement variation as well. However, over such a large dataset we assume that in terms of aggressive language the texts will be broadly well ordered by their attack scores. Table 1 shows examples randomly drawn from each attack score, zero to ten, along with the number of posts in each class, and the cumulative size of the corpus in reverse order from attack score ten to zero.

The curators of WikiComments used these annotated discussion posts to train a classifier and further label unseen posts in a larger collection of 63 million discussion posts, with a view to large-scale analyses of attacks by unregistered users, moderator actions in response to attacks, and more (Wulczyn et al., 2017). They experimented with different thresholds t where attack scores at or above t would be labelled as attacks, and those below t would not be attacks. They found that the optimal value for t balancing precision and recall was 4.25.

Our intention is to take the texts and attack scores from WikiComments to train a binary aggression classifier for use with other corpora. The question with such a classifier is how to partition the training data for true/false aggression labels: the cut-off could be any attack score value from one to ten. In the following sections we report on classification experiments with each attack score cut-off value and a test corpus sourced from Internet forums.

Our test data come from the CrimeBB Corpus[3], a dataset harvested from several hacking-related websites including HackForums, Antichat and Greysec (Pastrana et al., 2018). The corpus currently contains both English and Russian language data, with plans to incorporate other languages in future. We opted to work only with posts from the HackForums website[4], it being the most popular English language hacking site worldwide.

Among other author intents such as helpfulness,

[3] Available by application to the Cambridge Cybercrime Centre, https://www.cambridgecybercrime.uk
[4] https://hackforums.net

disapproval, sarcasm and gratitude, we manually labelled author aggression as indicated by abusive language in a total of 4123 posts randomly sampled from a selection of HackForums *bulletin boards* (themed discussion pages) from November 2007 to January 2018. All boards are related to hacking (such as 'Cryptography, Encryption, and Decryption', 'Keyloggers', and 'Remote Administration Tools'), as opposed to other interests represented on HackForums such as gaming, entertainment and graphics. Three annotators labelled 2200 posts and agreed to a 'moderate degree' according to Landis & Koch's framework for interpreting Fleiss's kappa (Fleiss, 1971; Landis and Koch, 1977) – i.e. $\kappa = 0.4$ to 0.6. We did not attempt to settle on single annotations for each post, but instead treated all judgements equally, allowing multiple labels both by individual annotators and across different annotators. A single annotator further labelled the remaining 1923 posts.

Posts with aggressive intent are uncommon on HackForums, with only 100 aggressive posts judged to be aggressive by at least one annotator in the total corpus of 4123 posts (2.4%). Note that profane language is more commonly found – which is unsurprising given the casual linguistic register – with 201 posts in this dataset featuring at least one of 'fuck, shit, cunt, jerk, crap, dick' (or derived forms). However, the profanity is often used for humorous purposes, or to defuse potentially confrontational conversations, or simply in a casual way for no purpose at all; it is not always used aggressively (hence the need for manual annotation). This observation underlines the distinction between offensive and aggressive language. Table 2 shows the size of the CrimeBB Corpus, the HackForums subset, and the annotated posts, along with examples of aggressive and non-aggressive posts from HackForums.

4 Classification experiments

We trained a binary aggression classifier on the WikiComments Corpus setting the true/false threshold t at each attack score from 1 to 10 and testing the classifier on our annotated set of 4123 HackForums posts from the CrimeBB Corpus.

4.1 Evaluation

We are interested in the successful classification of aggressive posts only and therefore, rather than reporting precision, recall and F-measures, we re-

Attack score	Example	N.posts	Cumulative n.posts
10	fuck u asshole go fuck your own mother fuck fuck fuck fuck a duck fucked a kangaroo you piece of shit go suck your own balls.	3223	3223
9	drop dead. you're a cancer on wikipedia, and i assume you're a cancer on the rest of the world as well. your baby will do better without you.	2842	6065
8	oh right, like "this article sucks and you know it." isn't abusive language. hypocrite. eat shit and die, loser.	2501	8566
7	the link is there. i have an idea. why not delete the page and then re create it a few days later you fucking retard? have you a life at all? is it your life to go around and delete everything here? why not go outside and build a snowman you loser?	2195	10,761
6	next time you remove a section without first following procedures, i will have you permanently barred from wikipedia. i wrote the section and it is completely accurate an unbiased as reported. you are a fool and a vandal and i will be closely monitoring your activities on anything i write.	2706	13,467
5	so this looks like a vendetta. it is stupid. you are pissing me off. this is not what we are here for.	2263	15,730
4	everybody!!! everybody!!!! *redacted* is the undigested part of a giant squid stuck in a sperm whales intestines and testicles	4133	19,863
3	hello, hoaxer. thank you for posting on my talk page. it appears that you enjoy wasting hours first hoaxing and then arguing about it with wikipedia editors on discussion and user pages. all one needs to is track your ip army to see that you are the hoaxer. nobody is falling for your nonsense, especially when you don't sign your posts.	6280	26,143
2	i am aware that most bible thumping christians want to burn this guy alive. i find your assessment far from neutral, i will agf here, but your tone is vitriolic.	9408	35,551
1	the new title doesn't convey what i wanted the section to be about, think of title that conveys the question not just the general subject matter.	22,548	58,099
0	in a legal brief, one might well exclude trial court opinions. in an encyclopedia article, it's a different story, especially when the trial court opinion predates the appellate decision by decades.	57,765	115,864

Table 1: Examples, the number of posts, and the cumulative size (in reverse order) for each attack score subset of the Wikipedia Comments Corpus (Wulczyn et al., 2017).

Corpus	Example	N.posts
CrimeBB		57,733,219
HackForums		40,152,443
Annotated dataset		4123
Non-aggressive	my bet would be install linux and then use spoofing via that	4023
Aggressive	kill yourself. most retarded advice you could give him	100

Table 2: Examples and the number of posts in subsets of the CrimeBB Corpus (Pastrana et al., 2018).

port accuracy as in equation (1):

$$\text{Accuracy} = \frac{\text{true positives}}{\text{true positives} + \text{false negatives}} \tag{1}$$

4.2 Method

All test and training texts were lower-cased and transformed into document-term matrices using the `text2vec` package for R (Selivanov and Wang, 2017). For each value of threshold t from 1 to 10, the training texts were assigned true and false labels according to their attack score s where aggression is true if $s \geq t$.

We trained an extreme gradient boosting (XG-Boost) classifier with the R package `xgboost` (Chen et al., 2018). Boosting is an additive technique whereby new models are added to correct the errors made by existing models thus far: models are added sequentially until no further improvements can be made. In gradient boosting, new models predict the residuals or errors of prior models using a gradient descent algorithm. XG-Boost is known to work well with sparse matrices, which is the kind of input associated with textual data, and in NLP terms has been shown to perform competitively in sentiment analysis shared tasks (Nasim, 2017; Jabreel and Moreno, 2018).

To avoid over-fitting we set parameters fairly conservatively, with a maximum tree depth of 6, the number of rounds at 10 and early stopping set to 5, gamma at 1, and the learning rate at 0.3. We report classifier accuracy according to equation (1) on gold aggression:true labels in our CrimeBB test corpus. Recall that we do not compare XGBoost with other classifiers, as our focus is on the training data rather than performance. In future work we can investigate other models including neural networks, though logistic regression has in some cases out-performed neural nets in the detection of abusive language (Park and Fung, 2017).

As the value of t increases the size of the aggression:true dataset decreases, as seen in Table 1. To ensure any change in accuracy is not due to the decrease in aggression:true training instances, we run a second experiment in which for all values of t both label subsets (aggression:true and aggression:false) are randomly reduced to 3223 instances – the size of the smallest attack score sub-corpus (per the cumulative n.posts column in Table 1). For this latter experiment we report accuracies averaged over one hundred runs to smooth variation in the random sampling process (identified as 'Acc.Control' in Table 3).

4.3 Results

Classification accuracies are shown in Table 3 [5]. It is apparent that in both training data settings – controlled and non-controlled ('all') – the accuracy of aggression identification reduces as the true/false cut-off threshold t increases. In the case of the controlled training data setting there is at first a small increase in accuracy as t rises from 1 to 3. This result suggests that the levels in the Wiki-Comments Corpus most closely matching the aggressive posts on HackForums are those in the attack score range 1 to 5, and that the optimal value of t is between 2 and 3.

To illustrate the rise and fall in classification accuracy as t increases, we plot accuracies as boxplots for the 100 runs in the controlled training data setting (Figure 4.3). The boxplots show medians (the thick horizontal bars), first and third quar-

---

[5]For comparison with the classifiers trained by Wulczyn et al (2017) we also calculated AUC (area under the curve) measures in the 'all' condition. Our best AUC was .739 with t at 2; Wulczyn et al's best model was a multi-layered perceptron estimating empirical distributions based on character n-grams and this achieved an AUC of .966.

t	N.True posts	Acc. All	Acc. Control
1	58,099	.80	.76
2	35,551	.63	.77
3	26,143	.54	.78
4	19,863	.41	.75
5	15,730	.35	.72
6	13,467	.32	.70
7	10,761	.27	.64
8	8566	.22	.60
9	6065	.19	.52
10	3223	.09	.42

Table 3: Classification accuracy for aggressive posts in the CrimeBB Corpus, with a varying true/false training threshold t from 1 to 10, the size of the aggression:true set in WikiComments for different values of t, accuracy for all training WikiComments instances, and a controlled experiment sampling 3223 true and false instances (averaged over 100 runs).

tiles (Q1, Q3, shown by the hinges), and whiskers extending as far as $1.5 * IQR$ where IQR is the inter-quartile range between Q1 and Q3. Datapoints beyond the whiskers are outliers and are plotted individually.

4.4 Discussion

It is evident from our classification experiments that levels of linguistic aggression in HackForums tend to be milder than those in WikiComments, if we take the optimal value of t to lie between 2 and 3 (Table 3) whereas for WikiComments it was found to be 4.25 (Wulczyn et al., 2017). A possible explanation for this finding may be the difference in purposes of the two sources for our test and training data: discussion of Wikipedia page edits often end up as arguments between contributors. The fact these arguments may become aggressive or personally offensive at times is unsurprising.

In HackForums, where our test data came from, users often have the intention of educating others, learning from others, buying and selling products, and in many cases discouraging others from acting illegally online (those with a so-called 'white hat' hacking ethos – hackers who identify security vulnerabilities and report them rather than exploit them). HackForums is not an oasis of calm, positive behaviour, however – on the con-

trary, users can often be off-hand in their comments, dismissive of 'noobs' and 'skids' (script kiddies – a novice or tinkerer), sarcastic and rude. These attitudes, where they do not cross the line into aggressive behaviour, map to our negative label for author intent. Debates about hacking techniques, authorship of code, and user behaviour (e.g. spam, posting out-of-date tutorials, offering hacking tools which don't work as advertised) are frequent. But on the whole, the forum exists for information and technology exchange and the white hat hackers, along with active administrators and a reputation scoring system, help to constrain user behaviour.

Indeed this highly active reputation scoring system may deter aggressive online harassment and allow for users to engender trust in what could otherwise be quite untrustworthy environments (Holt et al., 2016; Décary-Hétu and Leppänen, 2016). Furthermore, online deviant communities such as these tend to be rather homogeneous, particularly involving young males (Hutchings and Chua, 2017). Therefore the targets for any harassment may be off, rather than on, the forum.

Aside from aggression, we also labelled positive texts (which answer others' questions, contain laughter-related word tokens or emoticons, or praise the work of others), neutral texts, and negative texts (including users stating that others cannot or should not do something, sarcasm and arguments). These intent types are the majority labels in our 4123 post subset, with 1562 positive, 2566 neutral and 788 negative occurrences (the posts could be multiply labelled, hence these counts sum to more than 4123). Minority labels are aggression (n=100), users posting to moderate discussion (n=119), and requests to continue discussion in private messaging (n=238).

We further subdivide our set of 100 aggressive forum posts into seven classes: simply aggressive, personal denigration, alludes to violence, refers to disability, features misogyny, homophobia, racism. Personal denigration typically involves name-calling – dismissing someone as an idiot or moron, doubting their technical skills, and so on. The other classes indicate that the author of the post alludes to violence ("I'll cut your neck"), disability ("you're a retard"), misogyny ("stop bitching"), homophobia ("that's gay"), and racism ("fucking jew"). Note that, with the exception of 'simply aggressive' which tends to be

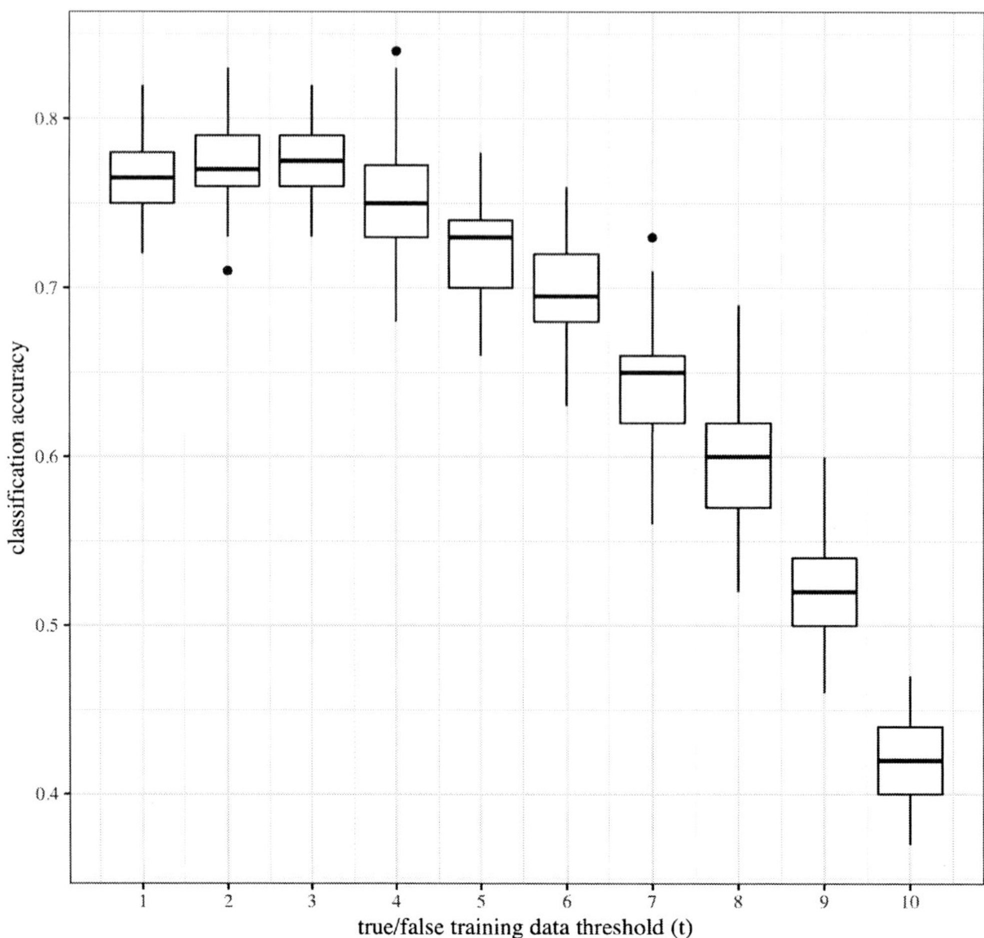

Figure 1: Classifying aggressive posts in the CrimeBB Corpus using controlled training data sizes; with the true/false training threshold t on the x-axis and accuracy on the y-axis, and each data point being 1 of 100 runs randomly sampling the training data.

a fallback if the post falls into no other class, the posts may be assigned multiple labels and that a single annotator undertook labelling. Label counts are shown in Table 4.

We find that most aggressive posts are just that – simply aggressive manners of writing which would be out of place in polite discourse. For example, authors add emphasis with the f-word, including formulaic phrases in acronym form ('gtfo', 'wtf', 'stfu'). The next most common aggression type is personal denigration: most often calling the addressee's intelligence into question, or doubting their motives. After that, the minority labels are those which might feature in hate speech: discriminating against women, homosexuals and ethnicities. In addition, the 'refers to dis-

Label	Count
Simply aggressive	48
Personal denigration	37
Refers to disability	7
Includes misogyny	4
Alludes to violence	2
Includes homophobia	1
Includes racism	1

Table 4: Aggression subclass counts in 100 HackForums posts with aggressive intent from the CrimeBB Corpus.

ability' label always involves the words 'retard' and 'retarded' in this 100 post sample. Finally, direct threats of violence are very rare, with only two examples found in this subcorpus.

5 Conclusions & Future work

We have shown that abusive language in an online hacking forum is relatively mild compared to that found in Wikipedia page edit comments. We propose that the tendency of forum users to on the whole engage in constructive and informative discourse results in positive behaviour and non-toxic language. WikiComments, on the other hand, is made up of debates about the rights and wrongs of page edits, and perhaps inevitably this adversarial set up allows more aggressive behaviours to manifest themselves in writing.

In future work we evidently need to annotate more data so that we have more than 100 examples of abusive language from CrimeBB. Due to the low hit rate for abusive language in CrimeBB texts (100 in 4123, for instance) we can investigate automatic annotation of further chunks of the data, along with supervised sampling from those new annotations to check their quality. These labelled data on a larger scale will allow us to analyse more general patterns of behaviour such as individual and community-wide trends over time, how aggression surfaces and is dealt with by moderators, and linguistic facets of aggressive behaviour such as homophobia, racism, misogyny and so on.

We can also investigate other Internet domains such as social media, other forums and potentially the Dark Web, but also other sections of CrimeBB, such as the reputation voting area within HackForums in which we might expect to find more vitriolic interactions given that votes can be both positive and negative and accompanied by review-like texts. Finally, we are also interested in applications of our research, including the questions of desired accuracy of any deployed system, the appropriate actions to take, and the ethics of data collection, analysis and intervention (Kennedy et al., 2017; Thomas et al., 2017). One option could be to create an alert system for forum moderators, thereby offering real-world impact for our work while allowing the appropriate authorities to take action when necessary (Kumar et al., 2018).

Acknowledgments

This work was supported by The Alan Turing Institute's Defence & Security Programme, and the U.K. Engineering & Physical Sciences Research Council. We thank Emma Lenton, Dr Alastair Beresford, and the anonymous reviewers for their support and advice.

References

Peter Bourgonje, Julian Moreno-Schneider, Ankit Srivastava, and Georg Rehm. 2018. Automatic classification of abusive language and personal attacks in various forms of online communication. In *Language Technologies for the Challenges of the Digital Age*. Springer International Publishing.

Tianqi Chen, Tong He, Michael Benesty, Vadim Khotilovich, and Yuan Tang. 2018. *xgboost: Extreme Gradient Boosting*. R package version 0.6.4.1.

Justin Cheng, Michael Bernstein, Cristian Danescu-Niculescu-Mizil, and Jure Leskovec. 2017. Anyone can become a troll: Causes of trolling behavior in online discussions. In *Proceedings of the 2017 ACM Conference on Computer Supported Cooperative Work and Social Computing*.

Justin Cheng, Cristian Danescu-Niculescu-Mizil, and Jure Leskovec. 2015. Antisocial behavior in online discussion communities. In *The 9th International AAAI Conference on Web and Social Media (ICWSM)*.

David Décary-Hétu and Anna Leppänen. 2016. Criminals and signals: An assessment of criminal performance in the carding underworld. *Security Journal*, 29:442–460.

Karthik Dinakar, Roi Reichart, and Henry Lieberman. 2011. Modeling the detection of textual cyberbullying. In *Fifth International AAAI Conference on Weblogs and Social Media*.

Darja Fišer, Tomaž Erjavec, and Nikola Ljubešić. 2017. Legal framework, dataset and annotation schema for socially unacceptable online discourse practices in Slovene. In *Proceedings of the First Workshop on Abusive Language Online*.

Joseph Fleiss. 1971. Measuring nominal scale agreement among many raters. *Psychological Bulletin*, 76:378–382.

Björn Gambäck and Utpal Kumar Sikdar. 2017. Using convolutional neural networks to classify hate-speech. In *Proceedings of the First Workshop on Abusive Language Online*.

Thomas Holt, Olga Smirnova, and Alice Hutchings. 2016. Examining signals of trust in criminal markets online. *Journal of Cybersecurity*, 2:137–145.

Alice Hutchings and Yi Ting Chua. 2017. Gendering cybercrime. In T. J. Holt, editor, *Cybercrime through an Interdisciplinary Lens*. Oxford: Routledge.

Mohammed Jabreel and Antonio Moreno. 2018. EiTAKA at SemEval-2018 Task 1: An ensemble of n-channels ConvNet and XGboost regressors for emotion analysis of tweets. In *Proceedings of The 12th International Workshop on Semantic Evaluation*.

George Kennedy, Andrew McCollough, Edward Dixon, Alexei Bastidas, John Ryan, Chris Loo, and Saurav Sahay. 2017. Technology solutions to combat online harassment. In *Proceedings of the First Workshop on Abusive Language Online*.

Srijan Kumar, William L. Hamilton, Jure Leskovec, and Dan Jurafsky. 2018. Community interaction and conflict on the Web. In *Proceedings of the 2018 World Wide Web Conference*.

Irene Kwok and Yuzhou Wang. 2013. Locate the hate: Detecting tweets against blacks. In *Twenty-Seventh AAAI Conference on Artificial Intelligence*.

J. Richard Landis and Gary G. Koch. 1977. The measurement of observer agreement for categorical data. *Biometrics*, 33:159–174.

Tai Ching Li, Joobin Gharibshah, Evangelos E. Papalexakis, and Michalis Faloutsos. 2017. TrollSpot: Detecting misbehavior in commenting platforms. In *Proceedings of the 2017 IEEE/ACM International Conference on Advances in Social Networks Analysis and Mining 2017*.

Hamdy Mubarak, Kareem Darwish, and Walid Magdy. 2017. Abusive language detection on Arabic social media. In *Proceedings of the First Workshop on Abusive Language Online*.

Zarmeen Nasim. 2017. IBA-Sys at SemEval-2017 Task 5: Fine-grained sentiment analysis on financial microblogs and news. In *Proceedings of the 11th International Workshop on Semantic Evaluation (SemEval-2017)*.

Chikashi Nobata, Joel Tetreault, Achint Thomas, Yashar Mehdad, and Yi Chang. 2016. Abusive language detection in online user content. In *Proceedings of the 25th International Conference on World Wide Web*.

Ji Ho Park and Pascale Fung. 2017. One-step and two-step classification for abusive language detection on twitter. In *Proceedings of the First Workshop on Abusive Language Online*.

Sergio Pastrana, Daniel Thomas, Alice Hutchings, and Richard Clayton. 2018. Crimebb: Enabling cybercrime research on underground forums at scale. In *Proceedings of the 27th International Conference on World Wide Web (WWW'18)*.

Stephanie Pieschl, Christina Kuhlmann, and Torsten Porsch. 2015. Beware of publicity! perceived distress of negative cyber incidents and implications for defining cyberbullying. *Journal of School Violence*, 14:111–132.

Manoel Horta Ribeiro, Pedro H. Calais, Yuri A. Santos, and Wagner Meira J Virgîl̦io A. F. Almeid and. 2018. "like sheep among wolves": Characterizing hateful users on Twitter. In *Proceedings of WSDM workshop on Misinformation and Misbehavior Mining on the Web (MIS2)*.

Dmitriy Selivanov and Qing Wang. 2017. *text2vec: Modern Text Mining Framework for R*. R package version 0.5.0.

Sara Owsley Sood, Elizabeth F. Churchill, and Judd Antin. 2012. Automatic identification of personal insults on social news sites. *Journal of the American Society for Information Science and Technology*, 63:270–285.

Daniel Thomas, Sergio Pastrana, Alice Hutchings, Richard Clayton, and Alastair Beresford. 2017. Ethical issues in research using datasets of illicit origin. In *Proceedings of the ACM Internet Measurement Conference (IMC'17)*.

William Warner and Julia Hirschberg. 2012. Detecting hate speech on the World Wide Web. In *Proceedings of the Second Workshop on Language in Social Media*.

Zeerak Waseem, Thomas Davidson, Dana Warmsley, and Ingmar Weber. 2017. Understanding abuse: A typology of abusive language detection subtasks. In *Proceedings of the First Workshop on Abusive Language Online*.

Zeerak Waseem and Dirk Hovy. 2016. Hateful symbols or hateful people? predictive features for hate speech detection on Twitter. In *Proceedings of the NAACL Student Research Workshop*.

Ellery Wulczyn, Nithum Thain, and Lucas Dixon. 2017. Ex Machina: Personal attacks seen at scale. In *Proceedings of the 26th International Conference on World Wide Web*.

Jun-Ming Xu, Benjamin Burchfiel, Xiaojin Zhu, and Amy Bellmore. 2013. An examination of regret in bullying tweets. In *Proceedings of the 2013 Conference of the North American Chapter of the Association for Computational Linguistics: Human Language Technologies*.

Dawei Yin, Zhenzhen Xue, Liangjie Hong, Brian D. Davison, April Kontostathis, and Lynne Edwards. 2009. Detection of harassment on Web 2.0. In *Proceedings of the Content Analysis in the WEB 2.0 (CAW2.0) Workshop at WWW2009*.

The Effects of User Features on Twitter Hate Speech Detection

Elise Fehn Unsvåg and **Björn Gambäck**
Department of Computer Science
Norwegian University of Science and Technology
NO-7491 Trondheim, Norway
elisefol@stud.ntnu.no, gamback@ntnu.no

Abstract

The paper investigates the potential effects user features have on hate speech classification. A quantitative analysis of Twitter data was conducted to better understand user characteristics, but no correlations were found between hateful text and the characteristics of the users who had posted it. However, experiments with a hate speech classifier based on datasets from three different languages showed that combining certain user features with textual features gave slight improvements of classification performance. While the incorporation of user features resulted in varying impact on performance for the different datasets used, user network-related features provided the most consistent improvements.

1 Introduction

Detecting hate speech has become an increasingly important task for online communities, but automatic hate speech detection is a challenging task, which the majority of the research in the field is targeting through textual features. However, as shown by, e.g., Gröndahl et al. (2018), there is a need for further efforts to improve the quality and efficiency of detection methods, motivating for studies on how non-textual features can be utilised to enhance detection performance.

The goal of this research is to investigate information related to users in the Twitter community that can be helpful in identifying online hate speech, and use this as features in hate speech classification. Information about the users could be either known factors, such as age and gender, or factors derived from behaviour. There exists research that investigates the impact of different features, and research about the personality and behaviour of users expressing hate speech. However, there is little research that combines the two topics.

Most early studies on automatic recognition of online hate speech focused on lexicon-based approaches for detecting "bad" words, with Kwok and Wang (2013) finding that 83% of their data was annotated racist due to the presence of offensive words. However, these approaches tend to give low precision by mistakenly classifying all messages containing specific terms as hate speech, which is particularly problematic on social media sites that have a relatively high prevalence of offensive words (Wang et al., 2014). After all, hate speech can be much more sophisticated than that.

Finding the features that best represent the underlying phenomenon of hate speech is challenging. Later studies have mainly focused on content-based text classification using features such as the appearance or frequency of words, spelling mistakes or semantic meaning, but while these methods perform relatively well, there is still need for improvements to increase the quality of detection.

The rest of the paper is structured as follows: Section 2 discusses previous studies related to the authors of hate speech and Section 3 presents the datasets used together with an analysis of user characteristics. Section 4 describes the classifier developed, while Section 5 details the experiments conducted to measure the impact of user features. Section 6 sums up the research contributions along with suggestions for potential future work.

2 Related Work

Including user information in methods for detecting hate speech is an under-researched area. However, related to hate speech detection are studies of the people that post hateful content online, including characteristics and behavioural traits that are typical of the authors behind aggressive behaviour, hate speech or trolling. Chen et al. (2012)

Proceedings of the Second Workshop on Abusive Language Online (ALW2), pages 75–85
Brussels, Belgium, October 31, 2018. ©2018 Association for Computational Linguistics

proposed a Lexical Syntactic Feature architecture to bridge the gap between detecting offensive content and potential offensive users in social media, arguing that although existing methods treat messages as independent instances, the focus should be on the source of the content. Waseem and Hovy (2016) stated that among various extra-linguistic features, only gender brought improvements to hate speech detection. Papegnies et al. (2017) mention a plan to use context-based features for abuse detection, and especially those based on the networks of user interactions. Several authors share this intention, but face the challenge that user information often is limited or unavailable.

Wulczyn et al. (2017) qualitatively analyzed personal attacks in Wikipedia comments, showing that anonymity increases the likelihood of a comment being an attack, although anonymous comments only contributed to less than half of the total attacks. The study also suggested that personal attacks cluster in time, which may be because one attack triggers another. In another qualitative analysis, Cheng et al. (2015) characterized forms of antisocial behaviour in online discussion communities, comparing the activity of users that have been permanently banned from a community to those that are not banned. The study found the banned users to use less positive words and more profanity, and to concentrate their efforts in a small amount of threads. They also receive more replies and responses than other users.

Hardaker (2010) defined a *troller* as a user who appears to sincerely wish to be part of a group, including professing, or conveying pseudo-sincere intentions, but whose real intentions are to cause disruption or to trigger conflict for the purposes of their own amusement. Buckels et al. (2014) studied the characteristic traits of Internet trolls by looking at commenting styles and personality inventories, and found strong positive relations among commenting frequency, trolling enjoyment and trolling behaviour and identity. Cheng et al. (2017) proposed that an individual's mood and seeing troll posts by others trigger troll behaviour.

Most similar to the objectives of the present work, Chatzakou et al. (2017) investigated user features that can be utilized to enhance the detection and classification of bullying and aggressive behaviour of Twitter users. They found that network-based features (such as the number of friends and followers, reciprocity and the position in the network) were particularly useful and effective in classifying aggressive user behaviour.

3   Data Analysis

Creating datasets of hate speech is time consuming, as the number of hateful instances in online communities is relatively low. The datasets available are also often created for different tasks, and from different types of media and languages, and therefore vary in characteristics and types of hate speech. Sources include Twitter (Waseem and Hovy, 2016; Fortuna, 2017; Ross et al., 2016), Wikipedia (Wulczyn et al., 2017), and Fox News (Gao and Huang, 2017). Furthermore, many datasets (from Yahoo, SpaceOrigin and Twitter) are not publicly available (Djuric et al., 2015; Nobata et al., 2016; Papegnies et al., 2017; Chatzakou et al., 2017), while others are available only under some restrictions (Davidson et al., 2017; Golbeck et al., 2017). This may be due to privacy issues or considering the content of the datasets: Pavlopoulos et al. (2017) made their Greek Gazzetta dataset available by using an encryptor to avoid directly publishing hate speech content.

Here, three datasets were used to investigate the characteristics of users for increased insight and to allow comparisons of the findings. All datasets have Twitter as their source, ensuring that the same information could be retrieved. However, the datasets differ in terms of annotations, size and characteristics, and come from three different languages: English (Waseem and Hovy, 2016), Portuguese (Fortuna, 2017), and German (Ross et al., 2016). The datasets contain tweet IDs that can be used to retrieve the actual text, information about the tweet or information about the user who has posted it. As user information is something that should be handled with care, it is important to mention that no attempt was made to directly identify the actual users.

Tweet IDs may become unavailable, either by the tweet having been deleted, or if the user who posted the tweet has become suspended or has deleted their account. Therefore, a review of the availability of the tweets in all datasets was conducted prior to the investigation of characteristics, and will be described first below, before going into details of the analysis of the user characteristics in the three datasets. The statistics of the actually available tweets and posting users in the datasets as included in this work are shown in Table 1.

Label	ENG		POR		GER	
	Tweets	Users	Tweets	Users	Tweets	Users
Hate	4,968	539	649	376	98	47
None	10,759	1,569	2,410	634	243	123
Total	15,727	2,108	3,059	1,010	341	170

Table 1: Available tweets and users in the datasets

3.1 Datasets

The English dataset by Waseem and Hovy (2016) is publicly available on GitHub.[1] The Twitter search API was used to collect the corpus, and in total 16,907 tweets (from 2,399 users) were annotated either as racist, sexist or neither. The dataset contains more instances of neutral than racist or sexist tweets. This unbalance was intended by the developers, to make the corpus more representative of the real world, where hate speech is a limited phenomenon. Since the dataset was developed in 2016, the Python library Tweepy was used here to filter out any unavailable tweets and users. Furthermore, the original "Sexism" and "Racism" classes were merged into one "Hate speech" class. 1,180 of the original tweets were no longer available, which also impacted the number of users in the dataset. The remaining tweets and users are presented in Table 1, in the 'ENG' column.

Fortuna (2017) developed a dataset consisting of 5,668 Portuguese tweets and made it available through the INESC TEC research data repository.[2] Tweets were collected through the Twitter API with searches based on keywords related to hate speech and Twitter profiles known for posting hate messages. Fortuna aimed to have a higher proportion of hate speech messages than other related datasets, and 22% of the tweets were annotated as hate speech. She annotated nine direct hate speech sub-classes, but in the present work those will be merged into one hate speech class. In total there are 5,668 annotated tweets by 1,156 distinct users; however, the distribution of users within the target classes was not specified. Today, close to half of the tweets in both classes are unavailable; however, as shown in the 'POR' column of Table 1, there are still 1,010 users available, meaning that the unavailability of tweets did not heavily affect the number of users. While the original dataset had a binary value for the presence of hate speech and subcategories as labels, the target classes were here changed to "Hate speech" and "None".

To investigate the issue of reliability concerning hate speech annotation, Ross et al. (2016) compiled a German hate speech corpus with tweets linked to the refugee crisis in Europe. By using known insulting or offensive hashtags, a total of 13,766 tweets were collected, 469 of which were annotated by two annotators for presence or absence of hate speech. In Table 1 the column 'GER' shows the availability of the tweets in the dataset and the number of users in each target class. It was beneficial to transform the labels of the dataset into binary classes, to equal the labelling of the other datasets. Therefore, a tweet that was labelled "Yes" by one or both of the annotators was assigned to the "Hate speech" class. Hence, the "Hate speech" class consists of 65 available tweets labelled as hate speech by one annotator, and 33 labelled hate speech by both annotators.

3.2 Characteristics

A quantitative analysis was conducted to better understand the characteristics of the users in the datasets, based on the proposed features in Section 2 and other information about the user available through the Twitter API. All datasets included several tweets from the same users; tweets that then can be present in both target classes. However, to better distinguish between users and avoid redundancy in the analysis, users who are present in both target classes are here only included as users within the "Hate speech" class.

Gender: Twitter does not require users to register their gender, so no explicit gender field is retrievable through the Twitter API. Finding the gender distribution for users in the dataset is therefore challenging. Waseem and Hovy (2016) investigated the distributions of gender in their original dataset through extracting gender information by looking up usernames and names in the user profiles, and then comparing these to known male or female given names. A similar approach was used here, by incorporating lists of common international, Portuguese, German, and English names. In addition, the user descriptions were also considered, as users often give a more detailed description there of who they are, e.g., "I am a mom of three boys". A risk with this approach is that names or descriptions may mistakenly be classified as the wrong gender, and therefore the gender findings may not be entirely accurate. Names that can be both female and male have been avoided.

---

[1] `github.com/ZeerakW/hatespeech`
[2] `rdm.inesctec.pt/dataset/cs-2017-008`

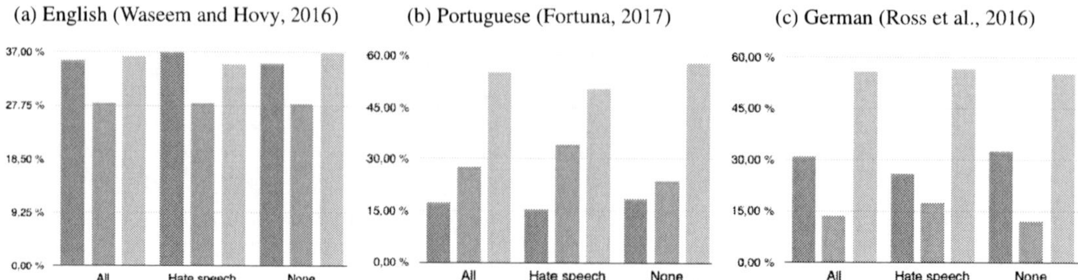

Figure 1: Gender distribution of users in the datasets: blue = male, green = female, beige = unidentified

Waseem and Hovy (2016) expressed that the gender of about half the users could not be identified by their approach, and that the male gender was over-represented in all categories. Figure 1a presents the gender distribution derived here, with significant differences to their findings. In particular, the female users are identified to a much larger degree, with the distribution of male, female and unidentified users being more equal; the fraction of unidentified users has decreased from 50% to 36%. Still, a higher amount of male users are identified than female, which is also the case for the dataset by Ross et al. (2016). In contrast, the gender distribution derived from the dataset by Fortuna (2017) shows a majority of the identified user genders to be female. In that dataset there is also a large number of unidentified genders (55%), which is equal to the number of unidentified users in the dataset by Ross et al. (2016).

User Network: The user networks are defined here as their social networks on Twitter, i.e., who a user follows (called 'following' or 'friends' on Twitter) and who follows that user ('followers'). Chatzakou et al. (2017) found network-based features to be very useful in classifying aggressive user behaviour. They investigated features such as the ratio of followers to friends, the extent to which users reciprocate the follow connections they receive from others, and the users' tendency to cluster with others.

In Figure 2a, the relationship between a user's friends and followers in the dataset by Waseem and Hovy (2016) is illustrated. The majority of users form a cluster in the area below 10,000 friends and 50,000 following. Beyond this cluster, it appears as users of the "None" class are most common, with the exception of one outlier of the "Hate speech" class with about 228,00 followers and no friends. It is difficult to say whether this trend can be generalized, or is caused by the uneven number of users in the two target classes.

Figure 2b shows the distribution of friends and followers for the users in the dataset by Fortuna (2017). A general observation is that the users of this dataset often tend to have more followers than friends. Furthermore, there is little that distinguishes the users of the two classes regarding the number of friends and followers. The number of users in the dataset by Ross et al. (2016) is considerably lower than the other datasets, and may explain the lower number of friends and followers for the users, as shown in Figure 2c. There is

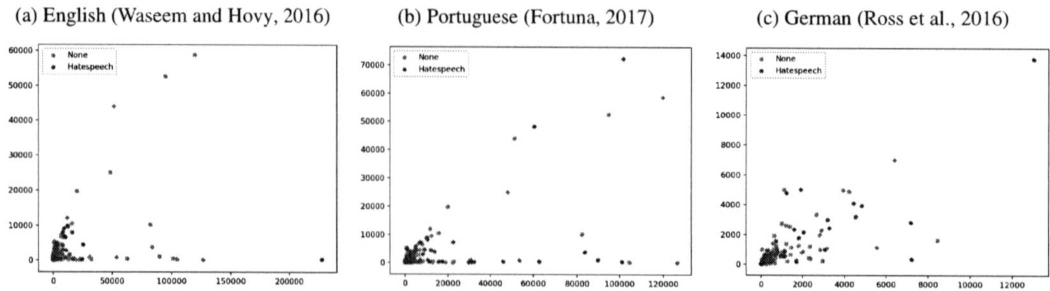

Figure 2: Distribution of users based on their network (number of friends vs number of followers)

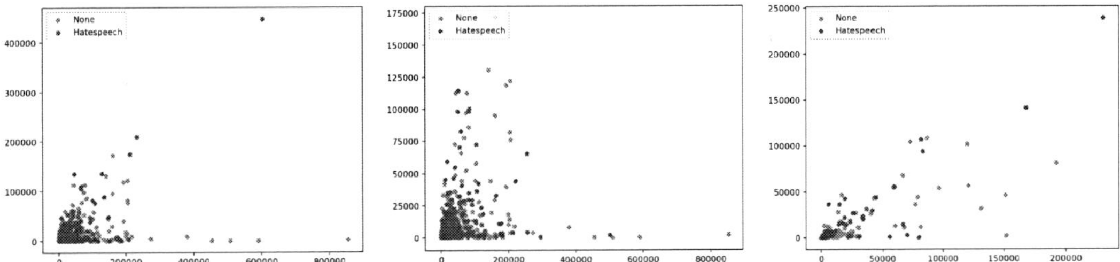

Figure 3: Distribution of users based on activity (number of favourites given vs number of status updates)

an outlier in the "Hate speech" class with about 13,000 followers and 14,000 friends, but the rest of the users are somewhat evenly distributed.

Activity: Previous research suggests that both high and low activity levels can be related to posting hate speech content. Buckels et al. (2014) found commenting frequency to be positively associated with trolling enjoyment and Cheng et al. (2015) suggested that frequently active users are often associated with anti-social behaviour online. In contrast, Wulczyn et al. (2017) found users that launched personal attacks on Wikipedia regardless of activity level. Here, activity is defined by the information that can be extracted through the Twitter API. Tweepy enables the retrieval of the number of tweets a user has posted (also known as 'status updates' on Twitter) and the number of 'favorites' they have given to tweets by others (corresponding to 'likes' in other online media).

In Figure 3 the relationship between a user's number of favourites given and total number of statuses is illustrated, showing that there is a general tendency to have a larger number of status updates than favourites. With the exception of one outlier in the "Hate speech" class with over 400,000 favourites and over 600,000 statuses, the majority of users in both classes of the English dataset form a cluster below 50,000 favourites and 200,000 statuses. In the Portuguese dataset, the users of both target classes are somewhat evenly distributed, and in general the users of this dataset have posted below 200,000 tweets and given below 25,000 favourites. The number of status updates and the number of favourites for the users in the German dataset are much lower than in the other datasets, and similarly to the findings investigating the users' network, there is no clear distinction between the activity characteristics of the users in the target classes.

	ENG		POR		GER	
Feature	Hate	None	Hate	None	Hate	None
Geotag	51.7	48.6	58.8	58.2	16.1	26.6
Profile	60.1	72.4	75.1	67.4	50.0	45.9
Image	98.1	96.2	99.6	98.2	98.4	98.2

Table 2: User profile characteristics (%)

User Profile: Twitter enables users to customize their profile pages, e.g., by changing theme colour, or by adding a profile or header picture. In addition, users can add a bio description, a geographical location or a web page link. Wulczyn et al. (2017) found personal attacks to be more prevalent among anonymous users than registered users. Therefore the elements of a user's profile that can be personalized were examined with the underlying assumption that personalizing the profile is contradicting to remaining anonymity. The elements retrieved were the number of public lists a user has joined, geotagging of tweets, the profile image, and whether or not the user has altered a default theme or background of the profile.

The users in the English data are somewhat equally divided between enabling and disabling of geotagging for both target classes, as seen in Table 2. The distribution is similar for the geotagging characteristic of users in the Portuguese data. However, the majority in both target classes in the German data have disabled geotagging, with a slightly higher percentage for the users in the "Hate speech" class. There is a tendency of the users in the English and Portuguese datasets to rather have a customized profile page than a standard, while the German data is more evenly distributed. Nearly all the users in the three datasets have changed their profile image. For all the datasets, the percentage of changed profile images is also marginally higher for the users in the "Hate speech" class than the users in the "None" class.

4 Classification Setup

The analysis of the datasets presented in the previous section indicated that none of the investigated user characteristics could be clearly used to differentiate textual tweets annotated "Hate speech" and "None". However, the impact of user features in detection may become more visible when tested through a classifier. To investigate the possible effects user features have on the performance of hate speech classification, a baseline hate speech classifier was implemented and trained only on the textual tweets from the datasets, and then compared to a classifier that also incorporated user features. Along with observing the overall effects of user feature inclusion, the impacts of the individual features and feature subsets were investigated.

A basic hate speech classifier needs to include preprocessing of the textual input, feature extraction, and a choice of actual classification model. These will be addressed in turn below, while classification results will be given in the next section.

Preprocessing: Text processing is a difficult task due to the noise contained in language and should be done with care, to avoid losing any important features. This is particularly proliferent in social media such as Twitter, which also introduces domain-specific challenges: the character limit in a tweet increases the use of abbreviations, while including non-textual content (e.g., URLs, images, user mentions and retweets) is common.

The Natural Language Toolkit (Bird et al., 2009) was used for preprocessing of the data, through: (i) removal of Twitter specific information (user mentions, emoticons, retweets, URLs, and hashtag symbols; only retaining textual content), (ii) tokenization, (iii) lowercasing, and (iv) stop word removal (with different stop word lists for the datasets, due to the different languages).

Feature Extraction and Representation: Having found many tweets to be annotated racist due to the appearance of offensive words, Kwok and Wang (2013) constructed a vocabulary using unigram features only. However, this fails to capture relationships between words, so Nobata et al. (2016) added syntactic features, while also employing n-grams and distributional semantic derived features. They found combining all features to yield the best performance, but character n-grams made the largest individual feature contribution. Mehdad and Tetreault (2016) specifically investigated character-based approaches and showed them to be superior to token-based approaches and other state-of-the-art methods.

Since n-grams thus have been shown to be very useful in hate speech classification, both character n-grams and word n-grams were tested here to represent the textual content of the tweets. A TF-IDF approach was used to represent the n-gram features, and ranges up to n=6 tested. Higher values of n were not considered due to the computational effort required. The most suitable type of n-gram and n-gram range were explored through a grid search, and finding different alternatives for representing the tweets suiting the different datasets.

Classification Model: Supervised machine learning classifiers have been the most frequently used approaches to hate speech detection, in particular Support Vector Machines (SVM) and Logistic Regression (LR). Davidson et al. (2017) found LR and linear SVM to perform better than other models, such as Naïve Bayes, Decision Trees, and Random Forests. A comparative study performed by Burnap and Williams (2015) concluded that an ensemble method seemed most promising. Deep learning methods have also been investigated, both Recurrent Neural Networks (Pavlopoulos et al., 2017; Mehdad and Tetreault, 2016), Convolutional Neural Networks (Gambäck and Sikdar, 2017), and combinations (Zhang et al., 2018). Badjatiya et al. (2017) used various deep learning architectures to learn semantic words embeddings and showed these to outperform character and word n-grams.

Here a Logistic Regression model was chosen due to its simplicity and its common usage in language classification. This is also in line with the note by Gröndahl et al. (2018) that a simple LR model performed on par with more complex models in their comparison of hate speech detection classifiers. As the aim here was not to implement the best performing classifier or to compare methods, but to investigate the effects of user features, no other classification models were tested.

5 Experiments and Results

The datasets were initially split into training data and test data to ensure that the model performance was evaluated on unseen data. A grid search with 10-fold cross-validation over the training data was used for selecting model parameters. The classification model with the chosen hyperparameters

n-gram	ENG		POR		GER	
	Word	Char	Word	Char	Word	Char
[1, 1]	.8166	.7399	**.7769**	.6927	.7227	.7185
[1, 2]	.8168	.8020	.7718	.7383	.7185	**.7269**
[1, 3]	.8147	.8201	.7688	.7525	.7227	.7101
[1, 4]	.8119	.8226	.7667	.7657	.7227	.7101
[1, 5]	.8117	**.8248**	.7637	.7698	.7227	.7143
[1, 6]	.8110	.8237	.7612	.7759	.7227	.7143

Table 3: Grid search of n-gram parameters

Class	ENG			POR			GER		
	P	R	F_1	P	R	F_1	P	R	F_1
None	.83	.94	.88	.79	.96	.87	.68	.99	.81
Hate	.82	.58	.68	.82	.40	.54	.50	.03	.06
Avg.	.83	.83	.83	.80	.79	.79	.62	.68	.65

Table 4: Baseline model performance on test data

Features	ENG			POR			GER		
	P	R	F_1	P	R	F_1	P	R	F_1
n-grams	.83	.83	.83	.80	.79	.79	.62	.68	.65
+ gender	.83	.83	.83	.80	.79	.79	.69	.70	.69
+ network	.84	.85	.84	.81	.81	.81	.63	.68	.65
+ activity	.83	.84	.83	.79	.79	.79	.68	.69	.68
+ profile	.83	.83	.83	.80	.80	.80	.71	.71	.71
+ all	.86	.86	.86	.79	.79	.79	.63	.68	.65

Table 5: Impact of different user feature sets

was then evaluated on the test set. This section first presents results from baseline classification with only n-gram features, and then discusses the effects of incorporating user features.

5.1 Classifier with Text Features

The dataset provided by Waseem and Hovy (2016) contained 15,727 available English tweets, that were split into a training set of 11,008 tweets and a test set containing 4,719 tweets, of which 3,275 were classified as non-hate speech. A grid search found that character n-grams in range [1,5] provided the best performance, as shown in the column 'ENG' in Table 3. Table 4 shows the performance metrics of the model, where 0.83 was the macro average F_1-score. Both the precision and recall values are higher for the "None" class. However, the recall value for the "Hate speech" class obtained for this dataset is higher than for the other datasets, most probably due to the larger amount of available training data.

3,059 tweets from the Portuguese dataset by Fortuna (2017) were used, with the training set containing 2,636 tweets and the test set 423, of which 126 were annotated as hate speech. Word unigrams yielded the best performance (Table 3), and the macro average F_1-score obtained for the test data was 0.79 (Table 4). The precision obtained for "Hate speech" is slightly higher than for the "None" class, while the recall is much lower.

The German dataset by Ross et al. (2016) is considerably smaller than the other datasets, containing only 341 tweets, that were split into a train-

ing set of 238 and a test set of 103 (33 hateful). A grid search of the n-gram parameters ('GER' in Table 3) showed a character n-gram with the range [1,2] produced the best 10-fold cross validation results on the training data. On the unseen test data, this model received a macro average F_1-score of 0.65 (Table 4), with the score severely hampered by the classifier only being able to identify 3% of the instances of the "Hate speech" class. This is most likely due to small the size of the dataset, resulting in an insufficient amount of training instances. Notably, Ross et al. (2016) did not develop this dataset primarily for classification, but for investigating hate speech annotation reliability. Their study concluded that the presence of hate speech perhaps should not be considered a binary yer-or-no decision; however, this is how the current classification model is operating.

5.2 Classifier with Text and User Features

In the second part of the experiments, the classifier was expanded to incorporate various user features and subsets. Four types of in total ten features were experimented with:

Gender: male and female,
Network: number of followers and friends,
Activity: number of statuses and favourites,
Profile: geo enabled, default profile, default image, and number of public lists,

where the "number of" features are integer valued, while all the other features are binary (boolean).

Table 5 repeats the performance of the baseline model (n-grams only, in row 1) and then shows n-grams along with various subsets of user features. Including all user features yielded the largest improvement over the baseline on the Waseem and Hovy (2016) dataset, with the 'Network' feature subset making the largest difference. 'Gender' did not improve performance at all, while 'Activity' and 'Profile' provided very slight improvements. Each individual feature was also tested along with

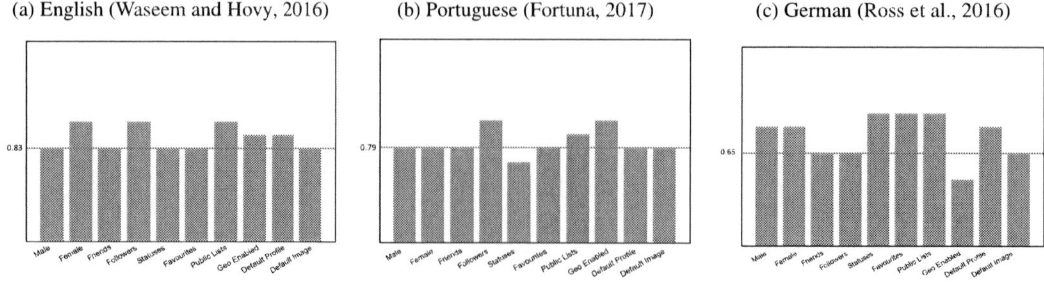

Figure 4: F_1 of individual features along with n-grams. (Red lines = average F_1 using n-grams only.)
[Features: Male, Female, Friends, Followers, Statuses, Favourites, Public Lists, Geo Enabled, Default Profile, Default Image.]

n-grams, as shown in Figure 4a. Half of the features had no impact on performance; 'Default profile' and 'Geo enabled' increased F_1 by 0.1, while 'Female', 'Followers' and 'Public lists' had the most impact, increasing F_1 by 0.2.

The incorporation of all user features on the Fortuna (2017) dataset resulted in a slightly worsened performance. This was also the case for inclusion of the 'Activity' subset, while including 'Network' improved performance. 'Gender' and 'Profile' made no major impact on the scores. Of the individual features, 'Followers' and 'Geo enabled' resulted in the largest F_1-score increase when used in combination with n-gram features, as shown in Figure 4b. In addition, the inclusion of 'Public lists' also slightly improved the F_1-score. Interestingly, the inclusion of 'Statuses' actually worsened model performance.

By only using word unigrams, the baseline classifier only received a recall value of 0.03 for the hate speech class of the dataset by Ross et al. (2016), as shown in Table 4. Looking at Table 5, we see that the 'Gender', 'Activity' and 'Profile' feature subsets resulted in improvements of the average F_1-score. The inclusion of all the features and the 'Network' subset had no effect on the average F_1 score. The inclusion of 'Activity' increased the F_1 by 0.02, 'Gender' increased it by 0.04, and 'Profile' had the largest impact by increasing F_1 by 0.06. These results are consistent with the testing of the individual features shown in Figure 4c, where 'Male', 'Female' and 'Profile' have a large impact on performance. However, the 'Statuses', 'Favourites', and 'Public lists' had the largest improvement by 0.4. Of the individual features included, only 'Geo Enabled' lead to a decreased F_1 score over the baseline.

The results are notably affected by the uneven distribution of instances in the target classes, as shown by significantly lower F_1-scores for "Hate speech" than "None" for all datasets. This was reflected clearly by a closer comparison of classifier output for the English data with n-grams and with all user features (i.e., the setup which yielded the best classifier performance on this dataset): the number of correctly labelled "Hate speech" instances increased from 623 to 1,048 (of 1,444) while the correctly labelled "None" instances decreased slightly, from 3,111 to 3,000 (of 3,275), as illustrated by the confusion matrices in Figure 5.

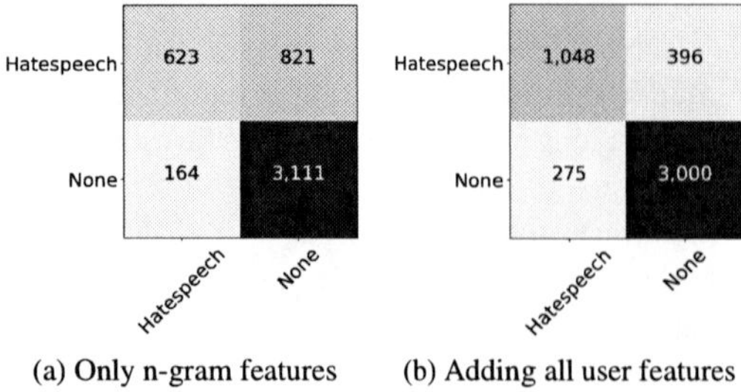

(a) Only n-gram features   (b) Adding all user features

Figure 5: English dataset confusion matrices

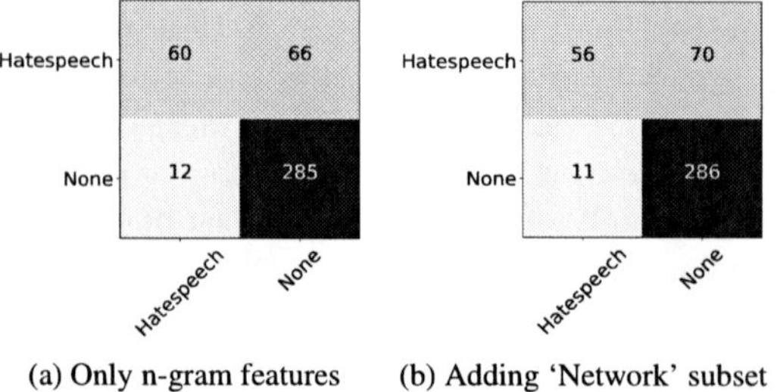

(a) Only n-gram features   (b) Adding 'Network' subset

Figure 6: Portuguese dataset confusion matrices

A similar pattern was observed also for the German data, for which the optimal classifier setup was to include the 'Profile' feature subset. However, for Portuguese where the best classifier utilised only the 'Network' user features, Figure 6 shows that adding those features produced a decrease of correctly labelled "Hate speech" (from 60 to 56 of 116) with marginally increased correctly labelled "None" instances (from 285 to 286 of 297), possibly since data sparsity made the model interpret the added features as noise.

6 Conclusion and Future Work

There are several challenges linked to the detection of harmful online behaviour, such as detection beyond simply recognising offensive words. Aiming to address this gap, the paper investigated the potential and effects of including user features in hate speech classification, focusing on Twitter. A quantitative analysis of three datasets in three different languages indicated that there were no particular characteristics distinguishing the users who have had tweets annotated as hate speech and those who have seemingly not.

However, systematically incorporating the user features into a Logistic Regression-based hate speech classifier in conjunction with word and character n-gram features allowed observations of the effects of individual features and feature subsets. Experimental results showed that the inclusion of specific user features, in addition to n-grams, caused a slight improvement of the baseline classifier performance.

Of all individually tested feature subsets, 'Network' (i.e., the number of followers and friends) caused the largest improvement of the classifier performance on the English and Portuguese datasets, corroborating the findings of Chatzakou et al. (2017) that network-based features are powerful for detecting aggressive behaviour. This subset improvement may have been affected by the individual feature (number of) 'Followers', which also increased the F_1-score on the two datasets. The other features had inconsistent effects on the different datasets, suggesting that the impact is highly dependent on the data or the subtask the data was created for. The experiments also found the inclusion of some user features to be detrimental to model performance, while some user features were ineffective alone, but improved model performance when combined with others.

Interestingly, the 'Gender' feature subset mainly failed to give any F_1-score improvements, in contrast to the result by Waseem and Hovy (2016). While other user features are easily retrievable through the Twitter API, user gender was derived from a comparative method, classifying more users by gender than in the work by Waseem and Hovy. However, also the method used here is still unable to identify the gender of a large amount of users in all datasets, so combinations with other gender identification methods would be needed to properly investigate the impact gender has in hate speech detection. As of now, it can be argued that gender is not a useful feature to include, at least where it cannot be directly extracted.

One limitation of using several datasets is that they were developed for different subtasks and languages, with different geographical areas of the users in the datasets, and in particular with different interpretations and annotations of hate speech. However, the main difference of the datasets is the size and hence number of instances available for model training, which probably is the main reason for the different results. Still, the results combine to show a potential for incorporating user features to improve hate speech detection performance.

There is a great amount of information related to the users of Twitter that was not used in the experiments, but that could be retrieved or derived from user behaviour. Examples include considering the time of tweeting, investigations of relationships with other users, communication with other users, and what content users are exposed to. It is in general important to not only consider who the users are or what they have written, but also their context and how they are affected by surrounding factors in their online communities, as well as combinations of those issues, since what can be considered as hate speech by one user in a specific context may be considered as non-hate speech if written by another user or in another context.

Acknowledgements

Thanks to Johannes Skjeggestad Meyer for fruitful discussions and to the providers of the datasets used in this work: Benjamin Cabrera, Guillermo Carbonell, Paula Fortuna, Dirk Hovy, Nils Kurowsky, Michael Rist, Björn Ross, Zeerak Waseem, and Michael Wojatzki.

References

Pinkesh Badjatiya, Shashank Gupta, Manish Gupta, and Vasudeva Varma. 2017. Deep learning for hate speech detection in tweets. In *Proceedings of the 26th International Conference on World Wide Web Companion*, pages 759–760, Perth, Australia. International World Wide Web Conferences Steering Committee.

Steven Bird, Ewan Klein, and Edward Loper. 2009. *Natural Language Processing with Python: Analyzing Text with the Natural Language Toolkit.* O'Reilly Media, Inc., Sebastopol, California.

Erin E. Buckels, Paul D. Trapnell, and Delroy L. Paulhus. 2014. Trolls just want to have fun. *Personality and Individual Differences*, 67:97–102.

Peter Burnap and Matthew Leighton Williams. 2015. Hate speech, machine classification and statistical modelling of information flows on Twitter: Interpretation and communication for policy decision making. *Policy and Internet*, 7(2):223–242.

Despoina Chatzakou, Nicolas Kourtellis, Jeremy Blackburn, Emiliano De Cristofaro, Gianluca Stringhini, and Athena Vakali. 2017. Mean birds: Detecting aggression and bullying on Twitter. In *Proceedings of the 2017 ACM on Web Science Conference*, pages 13–22, Troy, New York, USA. ACM.

Ying Chen, Yilu Zhou, Sencun Zhu, and Heng Xu. 2012. Detecting offensive language in social media to protect adolescent online safety. In *Proceedings of the 2012 ASE/IEEE International Conference on Social Computing and 2012 ASE/IEEE International Conference on Privacy, Security, Risk and Trust*, pages 71–80, Amsterdam, Netherlands. IEEE.

Justin Cheng, Michael Bernstein, Cristian Danescu-Niculescu-Mizil, and Jure Leskovec. 2017. Anyone can become a troll: Causes of trolling behavior in online discussions. In *Proceedings of the 2017 ACM Conference on Computer-Supported Cooperative Work and Social Computing*, pages 1217–1230, Portland, Oregon, USA. ACM.

Justin Cheng, Christian Danescu-Niculescu-Mizil, and Jure Leskovec. 2015. Antisocial behavior in online discussion communities. In *Proceedings of the 9th International Conference on Web and Social Media*, pages 61–70, University of Oxford, Oxford, UK. AAAI Press.

Thomas Davidson, Dana Warmsley, Michael Macy, and Ingmar Weber. 2017. Automated hate speech detection and the problem of offensive language. In *Proceedings of the 11th International Conference on Web and Social Media*, pages 512–516, Montréal, Québec, Canada. AAAI Press.

Nemanja Djuric, Jing Zhou, Robin Morris, Mihajlo Grbovic, Vladan Radosavljevic, and Narayan Bhamidipati. 2015. Hate speech detection with comment embeddings. In *Proceedings of the 24th International Conference on World Wide Web*, pages 29–30, Florence, Italy. ACM.

Paula Fortuna. 2017. Automatic detection of hate speech in text: an overview of the topic and dataset annotation with hierarchical classes. Master's thesis, Faculdade De Engenharia Da Universidade Do Porto, Porto, Portugal, June.

Björn Gambäck and Utpal Kumar Sikdar. 2017. Using convolutional neural networks to classify hate-speech. In *Proceedings of the First Workshop on Abusive Language Online*, pages 85–90, Vancouver, Canada. ACL.

Lei Gao and Ruihong Huang. 2017. Detecting online hate speech using context aware models. *CoRR*, abs/1710.07395.

Jennifer Golbeck, Zahra Ashktorab, Rashad O. Banjo, Alexandra Berlinger, Siddharth Bhagwan, Cody Buntain, Paul Cheakalos, Alicia A. Geller, Quint Gergory, Rajesh Kumar Gnanasekaran, Raja Rajan Gunasekaran, Kelly M. Hoffman, Jenny Hottle, Vichita Jienjitlert, Shivika Khare, Ryan Lau, Marianna J. Martindale, Shalmali Naik, Heather L. Nixon, Piyush Ramachandran, Kristine M. Rogers, Lisa Rogers, Meghna Sardana Sarin, Gaurav Shahane, Jayanee Thanki, Priyanka Vengataraman, Zijian Wan, and Derek Michael Wu. 2017. A large labeled corpus for online harassment research. In *Proceedings of the 2017 ACM Web on Science Conference*, pages 229–233, Troy, New York, USA. ACM.

Tommi Gröndahl, Luca Pajola, Mika Juuti, Mauro Conti, and N. Asokan. 2018. All you need is "love": Evading hate speech detection. *CoRR*, abs/1808.09115.

Claire Hardaker. 2010. Trolling in asynchronous computer-mediated communication: From user discussions to academic definitions. *Journal of Politeness Research*, 6(2):215–242.

Irene Kwok and Yuzhou Wang. 2013. Locate the hate: Detecting tweets against blacks. In *Proceedings of the 27th AAAI Conference on Artificial Intelligence*, pages 1621–1622, Bellevue, Washington. AAAI Press.

Yashar Mehdad and Joel R. Tetreault. 2016. Do characters abuse more than words? In *Proceedings of the 17th Annual Meeting of the Special Interest Group on Discourse and Dialogue*, pages 299–303, Los Angeles, USA. ACL/SIGDIAL.

Chikashi Nobata, Joel Tetreault, Achint Thomas, Yashar Mehdad, and Yi Chang. 2016. Abusive language detection in online user content. In *Proceedings of the 25th International Conference on World Wide Web*, pages 145–153, Montréal, Québec, Canada. International World Wide Web Conferences Steering Committee.

Etienne Papegnies, Vincent Labatut, Richard Dufour, and Georges Linares. 2017. Impact of content features for automatic online abuse detection. In *18th International Conference on Computational Linguistics and Intelligent Text Processing*, volume 10762 of *Lecture Notes in Computer Science*, Budapest, Hungary. Springer.

John Pavlopoulos, Prodromos Malakasiotis, and Ion Androutsopoulos. 2017. Deeper attention to abusive user content moderation. In *Proceedings of the 2017 Conference on Empirical Methods in Natural Language Processing*, pages 1125–1135, Copenhagen, Denmark. ACL.

Björn Ross, Michael Rist, Guillermo Carbonell, Benjamin Cabrera, Nils Kurowsky, and Michael Wojatzki. 2016. Measuring the reliability of hate speech annotations: The case of the European refugee crisis. In *Proceedings of NLP4CMC III: 3rd Workshop on Natural Language Processing for Computer-Mediated Communication*, volume 17 of *Bochumer Linguistische Arbeitsberichte*, pages 6–9, Bochum, Germany.

Wenbo Wang, Lu Chen, Krishnaprasad Thirunarayan, and Amit P. Sheth. 2014. Cursing in English on Twitter. In *Proceedings of the 17th ACM Conference on Computer Supported Cooperative Work & Social Computing*, pages 415–425, Baltimore, Maryland, USA. ACM.

Zeerak Waseem and Dirk Hovy. 2016. Hateful symbols or hateful people? Predictive features for hate speech detection on Twitter. In *Proceedings of the North American Chapter of the Association for Computational Linguistics (NAACL) Student Research Workshop*, pages 88–93, San Diego, California, USA. ACL.

Ellery Wulczyn, Nithum Thain, and Lucas Dixon. 2017. Ex machina: Personal attacks seen at scale. In *Proceedings of the 26th International Conference on World Wide Web*, pages 1391–1399, Perth, Australia. International World Wide Web Conferences Steering Committee.

Ziqi Zhang, David Robinson, and Jonathan Tepper. 2018. Detecting hate speech on Twitter using a convolution-GRU based deep neural network. In *15th European Semantic Web Conference*, pages 745–760, Heraklion, Greece. Springer.

Interpreting Neural Network Hate Speech Classifiers

Cindy Wang
Stanford University
Department of Computer Science
cindyw@cs.stanford.edu

Abstract

Deep neural networks have been applied to hate speech detection with apparent success, but they have limited practical applicability without transparency into the predictions they make. In this paper, we perform several experiments to visualize and understand a state-of-the-art neural network classifier for hate speech (Zhang et al., 2018). We adapt techniques from computer vision to visualize sensitive regions of the input stimuli and identify the features learned by individual neurons. We also introduce a method to discover the keywords that are most predictive of hate speech. Our analyses explain the aspects of neural networks that work well and point out areas for further improvement.

1 Introduction

We define hate speech as "language that is used to express hatred towards a targeted group or is intended to be derogatory, to humiliate, or to insult the members of the group" (Davidson et al., 2017). This definition importantly does not include all instances of offensive language, reflecting the challenges of automated detection in practice. For instance, in the following examples from Twitter (1) clearly expresses homophobic sentiment, while (2) uses the same term self-referentially:

> (1) Being gay aint cool ... yall just be confused and hurt ... **fags** dont make it to Heaven
>
> (2) me showing up in heaven after everyone told me god hates **fags**

As in many other natural language tasks, deep neural networks have become increasingly popular and effective within the realm of hate speech research. However, few attempts have been made to explain the underlying features that contribute to their performance, essentially rendering them black-boxes. Given the significant social, moral, and legal consequences of incorrect predictions, interpretability is critical for deploying and improving these models.

To address this, we contribute three ways of visualizing and understanding neural networks for text classification and conduct a case study on a state-of-the-art model for generalized hate speech. We **1)** perform occlusion tests to investigate regions of model sensitivity in the inputs, **2)** identify maximal activations of network units to visualize learned features, and **3)** identify the unigrams most strongly associated with hate speech. Our analyses explore the bases of the neural network's predictions and discuss common classes of errors that remain to be addressed by future work.

2 Related Work

Hate speech classification. Early approaches employed relatively simple classifiers and relied on manually extracted features (e.g. n-grams, part-of-speech tags, lexicons) to represent data (Dinakar et al., 2011; Nobata et al., 2016). Schmidt and Wiegand (2017)'s survey of hate speech detection describes various types of features used. The classification decisions of such models are interpretable and high-precision: Warner and Hirschberg (2012) found that the trigram "*<DET> jewish <NOUN>*" is the most significant positive feature for anti-semitic hate, while Waseem and Hovy (2016) identified predictive character n-grams using logistic regression coefficients. However, manually extracted feature spaces are limited in both their semantic and syntactic representational ability. Lexical features are insufficient when abusive terms take on various different meanings (Kwok and Wang, 2013; Davidson et al., 2017) or are not present at all in the case of implicit hate speech (Dinakar et al., 2011). Syntactic features such as part-of-speech sequences and typed dependencies fail to fully

Proceedings of the Second Workshop on Abusive Language Online (ALW2), pages 86–92
Brussels, Belgium, October 31, 2018. ©2018 Association for Computational Linguistics

capture complex linguistic forms or accurately model context (Waseem and Hovy, 2016; Warner and Hirschberg, 2012). Wiegand et al. (2018) used feature-based classification to build a lexicon of abusive words, which is similar to the interpretability task in this paper of identifying indicative unigram features. While their approach is primarily applicable to explicit abuse, they showed that inducing a generic lexicon is important for cross-domain detection of abusive microposts.

Neural network classifiers. The limitations of feature engineering motivate classification methods that can implicitly discover relevant features. Badjatiya et al. (2017) and Gambäck and Sikdar (2017) were the first to use recurrent neural networks (RNNs) and convolution neural networks (CNNs), respectively, for hate speech detection in tweets. A comprehensive comparative study by Zhang et al. (2018) used a combined CNN and gated recurrent unit (GRU) network to outperform the state-of-the-art on 6 out of 7 publicly available hate speech datasets by 1-13 F1 points. The authors hypothesize that CNN layers capture co-occurring word n-grams, but they do not perform an analysis of the features that their model actually captures. Deep learning classifiers have also been explored for related tasks such as personal attacks and user comment moderation (Wulczyn et al., 2017; Pavlopoulos et al., 2017). Pavlopoulos et al. (2017) propose an RNN model with a self-attention mechanism, which learns a set of weights to determine the words in a sequence that are most important for classification.

Visualizing neural networks. Existing approaches for visualizing RNNs largely involve applying dimensionality reduction techniques such as t-SNE (van der Maaten and Hinton, 2008) to hidden representations. Hermans and Schrauwen (2013) and Karpathy et al. (2015) investigated the functionality of internal RNN structures, visualizing interpretable activations in the context of character-level long short-term memory (LSTM) language models. We are interested in the high-level semantic features identified by network structures and are heavily influenced by the significant body of work focused on visualizing and interpreting CNNs. Zeiler and Fergus (2013) introduced a visualization technique that projects the top activations of CNN layers back into pixel space. They also used partial image occlusion to determine the area of a given image to which

Label	# Examples	% Examples
Hate	1430	5.8%
Offensive	19190	77.4%
Neither	4163	16.8%

Table 1: Distribution of class labels in the dataset.

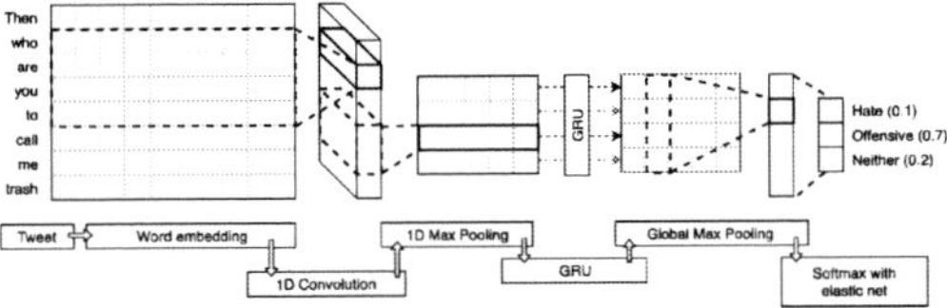

Figure 1: Illustration of the CNN-GRU architecture.

the network is most sensitive. Girshick et al. (2013) propose a non-parametric method to visualize learned features of individual neurons for object detection. We adapt these techniques to draw meaningful insights about our problem space.

3   Case Study

Dataset. We use the dataset of 24,802 labeled tweets made available by Davidson et al. (2017). The tweets are labeled as one of three classes: hate speech, offensive but not hate speech, or neither offensive nor hate speech. The distribution of labels in the resulting dataset is shown in Table 1. Out of the seven hate speech datasets publicly available at the time of this work,[1] it is the only one that is coded for general hate speech, rather than specific hate target characteristics such as race, gender, or religion.

CNN-GRU model. We utilize the CNN-GRU classifier introduced by Zhang et al. (2018), which achieves the state-of-the-art on most hate speech datasets including Davidson et al. (2017), and contribute a Tensorflow reimplementation for future study. The inputs to the model are tweets which are mapped to sequences of word embeddings. These are then fed through a 1D convolution and max pooling to generate input to a GRU. The output of the GRU is flattened by a global max pooling layer, then finally passed to the softmax output layer, which predicts a probability distribution over the three classes. The model architecture is shown in Figure 1 and described in detail in the original paper.

---

[1] For details and descriptions of all seven datasets, see Zhang et al. (2018).

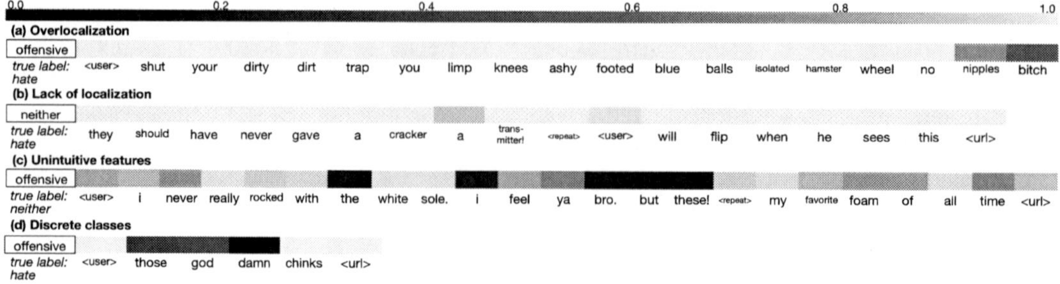

Figure 2: Partial occlusion heatmaps of test examples demonstrating four types of errors made by the CNN-GRU network. Heatmaps are plotted for the predicted class (boxed) while the true class is given below. Darker regions denote portions of the input to which the classifier prediction is most sensitive.

4 Visualization Techniques

4.1 Partial Occlusion

Previously applied to image classification networks, partial occlusion involves iteratively occluding different patches of the input image and monitoring the output of the classifier. We apply a modified version of this technique to our CNN-GRU model by systematically replacing each token of a given input sequence with an <unk> token.[2] We then plot a heatmap of the classifier probabilities of the true class (*hate*, *offensive*, or *neither*) over the tokens in the sequence.

The resulting visualizations reveal a few major types of errors made by the CNN-GRU (Figure 2). We observe **overlocalization** in many long sequences, particularly those misclassified as offensive. This occurs when the classifier decision is sensitive to only a single unigram or bigram rather than the entire context, as in Figure 2(a). The network loses sequence information during convolution and shows decreased sensitivity to the longer context as a result.

Lack of localization is the opposite problem in which the model is not sensitive to any region of the input, shown in Figure 2(b). It occurs mostly in longer and hate class examples. A possible explanation for this type of error is that convolving sequential data diffuses the signal of important tokens and n-grams.

For correctly classified examples, the sensitive regions intuitively correspond to features like n-grams, part-of-speech templates, and word dependencies. However, incorrectly classified examples

also demonstrate sensitivity to **unintuitive features** that are not helpful for classification. For instance, Figure 2(c) shows a sensitive region that crosses a sentence boundary.

Finally, we see a high rate of errors due to the **discretization of the *hate* and *offensive* classes**. While hate speech is largely contained within offensive language, the sensitive regions for the two classes are disparate. In Figure 2(d), the network's prediction that the example is offensive is highly sensitive to the sequence *"those god damn"*, but not the racial slur *"chinks,"* which is both hateful and offensive.

Some of the errors we identify, such as lack of localization and unintuitive features, can be addressed by modifying the model architecture. We can change the way long sequences are convolved, or restrict convolutions within phrase boundaries. More difficult to address are the errors in which our network is sensitive to the correct regions (or a reasonable subset thereof) but makes incorrect predictions. These issues stem from the nature of the data itself, such as the complex linguistic similarity between hate and offensive language. Moreover, many misclassified examples contain implicit characteristics such as sarcasm or irony, which limits the robustness of features learned solely from input text.

4.2 Maximum Activations

The technique of retrieving inputs that maximally activate individual neurons has been used for image networks (Zeiler and Fergus, 2013; Girshick et al., 2013), and we adapt it to the CNN-GRU in order to understand what features of the input stimuli it learns to detect. For each of the units in the final global max pooling layer of the CNN-

---

[2]<unk> indicates an out-of-vocabulary word. The word embedding for <unk> is random, whereas in-vocabulary word embeddings encode meaning via unsupervised pre-training.

Figure 3: Examples of interpretable units from the global max pool layer of the CNN-GRU. The inputs with the top eight activations for each neuron are shown, with relevant tokens bolded. In the interest of space, some examples here are abridged and the full version can be found in Appendix Figure 4.

GRU, we compute the unit's activations on the entire dataset and retrieve the top-scoring inputs.

Figure 3 displays the maximally activating examples for seven of 100 units in the global max pool. We verify that the model does indeed learn relevant features for hate speech classification, some of which are traditional natural language features such as the part-of-speech bigram *"you <NOUN PHRASE>."* Others, like a unit that fires on sports references and a unit that detects Dutch-language tweets (the result of querying for hate keywords *yankee* and *hoe,* respectively), reflect assumptions in data collection. Some units capture features that reflect domain-specific phenomena, such as repeated symbols or sequences of multiple abusive keywords.

Many units are too general or not interpretable at all. For instance, several units detect the hate term *bitch,* but none of them clearly capture the distinction between when it is used in sexist and colloquial contexts. Conversely, examples containing rarer and more ambiguous slurs like *cracker* do not appear as top inputs for any unit. Overall, the CNN-GRU discovers some interpretable lexical and syntactical features, but its final layer activations overrepresent common uni-

Category	Terms
Hatebase words	faggot, nigger, fag, coon, teabagger, cripple, spook, muzzie, mook, jiggaboo, mutt, redskin, dink
Hatebase plural	faggots, niggers, fags, crackers, coons, rednecks, hos, queers, coloreds, wetbacks, muzzies, wiggers, darkies
Pejorative nominalization	blacks, jews, commie, lightskins, negroes
Hate-related or offensive	racist, fugly, hag, traitor, chucks, goon, asss, blacc, eff, homophobic, racists, nogs, muhammed, fatherless, slurs
Hateful context words	arrested, yelled, smoked, joints, stoned, frat, celibate, catfished, wedlock, sliced, kappa, trappin, birthed, allegiance, menace, commander, stamp, cyber
Hashtags	*(see Table 4)*
Dialect variations	des, boutta, denna, waddup, boof, ont, bestf, playen, sav, erbody, prolli, deze, bougie
Pop culture	gram, tweakin, dej, uchiha, mewtwo, bios, fenkell, mikes, beavis, aeropostale
Other	en, waffle, moe, saltine, squid, pacer, sharpie, skyler, sockfetish, johns, lactose, ov, tater

Table 2: List of keywords discovered via synthetic test examples. Terms within each category appear in order of frequency in the corpus. Descriptions for hashtags are from blogs such as `www.socialseer.com` and cross-referenced on Twitter.

grams and fail to detect semantics at a more fine-grained level via surrounding context.

4.3 Synthetic Test Examples

Lastly, we propose a general technique to identify the the most indicative unigram features for a deep model using synthetic test examples and apply it to the CNN-GRU.

For each word in our corpus, we construct a sentence of the form *"they call you <word>"* and feed it as input to the CNN-GRU network. We choose this structure to grammatically accommodate both nouns and adjectives, and because it is semantically neutral compared to similar formulations such as *"you are <word>."* We then retrieve the words whose test sentences are classified as hate speech. After filtering out words that do not appear in two or more distinct tweets (retweets are indistinct) and words containing non-alphabetical characters,[3] this method returns 101 terms. We manually group the terms into nine categories and

---

[3] We inspect the output to confirm that this filtering eliminates only nonsense tokens and not intentional misspellings.

summarize them in Table 2.

As a quantitative heuristic for the quality of the discovered terms, we evaluate our method's recall on the hate speech lexicon Hatebase.[4] We measure the recall of Hatebase words, plural forms of Hatebase words, and tweets containing Hatebase terms and compare against a random baseline (Table 3). The recall of our method is approximately an order of magnitude better than random across all categories. Recall of plural forms is better than that of base forms, which may reflect the training data's definition of hate speech as language that targets a group. Notably, recall of Hatebase tweets[5] is lower than recall of individual terms regardless of form, meaning that the Hatebase terms discovered using our template method are not the ones that occur most commonly in the corpus. This is reasonable as several of the most common Hatebase terms such as *bitch* and *nigga* are ones that tend to be used colloquially rather than as slurs.

Of the non-Hatebase terms that our method discovers, four are pejorative nominalizations. These are neutral adjectives that take on pejorative meaning when used as nouns, such as *blacks* and *jews* (Palmer et al., 2017). We also find six domain-specific hate terms in the form of hashtags, which tend to be non-word acronyms and primarily used by densely connected, politically conservative Twitter users (see Table 4). The results also include dialect-specific terms and slang spellings, such as *des* and *boutta*, which mean *these* and *about to* respectively. While these terms co-occur frequently with hate speech keywords in our corpus, they are semantically neutral, suggesting that our model exhibits bias towards certain written vernaculars. While these terms co-occur frequently with hate speech keywords in our corpus, they are semantically neutral, suggesting that our model exhibits bias towards certain written vernaculars.

5 Conclusion

We presented a variety of methods to understand the prediction behavior of a neural network text classifier and applied them to hate speech. First,

	Recall (ours)	Recall % (ours)	Recall % (random)
Hb terms	13/182	7.14	1.05
Hb plurals	13/91	14.29	1.06
Both	26/273	9.52	1.04
Hb tweets	1453/ 24234	6.00	1.21

Table 3: Comparison between our method and a random baseline on recall of Hatebase lexicon terms and tweets containing Hatebase terms. The random baseline is averaged over 10,000 trials.

Hashtag	Meaning
#pjnet	Patriot Journalist Network
#lnyhbt	Let Not Your Heart Be Troubled, Sean Hannity's hashtag
#tgdn	Twitter Gulag Defense Network
#httr	Hail to the Redskins
#yeswedid	Reference to President Obama's motto
#acab	All Coppers Are Bastards

Table 4: Descriptions of discovered hashtag keywords, given by blogs such as `www.socialseer.com` and cross-referenced on Twitter.

we used partial occlusion of the inputs to visualize the sensitivity of the network. This revealed that the architecture loses representational capacity on long inputs and suffers from lack of class separability. We then analyzed the semantic meaning of individual neurons, some of which capture intuitively good features for our domain, though many still appear to be random or uninterpretable. Finally, we presented a way to discover the most indicative hate keywords for our model. Not all discovered terms are inherently hateful, revealing peculiarities and biases of our problem space.

Overall, our experiments give us better insight into the implicit features learned by neural networks. We lay the groundwork for future efforts towards better modeling and data collection, including active removal of linguistic discrimination.

Acknowledgments

Thanks firstly to Christopher Potts for many useful discussions that formed the foundation for this work in this paper. Thanks also to the three anonymous reviewers for their insightful feedback and constructive suggestions. This material is based in part upon work supported by the NSF under Grant No. BCS-1456077.

---

[4]Hatebase (`https://www.hatebase.org`) is an online, crowd-sourced hate speech lexicon. Davidson et al. (2017) use Hatebase queries to bootstrap the dataset we use in this paper.

[5]The number of tweets containing one of the 26 discovered terms divided by the number of tweets containing any Hatebase term.

References

Pinkesh Badjatiya, Shashank Gupta, Manish Gupta, and Vasudeva Varma. 2017. Deep learning for hate speech detection in tweets. In *WWW 2017 Companion*, pages 759–760. International World Wide Web Conference Committee.

Thomas Davidson, Dana Warmsley, Michael Macy, and Ingmar Weber. 2017. Automated hate speech detection and the problem of offensive language. In *Proceedings of the Eleventh International AAAI Conference on Web and Social Media*, pages 512–515.

Karthik Dinakar, Roi Reichart, and Henry Lieberman. 2011. Modeling the detection of textual cyberbullying. In *Fifth International AAAI Conference on Weblogs and Social Media Workshop on the Social Mobile Web*, pages 11–17.

Björn Gambäck and Utpal Kumar Sikdar. 2017. Using convolutional neural networks to classify hate-speech. In *Proceedings of the First Workshop on Abusive Language Online*, pages 85–90. Association for Computational Linguistics.

Ross B. Girshick, Jeff Donahue, Trevor Darrell, and Jitendra Malik. 2013. Rich feature hierarchies for accurate object detection and semantic segmentation. *CoRR*, abs/1311.2524.

Michiel Hermans and Benjamin Schrauwen. 2013. Training and analysing deep recurrent neural networks. In *Advances in Neural Information Processing Systems*, pages 190–198.

Andrej Karpathy, Justin Johnson, and Fei-Fei Li. 2015. Visualizing and understanding recurrent networks. *CoRR*, abs/1506.02078.

Irene Kwok and Yuzhou Wang. 2013. Locate the hate: Detecting tweets against blacks. In *Proceedings of the Twenty-Seventh AAAI Conference on Artificial Intelligence*, pages 1621–1622. Association for the Advancement of Artificial Intelligence.

Laurens van der Maaten and Geoffrey Hinton. 2008. Visualizing data using t-SNE. *Journal of Machine Learning Research*, 9:2579–2605.

Chikashi Nobata, Joel Tetreault, Achint Thomas, Yashar Mehdad, and Yi Chang. 2016. Abusive language detection in online user content. In *Proceedings of the 25th International Conference on World Wide Web*, WWW '16, pages 145–153.

Alexis Palmer, Melissa Robinson, and Kristy Phillips. 2017. Illegal is not a noun: Linguistic form for detection of pejorative nominalizations. In *Proceedings of the First Workshop on Abusive Language Online*, pages 91–100. Association for Computational Linguistics.

John Pavlopoulos, Prodromos Malakasiotis, and Ion Androutsopoulos. 2017. Deep learning for user comment moderation. In *Proceedings of the First Workshop on Abusive Language Online*, pages 25–35. Association for Computational Linguistics.

Anna Schmidt and Michael Wiegand. 2017. A survey on hate speech detection using natural language processing. In *Proceedings of the Fifth International Workshop on Natural Language Processing for Social Media*, pages 1–10.

William Warner and Julia Hirschberg. 2012. Detecting hate speech on the world wide web. In *Proceedings of the 2012 Workshop on Language in Social Media*, pages 19–26. Association for Computational Linguistics.

Zeerak Waseem and Dirk Hovy. 2016. Hateful symbols or hateful people? predictive features for hate speech detection on twitter. In *Proceedings of the 2016 Conference of the North American Chapter of the Association for Computational Linguistics: Human Language Technologies*, pages 88–93. Association for Computational Linguistics.

Michael Wiegand, Josef Ruppenhofer, Anna Schmidt, and Clayton Greenberg. 2018. Inducing a lexicon of abusive words–a feature-based approach. In *Proceedings of the 2018 Conference of the North American Chapter of the Association for Computational Linguistics: Human Language Technologies*, volume 1, pages 1046–1056. Association for Computational Linguistics.

Ellery Wulczyn, Nithum Thain, and Lucas Dixon. 2017. Ex machina: Personal attacks seen at scale. In *Proceedings of the 26th International Conference on World Wide Web*, pages 1391–1399. International World Wide Web Conferences Steering Committee.

Matthew D. Zeiler and Rob Fergus. 2013. Visualizing and understanding convolutional networks. *CoRR*, abs/1311.2901.

Ziqi Zhang, David Robinson, and Jonathan Tepper. 2018. Detecting hate speech on twitter using a convolution-gru based deep neural network. In *European Semantic Web Conference 2018*, pages 745–760.

A Appendix

True labels	Hate	Offensive	Neither
Hate	0.31	0.58	0.11
Offensive	0.04	0.94	0.03
Neither	0.02	0.13	0.85

Predicted labels

Table 5: A summary of performance for the CNN-GRU classifier on a held-out test set.

(a) Unit that detects sports references:

perhaps i'm not a diehard **yankee** fan but there's no more point in watching this debacle <hashtag> **yankees** <hashtag> **tigers** <hashtag> **mlb** <allcaps> <allcaps> so what else is on? lol <allcaps>

rt <allcaps> <user> : a <number> year old girl once struck out **babe ruth** and **lou gehrig** back to back and was banned from **baseball** for it <hashtag> **yankees** <sym>

<hashtag> mt <hashtag> commission <hashtag> gouache <hashtag> tiki <hashtag> wahine <hashtag> monkey <hashtag> tubed <hashtag> **surfing** <hashtag> **wavesliding** <hashtag> waterwalker <hashtag> notkook <url>

rt <allcaps> <user> : <hashtag> **yankees** lineup vs. **red sox**: [...] or get swept in motown lol <allcaps> <hashtag> **yankees** <hashtag> **tigers** <hashtag> **mlb** <allcaps> <allcaps>

rt <allcaps> <user> : **peyton manning**'s remarkable season:
  <sym> <number> **pass yds** (nfl <allcaps> record)
  <sym> <number> **pass td** <allcaps> (nfl <allcaps> **record**)
  <sym> <number> **completions**
  <sym> likely ho <sym>

rt <allcaps> <user> : the <hashtag> **cardinals** are <hashtag> mlb <allcaps> 's gold standard and there isn't even a close silver. <hashtag> **dodgers** <hashtag> **giants** <hashtag> **tigers** <hashtag> **yankees** <url> <sym>

it's gonna be a long season for the **yankees** if this simulation is right <hashtag> **bluejays** <hashtag> **rays** <hashtag> **yankees** <hashtag> **orioles** <sym> <url>

(b) Unit that detects anti-black racism:

watching the **nigger** movie menace<number>society. trying to learn more about the **enemy**. good reconnaissance.

  <user> <user>
i likes dat name. dem **sand niggers** needs to know dare place in da pecker order

hey my folk. this **nigger loving jew boy** <user> asked if i was making death threats against his goat fucking people. fuck him.

<number> white men in pick up trucks screaming **nigger** and my coach got the nerve to get mad i missed the free throw <sym> <sym> <sym> <hashtag> tweetlikepontiacholmes <sym>

i do the pontiac sprinkler. <repeat>

nigga nigga nigga nigga spic spic spic spic **nigga nigga nigga nigga**

  <user> **dumb haitian fake black faggots**. go to haiti and neck yourself.

  <user> ur pal <user> threat<number> apostate kufar> cld cut ur neck w / sword of islam &am<smile>watch u squeal like a bitch like daniel pearl

hey <user> **you're a nigger** <hashtag> racismisaliveandwellbro   learn from other blacks in the league on how to conduct yourself

(c) Unit that detects multiple symbols:

<sym> <sym> <sym> <sym> <sym> <sym> <sym> <sym> <sym> <sym> <sym> <sym> <user> : teanna trump probably cleaner than most of these twitter hoes but. <repeat>

  <sym> <sym> <sym> - your my bffl <allcaps> . i love you ya funcy bitch <sym> i went finna be faded &am<smile> shaded on ya c day <sym> <hashtag> wedemgirlz <allcaps> <allcaps> <sym> <sym> <sym> <sym> <sym> <sym> <sym> <sym> <sym> <sym> <sym> <sym> <sym> <sym> <sym> <sym> <sym> <sym> rt <allcaps> : mcnair had brisket sizzlin on the grill when his side hoe laid the uzi game down

  <sym> <sym> <sym> <sym> <sym> <sym> plus sheryl crow <url>
  <sym> <sym> <sym> <sym> <sym> <sym> <sym> <sym> <sym>
<sym> <user> : gay niggas couldn't wait to act like bitches tonight
<sym> <sym> <sym> <sym> <sym> <sym> <sym> <sym> <sym>
<sym> <user> : gay niggas couldn't wait to act like bitches tonight
  <sym> <sym> <sym> <sym> <sym> <sym> <sym> <sym>
<sym> <sym> this fucking bitch rachel needs to die please
rt <allcaps> <user> : are these hoes loyal?
  <sym> n
<sym> <sym> o
<sym> <sym> <sym> o
<sym> <sym> <sym> <sym> o [...]

(d) Unit that detects Dutch:

mam ren <sym> e doet in haar rol net of ze ongesteld is wat is ongesteld? van dat soort vragen waar je denkt: hoe leg ik die weer uit.

  <user> <user> nee dat is na langdurig gepest worden.zoals ik al zei:in d kiem smoren.is ook vb voor t kind hoe je moet optreden

  <user> <user> <user> <user> steek d morele vinger maar in j neus zelfde soort types bij nato <allcaps> stenigt vrouwen by bosjes

  <user> <user> <user> <user> goh d anoniemeaso meeting heeft weer pauze.nog steeds niet bij hoofdstuk:hoe haal ik m'n id <allcaps> ?

  <user> <user> &am<smile> als je over syrie tweet volg <user> maar zij komt er vandaan &am<smile> zal je precies uitleggen hoe of wat.

  <user> <user> ja moest van plisie niet meteen wild gaan denken.juistja willen wel meer mensen mij vertellen hoe k moet denken laat zihni ozdil met rust jullie gemene trollen hoe durven jullie zijn mening in twijfel te nemen! zijn zegje is wet en*kuch**kuch* . .water

  <user> <user> <user> <user> tegenwoordig weet je ook al niet wat voor vlees je eet voor je t weet is t zebra of een aap

(e) Unit that detects personal attacks:

  <user> what did you search? gay redneck episode <number> play?
  <user> - you know what you did **you faggot**. there are literally thousands of people that have you on their radar homo
  <user> : when you live this gay you can't be afraid of two black dicks in your butt **you fucking queer**
lol so since i'm from the south i automatically sound like a fucking redneck. hahahaha how about fuck **you stupid ass**.

i bet you think you a no-chill savage huh. **fucking faggot** <user>
  <user> omg gtfo **white faggot**
somebody please choke that fucking retard that keeps yelling mashed potatoes. what a tool! <hashtag> pgac <allcaps> hampionship
  <user> <user> fight me **you fucking obese niglet**

(f) Unit that detects sequences of abusive keywords:

bitch fuck yo nigga what's up with that **pussy!** <repeat>
  <user> ew **queer white** thirsty **bitch**
rt <allcaps> <user> : <user> <user> <user> get **fucked** you **racist inbred hillbilly fuck**
  <user> done that spell check we know you meant **fat liberal dyke feminist nazi bitches**

i would like to apologize to anyone i have called **fat stupid gay nigger jew** or **retarded**. i am truly sorry. <repeat>

jk <allcaps>
just trolling
fags
  <user> shut up **lizard faggot nigger cunt**
<hashtag> somethingig <allcaps> etalot are you. <repeat> asian? black? hawaiian? **gay? retarded?** drunk?
  <user> your a **fucking queer faggot bitch**

(g) Many units are not easily interpretable:

rt <allcaps> <user> : you're not the father ! what every mexican / nigger loves to hear.

  <user> : <user> lol haha hahahahahahahahahaaah deez nuts bitch don't worry about the nigga you see worry about the nigga you don <allcaps> 't see. <repeat> dat's da nigga fuckin yo bitch.

~~ruffled l ntac eileen dahlia - beautiful color combination of pink orange yellow &am<smile> white. a coll <url>

  <user> <user> bernstine is chi sox jew fag.
honestly i think i would trash that young man. and i'll fuck his bitch. and i'll smack his mother. prolly shot his ugly ass dog

  <user> : i hate that bitch &am<smile> the fact that oomf likes her. <repeat> just no <sym> retweeettt <number>x.

rt <allcaps> <user> : here's how your suggestion plays out <user> racist: ha those niggers stopped callin each other nigga the end

Figure 4: Version of Figure 3 with full text of each tweet. Examples of interpretable units from the global max pool layer of the CNN-GRU. The inputs with the top eight activations for each neuron are shown, with relevant tokens bolded.

Determining Code Words in Euphemistic Hate Speech Using Word Embedding Networks

Rijul Magu
Department of Computer Science
University of Rochester
Rochester, New York
rmagu2@cs.rochester.edu

Jiebo Luo
Department of Computer Science
University of Rochester
Rochester, New York
jluo@cs.rochester.edu

Abstract

While analysis of online explicit abusive language detection has lately seen an ever-increasing focus, implicit abuse detection remains a largely unexplored space. We carry out a study on a subcategory of implicit hate: euphemistic hate speech. We propose a method to assist in identifying unknown euphemisms (or code words) given a set of hateful tweets containing a known code word. Our approach leverages word embeddings and network analysis (through centrality measures and community detection) in a manner that can be generalized to identify euphemisms across contexts- not just hate speech.

1 Introduction

Euphemisms, as an instrument to mask intent, have long been used throughout history. For example, a rich lexicon of drug slang has developed over time, with entire communities subscribing to benign sounding words that allude to names of drugs, intake practices or other stakeholders (such as dealers). In these instances, the primary motive is often to get a message across while evading detection from authorities. The main obstacle in these cases is the inability to identify code words without gaining access to an explicit mapping between the words and their latent meanings. Often, these words are already embedded in such common parlance that they cannot be spotted without placing the correct context.

Notably, in late 2016, a number of users across social media platforms and internet forums (particularly 4chan) began a movement called 'Operation Google', a direct retaliation to Google announcing the creation of tools for the automated moderation of toxic content. Essentially, the idea was to create code words for communities within the context of hate speech, so that they would not be detected by such systems. The movement branched out to a number of social media platforms, and in particular Twitter (Magu et al., 2017). The complete list of all code words is presented in Table 1.

Recent work has begun to emerge on studying this instance of euphemistic hate speech. However, they deal largely with the impact of code words in hate speech. Our work instead focuses on moving towards automating the *discovery* of code words. The objective is to significantly decrease, or even eliminate the need for human effort required in manually evaluating what words could be euphemisms. That said, the solutions and processes we describe go beyond finding use within the hate speech context. While some parts of the preprocessing stages do benefit from being aware about hate speech associated issues, the fundamental approach is general enough to be applied to assist in extracting code words in any context that may be found in natural language.

Additionally, our technique, revolving around studying the structures of the word co-occurrence networks that emerge from instances of coded hate speech, also lies within a predominantly unexplored space. We find that the centralities of word nodes within such networks indirectly provide crucial hints about the context within which they arise.

2 Abusive Language

The past few years have witnessed an increased focus on abusive language (particularly hate speech) detection, with a variety of different approaches and applications to a diverse set of contexts. These have ranged from classification of hateful tweets using bag-of-words models and typed dependencies (Burnap and Williams, 2015), to using semantic structure of sentences to the study of tar-

93

Proceedings of the Second Workshop on Abusive Language Online (ALW2), pages 93–100
Brussels, Belgium, October 31, 2018. ©2018 Association for Computational Linguistics

Code Word	Actual Word
Google	Black
Yahoo	Mexican
Skype	Jew
Bing	Chinese
Skittle	Muslim
Butterfly	Gay
Fishbucket	Lesbian
Durden	Transsexual
Car Salesman	Liberal
A leppo	Conservative
Pepe	Alt-Right

Table 1: Some common code words.

gets of hate (Silva et al., 2016). Others have used related methods to study phenomena closely associated to hate speech such as cyberbullying (Raisi and Huang, 2017) and offensive language in general. From an application perspective, Magu et al. (2018) create models to predict the extent of hateful content in the comments section of news sources, using article titles and body information as input, indicating a relationship between the entities. Davidson et al. (2017), a recent work on hate speech detection, notes the difference between hate speech and offensive language.

Notably, Waseem et al. (2017) provide a typology of abusive language, categorizing abusive language across two dimensions: 1) target of abuse and 2) degree of abuse being explicit. In terms of target, they distinguish *directed* hate (hatred towards an individual. Example: 'Go kill yourself') and *generalized* hate (hatred towards a recognized group. Example: 'So an 11 year old n***er girl killed herself over my tweets? thats another n***er off the streets!!'). With regard to this, a number of studies have been carried out that measure and study this effect, particularly within the context of social media. For instance, ElSherief et al. (2018) deal with analyzing the characteristics of hate speech instigators and targets on Twitter.

For the second dimension, the authors differentiate between *explicit* (containing 'language that which is unambiguous in its potential to be abusive'. Examples could be language containing racial slurs) and *implicit* (containing 'language that does not immediately imply or denote abuse'. Example: 'Gas the skypes' (Magu et al., 2017)) hate. The authors discuss the role of *context* which is needed to correctly identify hate. As such,

they touch upon a fundamental mode of expression that displays implicit hate: euphemistic hate speech. Euphemistic hate speech stands separate from other forms of implicit hate speech (namely micro-aggressions) because in truth, they are often direct toxic attacks as opposed to veiled or context dependent ones. They are implicit because they make use of clever word substitutions in language to avoid detection. Even a classifier trained on a hate speech dataset containing instances of code words, can fail to identify hateful content if new code words (either intentionally or otherwise) start being used by the community. Indeed, currently, the only available option to recognize such instances manually, which is often inefficient and burdensome. Therefore, this motivates the exploration of more automated methods to detect euphemisms within the hateful context.

2.1 Euphemistic Hate Speech

To clearly define the problem of euphemistic hate speech, we start by looking at the general definition of hate speech as given by Davidson et al. (2017). They define hate speech as:

> *"language that is used to expresses hatred towards a targeted group or is intended to be derogatory, to humiliate, or to insult the members of the group."*

In this sense, we note that euphemistic offensive language also qualifies as hate speech because it targets communities based on race, religion and sexual orientation. As a result, *hate speech that relies on intentional word substitutions to evade detection* can be considered to be **euphemistic hate speech**.

As discussed earlier, one of the most prominent uses of euphemistic hate speech came as a result of Operation Google, ever since the movement started in 2016. For instance Hine et al. (2016) studied the usage patterns and behavior of a community on 4chan (where the movement first started) and Twitter. Finally, Magu et al. (2017) analyzed euphemistic hate speech on Twitter, creating a tool to automate the process of segregating tweets containing code words (eg. 'gas the skypes') from those containing code words, but benign in nature (eg. 'I like to make skype calls').

3 Dataset

We collected approximately 200,000 English tweets containing the code words using the Twitter Streaming API. The time range was crucial for us as we wanted to study the use of code words as they first propped up. Therefore, our extracted tweets were concentrated between September 2016 (when the code first gained prominence) up until November 2016 slightly after the election season in the United States of America. Next, we needed to select a single code word that could be used as a starting seed word for our analysis. Effectively, the aim was to retrieve other code words knowing only one code word beforehand. We chose the code word 'Skypes' (used in place of 'Jews') and manually extracted 850 random tweets that used it in a hateful context (for example saying 'Gas the Skypes' but not 'I like to Skype call him everyday'). From this point on, all of our analysis is carried out on this dataset of hate tweets containing the word 'Skype'. Note that the set of tweets can and do contain other code words also (example: *'If welfare state is a given it must go towards our own who needs. No Skypes, googles, or yahoos'*). As a proof of concept, we showcase the entire process starting with 'skypes' but this can be extended to other starting code words as well. While we recognize the value of a comprehensive study of the methodology across the entire spectrum of combinations (retrieving all other codes given any randomly selected initial word), it went beyond the exploratory nature of our work.

Importantly, as an artifact of the time range of the data (late 2016), we do not expect there to be any previously unidentified code words (or at least not ones used extensively by the community during that time) within the dataset. Therefore, to validate the working of our methodology, from this point on, we instead assume we have no knowledge of the existence of any other code word beside 'skype'. Indeed, our method does not incorporate or exploit any hints it may derive from knowing any of the other code words beforehand.

4 Baseline

To asses how well our method performed, we needed to establish a baseline method. Currently, the simplest way to identify code words in natural language would be to manually sift through a series of tweets of users belonging to known hate communities. Clearly, this is an arduous and ineffective process. A reasonable approach is to rank all the words in the corpus (on the basis of some metric) so that higher ranked words have a greater

Code Word	Rank
Google	10
Yahoo	67
Bing	195
Skittle	23
Butterfly	459
Fishbucket	998
Durden	471
Car Salesman	232
A leppo	667
Pepe	137

Table 2: Baseline ranks of code words.

chance of being code words than those lower on the list. For a small time frame like ours and without any prior information (note there might not be any qualifying indicator for a specific word to be a code word), a good bet would be to use word frequency as the metric. This is based on the idea that rarely used words would be unlikely candidates for code words. This method forms our baseline. As a result, the base ranks of our code words were the ranks of the words on this baseline list. Thus, we can quantify the performance of the method we develop by comparing evaluating the rank improvement of code words against their base ranks. Baseline ranks can be found in Table 1.

5 Preprocessing

We made use of a set of strong assumptions about hate code usage in natural language to inform our data processing decisions (visualized through Figure 1). It is worth considering that while these assumptions help immensely in narrowing the space of possibilities, they are general enough to be applied to any scenario involving coded speech. Additionally, it is important to note that the numbering of these assumptions does not indicate a sequential order of processing (in terms of trimming down words). This is because some of these steps benefit from having the entire, unaltered tweet available to them. Pruning is carried out after determinations are made for each word through all of the assumption steps. Thes assumptions are as follows:

- A1: The code words are nouns.

- A2: They are not words normally considered negative.

- A3: They are not either extremely generic nor are they very specific

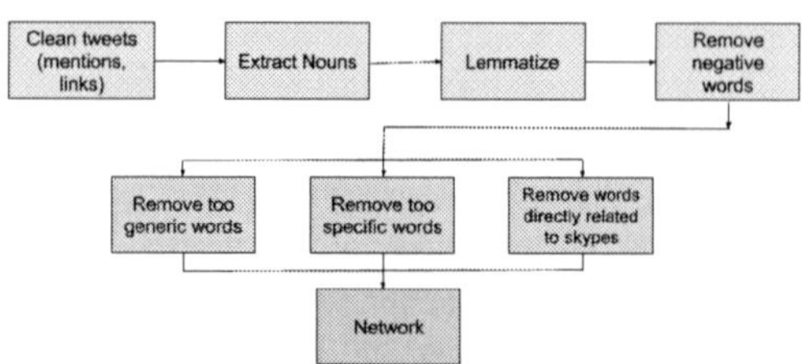

Figure 1: Flow chart depicting the pre-processing steps.

It is safe to assume that the words would be nouns, in the context they are written within tweets. It is to be noted that all code words are used in place of references to real communities, which in turn are necessarily nouns. As a result, although the references themselves are replaced, the syntactic structures of the tweets remain intact. Hence, the code words, like the communities themselves would be detected as nouns by syntactic parsing. Therefore we use part-of-speech tagging to extract the set of all nouns from the entire list of words tokens.

Next, we lemmatize these tokens to bring them to their base form. This is of critical importance because we would like to construct a network at some point, and without standardization, we would be left with multiple duplicate nodes and unclear results. Additionally, carrying out lemmatization at this stage considerably reduces the space of possibilities early on, allowing for faster computation during later stages.

We move onto our next assumption A2, namely 1code words are not words normally considered negative'. Using words that are already negative (for example, 'terrorist', 'vermin' etc) defeats the purpose of using code words to begin with, asides from immensely confusing readers. For instance, consider replacing 'Jews' with 'terrorists' in the sentence 'Kill the Jews'. In the new sentence, 'Kill the terrorists', even if 'terrorists' had been adopted as a code word, it would become impossible for the author to convey whether they meant killing of Jews or actually terrorists. Hence, we attempt to remove all negative words at this stage. We do this by importing the list of negative words assembled by Hu and Liu (2004) and removing words from our lemmatized set that match those in this list.

The third assumption A3 ('They are not either extremely specific nor are they very generic') is checked for next. Clearly, like in the previous case, it is very confusing if the code words are too broad. For instance, in each of the following cases 'These people are disgusting', 'These men are disgusting', 'Something is disgusting', the potential code words 'people', 'men' and 'something' have alternate meanings that fit well within the context, but are too generic to be used as code words. As a result, we discard all such instances. Similarly, sample 'This Hillary is stupid!' in place of 'This Jew is stupid'. It is hard to decipher whether the author refers to a particular individual ('Hillary' the name) or the target community ('Hillary' as a euphemism for Jew). In these cases, the words are too specific to be useful as code words. Therefore, we use a mix of named entity recognition and manual pruning to remove these tokens.

Next, it is imperative to also exclude words that are directly related to the known code word. For example, we need to remove instances like 'Jew', 'Gas', 'Holocaust' etc when using the dataset for skypes because these already exist within the context of anti-semitic hate speech and cannot be used as code words by definition. Yet they may affect our analysis because of their expectedly high common usage. This is the only part of the filtering process that requires some basic domain knowledge of the problem.

As a final step, we discard the word skypes itself, since it occurs in every single tweet and provides no additional information.

6 Detecting Euphemistic Hate Speech

The main idea behind how our system works, is that *code words are an abnormality within the context defined by hateful users*. Words like 'google', 'skype', 'yahoo' etc are not expected to occur regularly in tweets aiming to attack groups. For example, the occurrence of 'skypes' and 'googles' is an aberration with respect to the surrounding words within the following:

"fucking googles and skypes kill em all"

6.1 News Data Word Embeddings

As a result, we can exploit this effect by representing all of our word tokens by their word embeddings that have been pre-trained on a regular, not necessarily hateful context, and evaluating how dissimilar they are with respect to each other. For our purpose we use word2vec (Mikolov et al., 2013) embeddings trained on a Google news dataset (built on google news articles with over a 100 million words) and find the pairwise cosine distances for all words. Essentially, we can expect the code words to be further apart than other words which belong to the hate speech context. A subgraph, with a few representative nodes can be seen in Figure 2.

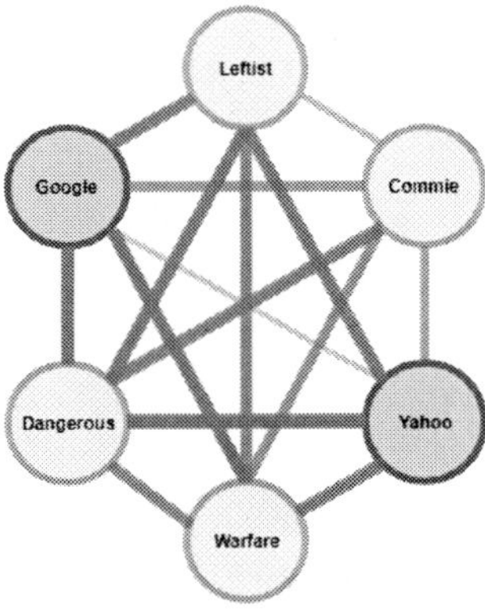

Figure 2: A subgraph of the network composed of some sample nodes. The red nodes are code words whereas the yellow nodes are non-code words. The diagram is for representation only and these labels are not provided beforehand.

The primary limitation to this approach is that some of the code words do not have representations within this pre-trained model and might be missed entirely. These words are 'leppos', 'fishbuckets' and 'durdens'.

6.2 Hate Network

Since 1) the pairwise relationships between words are now quantified and 2) that these relationships cannot be assumed to be independent of each other, an intuitive way to study this structure would be to model it as a network (seen in Figure 3). The degree distribution is graphically represented in Figure 4. Specifically, we created a network where each node represented a particular word, and the edges denoted the cosine distance between their respective word embeddings. In addition, we decided to leverage the fact that a sizable number of words did not co-occur together in tweets, thus providing us with additional information about context. As a result, we pruned all edges where the connected words did not ever occur together in any tweet. Some characteristics of the graph such as number of edges and average degree are given in Table 3.

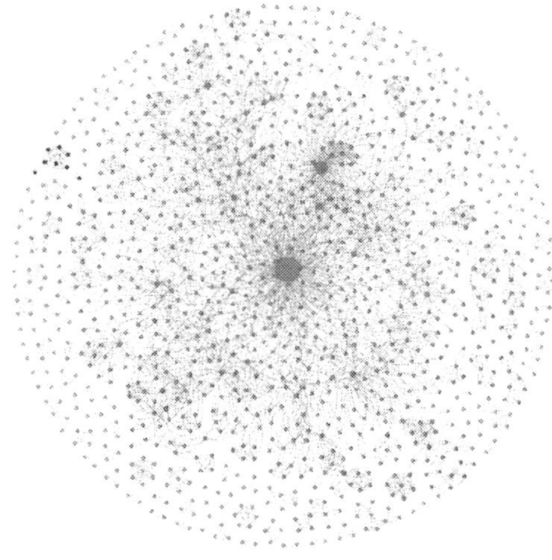

Figure 3: The hate word network. Note that the nodes are colored by the connected component they belong to. Those belonging to components insignificant in size are colored grey. The giant component is colored orange. Also, the size of the nodes corresponds to the degree. The largest node in the center is 'Google'.

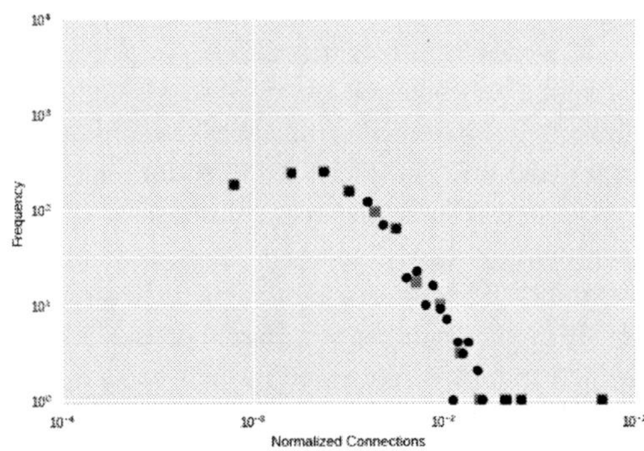

Figure 4: The degree distribution (in black) and log-binned degree distribution (in red) of the network.

The network displays characteristics typical of a complex network. For instance, the network shows the small world effect (Watts and Strogatz, 1998). We evaluated the value of the cluster coefficient (C) and mean shortest path length (L) for the network (as can be seen in Table 3) and then found the average of those metrics (C_r and L_r) across an ensemble of 100 random graphs with the same degree distribution. This allowed us to calculate the value of the small-world coefficient (σ), which is found using equation 1. The value was noted to

Metric	Value
Number of nodes	1129
Number of edges	2188
Average Degree	3.88
Clustering coefficient	0.76
Mean shortest path length	4.53

Table 3: Hate network properties. Clustering coefficient and mean shortest path length are for giant component.

Code Word	EC	IoB
Google	1	9
Yahoo	3	64
Bing	22	173
Skittle	2	21
Butterfly	215	244
Fishbucket	-	-
Durden	-	-
Car Salesman	4	228
A leppo	-	-
Pepe	30	107

Table 4: Centrality rank of code words in comparison to baseline. EC: Eigenvector Centrality Rank. IoB: Improvement over Baseline. Note that the centrality values and improvements for some words is absent since they did not have a word-embedding within the pre-trained model. As a result, they were removed at an earlier stage.

be 20.46 which is much greater than the required threshold of 1, for a graph to be expected to show the small world effect.

$$\sigma = \frac{C/C_r}{L/L_r} \tag{1}$$

6.3 Word Ranks

As noted by Magu et al. (2017), the code words tend to extensively co-occur with each other. There are a number of possible explanations for this effect. First, as people warm up to a new code, they are incentivized to use as many different words as possible so that the code gains traction amongst their followers. Using too few code words within tweets (at the very beginning of adoption) could lead to those words being overlooked, or be treated as mistakes. Second, the alt-right (the primary users of the code) tend to display blanket hate towards a number of different communities across spectrum of race, religion and sexuality. Therefore, their tweets often simultaneously target a number of different groups, a pattern which in turn is replicated in their code word usage.

In this circumstance, we decided to use eigenvector centralities (Bonacich, 1972a,b) words as our ranking metric. Intuitively, this was an appropriate choice. Eigenvector centrality estimating techniques attribute higher centrality values to nodes that are connected to other important nodes. This was very relevant to our context since we know that the existence of certain words (which are hard to pre-determine) within hate speech have an effect on whether surrounding words could be code words or not. The ranks of code words are shown in Table 4. As we can see all codewords (barring those without word embeddings) substantially move up the ranking order, when compared to the baseline model (with a mean jump of

134 positions). Interestingly, the improvement for 'butterfly' was not as dramatic (in terms of its final rank) likely because it might have occurred with words considerably different than those connected to the other code words.

6.4 Candidate Cluster

There is one major issue with the above discussed approach: manually moving down a ranked list to discover code words can be cumbersome. Additionally, there is no bound or limit till which we can expect to cover all or most code words. Therefore, perhaps a more useful technique could be to suggest a group or cluster of candidate words which have a high chance of being code words. Community detection analysis on the network is hence a viable approach.

First, since the graph is disconnected, we focus on the largest component (or the giant component) of the graph to further carry out our analyses (visualization in Figure 3). Since we know that the code words are likely to be closely connected to each other, we expect to find cliques (sets of completely connected subgraphs) within the network. Therefore, we applied the clique percolation method (Palla et al., 2005) on our graph to achieve overlapping communities of words. Essentially, the clique percolation method works by constructing communities from k-cliques (where k is a natural number). A community is obtained by finding the maximal union of k-cliques that are within reach from each other through a sequence

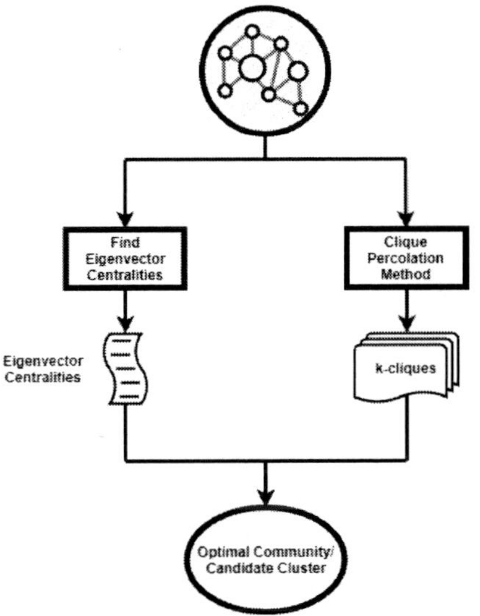

Figure 5: Finding the optimal community. This is a high level visualization of the approach used to determine a set of candidate nodes using community detection analysis.

of adjacent k-cliques. Here, adjacent k-cliques are those cliques which have k-1 nodes in common. Since we do not know the optimal value of k, we carried out separate analyses for each value of k starting from $k=4$ to $k=8$, which is the largest possible value such that no $(k+1)$ cliques exist in the graph. Judging by the extremely high clustering coefficient of the graph, there are an immensely large number of triangles in the graph. As a result, the algorithm is non-trivially affected because essentially, all or most nodes are grouped together into a single community. This is why values of k less than 4 were not considered.

Next, we needed to find the optimal community out of all the possible communities we have achieved for each value of k. A common approach is to simply select the largest community, which implies the community with the most number of nodes (largest length). This approach assumes each node to have the same weight (of value 1). However, since we know that eigenvector centralities serve as a useful indicator to finding the code words, we can weigh each node instead by its eigenvector centrality. As a result, in place of simply finding the community with the highest length, we summed over the eigenvector centralities of all nodes in every community and returned the one with the highest value. The resulting community was: ['blind', **'skittle'**, **'google'**, 'don', 'commie',

'car', 'salesman', 'youtube', 'yahoo', 'bings']. Figure 5 depicts a high level representation of the process.

The cluster is extremely tight- consisting of only 10 members. Yet, it contains all the code words that are present within the word2vec pre-trained model except 'pepe' and 'butterfly' with only a few outliers. While some of these are likely noise, the occurrence of terms like 'commie' is explainable. The left is frequently targeted by the alt-right, the most common users of the euphemisms. Therefore, these users seem to often group 'commies' (or communists) together with the other target communities (which have euphemisms) within their tweets. This is why they form part of the clique that was uncovered through our analysis. For example:

> "In theory, I agree, but with a congress filled with skypes , yahoos, googles, and commies, @realDonaldTrump won't get anything done"

Thus, other than providing us with a set of strong candidates for euphemisms, this approach also reveals useful information about the posting patterns of this community of hateful users.

7 Limitations

There are some limitations that we would like to work on in the future. The major drawback is that we need one starting seed code word to find others. We would like to be able to identify code words in a manner in which we require no prior information about any code words, even at the cost of robustness. Second, it would be useful if we could iteratively improve our performance. For example, if we are able to identify a second code word using our technique, the suggestions for the next candidates should adapt appropriately to generate better results. Finally, we wish to achieve the word embeddings on larger, varied datasets so that when they are used to find cosine distances, some important words are not automatically missed out on.

8 Conclusions

We discussed the problem of euphemistic hate speech and how we could transform the challenge of finding unknown code words into a network science problem. We presented insights that can be derived during the preprocessing stage (such as the code words being nouns and neither too generic nor too specific). Finally, we showed how by using cosine distances between word embeddings could be coupled with analyzing the structure of the resulting network to achieve likely candidates for code words.

Our approach can be used to detect code words not only within the context of hate speech, but anywhere else where a community may feel the need to use euphemisms within natural language.

References

Phillip Bonacich. 1972a. Factoring and weighting approaches to status scores and clique identification. *Journal of mathematical sociology*, 2(1):113–120.

Phillip Bonacich. 1972b. Technique for analyzing overlapping memberships. *Sociological methodology*, 4:176–185.

Pete Burnap and Matthew L Williams. 2015. Cyber hate speech on twitter: An application of machine classification and statistical modeling for policy and decision making. *Policy & Internet*, 7(2):223–242.

Thomas Davidson, Dana Warmsley, Michael Macy, and Ingmar Weber. 2017. Automated hate speech detection and the problem of offensive language. *arXiv preprint arXiv:1703.04009*.

Mai ElSherief, Shirin Nilizadeh, Dana Nguyen, Giovanni Vigna, and Elizabeth Belding. 2018. Peer to peer hate: Hate speech instigators and their targets. *arXiv preprint arXiv:1804.04649*.

Gabriel Emile Hine, Jeremiah Onaolapo, Emiliano De Cristofaro, Nicolas Kourtellis, Ilias Leontiadis, Riginos Samaras, Gianluca Stringhini, and Jeremy Blackburn. 2016. A longitudinal measurement study of 4chan's politically incorrect forum and its effect on the web. *arXiv preprint arXiv:1610.03452*.

Minqing Hu and Bing Liu. 2004. Mining and summarizing customer reviews. In *Proceedings of the tenth ACM SIGKDD international conference on Knowledge discovery and data mining*, pages 168–177. ACM.

Rijul Magu, Nabil Hossain, and Henry Kautz. 2018. Analyzing uncivil speech provocation and implicit topics in online political news. *arXiv preprint arXiv:1807.10882*.

Rijul Magu, Kshitij Joshi, and Jiebo Luo. 2017. Detecting the hate code on social media. In *Proceedings of the eleventh International AAAI Conference on Web and Social Media*, page 608.

Tomas Mikolov, Ilya Sutskever, Kai Chen, Greg S Corrado, and Jeff Dean. 2013. Distributed representations of words and phrases and their compositionality. In *Advances in neural information processing systems*, pages 3111–3119.

Gergely Palla, Imre Derényi, Illés Farkas, and Tamás Vicsek. 2005. Uncovering the overlapping community structure of complex networks in nature and society. *Nature*, 435(7043):814.

Elaheh Raisi and Bert Huang. 2017. Cyberbullying detection with weakly supervised machine learning. In *Proceedings of the IEEE/ACM International Conference on Social Networks Analysis and Mining*.

Leandro Silva, Mainack Mondal, Denzil Correa, Fabrício Benevenuto, and Ingmar Weber. 2016. Analyzing the targets of hate in online social media. *arXiv preprint arXiv:1603.07709*.

Zeerak Waseem, Thomas Davidson, Dana Warmsley, and Ingmar Weber. 2017. Understanding abuse: A typology of abusive language detection subtasks. *arXiv preprint arXiv:1705.09899*.

Duncan J Watts and Steven H Strogatz. 1998. Collective dynamics of small-worldnetworks. *nature*, 393(6684):440.

Comparative Studies of Detecting Abusive Language on Twitter

Younghun Lee[*]   **Seunghyun Yoon**[*]   **Kyomin Jung**
Dept. of Electrical and Computer Engineering
Seoul National University, Seoul, Korea
`younggnse@gmail.com {mysmilesh,kjung}@snu.ac.kr`

Abstract

The context-dependent nature of online aggression makes annotating large collections of data extremely difficult. Previously studied datasets in abusive language detection have been insufficient in size to efficiently train deep learning models. Recently, *Hate and Abusive Speech on Twitter*, a dataset much greater in size and reliability, has been released. However, this dataset has not been comprehensively studied to its potential. In this paper, we conduct the first comparative study of various learning models on *Hate and Abusive Speech on Twitter*, and discuss the possibility of using additional features and context data for improvements. Experimental results show that bidirectional GRU networks trained on word-level features, with Latent Topic Clustering modules, is the most accurate model scoring 0.805 F1.

1 Introduction

Abusive language refers to any type of insult, vulgarity, or profanity that debases the target; it also can be anything that causes aggravation (Spertus, 1997; Schmidt and Wiegand, 2017). Abusive language is often reframed as, but not limited to, offensive language (Razavi et al., 2010), cyberbullying (Xu et al., 2012), othering language (Burnap and Williams, 2014), and hate speech (Djuric et al., 2015).

Recently, an increasing number of users have been subjected to harassment, or have witnessed offensive behaviors online (Duggan, 2017). Major social media companies (i.e. Facebook, Twitter) have utilized multiple resources—artificial intelligence, human reviewers, user reporting processes, etc.—in effort to censor offensive language, yet it seems nearly impossible to successfully resolve the issue (Robertson, 2017; Musaddique, 2017).

The major reason of the failure in abusive language detection comes from its subjectivity and context-dependent characteristics (Chatzakou et al., 2017). For instance, a message can be regarded as harmless on its own, but when taking previous threads into account it may be seen as abusive, and vice versa. This aspect makes detecting abusive language extremely laborious even for human annotators; therefore it is difficult to build a large and reliable dataset (Founta et al., 2018).

Previously, datasets openly available in abusive language detection research on Twitter ranged from 10K to 35K in size (Chatzakou et al., 2017; Golbeck et al., 2017). This quantity is not sufficient to train the significant number of parameters in deep learning models. Due to this reason, these datasets have been mainly studied by traditional machine learning methods. Most recently, Founta et al. (2018) introduced *Hate and Abusive Speech on Twitter*, a dataset containing 100K tweets with cross-validated labels. Although this corpus has great potential in training deep models with its significant size, there are no baseline reports to date.

This paper investigates the efficacy of different learning models in detecting abusive language. We compare accuracy using the most frequently studied machine learning classifiers as well as recent neural network models.[1] Reliable baseline results are presented with the first comparative study on this dataset. Additionally, we demonstrate the effect of different features and variants, and describe the possibility for further improvements with the use of ensemble models.

2 Related Work

The research community introduced various approaches on abusive language detection. Razavi

---

* Equal contribution.

[1]The code can be found at: `https://github.com/younggns/comparative-abusive-lang`

101

Proceedings of the Second Workshop on Abusive Language Online (ALW2), pages 101–106
Brussels, Belgium, October 31, 2018. ©2018 Association for Computational Linguistics

et al. (2010) applied Naïve Bayes, and Warner and Hirschberg (2012) used Support Vector Machine (SVM), both with word-level features to classify offensive language. Xiang et al. (2012) generated topic distributions with Latent Dirichlet Allocation (Blei et al., 2003), also using word-level features in order to classify offensive tweets.

More recently, distributed word representations and neural network models have been widely applied for abusive language detection. Djuric et al. (2015) used the Continuous Bag Of Words model with paragraph2vec algorithm (Le and Mikolov, 2014) to more accurately detect hate speech than that of the plain Bag Of Words models. Badjatiya et al. (2017) implemented Gradient Boosted Decision Trees classifiers using word representations trained by deep learning models. Other researchers have investigated character-level representations and their effectiveness compared to word-level representations (Mehdad and Tetreault, 2016; Park and Fung, 2017).

As traditional machine learning methods have relied on feature engineering, (i.e. n-grams, POS tags, user information) (Schmidt and Wiegand, 2017), researchers have proposed neural-based models with the advent of larger datasets. Convolutional Neural Networks and Recurrent Neural Networks have been applied to detect abusive language, and they have outperformed traditional machine learning classifiers such as Logistic Regression and SVM (Park and Fung, 2017; Badjatiya et al., 2017). However, there are no studies investigating the efficiency of neural models with large-scale datasets over 100K.

3 Methodology

This section illustrates our implementations on traditional machine learning classifiers and neural network based models in detail. Furthermore, we describe additional features and variant models investigated.

3.1 Traditional Machine Learning Models

We implement five feature engineering based machine learning classifiers that are most often used for abusive language detection. In data preprocessing, text sequences are converted into Bag Of Words (BOW) representations, and normalized with Term Frequency-Inverse Document Frequency (TF-IDF) values. We experiment with word-level features using n-grams ranging from 1 to 3, and character-level features from 3 to 8-grams. Each classifier is implemented with the following specifications:

Naïve Bayes (NB): Multinomial NB with additive smoothing constant 1
Logistic Regression (LR): Linear LR with L2 regularization constant 1 and limited-memory BFGS optimization
Support Vector Machine (SVM): Linear SVM with L2 regularization constant 1 and logistic loss function
Random Forests (RF): Averaging probabilistic predictions of 10 randomized decision trees
Gradient Boosted Trees (GBT): Tree boosting with learning rate 1 and logistic loss function

3.2 Neural Network based Models

Along with traditional machine learning approaches, we investigate neural network based models to evaluate their efficacy within a larger dataset. In particular, we explore Convolutional Neural Networks (CNN), Recurrent Neural Networks (RNN), and their variant models. A pre-trained GloVe (Pennington et al., 2014) representation is used for word-level features.

CNN: We adopt Kim's (2014) implementation as the baseline. The word-level CNN models have 3 convolutional filters of different sizes [1,2,3] with ReLU activation, and a max-pooling layer. For the character-level CNN, we use 6 convolutional filters of various sizes [3,4,5,6,7,8], then add max-pooling layers followed by 1 fully-connected layer with a dimension of 1024.

Park and Fung (2017) proposed a HybridCNN model which outperformed both word-level and character-level CNNs in abusive language detection. In order to evaluate the HybridCNN for this dataset, we concatenate the output of max-pooled layers from word-level and character-level CNN, and feed this vector to a fully-connected layer in order to predict the output.

All three CNN models (word-level, character-level, and hybrid) use cross entropy with softmax as their loss function and Adam (Kingma and Ba, 2014) as the optimizer.

RNN: We use bidirectional RNN (Schuster and Paliwal, 1997) as the baseline, implementing a GRU (Cho et al., 2014) cell for each recurrent unit.

From extensive parameter-search experiments, we chose 1 encoding layer with 50 dimensional hidden states and an input dropout probability of 0.3. The RNN models use cross entropy with sigmoid as their loss function and Adam as the optimizer.

For a possible improvement, we apply a self-matching attention mechanism on RNN baseline models (Wang et al., 2017) so that they may better understand the data by retrieving text sequences twice. We also investigate a recently introduced method, Latent Topic Clustering (LTC) (Yoon et al., 2018). The LTC method extracts latent topic information from the hidden states of RNN, and uses it for additional information in classifying the text data.

3.3 Feature Extension

While manually analyzing the raw dataset, we noticed that looking at the tweet one has replied to or has quoted, provides significant contextual information. We call these, *"context tweets"*. As humans can better understand a tweet with the reference of its context, our assumption is that computers also benefit from taking context tweets into account in detecting abusive language.

As shown in the examples below, (2) is labeled abusive due to the use of vulgar language. However, the intention of the user can be better understood with its context tweet (1).

(1) I hate when I'm sitting in front of the bus and somebody with a wheelchair get on.
↳ (2) I hate it when I'm trying to board a bus and there's already an as**ole on it.

Similarly, context tweet (3) is important in understanding the abusive tweet (4), especially in identifying the target of the malice.

(3) Survivors of #Syria Gas Attack Recount 'a Cruel Scene'.
↳ (4) Who the HELL is "LIKE" ING this post? Sick people....

Huang et al. (2016) used several attributes of context tweets for sentiment analysis in order to improve the baseline LSTM model. However, their approach was limited because the meta-information they focused on—author information, conversation type, use of the same hashtags or emojis—are all highly dependent on data.

In order to avoid data dependency, text sequences of context tweets are directly used as

Labels	Normal	Spam	Hateful	Abusive
Number	42,932	9,757	3,100	15,115
(%)	(60.5)	(13.8)	(4.4)	(21.3)

Table 1: Label distribution of crawled tweets

an additional feature of neural network models. We use the same baseline model to convert context tweets to vectors, then concatenate these vectors with outputs of their corresponding labeled tweets. More specifically, we concatenate max-pooled layers of context and labeled tweets for the CNN baseline model. As for RNN, the last hidden states of context and labeled tweets are concatenated.

4 Experiments

4.1 Dataset

Hate and Abusive Speech on Twitter (Founta et al., 2018) classifies tweets into 4 labels, *"normal"*, *"spam"*, *"hateful"* and *"abusive"*. We were only able to crawl 70,904 tweets out of 99,996 tweet IDs, mainly because the tweet was deleted or the user account had been suspended. Table 1 shows the distribution of labels of the crawled data.

4.2 Data Preprocessing

In the data preprocessing steps, user IDs, URLs, and frequently used emojis are replaced as special tokens. Since hashtags tend to have a high correlation with the content of the tweet (Lehmann et al., 2012), we use a segmentation library[2] (Segaran and Hammerbacher, 2009) for hashtags to extract more information.

For character-level representations, we apply the method Zhang et al. (2015) proposed. Tweets are transformed into one-hot encoded vectors using 70 character dimensions—26 lower-cased alphabets, 10 digits, and 34 special characters including whitespace.

4.3 Training and Evaluation

In training the feature engineering based machine learning classifiers, we truncate vector representations according to the TF-IDF values (the top 14,000 and 53,000 for word-level and character-level representations, respectively) to avoid overfitting. For neural network models, words that appear only once are replaced as unknown tokens.

---

[2]WordSegment module description page: `https://pypi.org/project/wordsegment/`

	Normal			Spam			Hateful			Abusive			Total		
Model	Prec.	Rec.	F1	Prec.	Rec.	F1	Prec.	Rec.	F1	Prec.	Rec.	F1	Prec.	Rec.	F1
NB (word)	.776	.916	.840	.573	.378	.456	.502	.034	.063	.828	.744	.784	.747	.767	.741
NB (char)	.827	.805	.815	.467	**.609**	.528	.452	.061	.107	.788	.832	.803	.752	.751	.744
LR (word)	.807	.933	.865	.616	.365	.458	.620	.161	.254	.868	.844	.856	.786	.802	.780
LR (char)	.808	.934	.866	.618	.363	.457	.636	.183	.283	**.873**	.848	.860	.788	.804	.783
SVM (word)	.757	.967	.850	**.678**	.190	.296	**.836**	.034	.065	.865	.757	.807	.773	.775	.730
SVM (char)	.763	**.968**	.853	**.680**	.198	.306	**.805**	.070	.129	**.876**	.775	.822	.778	.781	.740
RF (word)	.776	.945	.853	.581	.213	.311	.556	.109	.182	.852	.819	.835	.757	.781	.745
RF (char)	.793	.934	.857	.568	.252	.349	.563	.150	.236	.853	.856	.854	.765	.789	.760
GBT (word)	.806	.921	.860	.581	.320	.413	.506	.194	.279	.854	.863	.858	.772	.794	.773
GBT (char)	.807	.913	.857	.560	.346	.428	.472	.187	.267	.859	.859	.859	.770	.791	.772
CNN (word)	.822	.925	.870	.625	.323	.418	.563	.182	.263	.846	.916	.879	.789	.808	.783
CNN (char)	.784	.946	.857	.604	.180	.264	.663	.124	.204	.848	.864	.856	.768	.787	.747
CNN (hybrid)	.820	.926	.869	.616	.322	.407	.628	.180	.265	.853	.910	.880	.790	.807	.781
RNN (word)	.856	.887	.870	.589	.514	.547	.577	.194	.287	.844	**.934**	**.887**	**.804**	**.815**	**.804**
RNN (char)	.606	**.999**	.754	.000	.000	.000	.000	.000	.000	.000	.000	.000	.367	.605	.457
RNN-attn (word)	.846	.898	**.872**	.593	.469	.520	.579	.194	.283	.849	.925	.886	.800	.814	.800
RNN-LTC (word)	**.857**	.884	**.871**	.583	.525	**.551**	.564	**.210**	**.302**	.846	.932	**.887**	**.804**	**.815**	**.805**
CNN (w/context)	.828	.910	.867	.609	.341	.429	.505	**.246**	**.309**	.840	.914	.875	.786	.804	.784
RNN (w/context)	**.858**	.880	.869	.577	**.527**	**.549**	.534	.175	.256	.840	**.937**	.885	.801	.813	.801

Table 2: Experimental results of learning models and their variants, followed by the context tweet models. The top 2 scores are marked as bold for each metric.

Since the dataset used is not split into train, development, and test sets, we perform 10-fold cross validation, obtaining the average of 5 tries; we divide the dataset randomly by a ratio of 85:5:10, respectively. In order to evaluate the overall performance, we calculate the weighted average of precision, recall, and F1 scores of all four labels, "*normal*", "*spam*", "*hateful*", and "*abusive*".

4.4 Empirical Results

As shown in Table 2, neural network models are more accurate than feature engineering based models (i.e. NB, SVM, etc.) except for the LR model—the best LR model has the same F1 score as the best CNN model.

Among traditional machine learning models, the most accurate in classifying abusive language is the LR model followed by ensemble models such as GBT and RF. Character-level representations improve F1 scores of SVM and RF classifiers, but they have no positive effect on other models.

For neural network models, RNN with LTC modules have the highest accuracy score, but there are no significant improvements from its baseline model and its attention-added model. Similarly, HybridCNN does not improve the baseline CNN model. For both CNN and RNN models, character-level features significantly decrease the accuracy of classification.

The use of context tweets generally have little effect on baseline models, however they noticeably improve the scores of several metrics. For instance, CNN with context tweets score the highest recall and F1 for "*hateful*" labels, and RNN models with context tweets have the highest recall for "*abusive*" tweets.

5 Discussion and Conclusion

While character-level features are known to improve the accuracy of neural network models (Badjatiya et al., 2017), they reduce classification accuracy for *Hate and Abusive Speech on Twitter*. We conclude this is because of the lack of labeled data as well as the significant imbalance among the different labels. Unlike neural network models, character-level features in traditional machine learning classifiers have positive results because we have trained the models only with the most significant character elements using TF-IDF values.

Variants of neural network models also suffer from data insufficiency. However, these models show positive performances on "*spam*" (14%) and "*hateful*" (4%) tweets—the lower distributed labels. The highest F1 score for "*spam*" is from the RNN-LTC model (0.551), and the highest for "*hateful*" is CNN with context tweets (0.309). Since each variant model excels in different metrics, we expect to see additional improvements with the use of ensemble models of these variants in future works.

In this paper, we report the baseline accuracy of different learning models as well as their variants on the recently introduced dataset, *Hate and Abusive Speech on Twitter*. Experimental results show that bidirectional GRU networks with LTC provide the most accurate results in detecting abusive language. Additionally, we present the possibility of using ensemble models of variant models and features for further improvements.

Acknowledgments

K. Jung is with the Department of Electrical and Computer Engineering, ASRI, Seoul National University, Seoul, Korea. This work was supported by the National Research Foundation of Korea (NRF) funded by the Korea government (MSIT) (No. 2016M3C4A7952632), the Technology Innovation Program (10073144) funded by the Ministry of Trade, Industry & Energy (MOTIE, Korea).

We would also like to thank Yongkeun Hwang and Ji Ho Park for helpful discussions and their valuable insights.

References

Pinkesh Badjatiya, Shashank Gupta, Manish Gupta, and Vasudeva Varma. 2017. Deep learning for hate speech detection in tweets. In *Proceedings of the 26th International Conference on World Wide Web Companion*, pages 759–760. International World Wide Web Conferences Steering Committee.

David M Blei, Andrew Y Ng, and Michael I Jordan. 2003. Latent dirichlet allocation. *Journal of machine Learning research*, 3(Jan):993–1022.

Peter Burnap and Matthew Leighton Williams. 2014. Hate speech, machine classification and statistical modelling of information flows on twitter: Interpretation and communication for policy decision making.

Despoina Chatzakou, Nicolas Kourtellis, Jeremy Blackburn, Emiliano De Cristofaro, Gianluca Stringhini, and Athena Vakali. 2017. Mean birds: Detecting aggression and bullying on twitter. In *Proceedings of the 2017 ACM on web science conference*, pages 13–22. ACM.

Kyunghyun Cho, Bart Van Merriënboer, Caglar Gulcehre, Dzmitry Bahdanau, Fethi Bougares, Holger Schwenk, and Yoshua Bengio. 2014. Learning phrase representations using rnn encoder-decoder for statistical machine translation. *arXiv preprint arXiv:1406.1078*.

Nemanja Djuric, Jing Zhou, Robin Morris, Mihajlo Grbovic, Vladan Radosavljevic, and Narayan Bhamidipati. 2015. Hate speech detection with comment embeddings. In *Proceedings of the 24th international conference on world wide web*, pages 29–30. ACM.

Maeve Duggan. 2017. Online harassment 2017. Pew Research Center; accessed 5-July-2018.

Antigoni Founta, Constantinos Djouvas, Despoina Chatzakou, Ilias Leontiadis, Jeremy Blackburn, Gianluca Stringhini, Athena Vakali, Michael Sirivianos, and Nicolas Kourtellis. 2018. Large scale crowdsourcing and characterization of twitter abusive behavior. In *Proceedings of the International AAAI Conference on Web and Social Media*.

Jennifer Golbeck, Zahra Ashktorab, Rashad O Banjo, Alexandra Berlinger, Siddharth Bhagwan, Cody Buntain, Paul Cheakalos, Alicia A Geller, Quint Gergory, Rajesh Kumar Gnanasekaran, et al. 2017. A large labeled corpus for online harassment research. In *Proceedings of the 2017 ACM on Web Science Conference*, pages 229–233. ACM.

Minlie Huang, Yujie Cao, and Chao Dong. 2016. Modeling rich contexts for sentiment classification with lstm. *arXiv preprint arXiv:1605.01478*.

Yoon Kim. 2014. Convolutional neural networks for sentence classification. *arXiv preprint arXiv:1408.5882*.

Diederik P Kingma and Jimmy Ba. 2014. Adam: A method for stochastic optimization. *arXiv preprint arXiv:1412.6980*.

Quoc Le and Tomas Mikolov. 2014. Distributed representations of sentences and documents. In *International Conference on Machine Learning*, pages 1188–1196.

Janette Lehmann, Bruno Gonçalves, José J Ramasco, and Ciro Cattuto. 2012. Dynamical classes of collective attention in twitter. In *Proceedings of the 21st international conference on World Wide Web*, pages 251–260. ACM.

Yashar Mehdad and Joel Tetreault. 2016. Do characters abuse more than words? In *Proceedings of the 17th Annual Meeting of the Special Interest Group on Discourse and Dialogue*, pages 299–303.

Shafi Musaddique. 2017. Artist stencils hate speech tweets outside twitter hq to highlight failure to deal with offensive messages. Independent; accessed 5-July-2018.

Ji Ho Park and Pascale Fung. 2017. One-step and two-step classification for abusive language detection on twitter. In *Proceedings of the First Workshop on Abusive Language Online*, pages 41–45.

Jeffrey Pennington, Richard Socher, and Christopher Manning. 2014. Glove: Global vectors for word representation. In *Proceedings of the 2014 conference on empirical methods in natural language processing (EMNLP)*, pages 1532–1543.

Amir H Razavi, Diana Inkpen, Sasha Uritsky, and Stan Matwin. 2010. Offensive language detection using multi-level classification. In *Canadian Conference on Artificial Intelligence*, pages 16–27. Springer.

Adi Robertson. 2017. Facebook explains why it's bad at catching hate speech. The Verge; accessed 5-July-2018.

Anna Schmidt and Michael Wiegand. 2017. A survey on hate speech detection using natural language processing. In *Proceedings of the Fifth International Workshop on Natural Language Processing for Social Media*, pages 1–10.

Mike Schuster and Kuldip K Paliwal. 1997. Bidirectional recurrent neural networks. *IEEE Transactions on Signal Processing*, 45(11):2673–2681.

Toby Segaran and Jeff Hammerbacher. 2009. *Beautiful Data: The Stories Behind Elegant Data Solutions*. O'Reilly Media.

Ellen Spertus. 1997. Smokey: Automatic recognition of hostile messages. In *AAAI/IAAI*, pages 1058–1065.

Wenhui Wang, Nan Yang, Furu Wei, Baobao Chang, and Ming Zhou. 2017. Gated self-matching networks for reading comprehension and question answering. In *Proceedings of the 55th Annual Meeting of the Association for Computational Linguistics*, volume 1, pages 189–198.

William Warner and Julia Hirschberg. 2012. Detecting hate speech on the world wide web. In *Proceedings of the Second Workshop on Language in Social Media*, pages 19–26. Association for Computational Linguistics.

Guang Xiang, Bin Fan, Ling Wang, Jason Hong, and Carolyn Rose. 2012. Detecting offensive tweets via topical feature discovery over a large scale twitter corpus. In *Proceedings of the 21st ACM international conference on Information and knowledge management*, pages 1980–1984. ACM.

Jun-Ming Xu, Kwang-Sung Jun, Xiaojin Zhu, and Amy Bellmore. 2012. Learning from bullying traces in social media. In *Proceedings of the 2012 conference of the North American chapter of the association for computational linguistics: Human language technologies*, pages 656–666. Association for Computational Linguistics.

Seunghyun Yoon, Joongbo Shin, and Kyomin Jung. 2018. Learning to rank question-answer pairs using hierarchical recurrent encoder with latent topic clustering. In *Proceedings of the 2018 Conference of the North American Chapter of the Association for Computational Linguistics: Human Language Technologies*, volume 1, pages 1575–1584.

Xiang Zhang, Junbo Zhao, and Yann LeCun. 2015. Character-level convolutional networks for text classification. In *Advances in neural information processing systems*, pages 649–657.

Boosting Text Classification Performance on Sexist Tweets by Text Augmentation and Text Generation Using a Combination of Knowledge Graphs

Sima Sharifirad
Department of computer science, Dalhousie University, Halifax, Canada
s.sharifirad@dal.ca
Borna Jafarpour
Huawei Technology, Toronto, Canada
borna.jafarpour@huawei.com
Stan Matwin
Department of computer science, Dalhousie University, Halifax, Canada
stan@cs.dal.ca

Abstract

Text classification models have been heavily utilized for a slew of interesting natural language processing problems. Like any other machine learning model, these classifiers are very dependent on the size and quality of the training dataset. Insufficient and imbalanced datasets will lead to poor performance. An interesting solution to poor datasets is to take advantage of the world knowledge in the form of knowledge graphs to improve our training data. In this paper, we use ConceptNet and Wikidata to improve sexist tweet classification by two methods (1) text augmentation and (2) text generation. In our text generation approach, we generate new tweets by replacing words using data acquired from ConceptNet relations in order to increase the size of our training set, this method is very helpful with frustratingly small datasets, preserves the label and increases diversity. In our text augmentation approach, the number of tweets remains the same but their words are augmented (concatenation) with words extracted from their ConceptNet relations and their description extracted from Wikidata. In our text augmentation approach, the number of tweets in each class remains

the same but the range of each tweet increases. Our experiments show that our approach improves sexist tweet classification significantly in our entire machine learning models. Our approach can be readily applied to any other small dataset size like hate speech or abusive language and text classification problem using any machine learning model.

1 Introduction

When it comes to machine learning algorithms, the dataset plays a pivotal role in the usability of those models. There are many problems where datasets are imbalanced, data is rare or data is hard to collect, hard to label or the overlap between the classes is high. One of the methods which handles these shortcomings in text classification is text generation. Text generation has been used widely for machine translation, summarization and dialogue generation (Sathish Indurthi et al., 2017) and (Uchimoto, K. et al. 2002). In addition, sentences contain different keywords and concepts. One way of understanding these concepts and getting more information about them is by using linked data and knowledge graphs. The popularity of the internet and advancements in linked data research has led to the development of internet-scale public domain knowledge graphs such as FreeBase, DBPedia, ConceptNet and Wikidata.

Proceedings of the Second Workshop on Abusive Language Online (ALW2), pages 107–114
Brussels, Belgium, October 31, 2018. ©2018 Association for Computational Linguistics

Knowledge in popular knowledge graphs is usually mined from available online resources such as Wikipedia using natural language understanding techniques or harvested by crowd sourcing or a combination of both. Knowledge graphs are used to represent concepts and their relationships in a computer understandable format. They have a wide range of application in the text analysis domain such as question answering (Xu, Q. et al., 2017) query expansion (Yao, Xuchen et al.,2014), recommendation engines (Voorhees, E, 1994) and many more.

ConceptNet is a common sense knowledge graph that represents approximately 21 million everyday concepts and their relationships using one of the 36 existing relationships such as IsA (e.g. jack IsA first name), UsedFor (e.g. car UsedFor driving) or PartOf (wheel PartOf car) (Dzmitry Bahdanau et al., 2015). Each fact in ConceptNet has a weight value which shows the degree of truthiness. Higher values show more confidence. In other words, it shows the closeness of the concpts to each other. Wikidata is a wiki project that is used to crowd source structured data which is consumable both by humans and machines. Wikidata contains 4400 types of relationships between more than 45 million concepts. ConceptNet and Wikidata are far from perfectly consistent and complete. Therefore, we use both of these knowledge graphs in our approach for better coverage of word knowledge with more consistency. An interesting source of information in Wikidata is concept descriptions. We use these descriptions for augmenting tweets. For the text generation task, we replace words in each tweet by words that they are connected to in ConceptNet using some of its 19 relations such as IsA, RelatedTo, HasA, HasProperty, etc.

Another approach for improving the classification is text augmentation, adding more information or enriching the text semantically for the purpose of achieving better classification results. Text augmentation has been widely used in bioinformatics, image processing, computer vision, video and audio processing (Björn Gambäck and Utpal Kumar Sikdar. 2017) and (X. Lu, 2006). Even though the most prevalent applications of text augmentation are in the fields of vision or audio, we believe that introducing simple but effective ideas can be useful for text classification tasks. In addition, they can help in reducing the scarcity of the data, avoiding over-fitting due to lack of data and increasing the generality power of the algorithm.

Our contribution in this paper is using ConceptNet, Wikidata and a combination of both for text generation and augmentation in order to improve sexist tweet classification. Even though we have used our approach for sexist tweet classification, it can be readily applied to other text classification problems using any of the existing text classification models. It can also be beneficial for hateful speech and abusive dataset where the data is scarce.

The rest of the paper is as follows: In the next section, we will discuss the prior work on sexism, text generation and text augmentation. Then, in the experiment part, we will go through the dataset, text preprocessing, classification algorithms, and the detailed method of text generation and text augmentation. In the results, we will show the result of text generation and text augmentation and finally the conclusion.

2   Related Work

2.1 Text generation

Text generation has been studied for many years and computational linguistic and diverse methods have been suggested ever since. Sentence structures are very different and these diversities expand in different types of social media whichmakes text generation harder. For instance, text in Wikipedia is well written and well structured. However, twitter sentences follow mandatory structures in being less than 280 characters (Robert Speer, 2017). Two directions for text generation systems have been suggested. The first method tries to keep the reusability and generality of the sentence without focusing on the structure of the sentence. The second approach tries to keep the structure and template of the sentence (Kingma & Welling, 2013). Uchimoto Kiyotaka et al. suggested their text generation method using keywords candidate coming from a dependency tree.

More recently, deep learning approaches have been utilized for this purpose. Deep generative models have been used for this task. One of these is to use Variational Autoencoders (VAEs). Kingma and Welling, 2013 took advantage of VAEs to encode the data examples to a latent representation and then new samples were generated from that latent space. There have been other works on text question and answer generation using knowledge graphs. Sathish Indurthi et al., 2017 produces the question and answer pair from a knowledge graph. They used

Freebase as their knowledge base to produce the triples and then used them for their question, answer pair. They argue that each triplet is a subject, predicate and an object set and these parts in the triplets can be used exchangeably in the question and answer.

2.2 Text Augmentation

Text augmentation is studied in many areas such as image processing, bioinformatics, and video and audio processing. One of the famous works in data augmentation is related to the study by (Krizhevsky et al., 2014). They tried to classify the images into many classes. They used data augmentation to avoid the problem of over fitting in their neural networks, having 60 million parameters. From a large image, they extracted all the smaller patches and used those patches along with the original image in the training. In addition, for other types of data augmentation, they accompanied the image with different intensities of the original image in the training phase. (Dosovitskiy et. al., 2014) tried data augmentation by first getting different batches from the original data; then they tried different transformations such as different scale, color and contrast on those batches and added them to that class. They trained a convolutional neural network and report higher accuracy using data augmentation. (Bouthillier et. al., 2015) suggested adding data from the same distribution as the original data in the training. They argue that it helps the classifier to have better generalization error. In line with the previous research, (Simard, Steinkraus and Platt, 2003), suggested text augmentation as their best practice in their article. They added different versions of the original data such as the rotated version of the data or random displacement fields to the data for training. They noticed an improvement in the classification error, training their convolutional neural network. In this article, we suggest text augmentation by adding concepts from Conceptnet and Wikidata and descriptions deprived from Wikidata. The detail of these methods is found in the following sections. In addition, we argue that the relations and the concepts in the ConceptNet are not complete and their combination with relation and concepts

from Wikidata are more useful and complete for this process. For this purpose, we present Fig.2. It shows the knowledge graphs from Wikidata and ConceptNet; we limit the number of nodes (concepts) to 10 and the number of relations for the purpose of clarity. We chose the word "bitch" because it was the most frequent non-stop-word in our corpus. Figure 1a, the image of the Wikidata knowledge graph around this word, shows the related concepts to which "bitch" is related , "profanity" and "insult", with the relation, IsA. Figure 1b, is a ConceptNet knowledge graph with more relations such as IsA, Synonym, relatedTo and CapableOf to words such as "sugar_baby", "cunt", "canine", "difficulty" and "backbite". Figure 1c. shows the combination of the two knowledge graphs.

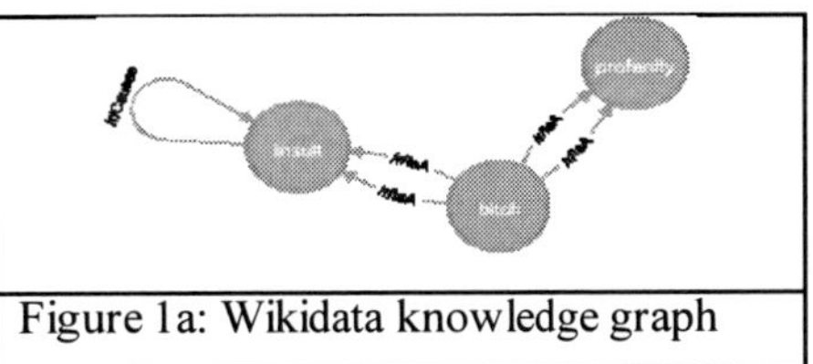

Figure 1a: Wikidata knowledge graph

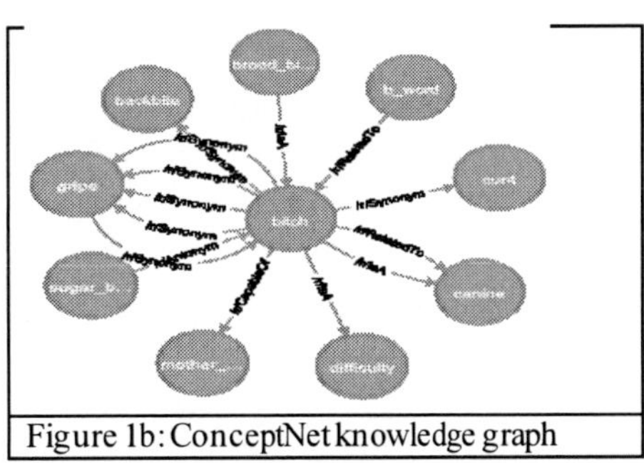

Figure 1b: ConceptNet knowledge graph

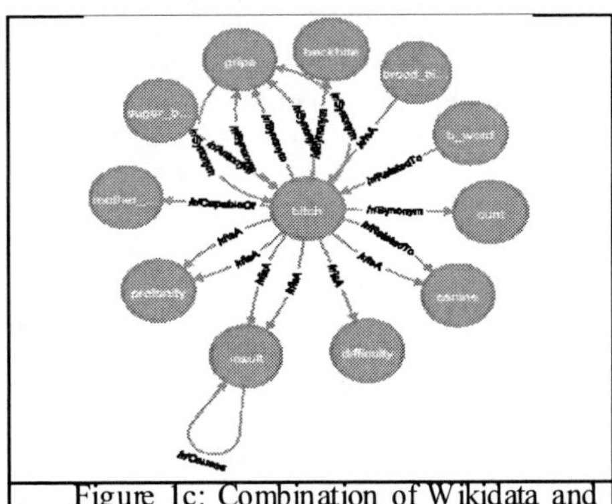

Figure 1c: Combination of Wikidata and ConceptNet knowledge graphs.

3 Experiment

3.1 Dataset

Z. Waseem and D. Hovy, 2016 were the first who collected hateful tweets and categorized them into sexism, racism or neither. Inspired by the study of McIntosh (Peggy McIntosh, 2003), Waseem categorized the tweets into being sexist or racist if they have any of the proposed 18 observations in the tweets such as the usage of any kind of slur to showing sexism racism, criticizing minorities and so forth. Jha and Mamidi 2017 (Jha, A., and Mamidi, R. 2017) solely focused on sexist tweets and proposed two categories of hostile and benevolent sexism. However, these categories were very general and simply ignored other types of sexism happening in social media. In one step further, Sharifirad S. and Matwin S 2018(S sharifirad and S Matwin, 2018), proposed complimentary categories of sexist language inspired from social science work. They categorized sexist tweets into the categories of (1) indirect harassment, (2) information threat, (3) sexual harassment and (4) physical harassment. Table 1 shows the distribution of the dataset along with the sample of tweets in each category mentioned in Table2.

Table 1: The detail information of the sexist data distribution.

Category	Number of tweets
Indirect harassment(#1)	260
Information threat(#2)	6
Sexual harassment(#3)	417
Physical harassment(#4)	123

Table 2: Sample of each category

category	sample
Indirect harassment	-'act like a woman think like a man' -'conservative and intelligent women did not take the day off' -'everybody knows that every girl should only want to marry a sane man as good as her sane father nobody can top a girl' - 'i am so sick amp tired of this attitude oh wow youre smart for a girl'
Physical harassment	-'a womans guide to st century sex naked paintball girls' -'correction katie and nikki are really the dumb blonde ones -'hoping to see the spice girls crash and burn'
	- 'how can such an ugly girl win a beauty competition she must have been the only one competing that year' - 'i ll never understand why pretty girls let below average guys treat them like shit' -'nobody fucking likes you you ugly stupid fat bitch'
Sexual harassment	-birch bitch d.ck tosser theres no enough words for him but dead man walking id say forged f..cking v -'bitch shut yall dumbasses up cosigning on bullshit' -chloe and kelly you are a pack of cunts' -'f..ck on that bitch and we lay up' -'caramel girl misionary position naked girls', -caribbean girls getting f..cked best porn shot',

In this study, we focused on the sexual harassment tweets gathered by (Sharifirad and Matwin, 2018, 2018).

3.2 Text preprocessing

Preprocessing of the tweets involves removal of the punctuation, hyperlinks/URLs, emojis and tags. Before training the classification models, Wordnet lemmatization from NLTK library is applied on all the tweets. We set the maximum size of each tweet to 40 words, and padded the tweets of shorter length with zeroes. Next, tweets are converted into vectors using Word2vec (T. Mikolov , 2013), all with the length 300. For the out-of-vocabulary words, we use their character vectors and concatenate them to have the final representation of the word. Classification algorithms For multiclass classification, we considered a baseline along with some traditional classification algorithms utilized for this purpose and deep learning algorithms. We used one-vs-rest (OVR), and trained and evaluated K independent binary classifiers for each class separately. We considered all the samples in that class positive and the rest were all negative samples using LinearSVC in the Sklearn python package. We also considered Support vector Machines (SVM) and Naive Bayes (NB) as the traditional methods and Long-short-term-memory (LSTM) and Convolutional Neural network (CNN) for the choice of deep learning methods (Björn Gambäck and Utpal Kumar Sikdar. 2017).

3.3 Text Generation

We generated new tweets using ConceptNet in order to improve coverage of our classes using three methods and compared their performance of classification using machine learning models. In the first approach which we call "All Words Replacement (AWR)", tweets were tokenizedand then each token (except for stop words), regardless of its grammatical role, was replaced with all their FromOf and IsA relationships target in ConceptNet whose weight is greater than 1.0. We started from the first token and went forward until a specific number of new tweets had been generated. Relationships other than the ones listed in table 3 led to meaningless tweets that did not represent the original tweet. As an example, the output of Conceptnet for the query of the word "girl" is as follows: [{'relationship': 'IsA', 'target': 'woman', 'weight': 2.0}, {'relationship': 'IsA', 'target': 'female person', 'weight': 1.0}, {'relationship': 'IsA', 'target': 'female young human', 'weight': 1.0}]. We then replaced the word "girl" with the words "women", "female person" and "female young human". The second method which we call "Verb Replacement (VR)" was to first tokenize the tweet and replace the verb by its synonyms in ConceptNet. The third method is called "Noun Replacement (NR)"; the process is the same as with the second approach, VR, but with the difference that we replaced only the nouns with the concepts coming from ConceptNet. Table3 shows the summary of the relation, the selected words and the generated sentence. For each sentence we show only one example out of many of the newly generated tweet. Table 4 shows the result of classification algorithms on the generated tweets.

Table 3: Sample of generated sentence along with the relation type.

	Sentence sample	Types of relation	Generated sentence
AWR	"Kathy you **bitch need** to **slap** your **daughter**"	FromOf IsA	"Kathy you **cunt want** to **hit** your **mom**"
VR	"Kathy you bitch **need** to slap your daughter"	Synonym	Kathy you bitch **want** to smack your daughter
NR	"Kathy you bitch need to slap your **daughter**"	Synonym Related To	Kathy you bitch need to slap your **mother**

Table 4: Classification results on the original and on the generated texts.

	OVR	SVM	Naive Bayes	LSTM	CNN
The original data	0.52	0.68	0.60	0.74	0.75
AWR	0.79	0.94	0.92	0.98	0.98
NR	0.77	0.83	0.85	0.92	0.91
VR	0.82	0.88	0.88	0.97	0.95

3.4 Text augmentation

For text augmentation, we added the concepts from ConceptNet for the first proposed method. In the second method, we considered the concepts from ConceptNet and Wikidata in a smart procedure. The first method is based on adding the related concepts to the original tweets. We tokenized each tweet, then considered "IsA" as the relation and chose the top ten related concepts based on their weight from ConceptNet and added them to the end of the tweet. Even though the number of tweets remained the same the length of the tweets increased to the length of a paragraph. Table 5 shows an example of text augmentation. In the second approach, in addition to the augmentation of tweets using ConceptNet, we augmented tweets by the definition of their tokens in Wikidata. We tokenized the sentence, then added the top related concepts from ConceptNet based on the sorted weight. After that, we combined ConceptNet with Wikidata. The output of the Wikidata around the word query "girls" is 39 tuples; we mention 4 of them as follows: [{'q1.description': 'painting by Lisa Milroy', 'relationship': 'IsA', 'target': 'painting' },{'q1.description': 'painting by Henri-Jean-Guillaume Martin','relationship': 'IsA', 'target': 'painting' }, , {'q1.description': 'young female human', 'relationship': 'IsA', 'target': 'female' }, {'q1.description': 'young female human', etc. Of all these concepts in Wikidata, only one of them is pertaining to the concept "girl" in ConceptNet. To choose the right concept from Wikidata, we first chose the top 10 concepts sorted by the weight, then calculated the cosine similarity between the averaged word vectors of these concepts using Word2vec and the averaged vector of the words in the description from Wikidata. After sorting the descriptions based on the similarity score, we added the most similar description to that tweet.

Table 5: Sample of text augmentation

Original tweet	Augmented tweet
"local girls near you that are down to fuck rt what links do yall keep clicking on to get hacked"	local girls near you that are down to fuck rt what links do yall keep clicking on to get hacked public transport local organization smaller than national agent non geographical animanga character area unit passive verb feather hair highland strike get better of direction turn soft feather from goose hair feather mood landscape semisolid sexual intercourse rude word television station dehydrated may rehydrated right best human ear good all-purpose life but seeing difference film television show situation software solfa syllable travel create proceed carry through musical artist record confine have store stronghold grow lodge protect stay sound emission communicate destroy make buy return catch annoy touch hit seize get"

4 Results

4.1 Experimental Setup

We made bigrams using the python NLTK package and changed them into vectors using word2vec. For word2vec, we used the genism library trained using CBOW and concatenated the vectors of length 300 to get a vector for the each tweet. We used multi-class Naïve Bayes in Scikit learn python, multiclass LSTM and multi-class CNN using Keras for the choice of classifiers. We divided the dataset into 70% train and 30% set. For each tweet, we made the labels in the form of one-hot encoding of length four and we used the same labels for all the classification process. We applied a CNN-based approach to automatically learn and classify sentences into one of the four categories. During the evaluation, a grid search was applied to get the optimal number of filters and filter sizes. Also, we tried with multiple configurations of convolutional layers of 2, 4 and 6. The best performance consisted of two convolutional layers of each followed by a max pooling layer. Convolutional of size 256 with filter size 5 applied for all the convolutional layers. A dropout rate of 0.5 was implemented to avoid over fitting. A fully connected layer with a length of 128 was followed by a second dropout function. This was followed by a dense layer with a size of 4 to represent the number of classification classes using the Softmax function. Our implementation was similar to the model presented in (Björn Gambäck and Utpal Kumar Sikdar. 2017). We trained a simple LSTM model including one hidden layer containing 256 nodes and rectifier activation on the hidden layer, sigmoid activation on the output layer ADAM gradient descent, and a negative likelihood loss function. We created 300 epochs and batch sizes of 5. Table 6 shows the results of the text generation. Our first classification experiment was over the original dataset with three classes, since in the original dataset, the second class, indirect harassment, had only 6 tweets and in comparison to the other classes, it didn't have enough tweets; thus we removed this class and performed our classification algorithm on the rest of three classes. Our second classification approach, verb replacement (VR), was based on the four balanced classes each having about 996 tweets, coming from the first text generation method, all word replacement (AWR). The third classification experiment, noun replacement (NR), was on the four balanced datasets coming from the second method of text generation, each class having about one thousand data points and the last experiment coming from the third approach for text generation; each class having the same number of tweets. We used five classification algorithms, the one-versus-all algorithm as the baseline, naive Bayes and SVM as more traditional classification algorithms and then two artificial neural network approaches, Recurrent Neural Network (RNN) and Convolutional Neural Network (CNN). On the original dataset, the highest accuracy, we achieved was 75% using CNN (for more results please see Table 6). We believe this poor performance was due to poor coverage of our dataset and the imbalanced nature of the dataset. We aimed to alleviate these issues using ConceptNet. Experimenting on the second dataset, which was the generated data with all word replacement (AWR), showed a considerably higher performance in comparison to the original dataset. In this dataset, all four classes are balanced. LSTM and CNN both have the same high performance on the classes. The second performance relates to the SVM and the last one relates to the one-versus-all classification algorithm. In the third generated dataset, noun replacement, the highest performance relates to the LSTM and the second highest relates to the CNN with a very small margin. The highest performance is related to the LSTM for the third method of generated data, followed by CNN and the SVM and Naive Bayes. We ran different text generated methods to know the best way to increase the number of tweets in each class and to balance it. It seems all word replacement (AWR) of the sentence elements with specific relations from ConceptNet in combination with neural network yields the highest performance boost. As mentioned in table 5. All the generated methods have better performance in comparison to the raw data. VR has better performance in comparison to the NR. The best performance for the text generation method is AWR (all Word Replacement) using ConceptNet as the generation method and LSTM and CNN as the classification method. In addition, all the augmentation methods have better performance in comparison to the original data. The method in which we augment the concepts from Wikidata and ConceptNet along with the description from Wikidata has better performance in comparison to the augmentation with ConceptNet. However, the performance is not as good as the text generation method.

Table 6: Augmentation classification results					
Method s	**OVR**	**SV M**	**Naive Baye s**	**LST M**	**CN N**
Augmen ted with Concept Net	0.55	0.65	0.64	0.90	0.88
Augmen tation with Concept Net and Wikidat a	0.60	0.69	0.70	0.93	0.91

5 Conclusion

In this article we introduced simple but effective methods for text generation and text augmentation using general purpose knowledge graphs. For text generation we solely used ConceptNet and for text augmentation we used both ConceptNet separately and both ConceptNet and wikidata. Since there is no mapping between ConceptNet and wikidata, we used the cosine similarity of word vectors of related concepts in ConceptNet and words in description of wikidata in order to establish mappings between their concepts. Application of our method to the problem of sexist tweet classification shows drastic improvements in classification results. Our approach can be applied without any modifications to any other text classification problem. As the future work, it is interesting to add words and descriptions from Wikidata for the text augmentation task. We would like to try this method on other abusive and hate speech datasets. It would also be interesting to combine ConceptNet, Wikidata and Emoji ontology for the text augmentation and text generation task. Also, investigating the impact of the methods on larger datasets are an interesting future work direction.

References:

Z. Waseem and D. Hovy. 2016. Hateful symbols or hateful people? predictive features for hate speech detection on twitter. *In Proceedings of the NAACL Student Research Workshop, pages 88–93. Association for Computational Linguistics.*

Jha, A., and Mamidi, R. 2017. When does a compliment become sexist? analysis and classification of ambivalent sexism using twitter data. *In Proceedings of the Second Workshop on NLP and Computational Social Science, 7–16.*

S sharifirad and S Matwin, 2018. Different types of sexist language on Twitter and the gender footprint, CICLing 2018.

Dzmitry Bahdanau, Kyunghyun Cho, and Yoshua Bengio. 2015. Neural machine translation by jointly learning to align and translate. *In ICLR.*

Yonghui Wu, Mike Schuster, Zhifeng Chen, Quoc V. Le, Mohammad Norouzi, Wolfgang Macherey, Maxim Krikun, Yuan Cao, Qin Gao, Klaus Macherey, Jeff Klingner, Apurva Shah, Melvin Johnson, Xiaobing Liu, Lukasz Kaiser, Stephan Gouws, Yoshikiyo Kato, Taku Kudo, Hideto Kazawa, Keith Stevens, George Kurian, Nishant Patil, Wei Wang, Cliff Young, Jason Smith, Jason Riesa, Alex Rudnick, Oriol Vinyals, Greg Corrado, Macduff Hughes, and Jeffrey Dean. 2016. Google's neural machine translation system: Bridging the gap between human and machine translation. CoRR abs/1609.08144.

Iulian Vlad Serban, Alessandro Sordoni, Ryan Lowe, Laurent Charlin, Joelle Pineau, Aaron C. Courville, and Yoshua Bengio. 2016. A hierarchical latent variable encoder-decoder model for generating dialogues. CoRR abs/1605.06069.

Sathish Indurthi , Dinesh Raghu , Mitesh M. Khapra and Sachindra Joshi. 2017. Generating Natural Language Question-Answer Pairs from a Knowledge Graph Using a RNN Based Question Generation Model, *in EACL.*

Uchimoto, K., Sekine, S. & Isahara, H. 2002. Text Generation from Keywords. In Proc. COLING (pp. 1037-1043).

N. Srivastava, G. Hinton, A. Krizhevsky, I. Sutskever, and R. Salakhutdinov. 2014. Dropout: A simple way to prevent neural networks from over fitting. *The Journal of Machine Learning Research.*

Patrice Y Simard, Dave Steinkraus, and John C Platt. 2003. Best practices for convolutional neural networks applied to visual document analysis. In Proceedings of the Seventh International Conference on Document Analysis and Recognition-Volume 2, page 958. IEEE Computer Society.

T. Mikolov, I. Sutskever, K. Chen, G. Corrado, and J. Dean. 2013. Distributed Representations of Words and Phrases and their Compositionality. *Accepted to NIPS*.

C. Cortes and V. Vapnik. 1995.Support vector networks. Machine Learning, 20:273–297.

Björn Gambäck and Utpal Kumar Sikdar. 2017. Using Convolutional Neural Networks to Classify Hate-Speech. *In Proceedings of the First Workshop on Abusive Language Online.* 85–90.

X. Lu, B. Zheng, A. Velivelli, and C. Zhai. 2006. Enhancing text categorization with semantic-enriched representation and training data augmentation. *Journal of the American Medical Informatics Association,* 13(5):526–535.

Xu, Q., Qin, Z., Wan, T. 2017. Generative cooperative net for image generation and data augmentation. arXiv preprint arXiv:1705.02887.

Yao, Xuchen and Benjamin Van Durme. 2014. Information extraction over structured data: Question answering with freebase. *In Proceedings of the 52nd Annual Meeting of the Association for Computational Linguistics. Baltimore, Maryland, USA,* pages 956–966.

Voorhees, E. 1994. Query expansion using lexical-semantic relations. *In Proceedings of A CM SIGIR International Conference on Research and Development in Information Retrieval,* pp. 61-69.

Sergio Oramas, Vito Claudio Ostuni, Tommaso Di Noia, Xavier Serra, and Eugenio Di Sciascio. 2017. Sound and Music Recommendation with Knowledge Graphs. ACM TIST 8, 2, 21:1–21:21.

Robert Speer, Joshua Chin, and Catherine Havasi. 2017. Conceptnet 5.5: An open multilingual graph of general knowledge. *In Proceedings of AAAI.* San Francisco, USA.

Peggy McIntosh, 2003. Understanding prejudice and discrimination. Chapter White privilege: Unpacking the invisible knapsack, pages 191–196. McGrawHill.

Diederik P. Kingma and Max Welling. 2013. Autoencoding variational bayes. CoRR abs/1312.6114.

Alexey Dosovitskiy, Jost Tobias Springenberg, Martin Riedmiller, and Thomas Brox. 2014. Discriminative unsupervised feature learning with convolutional neural networks. In Advances in Neural Information Processing Systems, pages 766:774.

K. Konda, X. Bouthillier, R. Memisevic, and P. Vincent,. 2015. Dropout as data augmentation," arXiv preprint arXiv:1506.08700.

Learning Representations for Detecting Abusive Language

Magnus Sahlgren
RISE AI and FOI
Box 1263, 164 29 Kista
Sweden
magnus.sahlgren@ri.se

Tim Isbister
FOI
164 90 Stockholm
Sweden
tim.isbister@foi.se

Fredrik Olsson
FOI
164 90 Stockholm
Sweden
fredrik.olsson@foi.se

Abstract

This paper discusses the question whether it is possible to learn a generic representation that is useful for detecting various types of abusive language. The approach is inspired by recent advances in transfer learning and word embeddings, and we learn representations from two different datasets containing various degrees of abusive language. We compare the learned representation with two standard approaches; one based on lexica, and one based on data-specific n-grams. Our experiments show that learned representations *do* contain useful information that can be used to improve detection performance when training data is limited.

1 Introduction

Abusive language is prevalent on the Internet of today. Many users of social media can attest to the frequent occurrence of negative slurs, racist and sexist comments, hate speech, cyberbullying, and outright threats. Commentary fields of news outlets, discussion forums, blogs, and normal websites are overflooded by abusive language, forcing administrators to restrict the possibility to comment on content, and in many cases removing this possibility altogether. As unfortunate as this development may be, it is hardly surprising. Our current information landscape has been designed to maximize the *effectiveness* of human communication, and factors such as transparency, trust and credibility have remained of peripheral concern for service providers. The combination of accessibility and anonymity of many online services provides the perfect conditions for "dark triad" behavior (Paulhus and Williams, 2002) to flourish. Even traditional news media, which have been seen as the last bastion for credibility and trust, are nowadays driven by the need for fast updates, sensationalism, and the hunt for clicks. It should serve as a

cautionary observation that even fringe phenomena such as *trolling* fit comfortably in the current media landscape on the Internet (Phillips, 2015).

Our research focus in this paper is the question whether an inherently abusive environment such as a discussion forum or a white supremacist website can be used to learn a generic representation of abusive language, and whether such a representation can be used in supervised methods for detecting abusive language. Our work is inspired on the one hand by recent advances in transfer learning and pre-training of deep neural networks (Pan and Yang, 2010; Erhan et al., 2010; Peters et al., 2018), and on the other hand the use of embeddings as representation layer in text classification (Sahlgren and Cöster, 2004; Jin et al., 2016). We use two different data sources for learning representations (Stormfront and Reddit, further detailed in Section 4.1) and three different representation learning mechanisms (character-enhanced word embeddings, document-enhanced word embeddings, and a character-level language model, all further detailed in Section 3.3). We compare the proposed approaches with standard lexicon-based classification as well as supervised classification using Bag-of-Words n-gram representations.

2 Previous Work

The widespread occurrence of abusive language and behavior in online environments makes it necessary to devise detection methods to identify and mitigate such phenomena. Where the occurrence of abusive language is an increasing nuisance that may have economic consequences for service providers, it can be a matter of life and death for individuals and organizations who are targeted with more extreme forms of abusive language, such as explicit death threats. There has

Proceedings of the Second Workshop on Abusive Language Online (ALW2), pages 115–123
Brussels, Belgium, October 31, 2018. ©2018 Association for Computational Linguistics

been a fair amount of previous work on detecting various forms of abusive language. In particular the general concept of hate speech, which may include anything from negative remarks and racist comments to threats, has enjoyed a considerable amount of previous research (see e.g. Warner and Hirschberg (2012); Wester et al. (2016); Ross et al. (2016); Waseem and Hovy (2016); Davidson et al. (2017); Isbister et al. (2018)), demonstrating both the complexity of such a general problem as manifested by low inter-annotator agreement scores, but also the viability of using machine learning for detecting specific instances of hate speech in online conversations. Several researchers have focused on more specific types of abusive language, such as cyberbullying (see e.g. Reynolds et al. (2011); Nandhini and Sheeba (2015); Murnion et al. (2018)) and threats (e.g. Hammer (2014); Wester et al. (2016)), demonstrating the applicability of machine learning for detection purposes. The somewhat related, but more general, tasks of sentiment analysis and stance detection have a long history in Natural Language Processing (NLP), with a large body of literature on both theoretical and practical issues related to detection and monitoring (see e.g. Turney (2002); Pang and Lee (2008); Liu (2012); Pozzi et al. (2016); Kucher et al. (2017)).

3 Text Representations

Our primary interest in this study is the effect of text representations for the task of detecting abusive language. We consider three inherently different approaches: predefined sets of keywords (i.e. lexica), data-specific n-grams (i.e. Bag-of-Words), and pretrained embeddings. The following sections provide more details regarding the different approaches.

3.1 Lexica

The arguably most simplistic representation for detecting abusive language is to use a set of keywords (i.e. a lexicon) of abusive terms, possibly augmented by weights that quantify the relative importance of lexicon items. As an example, a lexicon with negative slurs may list terms such as "idiot", "redneck" and "white trash", and weights may be assigned that give higher importance to occurrences of "idiot" and "white trash" than to occurrences of "redneck". It is obvious that the coverage of the lexicon will be dependent on the in-

ventiveness of the lexicographer. Coming up with an exhaustive list of all possible negative slurs is a daunting task, and (the almost certain) failure to do so will affect the coverage of the method. One way to alleviate this *synonymy* problem is to use unsupervised (or semi-supervised) machine learning to augment the compiled lexicon (Gyllensten and Sahlgren, 2018). Another obvious problem with keyword matching is *polysemy*, or the fact that words can have several different meanings. As an example, consider a statement such as "you should use the white trash can", which contains the abusive keyword "white trash", but does not signal negativity. Accounting for such context-sensitivity is a challenging problem (referred to as *word-sense disambiguation* in NLP) that affects the precision of the classification.

Despite these apparent drawbacks, lexicon-based classification is common in both sentiment analysis (see e.g. Taboada et al. (2011); Jurek et al. (2015)), and in hate speech detection (e.g. Njagi et al. (2015); Schmidt and Wiegand (2017); Isbister et al. (2018)). The two main reasons for this is simplicity and transparency. Simply defining a set of keywords and counting their occurrences in text is a quick and easy way to get an impression of the prevalence of some phenomenon. Furthermore, being able to precisely identify the matching keywords in text is a transparent and simple way to explain a classification decision to a user. Such explainability can be a very important consideration in practical applications.

In the following experiments, we use four previously published lexica relating to abusive language. We use the `baseLexicon` containing 537 tokens, and the `expandedLexicon` containing 2,680 tokens from (Wiegand et al.)[1], and the `hatebaseLexicon` containing 1,018 tokens, and the `refined_ngramLexicon` containing 178 tokens from (Davidson et al., 2017)[2]. We refer to these lexica simply as Lexicon #1, Lexicon #2, Lexicon #3, and Lexicon #4 in the remainder of this article. The original lexica are modified such that only terms that are certain to convey abusiveness, according to the lexicon creators, are retained and word class information is discarded. That is, in Lexicon #1, all terms labeled FALSE by the annotators are removed, and in Lexicon #2 all terms with a positive score (in-

---

[1] https://github.com/uds-lsv/lexicon-of-abusive-words
[2] https://github.com/t-davidson/hate-speech-and-offensive-language

dicating abusiveness) are kept. Lexicon #3 and #4 are used as-is. For the classification tasks using the lexica, a text is considered as abusive if it contains at least one term from a lexicon. Examples of abusive lexical entries include: "linthead", "alligator bait", and "you fuck wit".

3.2 Bag-of-Words

In contrast to a priori defining a set of representative terms, a *Bag-of-Words* (BoW) representation identifies informative terms directly from the training data. A BoW representation is an unordered collection of terms, in which each text is represented as an n-dimensional vector, where n is the size of the vocabulary, and each dimension encodes the weight (or *informativeness*) of a specific word in the current text. The standard term weight is some variant of TF-IDF (Sparck Jones, 1988), which combines a measure of the representativeness of a word for a text (often simply the frequency of the word in the text, TF) with a measure of how discriminative words are (often the inverse document frequency of a word, IDF). This "simple and proven" (Robertson and Jones, 1994) method for representing text is often employed in practical document processing applications, such as text categorization, document clustering, and information retrieval.

The main benefit of using BoW representations is that does not require any a priori knowledge, and that it operates completely on the given data. As such, a BoW representation may learn to use features that are not obvious for a lexicographer, and it may learn to use certain features in combination (e.g. that the occurrence of "can" in conjunction with "white trash" signals absence rather than presence of abusiveness). On the other hand, a BoW representation will be sensitive to out-of-vocabulary items, and it may learn to use features that do not make sense for a human analyst, which obviously decreases the explainability of the method.

In the following experiments, we augment standard BoW unigram features with character n-grams. This is normally done in order to account for morphological variation; if a training example contains the word "abuse" but a test example contains the word "abusive", a standard BoW representation will allocate different vector dimensions for these two words, and consequently there will be no similarity between the BoW representa-

tions for these texts. Using character n-grams, we would instead represent these words by their component character n-grams (up to some size of n), which would allocate the same vector dimensions to shared n-grams such as "abus", thus inducing similarity between their representations.

We use up to 4-grams for the character sequences, and we also allow for word bigrams in the representations. Word bigrams can be helpful to distinguish the use of collocations from use of the component terms. As an example, we would assign very different abusive scores to the two statements "you can use the trash can that is white" and "you are white trash"; it is not the individual occurrences of the words "white" and "trash" that is significant here, but the collocation "white trash". We weight the dimensions of the resulting representations using standard TF-IDF. For the classification tasks, the weighted n-gram representations are fed into a Logistic Regression classifier with L2 penalization.

3.3 Embeddings

While a lexicon relies completely on prior knowledge about the task and the domain, a BoW representation relies exclusively on task-dependent features. The idea of using pre-trained embeddings is a way to combine these two perspectives; we use bag-of representations to encode task-specific features, but take prior knowledge about the domain into account by learning a representation from representative data, which (in the best case) encodes latent variables that may be useful for relevant classification tasks.

This approach is inspired by recent advances in transfer learning and pre-training of deep neural networks (Pan and Yang, 2010; Erhan et al., 2010; Peters et al., 2018), in which a model that has been learned on some data is used as the foundation for learning a new model on new data. By doing so, the new model can take advantage of the previous knowledge already encoded in the representations of the pre-trained model. This is conceptually the same idea as using pre-trained word embeddings as representation layer in text classification (Sahlgren and Cöster, 2004; Jin et al., 2016), where the hope is that the embeddings can provide useful generalizations in comparison with only using standard BoW.

We investigate three flavors of this idea. The first flavor relies on character-enhanced word embeddings trained using the FastText model (Bojanowski et al., 2017), which uses the character n-grams of a set of context words to predict a target word. For those who are familiar with the word2vec model (Mikolov et al., 2013), this is essentially the same idea as the CBOW architecture, but using character n-grams instead of only word tokens. The resulting embeddings are used to produce text representations by simply averaging the TF-IDF-weighted vectors for all words in a text. For the embeddings, we use 300-dimensional vectors using the CBOW architecture with character n-grams, where n ranges between 3 to 6 characters. We use a window size of 5 tokens, and discard tokens that occur less than 100 times in the training data. These parameter settings are standard in the literature on embeddings, and are based on experience and trial and error.

The second flavor uses document-enhanced word embeddings trained using the Doc2Vec model (Le and Mikolov, 2014), which also relies on the architectures from word2vec, but adds a document id as input signal in addition to the word tokens. In this case, we use the distributed bag-of-words architecture, which predicts a set of word vectors based on a document vector (i.e. a document-based version of the SkipGram architecture). We use 300 dimensions for the embeddings, and the distributed bag-of-words architecture with a window size of 5, including only tokens that occur more than 100 times in the training data.

The third flavor uses a character-level language model that is trained to predict the next character given an input sequence of characters. We use a simple architecture consisting of one recurrent layer with Gated Recurrent Units (GRU) (Cho et al., 2014) using recurrent dropout, followed by a dense output layer using softmax activation. For training the network, we use adam optimization with learning rate decay, and a context size of 32 characters. For producing input vectors for training examples in the supervised classification experiments, we split the examples into consecutive chunks of 32 characters, and average the activations of the GRU layer over all chunks.

Despite being conceptually similar, there is an important difference between these three approaches that concerns the compositionality of the text representations. In the case of character-enhanced and document-enhanced word embeddings, we are essentially using bag-of represen-

tations that disregard the sequential nature of the data. That is, the average embedding for the sequences "Bob hates Mary" and "Mary hates Bob" will be exactly the same. This is not the case for the language model, which operates on the character sequences, and therefore will produce different compositional representations for these two sequences. It is an empirical question whether this difference is of practical importance when using the resulting representations as input to a supervised classifier.

4 Experiments

In order to compare the viability for detecting abusive language of the representations described in the previous sections, we use two different datasets for building embeddings, and four different datasets for validating classifiers based on the representations. Since our main focus in this paper is to study the effect of the representations rather than pursuing state of the art results, we use the same supervised classifier in all cases; a Logistic Regression classifier with L2 penalization. Before turning to the results, we describe the various datasets used in the experiments.

4.1 Data for Pre-Training

The three types of embeddings are trained on two different data sets; a collection of roughly 5 million posts from the white supremacist website Stormfront, and a random sample of approximately 54 million comments from the discussion forum Reddit. Both datasets were crawled specifically for these experiments.

The reason for selecting these data is that they can be expected to contain various levels of abusive language. In the case of Stormfront, which has been classified as a hate site (Levin, 2002), we can expect to find a wide diversity of abusive language, ranging from negative slurs of various sorts (racial, sexual, religious, political) to explicit threats and targeted hate. Reddit, on the other hand, is mainly a discussion forum where registered users discuss anything from general life style topics such as movies, gaming, and music, to very specialized topics such as machine learning and survivalism. Due to its diverse and inherently conversational nature, Reddit can also be expected to contain a fair amount of controversial topics and abusive language. However, it seems reasonable to assume that Stormfront contains a wider spectrum

Dataset	Token ratio	Doc. ratio
Stormfront	0.043	6.237
Reddit	0.041	1.497

Table 1: Ratios of occurrences of lexicon items in Stormfront vs. Reddit.

of abusive language, due to the fact that subjects who are active in white-supremacist environments tend to exhibit not only racial prejudice but *generalized prejudice*, which means we can also expect to find a substantial amount of sexism, homophobia, islamophobia, and so on.

As a simple demonstration of this, Table 1 shows the proportion of occurrences of terms from the various lexica introduced in Section 3.1 in Stormfront vs. Reddit. We count ratios of the occurrence of lexical items over both tokens and documents to account for differences in document length (comments on Stormfront are on average 143 words long, but only 36 words long on Reddit). The ratios in Table 1 demonstrate a slightly higher concentration of abusive terminology (especially when considering document ratio) in Stormfront compared to Reddit.

4.2 Data for Classification

Table 2 shows the four different datasets used to evaluate the viability of the different representations for detecting various forms of abusive language. The columns **Pos. used** and **Neg. used** specify the number of examples included in our experiments; we delimit all datasets to 10,000 data points (by random sampling) for efficiency reasons, and in order to use an equal amount of data in all experiments. Note that all datasets are highly imbalanced between the classes. This means that one could achieve high accuracy by simply guessing the majority class (i.e. the negative examples). To address this, we use weighted F1 score, which calculates F1 for each label and then their average is weighted by support – i.e. the number of true instances for each label. Note that the use of

weighted F1 can result in an F-score that does not lie in between precision and recall. We also provide a baseline method similar to random guessing by using a stratified dummy classifier that generates predictions by respecting the training set's class distribution.

4.3 Results

The results for the various representations on the various datasets are shown in Table 3 (next side). It is obvious that all representations beat the baseline, which demonstrates that they all provide useful information. Starting with the lexica, it is interesting to note that Lexicon #1 (the `baseLexicon` containing 537 tokens) outperforms the other lexica in all Wikipedia datasets, despite Lexicon #2 and #3 being significantly bigger. Lexicon #4, which is the `refined_ngramLexicon` containing merely 178 tokens, performs only slightly worse than the other lexica. The biggest lexicon, the `expandedLexicon` with 2,680 tokens, performs best on the Twitter Hatespeech data. These differences demonstrate that lexica in general do not generalize well.

The best-performing lexicon for each dataset outperforms the character-level language model representations. However, none of the lexica beat the GRU representations on all datasets, which indicates that pretrained representations have better generalization capabilities than simple keyword matching approaches. This is further corroborated by the fact that the FastText representations consistently outperform the lexica (and the language model). The best performing embeddings are the Doc2Vec representations, which produce competitive results in particular for the Wikipedia datasets (aggression, attack, and toxicity).

However, the standard BoW n-gram representations outperform all other representations on all datasets. We include three variants of the BoW vectors. The row labeled "n-grams" contain results from data-specific BoW representa-

Dataset	Reference	Pos. available	Pos. used	Neg. available	Neg. used
Twitter Hatespeech	Waseem and Hovy (2016)	2,989*	2,989	8,270*	7,011
Wikipedia Aggression	Wulczyn et al. (2017)	21,496	1,647	94,368	8,353
Wikipedia Attack	Wulczyn et al. (2017)	19,627	1,492	96,237	8,508
Wikipedia Toxicity	Wulczyn et al. (2017)	23,023	1,205	136,663	8,795
*Note that since the publishing of Waseem and Hovy (2016), more than 5,000 tweets in the original corpus have become unavailable, and are thus not included in our experiment.					

Table 2: Datasets used for evaluating the representations in supervised classification of abusive language.

Representation	Hatespeech	Aggression	Attack	Toxicity
Baseline	0.610	0.700	0.720	0.753
Lexicon #1	0.664	0.795	0.806	0.831
Lexicon #2	0.729	0.751	0.758	0.783
Lexicon #3	0.647	0.777	0.798	0.824
Lexicon #4	0.626	0.749	0.771	0.804
n-grams	**0.871**	0.831	0.848	0.870
n-grams-Reddit	0.854	0.833	0.850	0.870
n-grams-Stormfront	0.851	0.826	0.844	0.869
n-grams-Doc2Vec-Reddit	0.857	**0.841**	**0.857**	**0.878**
FastText-Stormfront	0.749	0.796	0.814	0.843
FastText-Reddit	0.738	0.804	0.824	0.848
Doc2Vec-Stormfront	0.820	0.817	0.840	0.862
Doc2Vec-Reddit	0.816	0.824	0.846	0.869
GRU-Stormfront	0.719	0.780	0.798	0.828
GRU-Reddit	0.711	0.774	0.791	0.824

Table 3: Results for the various representations on the datasets used in these experiments. The baseline is based on random guessing in proportion to the class distributions, and the lexica use simple Boolean matching (i.e. presence or absence of lexicon terms). All other results are produced by feeding the representations to a Logistic Regression classifer with L2 penalization.

tions (i.e. n-grams collected from the training data), while the "n-grams-Reddit" and the "n-grams-Stormfront" use vocabulary collected from the Reddit and Stormfront data, respectively. The point of including all three variants is to study the effect of data-specific vocabulary, which only seems to have a clear positive effect on the Twitter Hatespeech data. This is hardly surprising, since the Twitter data features a lot of domain-specific terminology such as hashtags and @-mentions.

In order to investigate whether the best-performing embeddings (Doc2Vec) contribute additional information in comparison with the data-specific BoW n-grams, we also include results with a model that concatenates the data-specific BoW n-grams with the Doc2Vec-Reddit model. These augmented representations produce the best results on all the Wikipedia datasets, but lowers the score for the Twitter Hatespeech data. This demonstrates that the document-based embeddings *do* contribute useful information in addition to the BoW n-grams, but that domain-specific vocabulary is important to include. It could be interesting in future research to investigate whether Doc2Vec representations that have been trained on Twitter data would improve the results for the Twitter Hatespeech dataset.

Note that the FastText and Doc2Vec embeddings trained on Stormfront produce slightly bet-ter results for the Twitter Hatespeech data than the ones trained on Reddit, but the opposite is true for the Wikipedia data. One interpretation of this is that the Wikipedia data is more similar in nature to Reddit than to Stormfront; both Wikipedia discussions and Reddit are essentially conversational in nature, and typically do not contain explicit hatespeech to the extent present in the Twitter Hatespeech data and in the white supremacist website Stormfront. This analysis does not hold for the GRU language model, however, where the model trained on Stormfront produces slightly better results on all datasets. Although the differences in the results produced with the representations learned from Stormfront and Reddit are very small, they indicate that the choice of background data can have an influence on the suitability of the learned representations for specific classification tasks.

In order to further investigate the effect of using pretrained representations, we compute learning curves for the Logistic Regression classifier using the various representations, shown in Figures 1 to 4 (next side). The score for each set of training examples in these Figures is the average of 10 cross-validations. Note that the number of training examples on the x axis is log scale, since we want to investigate how the representations perform on limited amounts of training data. Note also the

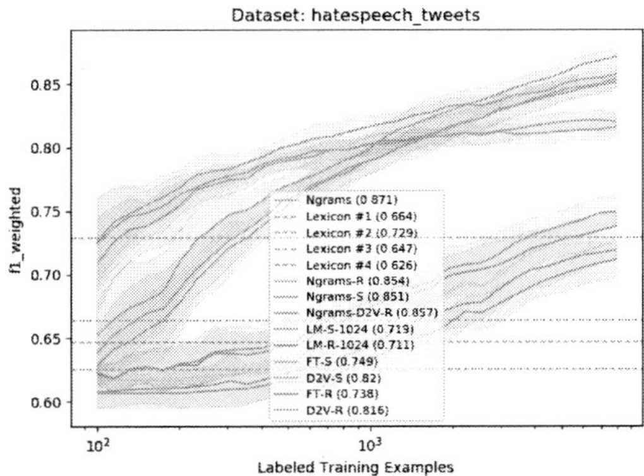

Figure 1: Learning curves for the Twitter Hatespeech data using different representations with a Logistic Regression classifier.

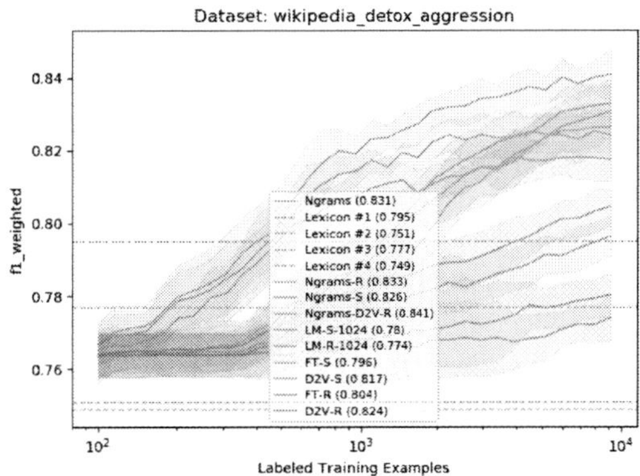

Figure 2: Learning curves for the Wikipedia Aggression data using different representations with a Logistic Regression classifier.

straight lines for the Baseline and Lexicon representations, which do not rely on training data.

The arguably most interesting aspect of the learning curves is the fact that the Doc2Vec representations lead to the best performance for all datasets when the amount of training data is limited. Up to a couple of hundred training examples, the Doc2Vec representation outperforms the BoW n-grams by a large margin. This does not apply for the other types of embeddings, however, which seem to require substantial amounts of training data in order to produce useful results. This suggests that when there is limited training data available, it is beneficial to utilize pretrained document-based embeddings as representation layer.

Note also that very few labelled examples are needed to beat the best-performing lexicon when using Doc2Vec embeddings. In the case of the Twitter Hatespeech data, only a hundred labelled examples are needed to beat the best lexicon. For the Wikipedia datasets, a couple of hundred examples are needed. This observation seems inconsistent with claims that lexica are more efficient to compile than collecting training data. Compiling a suitable lexicon with a couple of hundred relevant terms is hardly an easier, or more efficient, task than collecting a couple of hundred data samples. It could be an interesting future study to quantify the relative efforts involved in lexicon construction vs. data annotation.

5 Conclusions

This paper has investigated the question whether an inherently abusive environment such as a dis-

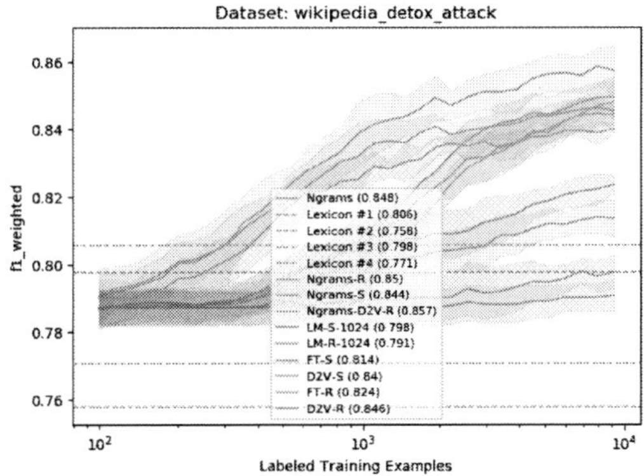

Figure 3: Learning curves for the Wikipedia Attack data using different representations with a Logistic Regression classifier.

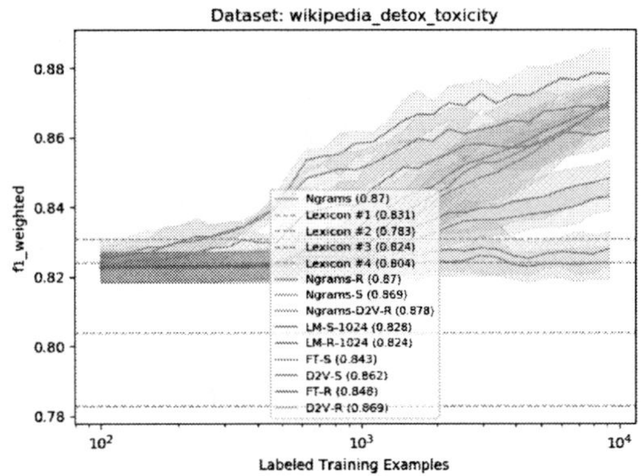

Figure 4: Learning curves for the Wikipedia Toxicity data using different representations with a Logistic Regression classifier.

cussion forum or a white supremacist website can be used to learn a generic representation of abusive language, and whether such a representation can be used in supervised methods for detecting abusive language. The answer seems to be yes.

Our main result is the fact that pretrained embeddings, in particular Doc2Vec representations, trained on some relevant background data produce better results than standard BoW n-grams when training data is limited. We hypothesize that the results produced with the Doc2Vec representations will be very difficult to beat even when using state of the art methods if the classifier can only use a couple of hundred training examples. The fact that Doc2Vec representations produce more useful results than the other embeddings suggests that it could be interesting to investigate the use of more traditional document-based embedding techniques such as Latent Semantic Analysis (LSA) or Latent Dirichlet Allocation (LDA). We leave this as a suggestion for future research.

We acknowledge the fact that other machine learning methods may be more suitable to use for the input representations included in these experiments. We use Logistic Regression mainly for its simplicity and its well-known effectiveness. There have been many successful results using (deep) neural networks with pretrained embeddings, but these models learn complex internal representations that are difficult to interpret, which means that such models are less suitable to use when studying the effect of the input representations on the classification performance. Even so, it could be interesting to investigate whether the Doc2Vec embeddings produce the best results also when using other (deep) machine learning models.

Our results also show that lexica do not generalize well across tasks, and that only a couple of hundred training examples are needed for a supervised classifier based on pretrained document-based embeddings to beat the best-performing lexicon.

References

Piotr Bojanowski, Edouard Grave, Armand Joulin, and Tomas Mikolov. 2017. Enriching word vectors with subword information. *Transactions of the Association for Computational Linguistics*, 5:135–146.

Kyunghyun Cho, Bart van Merrienboer, Caglar Gulcehre, Dzmitry Bahdanau, Fethi Bougares, Holger Schwenk, and Yoshua Bengio. 2014. Learning phrase representations using rnn encoder–decoder for statistical machine translation. In *Proceedings of EMNLP 2014*, pages 1724–1734. Association for Computational Linguistics.

Thomas Davidson, Dana Warmsley, Michael W. Macy, and Ingmar Weber. 2017. Automated hate speech detection and the problem of offensive language. In *Proceedings of the Eleventh International Conference on Web and Social Media*, pages 512–515.

Dumitru Erhan, Yoshua Bengio, Aaron Courville, Pierre-Antoine Manzagol, Pascal Vincent, and Samy Bengio. 2010. Why does unsupervised pre-training help deep learning? *Journal of Machine Learning Research*, 11:625–660.

Amaru Cuba Gyllensten and Magnus Sahlgren. 2018. Distributional term set expansion. In *Proceedings of LREC 2018*.

H. L. Hammer. 2014. Detecting threats of violence in online discussions using bigrams of important words. In *2014 IEEE Joint Intelligence and Security Informatics Conference*, pages 319–319.

Tim Isbister, Magnus Sahlgren, Lisa Kaati, Milan Obaidi, and Nazar Akrami. 2018. Monitoring targeted hate in online environments. In *Second Workshop on Text Analytics for Cybersecurity and Online Safety (TA-COS 2018)*.

Peng Jin, Yue Zhang, Xingyuan Chen, and Yunqing Xia. 2016. Bag-of-embeddings for text classification. In *Proceedings of IJCAI 2016*, pages 2824–2830. AAAI Press.

Anna Jurek, Maurice D. Mulvenna, and Yaxin Bi. 2015. Improved lexicon-based sentiment analysis for social media analytics. *Security Informatics*, 4(1):9.

Kostiantyn Kucher, Carita Paradis, Magnus Sahlgren, and Andreas Kerren. 2017. Active learning and visual analytics for stance classification with alva. *ACM Transactions on Interactive Intelligent Systems*, 7(3):14:1–14:31.

Quoc Le and Tomas Mikolov. 2014. Distributed representations of sentences and documents. In *Proceedings of ICML 2014*, ICML'14, pages II–1188–II–1196. JMLR.org.

Brian Levin. 2002. Cyberhate: A legal and historical analysis of extremists' use of computer networks in america. *American Behavioral Scientist*, 45(6):958–988.

Bing Liu. 2012. *Sentiment Analysis and Opinion Mining*. Morgan & Claypool Publishers.

Tomas Mikolov, Ilya Sutskever, Kai Chen, Gregory S. Corrado, and Jeffrey Dean. 2013. Distributed representations of words and phrases and their compositionality. In *NIPS*, pages 3111–3119.

Shane Murnion, William J. Buchanan, Adrian Smales, and Gordon Russell. 2018. Machine learning and semantic analysis of in-game chat for cyberbullying. *Computers & Security*, 76:197 – 213.

B. Sri Nandhini and J.I. Sheeba. 2015. Online social network bullying detection using intelligence techniques. *Procedia Computer Science*, 45:485 – 492. International Conference on Advanced Computing Technologies and Applications (ICACTA).

Dennis Njagi, Z Zuping, Damien Hanyurwimfura, and Jun Long. 2015. A lexicon-based approach for hate speech detection. 10:215–230.

Sinno Jialin Pan and Qiang Yang. 2010. A survey on transfer learning. *IEEE Transactions on Knowledge and Data Engineering*, 22(10):1345–1359.

Bo Pang and Lillian Lee. 2008. Opinion mining and sentiment analysis. *Foundations and Trends in Information Retrieval*, 2(1-2):1–135.

Delroy L Paulhus and Kevin M Williams. 2002. The dark triad of personality: Narcissism, machiavellianism, and psychopathy. *Journal of Research in Personality*, 36(6):556 – 563.

Matthew Peters, Mark Neumann, Mohit Iyyer, Matt Gardner, Christopher Clark, Kenton Lee, and Luke Zettlemoyer. 2018. Deep contextualized word representations. In *Proceedings of NAACL: HLT*, pages 2227–2237. Association for Computational Linguistics.

Whitney Phillips. 2015. *This Is Why We Can'T Have Nice Things: Mapping the Relationship Between Online Trolling and Mainstream Culture*. The MIT Press.

Federico Alberto Pozzi, Elisabetta Fersini, Enza Messina, and Bing Liu. 2016. *Sentiment Analysis in Social Networks*, 1st edition. Morgan Kaufmann Publishers Inc., San Francisco, CA, USA.

K. Reynolds, A. Kontostathis, and L. Edwards. 2011. Using machine learning to detect cyberbullying. In *2011 10th International Conference on Machine Learning and Applications and Workshops*, volume 2, pages 241–244.

Stephen Robertson and K. Sparck Jones. 1994. Simple, proven approaches to text retrieval. Technical report.

Björn Ross, Michael Rist, Guillermo Carbonell, Benjamin Cabrera, Nils Kurowsky, and Michael Wojatzki. 2016. Measuring the reliability of hate speech annotations: The case of the european refugee crisis. In *Proceedings of NLP4CMC III*. Bochumer Linguistische Arbeitsberichte.

Magnus Sahlgren and Rickard Cöster. 2004. Using bag-of-concepts to improve the performance of support vector machines in text categorization. In *Proceedings of COLING 2004*, Stroudsburg, PA, USA. Association for Computational Linguistics.

Anna Schmidt and Michael Wiegand. 2017. A survey on hate speech detection using natural language processing. In *Proceedings of the Fifth International Workshop on Natural Language Processing for Social Media*, pages 1–10. Association for Computational Linguistics.

Karen Sparck Jones. 1988. Document retrieval systems. chapter A Statistical Interpretation of Term Specificity and Its Application in Retrieval, pages 132–142. Taylor Graham Publishing, London, UK, UK.

Maite Taboada, Julian Brooke, Milan Tofiloski, Kimberly Voll, and Manfred Stede. 2011. Lexicon-based methods for sentiment analysis. *Computational Linguistics*, 37(2):267–307.

Peter D. Turney. 2002. Thumbs up or thumbs down?: Semantic orientation applied to unsupervised classification of reviews. In *Proceedings of ACL 2002*, ACL '02, pages 417–424, Stroudsburg, PA, USA. Association for Computational Linguistics.

William Warner and Julia Hirschberg. 2012. Detecting hate speech on the world wide web. In *Proceedings of the Second Workshop on Language in Social Media*, LSM '12, pages 19–26, Stroudsburg, PA, USA. Association for Computational Linguistics.

Zeerak Waseem and Dirk Hovy. 2016. Hateful symbols or hateful people? predictive features for hate speech detection on twitter. In *Proceedings of the Student Research Workshop, SRW@HLT-NAACL 2016*, pages 88–93.

Aksel Wester, Lilja Øvrelid, Erik Velldal, and Hugo Lewi Hammer. 2016. Threat detection in online discussions. In *Proceedings of the 7th Workshop on Computational Approaches to Subjectivity, Sentiment & Social Media Analysis*, pages 66–71, San Diego, USA.

Michael Wiegand, Josef Ruppenhofer, Anna Schmidt, and Clayton Greenberg. Inducing a lexicon of abusive words – a feature-based approach. In *Proceedings of NAACL: HTL*, pages 1046–1056. Association for Computational Linguistics.

Ellery Wulczyn, Nithum Thain, and Lucas Dixon. 2017. Wikipedia Talk Labels: Personal Attacks.

Datasets of Slovene and Croatian Moderated News Comments

Nikola Ljubešić
Jožef Stefan Institute
Jamova cesta 39,
1000 Ljubljana, Slovenia
nikola.ljubesic@ijs.si

Tomaž Erjavec
Jožef Stefan Institute
Jamova cesta 39,
1000 Ljubljana, Slovenia
tomaz.erjavec@ijs.si

Darja Fišer
Faculty of Arts,
University of Ljubljana
Aškerčeva cesta 2, 1000 Ljubljana, Slovenia
darja.fiser@ff.uni-lj.si

Abstract

This paper presents two large newly constructed datasets of moderated news comments from two highly popular online news portals in the respective countries: the Slovene RTV MCC and the Croatian 24sata. The datasets are analyzed by performing manual annotation of the types of the content which have been deleted by moderators and by investigating deletion trends among users and threads. Next, initial experiments on automatically detecting the deleted content in the datasets are presented. Both datasets are published in encrypted form, to enable others to perform experiments on detecting content to be deleted without revealing potentially inappropriate content. Finally, the baseline classification models trained on the non-encrypted datasets are disseminated as well to enable real-world use.

1 Introduction

With the rapid rise of user-generated content, there is increased pressure to manage inappropriate on-line content with (semi)automated methods. The research community is by now well aware of the multiple faces of inappropriateness in on-line communication, which preclude the use of simple vocabulary-based approaches, and are therefore turning to more robust machine learning methods (Pavlopoulos et al., 2017). These, however, require training data.

Currently available datasets of inappropriate on-line communication are primarily datasets of English, such as a Twitter dataset annotated for racist and sexist hate speech (Waseem and Hovy, 2016)[1], the Wikimedia Toxicity Data Set (Wulczyn et al., 2017)[2], the Hate Speech Identifica-tion dataset containing tweets annotated as hate speech, offensive language, or neither (Davidson et al., 2017)[3], and the SFU Opinion and Comment Corpus consisting of online opinion articles and their comments annotated for toxicity[4].

Datasets in other languages have recently also started to emerge, with a German Twitter dataset focused on the topic of refugees in Germany (Ross et al., 2017)[5] and a Greek Sport News Comment dataset containing moderation metadata (Pavlopoulos et al., 2017)[6].

In this paper we present two new and large datasets of news comments, one in Slovene, and one in Croatian. Apart from the texts, they also contain various metadata, the primary being whether the comment was removed by the site administrators. Given the sensitivity of the content, we publish the datasets in full-text form, but with user metadata semi-anonymised and the comment content encrypted via a simple character replacement method using a random, undisclosed bijective mapping, similar to the encryption method applied to the Gazzetta Greek Sport News Comments dataset[7] introduced in Pavlopoulos et al. (2017). The two datasets presented in this paper are aimed at further enriching the landscape of datasets on inappropriate online communication overall, but especially the dimension of multilinguality and multiculturality.

---

[1]https://github.com/ZeerakW/hatespeech
[2]https://figshare.com/projects/Wikipedia_Talk/16731
[3]https://data.world/crowdflower/hate-speech-identification
[4]https://github.com/sfu-discourse-lab/SOCC
[5]https://github.com/UCSM-DUE/IWG_hatespeech_public
[6]https://straintek.wediacloud.net/static/gazzetta-comments-dataset/gazzetta-comments-dataset.tar.gz
[7]https://straintek.wediacloud.net/static/gazzetta-comments-dataset/README.txt

Proceedings of the Second Workshop on Abusive Language Online (ALW2), pages 124–131
Brussels, Belgium, October 31, 2018. ©2018 Association for Computational Linguistics

The contributions of this paper are the following: (1) we introduce two new datasets annotated for content inappropriateness, (2) we perform a basic analysis of the type of the deleted content, (3) we investigate whether the deleted content is more dependent on specific users, threads or locations in a thread, (4) we build baseline predictive models on these datasets and (5) we publish the full but semi-anonymised and encrypted datasets, as well as the models built on the non-encrypted data ready to be used in real-life scenarios.

2 Dataset description

This section gives a description of the two datasets, which we obtained from two different sources from different countries and in different languages. Both datasets are comprehensive in the sense that they contain all the comments from the given time period. Their main value in the context of studying inappropriate content lies in the fact that they also contain all the comments that were deleted by the moderators of the two sites.

The Slovenian **MMC** dataset contains comments on news articles published on the MMC RTV web portal[8], the on-line portal of the Slovenian national radio and television. The dataset comprises all the comments from the beginning of 2010 until the end of 2017, i.e. eight years' worth of content, including deleted comments. The portal is monitored by moderators who delete comments that contain hate speech but also those that are not relevant for the thread or are spam by advertisers.

We obtained the dataset as a CSV file, where we deleted comments with formatting errors, removed illegal UTF-8 characters and remnants of formatting, and then converted the dataset into XML. Apart from the text itself, each comment contains the following metadata: comment ID; ID of the news article that is commented (note, however, that we did not receive the news articles themselves due to copyright limitations); user ID; time stamp; whether the comment was deleted or not; and the number of up- and down-votes.

The Croatian **STY** dataset contains comments on articles from the news portal 24sata[9] which is owned by Styria Media International. They comments in the dataset span from 2007-09-12 to 2017-07-21, i.e. almost ten years of content. Until

2016 the portal was monitored by one moderator, with the last two years of content being moderated by two moderators. Both hate speech and spam are deleted, and the respective users are banned for an amount of time depending on the frequency of their misbehavior.

We received the dataset as a SQL database dump, where we, similarly to MMC, cleaned the file and converted it to a similar XML as the MMC one. Here, the metadata was somewhat different, comprising: comment ID; ID of the news article that is commented (again, we did not receive the news articles themselves); where applicable, ID of comment that is being replied to; the ID of the thread to which the comment belongs; the user ID; the user name; time stamp; whether the comment was deleted or not; and the number of replies to the comment.

2.1 The datasets in numbers

Table 1 gives the sizes of the two datasets in users, texts (comments) and words, split into retained and deleted comments, and overall. As can be seen, both datasets are substantial, having together almost 25 million comments, and over 700 million words. The two datasets have a similar size per year, but given that the STY dataset has a longer time span it is also larger, with over 407 million words, against 325 million words in MMC. Interestingly, given their comparable size, the STY dataset has many more comments (17 million, as opposed to only 7.6 million of MMC) as well as many more users (185 thousand as against 42 thousand of MMC). On the other hand, MMC users write significantly longer texts.

As for the deleted comments, we first note that for a user to be classified into either of the Yes/No deleted row, it suffices that one of their comments has been deleted (or not), so the two percentages do not sum to 100%. The percentages reveal that the two portals adopt somewhat different deletion policies: for MMC almost half of the users had at least one comment deleted, while under 10% had a comment deleted in STY. Similarly for texts, the MMC portal deleted over 8% of the texts, while STY deleted under 2%. The proportion of the number of deleted words is lower for MMC and higher for STY, meaning that with MMC the deleted comments are typically shorter than the retained texts, while for STY they are slightly longer.

[8]http://www.rtvslo.si/
[9]https://www.24sata.hr/

Corpus	Deleted	Users		Texts		Words	
MMC	No	41,142	96.8%	6,965,725	91.7%	302,123,513	92.9%
MMC	Yes	20,086	47.3%	630,961	8.3%	23,102,063	7.1%
MMC	Σ	42,502	100.0%	7,596,686	100.0%	325,225,576	100.0%
STY	No	181,626	98.0%	16,732,818	98.2%	399,214,351	98.0%
STY	Yes	17,810	9.6%	310,147	1.8%	8,334,776	2.0%
STY	Σ	185,266	100.0%	17,042,965	100.0%	407,549,127	100.0%
Σ	No	222,768	97.8%	23,698,543	96.2%	701,337,864	95.7%
Σ	Yes	37,896	16.6%	941,108	3.8%	31,436,839	4.3%
Σ	Σ	227,768	100.0%	24,639,651	100.0%	732,774,703	100.0%

Table 1: Sizes of MMC and STY datasets.

	MMC	STY
Calumination	6	8
Discrimination	11	10
Disrespect	**37**	21
Insult	10	**42**
Irony	19	10
Swearing	3	14
Other	19	18
Σ	105	124

Table 2: Categories of deleted comments.

2.2 Types of inappropriate content

To gain more insight into the nature of the deleted comments, we manually classified 100 random deleted comments from each datasets into the 9 categories proposed by Pavlopoulos et al. (2017): calumniation, discrimination, disrespect, hooliganism, insult, irony, swearing, threat and other. Both samples were annotated by the same annotator. Where required, multiple labels were assigned to a comment.

As shown in Table 2, there are many differences between the two datasets. In the MMC sample, the most frequently represented category is disrespect (37) while swearing is the least frequent (3). Only 5 of the 100 comments were annotated with double labels. In the STY sample, on the other hand, 17 received a double and 1 a triple label (most frequent combinations being insult and swearing). The most frequent category in the STY sample is insult (42) and the least frequent one threat (1), which does not appear in the MMC sample. In general, the Croatian sample of deleted comments contains worse forms of inappropriate content compared to the Slovene one (e.g., many more cases of insults and swearing compared to

more subtle irony which is particularly common in the Slovene sample). Beyond the types of inappropriate comments, we have also observed differences in the persons, groups and institutions towards which the disrespectful comments are targeted. Whereas the targets are the expected "culprits" in the Croatian sample (e.g. marginalized members of the society), in the Slovenian sample, most of them are targeted at the national broadcasting service, its journalists or the administrators of the on-line comments, especially in the category of disrespectful comments.

The reasons for these differences could lie in the different positions of the two media (one national and the other one private) and their subsequently different policies for the treatment of inappropriate content, with MMC deleting more and STY only the most blatant examples of inappropriate comments. Another reason could also be cultural differences, such as more widespread swearing in public discourse in Croatia compared to Slovenia. Interestingly, in both samples a substantial amount (19 vs. 18) of the analysed comments did not belong to any of the categories specified by Pavlopoulos et al. (2017), suggesting that the annotation schema might benefit from further refinements.

3 Dataset Analysis

This section presents a basic analysis of deleted vs. retained content in both datasets. We analyze (1) the distribution of deleted vs. retained content through the years, (2) the distribution of deleted content among users, (3) the distribution of deleted content in threads, and (4) the distribution of the relative positions of the deleted comments in a thread. We compare the distributions (2)-(4) with their random counterparts to see

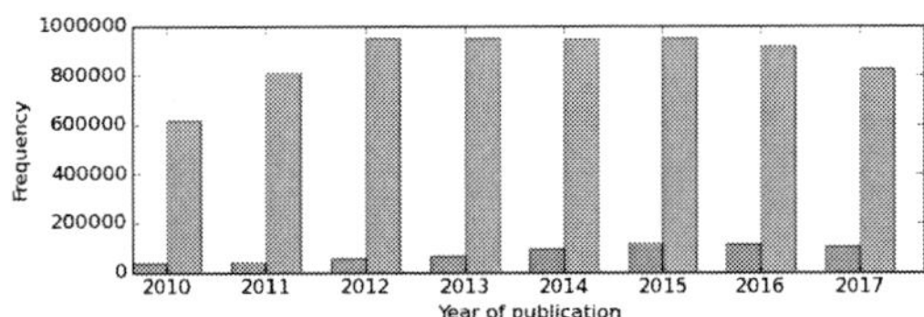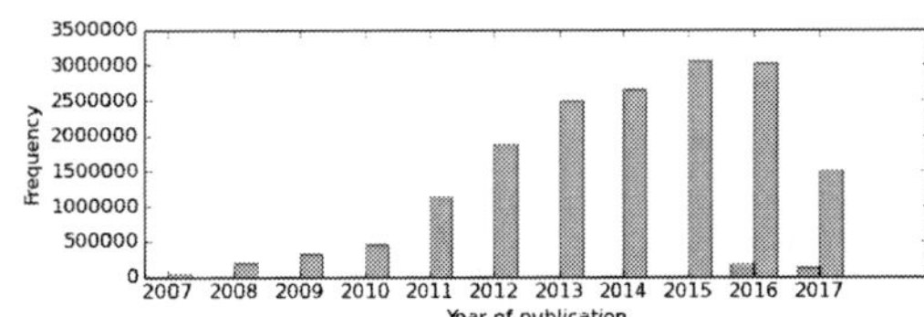

Figure 1: Distribution of deleted (red) and retained (green) comments throughout the publication years for MMC (left) and STY (right).

whether there is a dependence of comment deletion on these three phenomena: user, thread, and location in a thread.

3.1 Distribution through time

Figure 1 shows the distribution of the deleted and retained comments in each dataset throughout the publication years. The trends in the two datasets are quite different. While the STY dataset has an obvious increase in the number of comments throughout the years, the number of comments in the MMC dataset is rather stable. The number of the deleted comments throughout the years is even more different in the two datasets. Most of the deleted content in the STY dataset is from 2016 and 2017, which indicates an obvious change in the policy of content deletion.[10] In the MMC dataset, on the other hand, the percentage of the filtered content is rather stable throughout the years, with only a slight increase through time. The observed difference can be followed back to the type of publishers: STY is a commercial publisher, freely modifying filtering rules, whereas MMC is a national broadcasting company and is as such required to have a much more elaborate and strict, as well as more stable code of conduct.

3.2 Distribution per user

Figure 2 depicts the distribution of the percentage of comments deleted from each user, taking into account only users that published 10 or more comments to ensure a proper representation of the percentages on a histogram with 10 bins. The plot shows similar trends in both languages, with most users having 10% or less of their comments deleted. In both datasets we see an increase in the percentage of users having all their comments

deleted. This phenomenon can be followed back to the practice of deleting users and all their corresponding content.

We hypothesize that this distribution is significantly different from a random one, i.e., that there are users whose comments are deleted more often than by chance. Put in simpler terms, we assume that inappropriate comments are not a blunder that happens to everyone now and then but that there are consistently "non-conforming" users whose comments are deleted more often than those of other users. We test our hypothesis by applying the Kolmogorov-Smirnov non-parametric two-tailed test (Massey, 1951) of the equality of two distributions, with the null hypothesis that there is no difference between the observed and the expected random distribution. We calculate the expected, random distribution by calculating the probability of a comment to be deleted in a dataset and generating a dataset with the identical distribution of comments among users, calculating whether the comment is deleted via a random function with the deletion probability as estimated on the real dataset. On the MMC test we obtain a statistic of 0.274 with the p-value, i.e., the probability that we might falsely reject the null hypothesis that the two distributions are identical being close to 0.0. For the STY dataset we obtain a statistic of 0.371, with a p-value being close to 0.0. These results show that in each dataset some users' comments are being deleted more often than by chance.

To measure to what amount each of the distributions are different to a random one, we calculate the Wasserstein distance (Ramdas et al., 2017) between the observed and the random distributions. While we obtain a distance of 0.068 for the MMC distribution, this distance for the STY distribution is 0.032.[11] This inspection shows that in the

---

[10]The increase in the amount of deleted content can be followed back to the internal decision of the newspaper to make the moderation model more strict, resulting in greater identification of inappropriate content, but also an increase in the amount of inappropriate content aimed at the moderators.

[11]We repeat the calculation on the STY dataset only on the data from 2016 and 2017 to control for the different approach to deleting comments before and from 2016, obtaining

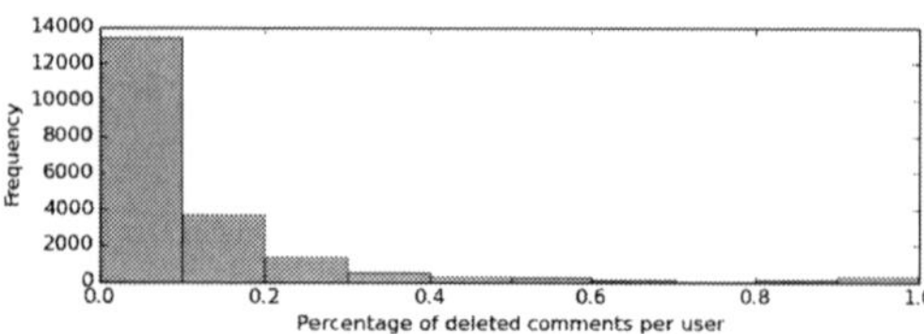 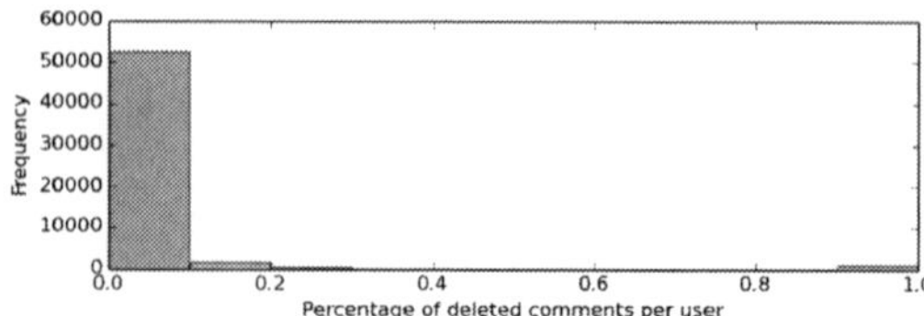

Figure 2: Distribution of the percentage of comments deleted per user publishing 10 or more comments for MMC (left) and STY (right).

Slovene MMC dataset the phenomenon of deleting content of specific users is more prominent than in the Croatian STY dataset.

3.3 Distribution per thread

In this subsection we repeat the calculations performed in the previous subsection on user-focused distributions of deleted content, only that this time we utilize the thread structures which are available in both datasets. For this analysis, as well as the following one presented in Section 3.4, we take into account only threads with at least 10 comments, again to ensure a proper representation on a 10-bin histogram.

In Figure 3 we plot the probability distribution of the percentage of comments deleted in each thread, obtaining a similar, long-tailed distribution as with the user-focused distribution. As with the user distributions, the MMC dataset has a larger number of threads with slightly higher percentage of deleted content (higher than 10%), indicating a less random deletion process in the MMC dataset, i.e., that there are threads that have more content deleted than would be expected by chance.

Similar to our previous calculations, we first calculate whether the obtained distributions are different from distributions obtained by randomly deleting comments in threads by applying the Kolmogorov-Smirnov test of the equality of two distributions. We then quantify the distance of the observed distributions to the random distributions via the Wasserstein distance.

When applying the Kolmogorov-Smirnov test on the MMC dataset, we obtain a statistic of 0.292 with a p-value close to 0.0, while on the STY dataset the obtained statistic is 0.333 with a p-value also close to 0.0. Based on this we can reject the null hypothesis that the random and the observed probability distributions are the same on both datasets. In other words, deletion on some

threads is more prominent than on others.

We continue by calculating the Wasserstein distance metric between the observed and the random distribution, with an obtained distance of 0.036 on the MMC dataset and a distance of 0.010 on the STY dataset. Similar to the previous measurements on the percentage of users' deleted content, a stronger difference between the two distributions is again observed on the MMC dataset, showing the deletion on that dataset to be less random. Furthermore, the distances obtained on the thread-dependent distributions are almost half the size of the distances calculated on the user-dependent distributions, showing that comments of specific users are deleted more often than comments on specific threads, which is an interesting result. Note that the user-focused and thread-focused distances are directly comparable as both distributions are defined on the same scale between 0 and 1.

3.4 Distribution per location in thread

Finally, we inspect the distributions of the deleted comments as per their relative location in a discussion thread. We apply the same calculations as with the user-focused and thread-focused analyses presented in the previous two subsections.

We first analyze the plot of the distribution of the relative location in a thread where a comment is deleted, which is given in Figure 4. Our expectation was that more comments will be deleted in the middle and at the end of the thread because discussions get heated gradually. Both distributions seem very similar, with a close to uniform distribution. However, on both distributions we observe a trend that is opposite to our expectations, namely that comments are deleted more often at the beginning of a thread. The Kolmogorov-Smirnov test of the equality of the random and the observed distribution gives the test statistic of 0.027 and the p-value of $1.448 * 10^{-199}$ on

---

an identical distance.

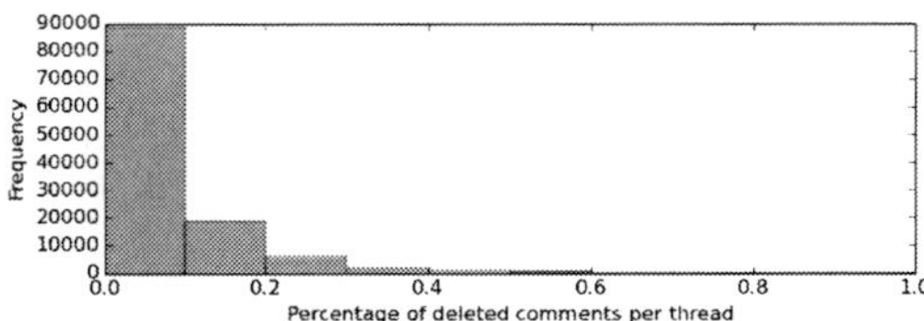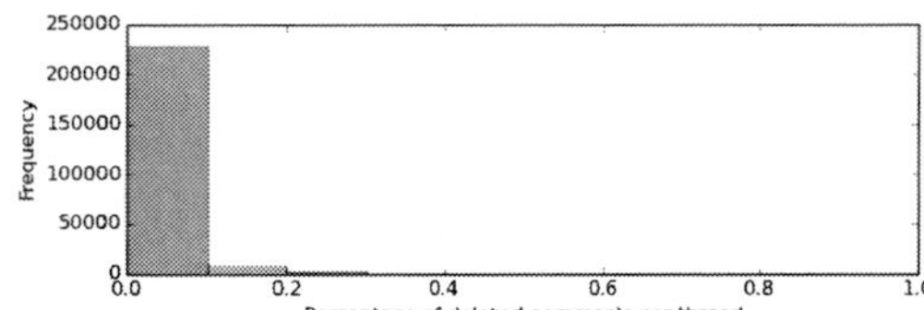

Figure 3: Distribution of the percentage of comments deleted in each thread containing 10 or more comments for MMC (left) and STY (right).

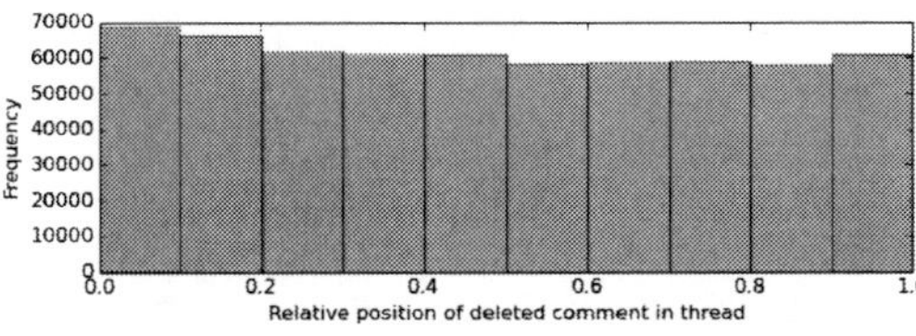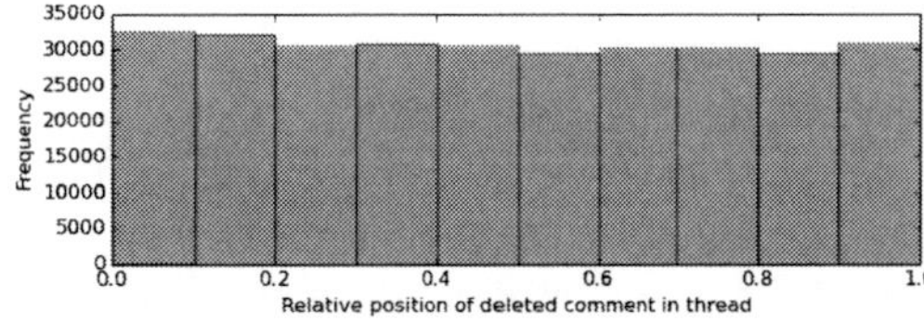

Figure 4: Distribution of the relative position of comments deleted in a thread containing 10 or more comments for MMC (left) and STY (right).

the MMC dataset, while the test statistic on the STY dataset is 0.017 and the p-value $3.26 * 10^{-39}$. The differences between the observed and the random distribution are still highly significant, but less than with the other analyses. Again, the STY dataset appears more random-like than the MMC dataset. We double-check these observations by calculating the Wasserstein distance between observed and random distributions. On the MMC dataset the distance is 0.018, while on the STY dataset it is 0.011. On the MMC dataset this is the smallest distance measured, while on the STY distance this distance is similar to the one calculated on the thread-dependent distribution. The distance to a random distribution is, again, smaller on the STY dataset than on the MMC dataset.

3.5 Discussion

Regarding the three analyses performed, namely the analysis of content deletion among users, threads and relative locations in threads, we can conclude that on the MMC dataset all the distributions are further away from random distributions than on the STY dataset, hinting at a more careful supervision of comments on that dataset. However, we must be careful about drawing such a conclusion because a less random behavior might also point towards targeting specific users (e.g., previously misbehaving users), threads (e.g., threads on specific topics) or locations of the comment in the thread (e.g., the beginning of the thread).

With these three levels of analysis we have shown that the user-dependent distribution of deleted comments is the least random, followed by the thread-dependent distribution, with the location of the comment in the thread being closest to random. In other words, specific users seem to be the most filtered, followed by specific threads, with specific locations in the thread being least prone to filtering. The observation that comments of specific users are more prone to deletion than comments in specific threads is interesting and should be compared to the distributions in other datasets. Given that we observe the same phenomenon in two datasets of different origin, we assume that such regularity would hold in other datasets as well.

4 Availability of data and baseline model

4.1 Data availability

Both datasets are published on the CLARIN.SI repository with all the metadata pseudo-anonymised, and the text encrypted via a simple character replacement method using a random, undisclosed bijective mapping to comply with the terms-of-use of our data providers as well as to mitigate propagation of inappropriate content. The Slovene dataset, published together with the baseline model described in the following subsection, is available from `http://hdl.handle.net/11356/1201,` while the Croatian counterpart is available from

4.2 Model availability

Given that the distributed datasets are encrypted, because of which only in-vitro experiments on inappropriate content identification can be run, but the final systems cannot be applied on real data, we have also published baseline models trained on the non-encrypted data. While these models are capable of identifying potentially inappropriate content, by sharing them we do not propagate inappropriate content above the token level.

For building the baseline models, we split each dataset into training, development and testing portions in a 8:1:1 distribution, and trained, tuned and evaluated fastText (Joulin et al., 2016) classification models on that data split. The published fastText models were trained on the full datasets.

When splitting the data into train, dev and test, we randomly shuffled on the thread level, ensuring that there is no spillover between threads, i.e., that there are no portions of the same thread to be found in train and dev or test data.

During tuning, we optimized the following fastText hyperparameters: word n-gram length (default is 1), minimum and maximum character n-gram length (no character n-grams are used by default) and number of epochs (default is 5). We optimize them by training on the train portion and evaluating on the dev portion. In Table 3 we give the results of the best-performing non-default values on each of the hyperparameters. We evaluate via the ROC AUC score, i.e., the area under the ROC curve, which is 0.5 in case of random results and 1 for perfect results where all positive instances are ranked higher than all negative instances. The presented results show that most impact can be obtained with adding character n-grams to the word, i.e., text representation procedure. By adding character n-grams of length 3 to 7 we lower the error rate on both datasets by 18%. Adding word n-grams longer than 1 does not have a positive impact on performance of fastText. Optimizing the number of epochs has a slight positive impact as long as other hyperparameters are kept default. If we combine optimal character n-gram and epoch hyperparameter values (last row in Table 3, there is no significant difference to using optimal character n-grams only. This is why we decided to use for our final setting all default hyperparameters, except for the character n-gram

lengths that we set between 3 and 7.

We evaluate our final system setting on the test set and obtain a ROC AUC result of 0.794 for the MMC dataset and 0.793 for the STY dataset. These results are more than half way from random to perfect, which is still far from satisfying. We leave the task of building stronger prediction models to future work.

The baseline fastText models trained on the full non-encrypted datasets with optimal hyperparameter values can be obtained from the CLARIN.SI repository together with the encrypted datasets, as mentioned above.

	MMC	STY
default (ngram=1;epoch=5)	0.755	0.746
ngram=2	0.717	0.711
charngram=3,7	**0.798**	**0.791**
epoch=3	0.762	0.753
charngram=3,7;epoch=3	**0.796**	**0.792**

Table 3: Results of tuning hyperparameters on both datasets. Results are ROC AUC scores.

5 Conclusions

In this paper we have introduced two new large on-line news comment datasets annotated for inappropriate content by the content providers for Slovene and Croatian, languages typically rarely represented in similar datasets, making them all the more valuable for the research community.

We have performed a small manual analysis of the kinds of comments that get deleted in each of the datasets. The Croatian deleted comments contain more severe types of inappropriate content, such as insults, as well as more swearing. The Slovene ones, on the other hand, are more covert, formulated as irony, and are frequently aimed at the broadcaster or are off-topic, which indicates differences in the policy of handling user comments by the two media outlets.

The initial statistical analysis of the distribution of filtering among users, threads and locations in threads, has shown that all the distributions are less random on the MMC dataset than on the STY dataset, which is probably caused by more constant and vigilant moderation on the MMC RTV portal. Regarding the three levels of analysis, we showed that the distribution of deleted content among users is the least random, followed by the distribution of that content among threads, with the location of the deleted content being closest to random. This shows that specific users seem to be the most deleted, followed by specific threads, with specific locations in the thread being least prone to deletion.

Finally, by building baseline models on the new datasets, we have shown that fastText classifiers can be improved most easily by adding character n-gram information to the text representation. The obtained results are promising, but still far from production-ready, at least for most usages. However, we have published not only the datasets with metadata pseudo-anonymised and texts encrypted, but also the baseline models trained on the non-encrypted full text of each dataset. We expect that our baseline classification models will not serve just as a point of comparison, but will also be used in real world scenarios, either for feature extraction and text representation for similar tasks, or for the task of ranking or classifying inappropriate content directly.

Acknowledgments

We would like to thank MMC RTV and Styria Media International for providing their databases of comments. The work presented in this paper was funded by the Slovenian Research Agency within the national basic research project Resources, methods and tools for the understanding, identification and classification of various forms of socially unacceptable discourse in the information society (J7-8280, 2017-2020).

References

Thomas Davidson, Dana Warmsley, Michael W. Macy, and Ingmar Weber. 2017. Automated Hate Speech Detection and the Problem of Offensive Language. *CoRR*, abs/1703.04009.

Armand Joulin, Edouard Grave, Piotr Bojanowski, and Tomas Mikolov. 2016. Bag of Tricks for Efficient Text Classification. *arXiv preprint arXiv:1607.01759*.

F. J. Massey. 1951. The Kolmogorov-Smirnov test for goodness of fit. *Journal of the American Statistical Association*, 46(253):68–78.

John Pavlopoulos, Prodromos Malakasiotis, and Ion Androutsopoulos. 2017. Deeper Attention to Abusive User Content Moderation. In *Proceedings of the 2017 Conference on Empirical Methods in Natural Language Processing, EMNLP 2017, Copenhagen, Denmark, September 9-11, 2017*, pages 1125–1135.

Aaditya Ramdas, Nicols Garca Trillos, and Marco Cuturi. 2017. On Wasserstein Two-Sample Testing and Related Families of Nonparametric Tests. *Entropy*, 19(2).

Björn Ross, Michael Rist, Guillermo Carbonell, Benjamin Cabrera, Nils Kurowsky, and Michael Wojatzki. 2017. Measuring the Reliability of Hate Speech Annotations: The Case of the European Refugee Crisis. *CoRR*, abs/1701.08118.

Zeerak Waseem and Dirk Hovy. 2016. Hateful Symbols or Hateful People? Predictive Features for Hate Speech Detection on Twitter. In *Proceedings of the Student Research Workshop, SRW@HLT-NAACL 2016, The 2016 Conference of the North American Chapter of the Association for Computational Linguistics: Human Language Technologies, San Diego California, USA, June 12-17, 2016*, pages 88–93.

Ellery Wulczyn, Nithum Thain, and Lucas Dixon. 2017. Ex machina: Personal attacks seen at scale. In *Proceedings of the 26th International Conference on World Wide Web*, WWW '17, pages 1391–1399, Republic and Canton of Geneva, Switzerland. International World Wide Web Conferences Steering Committee.

Cross-Domain Detection of Abusive Language Online

Mladen Karan and **Jan Šnajder**

Text Analysis and Knowledge Engineering Lab
Faculty of Electrical Engineering and Computing, University of Zagreb
Unska 3, 10000 Zagreb, Croatia
{mladen.karan,jan.snajder}@fer.hr

Abstract

We investigate to what extent the models
trained to detect general abusive language generalize between different datasets labeled with
different abusive language types. To this end,
we compare the cross-domain performance of
simple classification models on nine different
datasets, finding that the models fail to generalize to out-domain datasets and that having at least some in-domain data is important. We also show that using the frustratingly
simple domain adaptation (Daume III, 2007)
in most cases improves the results over in-
domain training, especially when used to augment a smaller dataset with a larger one.

1 Introduction

Abusive language online (Waseem et al., 2017)
is an increasing problem in modern society. Although abusive language is undoubtedly not a new
phenomenon in human communication, the rise
of the internet has made it concerningly prevalent.
The main reason behind this is the cloak of relative anonymity offered when commenting online,
which lowers the inhibitions of individuals prone
to abusive language and removes some of the social mechanisms present in real life that serve to
protect potential victims. Moreover, this type of
psychological violence can occur at any time and
regardless of the physical distance between the persons involved. While abusive language online can
probably never be weeded out entirely, its effect can
certainly be lessened by locating abusive posts and
removing them before they cause too much harm.
Training supervised machine learning models to
recognize abusive texts and alert human moderators can make this process much more efficient.
However, retaining humans in the loop is crucial,
since blindly relying on model predictions would
in effect turn every false positive prediction into
infringement of free speech. This would defeat the
initial purpose of using machine learning models
to facilitate a free and civilized online discussions.

Detecting abusive language online is a subject
of much ongoing research in the NLP community.
Different studies have zeroed in on different types
of abusive language (e.g., aggressive language,
toxic language, hate speech) and have yielded a
number of different datasets collected from various
domains (e.g., news, Twitter, Wikipedia). However,
from a practical perspective – if one simply wishes
to build a classifier for detecting general abusive
language in a given domain – the question arises as
to which of these datasets to use for training. More
generally, the question is to what extent abusive
language detection transfers across domains, and
how much, if anything, can be gained from a simple domain adaptation technique that combines the
source and the target domain.

This paper investigates the question to what extent abusive language detection can benefit from
combining training sets and sharing information between them through domain adaptation techniques.
Our contribution is twofold. First, we compare the
cross-domain performance of simple classification
models on nine different English datasets of abusive language. Second, we explore whether the
framework of frustratingly simple domain adaptation (FEDA) (Daume III, 2007) can be applied to
improve classifier performance, in particular for
smaller data sets. In addition, we show how a simple post-hoc feature analysis can reveal which features are specific to a certain domain and which are
shared between two domains. We make our code
and links to the used datasets available online.[1]

2 Related Work

A bewildering plethora of different types of abusive language can be found online. Some of the

---

[1] http://takelab.fer.hr/alfeda

Proceedings of the Second Workshop on Abusive Language Online (ALW2), pages 132–137
Brussels, Belgium, October 31, 2018. ©2018 Association for Computational Linguistics

types dealt with in related work include but are not limited to sexism, racism (Waseem and Hovy, 2016; Waseem, 2016), toxicity (Kolhatkar et al., 2018), hatefulness (Gao and Huang, 2017), aggression (Kumar et al., 2018), attack (Wulczyn et al., 2017), obscenity, threats, and insults. A typology of abusive language detection subtasks was recently proposed by Waseem et al. (2017).

Traditional machine learning approaches to detecting abusive language include the naive Bayes classifier (Kwok and Wang, 2013; Chen et al., 2012; Dinakar et al., 2011), logistic regression (Waseem and Hovy, 2016; Davidson et al., 2017; Wulczyn et al., 2017; Burnap and Williams, 2015), and support vector machines (SVM) (Xu et al., 2012; Dadvar et al., 2013; Schofield and Davidson, 2017). The best performance is most often attained by deep learning models, the most popular being convolutional neural networks (Gambäck and Sikdar, 2017; Potapova and Gordeev, 2016; Pavlopoulos et al., 2017) and variants of recurrent neural networks (Pavlopoulos et al., 2017; Gao and Huang, 2017; Pitsilis et al., 2018; Zhang et al., 2018). Some approaches (Badjatiya et al., 2017; Park and Fung, 2017; Mehdad and Tetreault, 2016) also rely on combining different types of models.

In this paper we explore combining different datasets from different domains to improve model performance. This idea is well established in the machine learning community under the name of transfer learning; we refer to (Weiss et al., 2016; Lu et al., 2015) for overviews. The work closest to ours is (Waseem et al., 2018), where multi-task learning is used to build robust hate-speech detection models. Our approach is very similar, but we consider more datasets and use a simpler, more easily interpretable transfer learning scheme.

3   Datasets

For our study we use nine publicly available datasets in English; Table 1 summarizes their main characteristics. For reasons of efficiency and comparability, we use a fixed split on each of the datasets into a train, development, and test portions. We respected the official splits where they were provided. As we are interested in detecting the presence of general abusive language, rather than in discerning among its many subtypes, we binarize the labels on all datasets into *positive* (abusive language) and *negative* (not abusive language).

We do this by labeling all classes typeset in bold in Table 1 as *positive* and all other classes as *negative*. There are two exceptions to this rule. First, on the Kol dataset, we consider as *positive* those examples for which at least one annotator gave a rating higher than 1. Second, on the Kaggle dataset, which uses a multilabeling scheme, we consider as *positive* all instances annotated with at least one of the six harmful labels, and as *negative* all instances without any labels. We perform only the very basic preprocessing by lowercasing all words and lemmatizing them using NTLK (Loper and Bird, 2002).

While these modifications to original datasets make a comparison to previous work difficult, they allow a direct comparison across the datasets and a straightforward application of FEDA.

4   Exp. 1: Cross-Domain Performance

The goal of this experiment is to asses how well the models trained on a particular dataset of abusive language perform on a different dataset. The differences in performance can be traced back to two factors: (1) the difference in the types of abusive language that the dataset was labeled with and (2) the differences in dataset sizes. In this work we observe the joint effect of both factors.

4.1   Experimental Setup

We use a linear Support Vector Machine (SVM), which has already been successfully applied to the task of abusive text classification (Schofield and Davidson, 2017). The main motivation for using an SVM, rather than more complex deep learning models, is that in this study we favor model interpretability, even if this means sacrificing performance.[3] Having interpretable models makes it easier to identify the biases that the models might have learned from data and how domain adaptation affects such biases. While, from a practical perspective, we might want to retain those biases for the sake of improving performance, it is important that we are aware that they exist, and thus have the option to correct them if necessary.

For the same reason, we rely on the most simple text representation with unigram counts, which makes it possible to directly correlate word salience to feature weights obtained from the SVM.

---

[3]We acknowledge that there are other competitive and yet interpretable models, such as deep neural networks with attention mechanisms. We leave the investigation of such models for future work.

---

[2]Available at https://tinyurl.com/y7qmd81m

	Source	Train	Dev	Test	BR	Labels
Kol (Kolhatkar et al., 2018)	Newspaper	730	104	209	.627	toxicity rating: 1,**2**,**3**,**4**
Gao (Gao and Huang, 2017)	Fox news	1069	153	306	.284	non-hateful, **hateful**
TRAC (Kumar et al., 2018)	Twitter	11999	3001	916	.566	non-aggressive, **covertly-aggressive, openly-aggressive**
Was2 (Waseem, 2016)	Twitter	4836	691	1382	.153	none, **racism, sexism, both**
Was1 (Waseem and Hovy, 2016)	Twitter	11835	1691	3381	.319	none, **racism, sexism**
Wul1 (Wulczyn et al., 2017)	Wikipedia	69526	23160	23178	.146	non-aggressive, **aggressive**
Wul2 (Wulczyn et al., 2017)	Wikipedia	69526	23160	23178	.134	non-attack, **attack**
Wul3 (Wulczyn et al., 2017)	Wikipedia	95692	32128	31866	.115	non-toxic, **toxic**
Kaggle [2]	Wikipedia	143614	15957	63978	.101	**toxic, severe_toxic, obscene, threat, insult, identity_hate**

Table 1: Nine abusive language datasets: the source, the number of instances in the train, development, and test set, positive instance base rate (BR), and label sets. We mapped the boldface labels to the positive label.

When an SVM model trained on dataset X is applied to dataset Y, we first train the model on training set X optimizing the hyperparameter C in the range $\{2^{-10}, ..., 2^6\}$ to maximize performance on the development set of X. We then train the SVM with the optimal hyperparameters on the union of training and development sets of X, and then use the model to label the test set of Y, obtaining the final score. We measure the performance using the standard two-class F1 score.

4.2 Results

Results are given in Table 2. The rows correspond to different training sets, while the columns correspond to different test sets. For each test set, the best performance is shown in bold. The diagonal cells correspond to the cases of in-domain model testing. For each model X tested on each out-domain dataset Y (off-diagonal cells), we test the statistical significance between that model's in-domain and out-domain performance using a two-tailed bootstrap resampling test at $\alpha = 0.05$.

Expectedly, most models perform best on the in-domain test sets. Exceptions are the Wikipedia-based data sets, where the model trained on Kaggle performs the best on all test sets. This can be attributed to the an overlap that exists between these data sets: Wul1 and Wul2 contain almost identical texts, Wul3 has 68% overlap with them and Kaggle has 1.5% and 3% overlap with Wul1/Wul2 and Wul3, respectively. We mark in gray the corresponding portion of the tables, and refrain from drawing any conclusions from this data.

Another observation is that the performance on out-domain data sets is considerably lower. When applying models to a different test set the performance often drops by more than 50% of F1 score, which indicates that the models do not generalize

well to different datasets. In cases when the size of X is small compared to the size of Y, the training portion of X will also be smaller than the training portion of Y, and it could be argued that the drop in performance is simply due to the model having less training data. However, considerable performance drops are also observable when going from a large X to a small Y, which suggests that the gains from having more training instances in X are counterbalanced by the domain differences between X and Y, and the net result is a loss in performance. Our experiments thus show that having a smaller dataset for a particular domain of abusive language is better than having a very large dataset from a different one. In the following experiment we explore whether a large dataset from a different domain can still be leveraged in a different way.

5 Exp. 2: Domain Adaptation

5.1 Experimental Setup

We investigate the potential of applying domain adaptation to augment the original domain with the information from a different domain. To this end, we employ the FEDA framework (Daume III, 2007), which works by copying features several times to account for different domains, allowing the model to learn domain-dependent weights for each feature.

Let the dataset from the original domain be denoted as O and the data set from an augmentation domain as A. We generate a joint train set as a union of train sets of O and A by keeping three copies of each feature: (1) a general copy, which is unaltered for instances from both domains, (2) an O-specific copy, which is set to 0 for all instances not from O, and (3) an A-specific copy, which is set to 0 for all instances not from A. In the same

	Kol	Gao	TRAC	Was2	Was1	Wul1	Wul2	Wul3	Kaggle
Kol	**0.816**	0.423	0.475*	0.280*	0.479*	0.251*	0.233*	0.204*	0.178*
Gao	0.362*	**0.493**	0.249*	0.181*	0.399*	0.184*	0.177*	0.168*	0.139*
TRAC	0.697*	0.421	**0.548**	0.283*	0.484*	0.307*	0.288*	0.259*	0.225*
Was2	0.088*	0.023*	0.091*	**0.680**	0.174*	0.108*	0.109*	0.098*	0.094*
Was1	0.432*	0.348*	0.238*	0.421*	**0.739**	0.236*	0.229*	0.208*	0.186*
Wul1	0.092*	0.118*	0.316*	0.190*	0.236*	0.701	0.718	0.746	0.602*
Wul2	0.115*	0.078*	0.318*	0.248*	0.226*	0.694	0.710	0.757	0.613*
Wul3	0.139*	0.159*	0.320*	0.263*	0.316*	0.773*	0.784*	0.753	0.626*
Kaggle	0.054*	0.132*	0.296*	0.249*	0.300*	**0.782***	**0.800***	**0.860***	**0.640**

Table 2: Results of cross-domain model performance. Rows are the training datasets and columns are the test datasets. The best performance for each test set (column) is shown in bold. "*" indicates statistical significance at significance level $\alpha = 0.05$ with respect to the diagonal cell.

	None	Kol	Gao	TRAC	Was2	Was1	Wul1	Wul2	Wul3	Kaggle
Kol	**0.816**	–	0.654*	0.775*	0.605*	0.615*	0.627*	0.651*	0.622*	0.605*
Gao	0.493	0.500	–	0.460	**0.534**	0.507	0.441	0.415	0.463	0.455
TRAC	0.548	0.548	0.554	–	0.567	0.568	**0.575**	0.573	0.557	0.565
Was2	0.680	0.703	0.661	**0.730***	–	0.711	0.706	0.714*	0.715*	0.724*
Was1	0.739	0.744	0.743	**0.755***	0.743	–	0.749	0.747	0.749	0.752*
Wul1	0.701	0.701	0.699	0.708*	0.701	0.699	–	0.701	**0.717***	**0.717***
Wul2	0.710	0.709	0.709	0.719*	0.710	0.715	0.716*	–	0.734*	**0.736***
Wul3	0.753	0.753	0.753	0.758*	0.752	0.754	0.764*	0.763*	–	**0.788***
Kaggle	0.640	0.640	0.640	**0.643***	0.639	0.639	0.640	0.640	0.638	–

Table 3: FEDA domain adaptation results. Rows correspond to original datasets and columns to augmentation datasets. The best performance for each original dataset (row) is shown in bold. "*" indicates statistical significance at significance level $\alpha = 0.05$ against the "None" column, which is equivalent to the diagonal of Table 2.

way we generate joint development and test sets. The intuition behind why this effectively leads to domain adaptation is that it allows the underlying machine learning model to differentiate features (words) that are generally useful from those that are useful in only one of the domains. Consequently, it can better learn the similarities and differences of the domains and how to exploit them to maximize performance. For example, a word such as *moron* is almost universally abusive in all domains and would generalize well. On the other hand, a word like *fruit* is almost always completely non-abusive except in specific domains where it might denote a derogatory slang for a homosexual person.

As before, the SVM is trained on the joint training set, with model selection on the joint development set. The model is then trained using optimal hyperparameters on the union of joint training and joint development set and applied to the joint test set. Note that the joint test set contains test instances from both O and A. We evaluate the model only on the test instances from O, as the goal is to determine whether augmentation with A improves performance on the dataset from the original domain O.

5.2 Results

Results are given in Table 3. Each row represents an original domain dataset and each column an augmentation domain dataset. The "None" column corresponds to the results obtained using no augmentation. We use two-tailed bootstrap resampling with $\alpha = 0.05$ to test the statistical significance of each result to the one on the same original dataset without augmentation. The main observation is that for most datasets FEDA leads to performance improvements, and for six out of nine datasets there is at least one augmentation dataset which gives a statistically significant performance improvement. For the five smallest datasets, (Kol, Gao, TRAC, Was1, and Was2) domain adaptation improves the performance on four, and for two the improvements are statistically significant. These results indicate that domain adaptation has the potential to improve results on smaller datasets. Augmenting Wul1, Wul2, and Wul3 with Kaggle yields considerable improvements, which again can be attributed to the overlap between these datasets. An exception is Kol, on which models do not benefit from FEDA. The possible reasons for this might be its small size or high base rate.

No FEDA	General	Was2	TRAC
anti_feminazi_movement	motherfucker	feminazi	fuck
feminazi	cocksucker	west	idiot
feminazi_front	dickhead	howtospotafeminist	asshole
models	douchebag	feminazi_front	ass
howtospotafeminist	cunt	blondes	bitch
prowomanchoice	assholes	anti_feminazi_movement	motherfucker
raging	fuckers	coon	cocksucker
blondemoment	fuckhead	killerblondes	dickhead
prove	feminazi	asian	shit
adorable	coward	hold	douchebag

Table 4: Top 10 features by SVM weights for the Was2 data set without FEDA and with FEDA using TRAC as the augmentation dataset and three feature variants (General, Was2-specific, and TRAC-specific)

5.3 Feature Analysis

FEDA offers a convenient way to analyze which features are generic and signal abusive language in both domains, and which are specific to each. The former features will have high merit for their general copies, while the latter will have high merit for domain-specific copies. In Table 4 we list the top 10 features for the case where we observed the highest improvement: Was2 as the original and TRAC as the augmentation dataset. The results show that the model does indeed learn to differentiate between the sexism/racism domain of Was2 and the aggression focused domain of TRAC, while also learning the general features useful on both datasets.

When not using FEDA, the most indicative features are, expectedly, focused mostly on the sexism/racism aspects of the Was2 dataset. However, when introducing the augmentation domain TRAC dataset, which focuses on aggressive/non-aggressive texts, the features discern between different aspects of abusive language. Words in the *General* column of Table 4 are indeed generally abusive words and can be viewed as indicative of the abusive class for both datasets. On the other hand, the domain-specific features reflect the specific properties of each dataset. For the Was2 dataset these include words correlated with sexism or racism (but not useful for aggression detection on TRAC) such as *feminazi*. On the TRAC dataset domain-specific features are words that are indicative of aggression (but not of sexism/racism in the Was2 dataset), such as *shit*.

6 Conclusion

We compared the performance of abusive language classifiers across datasets from different sources and types of abusive language. We found that the models considered do not generalize well to different-domain datasets, even when trained on a much larger out-domain data. This indicates that having in-domain data, even if not much of it, is crucial for achieving good performance on this task. Furthermore, the experiments have shown that frustratingly simple domain adaptation (FEDA) in most cases improves the results over in-domain training, especially when smaller datasets are augmented with a larger datasets from a different domain.

We found FEDA to be a useful tool to compare the differences between various domains of abusive language and believe that related techniques might lead to new interesting insights into the phenomenon of abusive language.

References

Pinkesh Badjatiya, Shashank Gupta, Manish Gupta, and Vasudeva Varma. 2017. Deep learning for hate speech detection in tweets. In *Proceedings of the 26th International Conference on World Wide Web Companion*, pages 759–760. International World Wide Web Conferences Steering Committee.

Pete Burnap and Matthew L Williams. 2015. Cyber hate speech on Twitter: An application of machine classification and statistical modeling for policy and decision making. *Policy & Internet*, 7(2):223–242.

Ying Chen, Yilu Zhou, Sencun Zhu, and Heng Xu. 2012. Detecting offensive language in social media to protect adolescent online safety. In *Privacy, Security, Risk and Trust (PASSAT), 2012 International Conference on and 2012 International Conference on Social Computing (SocialCom)*, pages 71–80. IEEE.

Maral Dadvar, Dolf Trieschnigg, Roeland Ordelman, and Franciska de Jong. 2013. Improving cyberbullying detection with user context. In *Advances in Information Retrieval*, pages 693–696. Springer.

Hal Daume III. 2007. Frustratingly easy domain adaptation. In *Proceedings of the 45th Annual Meeting of the Association of Computational Linguistics*, pages 256–263.

Thomas Davidson, Dana Warmsley, Michael Macy, and Ingmar Weber. 2017. Automated Hate Speech Detection and the Problem of Offensive Language. In *Proceedings of ICWSM*.

Karthik Dinakar, Roi Reichart, and Henry Lieberman. 2011. Modeling the detection of textual cyberbullying. In *The Social Mobile Web*, pages 11–17.

Björn Gambäck and Utpal Kumar Sikdar. 2017. Using Convolutional Neural Networks to Classify Hate-speech. In *Proceedings of the First Workshop on Abusive Language Online*, pages 85–90.

Lei Gao and Ruihong Huang. 2017. Detecting online hate speech using context aware models. In *Proceedings of Recent Advances in Natural Language Processing (RANLP)*, pages 260–266, Varna, Bulgaria.

Varada Kolhatkar, Hanhan Wu, Luca Cavasso, Emilie Francis, Kavan Shukla, and Maite Taboada. 2018. The SFU opinion and comments corpus: A corpus for the analysis of online news comments.

Ritesh Kumar, Aishwarya N. Reganti, Akshit Bhatia, and Tushar Maheshwari. 2018. Aggression-annotated corpus of Hindi-English code-mixed data. In *Proceedings of the 11th Language Resources and Evaluation Conference (LREC)*, pages 1425–1431, Miyazaki, Japan.

Irene Kwok and Yuzhou Wang. 2013. Locate the hate: Detecting tweets against blacks. In *Twenty-Seventh AAAI Conference on Artificial Intelligence*.

Edward Loper and Steven Bird. 2002. NLTK: The natural language toolkit. In *Proceedings of the ACL-02 Workshop on Effective Tools and Methodologies for Teaching Natural Language Processing and Computational Linguistics - Volume 1*, ETMTNLP '02, pages 63–70, Stroudsburg, PA, USA. Association for Computational Linguistics.

Jie Lu, Vahid Behbood, Peng Hao, Hua Zuo, Shan Xue, and Guangquan Zhang. 2015. Transfer learning using computational intelligence: a survey. *Knowledge-Based Systems*, 80:14–23.

Yashar Mehdad and Joel Tetreault. 2016. Do characters abuse more than words? In *Proceedings of the 17th Annual Meeting of the Special Interest Group on Discourse and Dialogue*, pages 299–303.

Ji Ho Park and Pascale Fung. 2017. One-step and two-step classification for abusive language detection on twitter. In *Proceedings of the First Workshop on Abusive Language Online*, pages 41–45.

John Pavlopoulos, Prodromos Malakasiotis, and Ion Androutsopoulos. 2017. Deep learning for user comment moderation. In *Proceedings of the First Workshop on Abusive Language Online*, pages 25–35.

Georgios K Pitsilis, Heri Ramampiaro, and Helge Langseth. 2018. Detecting offensive language in tweets using deep learning. *arXiv preprint arXiv:1801.04433*.

Rodmonga Potapova and Denis Gordeev. 2016. Detecting state of aggression in sentences using CNN. *arXiv preprint arXiv:1604.06650*.

Alexandra Schofield and Thomas Davidson. 2017. Identifying hate speech in social media. *XRDS: Crossroads, The ACM Magazine for Students*, 24(2):56–59.

Zeerak Waseem. 2016. Are you a racist or am I seeing things? Annotator influence on hate speech detection on Twitter. In *Proceedings of the first workshop on NLP and computational social science*, pages 138–142, Austin, Texas.

Zeerak Waseem, Thomas Davidson, Dana Warmsley, and Ingmar Weber. 2017. Understanding Abuse: A Typology of Abusive Language Detection Subtasks. In *Proceedings of the First Workshop on Abusive Langauge Online*.

Zeerak Waseem and Dirk Hovy. 2016. Hateful symbols or hateful people? Predictive features for hate speech detection on Twitter. In *Proceedings of the NAACL student research workshop*, pages 88–93, San Diego, California.

Zeerak Waseem, James Thorne, and Joachim Bingel. 2018. Bridging the gaps: Multi task learning for domain transfer of hate speech detection. In *Online Harassment*, pages 29–55. Springer.

Karl Weiss, Taghi M Khoshgoftaar, and DingDing Wang. 2016. A survey of transfer learning. *Journal of Big Data*, 3(1):9.

Ellery Wulczyn, Nithum Thain, and Lucas Dixon. 2017. Ex machina: Personal attacks seen at scale. In *Proceedings of the 26th International Conference on World Wide Web*, pages 1391–1399. International World Wide Web Conferences Steering Committee.

Jun-Ming Xu, Kwang-Sung Jun, Xiaojin Zhu, and Amy Bellmore. 2012. Learning from bullying traces in social media. In *Proceedings of the 2012 conference of the North American chapter of the association for computational linguistics: Human language technologies*, pages 656–666. Association for Computational Linguistics.

Ziqi Zhang, David Robinson, and Jonathan Tepper. 2018. Detecting hate speech on Twitter using a convolution-GRU based deep neural network. In *Lecture Notes in Computer Science*. Springer Verlag.

Did you offend me?
Classification of Offensive Tweets in Hinglish Language

Puneet Mathur
NSIT-Delhi
pmathur3k6@gmail.com

Ramit Sawhney
NSIT-Delhi
ramits.co@nsit.net.in

Meghna Ayyar
IIIT-Delhi
meghnaa@iiitd.ac.in

Rajiv Ratn Shah
IIIT-Delhi
rajivratn@iiitd.ac.in

Abstract

The use of code-switched languages (*e.g.*, Hinglish, which is derived by the blending of Hindi with the English language) is getting much popular on Twitter due to their ease of communication in native languages. However, spelling variations and absence of grammar rules introduce ambiguity and make it difficult to understand the text automatically. This paper presents the Multi-Input Multi-Channel Transfer Learning based model (MIMCT) to detect offensive (hate speech or abusive) Hinglish tweets from the proposed Hinglish Offensive Tweet (HOT) dataset using transfer learning coupled with multiple feature inputs. Specifically, it takes multiple primary word embedding along with secondary extracted features as inputs to train a multi-channel CNN-LSTM architecture that has been pre-trained on English tweets through transfer learning. The proposed MIMCT model outperforms the baseline supervised classification models, transfer learning based CNN and LSTM models to establish itself as the state of the art in the unexplored domain of Hinglish offensive text classification.

1 Introduction

Increasing penetration of social media websites such as Twitter in linguistically distinct demographic regions has led to a blend of natively spoken languages with English, known as code-switched languages. Social media is rife with such offensive content that can be broadly classified as abusive and hate-inducing on the basis of severity and target of the discrimination. *Hate speech (Davidson et al., 2017) is an act of offending a person or a group as a whole on the basis of certain key attributes such as religion, race, sexual orientation, gender, ideological background, mental and physical disability.* On the other hand, *abusive speech is offensive speech with a vague target and mild intention to hurt the sentiments of the receiver.* Most social media platforms delete such offensive content when: (i) either someone reports manually or (ii) an offensive content classifier automatically detects them. However, people often use such code-switched languages to write offensive content on social media so that English trained classifiers can not detect them automatically, necessitating an efficient classifier that can detect offensive content automatically from code-switched languages. In 2015, India ranked fourth on the Social Hostilities Index with an index value of 8.7 out of 10 (Grim and Cooperman, 2014), making it imperative to filter the tremendously high offensive online content in Hinglish.

Hinglish has the following characteristics: (i) it is formed of words spoken in Hindi (Indic) language but written in Roman script instead of the standard Devanagari script, (ii) it is one of the many pronunciations based pseudo languages created natively by social media users for the ease of communication and (iii) it has no fixed grammar rules but rather borrows the grammatical setup from native Hindi and compliments it with Roman script along with a plethora of slurs, slang and phonetic variations due to regional influence. Hence, such code-switched language presents challenging limitations in terms of the randomized spelling variations in explicit words due to a foreign script and compounded ambiguity arising due to the various interpretations of words in different contextual situations. For instance, the sentence: *Main tujhe se pyaar karta hun* is in Hinglish language which means *I love you.* Careful observation highlights how the word *pyaar* meaning 'love' can suffer from phonetic variations due to multiple possible pronunciations such as *pyar, pyaar* or *pyara.* Also, the explicit word by word translation of the above sentence, *I you love do*, is grammatically incorrect in English.

Proceedings of the Second Workshop on Abusive Language Online (ALW2), pages 138–148
Brussels, Belgium, October 31, 2018. ©2018 Association for Computational Linguistics

We present deep learning techniques that classify the input tweets in Hinglish as: (i) non-offensive, (ii) abusive and (iii) hate-inducing. Since transfer learning can act as an effective strategy to reuse already learned features in learning a specialized task through cross domain knowledge transfer, hate speech classification on a large English corpus can act as source tasks to help in obtaining pre-trained deep learning classifiers for the target task of classifying tweets translated in English from Hinglish language.

Representation vectors constructed by CNN consider local relationship values while the feature vectors constructed by LSTM stress on overall dependencies of the whole sentence. The proposed MIMCT model employs both CNN and LSTM as concurrent information channels that benefit from local as well as overall semantic relationship and is further supported by primary features (multiple word embeddings) and secondary external features (LIWC feature, profanity vector and sentiment score), as described in Section 3.3. The complete MIMCT model is pre-trained on English Offensive Tweet (EOT) dataset, which is an open source dataset of annotated English tweets that was obtained from CrowdFlower[1] and is an abridged version of the original dataset created by Davidson et al. (2017), followed by re-training on the proposed HOT dataset.

The main contributions of our work can be summarized as follows:

- Building an annotated Hinglish Offensive Tweet (HOT) dataset[2].

- We ascertain the usefulness of transfer learning for classifying offensive Hinglish tweets.

- We build a novel MIMCT model that outperforms the baseline models on HOT.

The remainder of this paper is organized as follows. Sections 2 and 3 discuss the related work and methodologies in detail, respectively. Discussions and evaluations are done in Section 4 followed by conclusion and future work in Section 5.

2   Related Work

One of the earliest works on code switched languages was presented by Bhatia and Ritchie (2008) demonstrating cross-linguistic interaction on a semantic level. Several attempts to translate the Hindi-English mixed language into pure English have been made previously, but a major hindrance to this progress has been the fact that the structure of language varies due to relative discrepancies in grammatical features (Bhargava et al., 1988). Ravi and Ravi (2016) proved that a combination of TF-IDF features, gain ratio based feature selection, and Radial Basis Function Neural Network work best for sentiment classification in Hinglish text. Joshi et al. (2016) used sub-word level LSTM models for Hinglish sentiment analysis. Efforts to detect offensive text in online textual content have been undertaken previously for other languages as well like German (Ross et al., 2017) and Arabic (Mubarak et al., 2017).

Gambäck and Sikdar (2017) used a multi-channel HybridCNN architecture to arrive at promising results for hate speech detection in English tweets. Badjatiya et al. (2017) presented a gradient boosted LSTM model with random embeddings to outperform state of the art hate speech detection techniques. Vo et al. (2017) demonstrated the use of multi-channel CNN-LSTM model for Vietnamese sentiment analysis. The use of transfer learning enables the application of feature-based knowledge transference in domains with disparate feature spaces and data distribution (Pan and Yang, 2010). Pan et al. (2012) gave a detailed explanation about the application of transfer learning for cross-domain, instance-based and feature-based text classification. An important work in this direction of Hinglish offensive text classification was done by by Mathur et al. (2018b) by effectively employing transfer learning.

3   Methodology

3.1   Pre-processing

The tweets obtained from data sources were channeled through a pre-processing pipeline with the aim to transform them into semantic feature vectors. The transliteration process was broken into intermediate steps:

Step 1: The first pre-processing step was the removal of punctuations, URLs, user mentions {@mentions} and numbers {0-9}. Hash tags and emoticons were suitably converted by their textual counterparts along with conversion of all tweets into lower case. Stop words corpus obtained from

---

[1] https://www.crowdflower.com/

[2] The dataset and source code is available for research purposes at www.github.com/pmathur5k10/Hinglish-Offensive-Text-Classification

NLTK was used to eliminate most unproductive words which provide little information about individual tweets. This was followed by transliteration and then translation of each word in Hinglish tweet into the corresponding English word using the Hinglish-English dictionary mentioned in Section 4.1. At this step, the syntax and grammatical notions of the target language were ignored and the resultant tweet was treated as an assortment of isolated words and phrases to make them eligible for conversion into word vector representation.

Step 2: We used multiple word embedding representations such as Glove (Pennington et al., 2014), Twitter word2vec (Godin et al., 2015), and FastText (Bojanowski et al., 2016) embeddings for creating the word embedding layers and to obtain the word sequence vector representations of the processed tweets. Finally, the train-test split of both the datasets was been kept in the ratio of 80:20 for all experiments described in this paper.

3.2 Transfer Learning based Offensive Text Classification

Recently, Badjatiya et al. (2017) performed state of the art classification of tweets in English language as racist, sexist or neither using multiple deep learning techniques motivating exploration of similar models for our task. The problem of hate speech classification in Hinglish language is similar to that in English due to the semantic parallelism but suffers from the drawback of syntactic disassociation when Hinglish is translated into English. The proposal to apply transfer learning is inspired by the fact that despite having a small-sized dataset, it provides relative performance increase at a reduced storage and computational cost (Bengio, 2012). Deep learning models pre-trained on EOT learn the low-level features of the English language tweets. The weights of initial convolutional layers are frozen while the last few layers are kept trainable such that when the model is retrained on the HOT dataset, it learns to extract high level features corresponding to syntax variations in translated Hinglish language.

One major drawback of CNN models is the fact that it finds only the local optimum in weighted layers. This disadvantage is somewhat overcome by LSTM's since they are well-suited to classify, process and capture long term dependencies in text. This makes them an excellent choice to learn long-range dependencies from higher-order

sequential features. The aim of three-label offensive tweet classification is achieved by using both CNN and LSTM models, respectively. In the first stage of experiments, the respective models are trained and tested on HOT to serve as a benchmark. The same models are reinitialized and run from scratch on the EOT dataset followed by retraining on the HOT dataset by keeping only the last dense layers as trainable. The models are finally then tested on the testing section of HOT and results compiled in Table 7. We hypothesize that the performance of both CNN and LSTM should comparatively enhance due to transfer learning as compared to the benchmark due to syntactical degradation of tweets during the pre-processing step. If this process leads to an overall enhancement of model performance on HOT dataset, then the intuition to use transfer learning for transferring pre-learnt semantic features between two syntactically obscure language would hold ground. As per (Park and Fung, 2017), proposed CNN and LSTM architecture for these experiments were designed to have shallow layers as the small size of our dataset runs the risk of overfitting on the data.

3.3 MIMCT Model

The architecture of the MIMCT model is shown in Figure 1, consisting of two main components: (i) primary and secondary inputs and (ii) CNN-LSTM binary channel neural network. The following subsection describes the application of primary and secondary inputs in MIMCT.

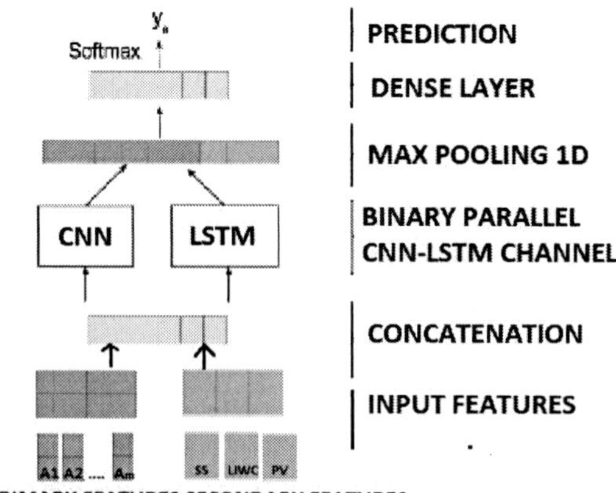

Figure 1: The MIMCT model

3.3.1 Primary and Secondary Inputs

Word embeddings help to learn distributed low-dimensional representations of tweets and different embeddings induced using different models, corpora, and processing steps encode different aspects of the language. While bag of words statistics based embeddings stress on word associations (doctor-hospital), those based on dependency-parses focus on similarity in terms of use (doctor-surgeon). Inspired by the works of (Mahata et al., 2018b), it is natural to consider how these embeddings might be combined to obtain the set of most promising word embeddings amongst Glove, Twitter Word2vec and FastText. Assuming m word embeddings with corresponding dimensions d_1, d_2, ...d_m are independently fed into the MIMCT model as primary inputs. Thus the input to MIMCT will comprise of multiple sentence matrices A_1, A_2, ...A_m, where each $A_l \in R^{s*d_l}$ having s as zero-padded sentence length and d_l as dimensionality of the embedding. Keeping the embedding dimension constant to 200 in each case, we obtained independent feature vectors for each set of embeddings that are known as primary inputs. Apart from the regular embedding inputs, additional hierarchical contextual features are also required so as to complement the overall classification of the textual data. These features additionally focus on the sentiment and tailor-made abuses that may not be present in regular dictionary corpus. This helps to overcome a serious bottleneck in the classification task and could be one of the prominent reasons for high misclassification of abusive and hate-inducing class in baseline and basic transfer learning approaches. The multiple modalities added to the MIMCT model as secondary inputs are:

- **Sentiment Score (SS)**: We have used tweet sentiment score evaluated using SentiWord-Net (Baccianella et al., 2010) as a feature to stress on polarity of the tweets. The SS input will be a unidimensional vector denoted by +1 for positive, 0 for neutral and -1 for negative sentiment.

- **LIWC Features**: Inspired by (Sawhney et al., 2018a), Linguistic Inquiry and Word Count (Pennebaker et al., 2007) throws light on various language modalities expressing the linguistic statistical make-up of each text. Table 1 portrays the cumulative linguistic attributes calculated by LIWC2007 to form a LIWC attribute vector of 67 dimension (67D). Moreover, we have excluded numbers and punctuation in LIWC features as these are removed in pre-processing steps.

- **Profanity Vector**: Swearing is a form of expressing emotions, especially anger and frustration (Jay and Janschewitz, 2008). Section 4.1 describes the Hinglish Profanity list with corresponding English translation. An integer vector of dimension 210 (210D) is constructed for each tweet such that the presence of a particular bad word is demarcated by its corresponding profanity score while its absence is demarcated by null value to emphasize the presence of contextually subjective swear words.

4 Evaluation

We provide an extensive description of the sources, ground truth annotation scheme and statistics of the proposed Hinglish Offensive Tweets (HOT) dataset in Section 4.1. Next, we discuss implementation details of baseline, transfer learning and MIMCT model in Section 4.2 followed by results analysis in Section 4.3.

4.1 Dataset

Table 2 spells out tweet distributions across EOT and HOT datasets. HOT is a manually annotated dataset that was created using the Twitter Streaming API[3] by selecting tweets having more than 3 Hinglish words. The tweets were collected during the interval of 4 months of November 2017 to February 2018. The tweets were mined by imposing geo-location restriction such that tweets originating only in the Indian subcontinent were made part of the corpus. Inspired by the work of Rudra et al. (2016), tweets were mined from popular Twitter hashtags of viral topics popular across the news feed. Bali et al. (2014) pointed out that Indian social media users have high activity on Facebook pages of a few listed prominent public entities. Hence, we crawled tweets and responses from Twitter handles of sports-persons, political figures, news channels and movie stars. The collected corpus of tweets initially had 25667 tweets which was filtered down to remove tweets containing only URL's, only images and videos, having less than 3 words, non-English and non-Hinglish scripts and duplicates. The annotation of

---

[3]`https://developer.twitter.com/`

LIWC Categories	Attributes
Linguistic Statistics	word count (mean), words per sentence, dictionary words, total pronouns, words >6 letters, total functional words, personal pronouns
Grammatical Structures	1st person singular, 1st person plural,2nd person, 3rd person singular, 3rd person plural, impersonal pronouns, articles, common verbs, auxiliary verbs, past, present and future tense, adverbs, prepositions, conjunctions, negotiations, quantifiers, swear words
Textual Category	sexual, body, health, ingestion, relativity, motion, space, time,
Psychological Processes	social processes, family, friends, humans, effective processes, negative and positive emotions, anxiety, anger, sadness, cognitive processes, insight, causation, discrepancy, tentativeness, certainty, inhibition, inclusive, exclusive, perceptual processes, see, hear feel, biological processes,
Current Concerns	work, achievement, leisure, home, money, religion, death
Spoken Categories	assent, non-fluencies, fillers

Table 1: LIWC linguistic attributes used in the MIMCT model

Label	EOT	HOT
Non-Offensive	7274	1121
Abusive	4836	1765
Hate-inducing	2399	303
Total	**14509**	**3189**
Train	11608	2551
Test	2944	637

Table 2: Tweet distributions in EOT and HOT.

Tweet	Label
(i) Tum ussey pyar kyun nahin karti? (ii) Why don't you love him? (iii) you him love why no	Non-offensive
(i) Ch*d! Yeh sab ch*tiye hain! :/ (ii) F**k! They all are c*nts! :/ (iii) F**k they all c*nts are	Abusive
(i) M*d*rch*d Mus*lm**n sE nafrat (ii) m*therf*ck*r m*sl*m hate (iii) m*therf*ck*r m*s*l*m**n hate	Hate-inducing

Table 3: Examples of tweets in the HOT dataset. Categories (i), (ii) and (iii) denote the Hinglish tweet, its corresponding English meaning and its transliterated and translated version. The authors have modified some bad words in original tweets with '*' to not offend the readers.

HOT tweets were done by three annotators having sufficient background in NLP research. The tweets were labeled as hate speech if they satisfied one or more of the conditions: (i) tweet used sexist or racial slur to target a minority, (ii) undignified stereotyping or (iii) supporting a problematic hashtags such as #ReligiousSc*m. The label chosen by at least two out of three independent annotators was taken as final ground truth for each tweet. In case of conflict amongst the annotators, an NLP expert would finally assign the ground truth annotation for ambiguous tweets. In this way, 386 tweets needed expert annotation, while 2803 tweets were labeled through consensus of annotators with an average value of Cohen Kappa's inter-annotator agreement $\kappa = 0.83$. Table 5 shows the internal agreement between our annotators.

A curated list of profane words was extracted to form the Hinglish profanity list[4], which was created by accumulating Hinglish swear words from curated social media blog posts (Rizwan, 2016) and dedicated swear word forums[5]. Each swear word was assigned an integer score on the scale of (1-10) based on the degree of profanity. This assignment of profanity scores was accomplished through discussion amongst four independent code-switching linguistic experts having an extensive background in social media analysis.

The task of transliterating Hinglish words into

Devanagari Hindi was achieved using datasets provided by Khapra et al. (2014). The words so obtained were further translated into Roman script using a Hindi-English dictionary consisting of 136110 word pairs mined from CFILT, IIT Bombay[6]. Additionally, the English translations present of the words in Hinglish Profanity list were added to form a map based Hinglish-English dictionary. A pertinent challenge in dealing with Hinglish language was the presence of spelling variants, homophones and homonyms that are used frequently in a loose context. Thus the spelling variations of various popular Hinglish words were added to the corpus. The Hinglish-English dictionary thus formed, comprising of 7193 word pairs, was used as the basis for all further Hinglish to English tweet conversions. Table 4 gives detailed examples of word pairs in Hinglish-English dictionary along with a few swear words and their profanity scores.

Approximately, 29% of the tokens in pre-processed tweets are in Hinglish, a whopping 65% of the tokens are in English, while the remaining are Hinglish named entities like persons, events, organizations or places. The higher instances of

---

[4]www.github.com/pmathur5k10/
Hinglish-Offensive-Text-Classification
[5]http://www.hindilearner.com/hindi_
words_phrases/hindi_bad_words1.php

[6]http://www.cfilt.iitb.ac.in/~hdict/
webinterface_user/

Hinglish	English	Tag
acha	good	adjective
neeche	under	adposition
abhi	now	adverb
aur	and	conjunction
nahin	no	determiner
ghar	home	noun
ek	one	numeral
saath	with	particle
tum	you	pronoun
pyar	love	verb
*s**la*	blo*dy	swear (1)
*k*tta*	dog	swear (2)
*s**ver*	pig	swear (3)
*har**mi*	bast*rd	swear (4)
*ch*tiya*	f*cker	swear (5)
*bh*dve*	p*mp	swear (6)
*g**nd*	a*s	swear (7)
*r*ndi*	ho*oker	swear (8)
*b*h*nch*d*	s*sterf*ck*r	swear (8)
*m*d*rch*d*	m*therf*ck*r	swear (10)

Table 4: Examples of word pairs in Hinglish-English dictionary and Hinglish Profanity List with their profanity score

the named-entities in the HOT dataset is a result of the way the data is sourced. Around 1.4% of Hinglish words in HOT share the same spellings with some English words because of transliteration of Hindi text to Roman script. The t-SNE (Maaten and Hinton, 2008) plot of the HOT dataset shows the probability distribution of words in terms of the tokens used in tweets as represented by Figure 2. We also computed a few metrics to understand code-switching patterns in our dataset, so as to rationalize the performance of the classification models.

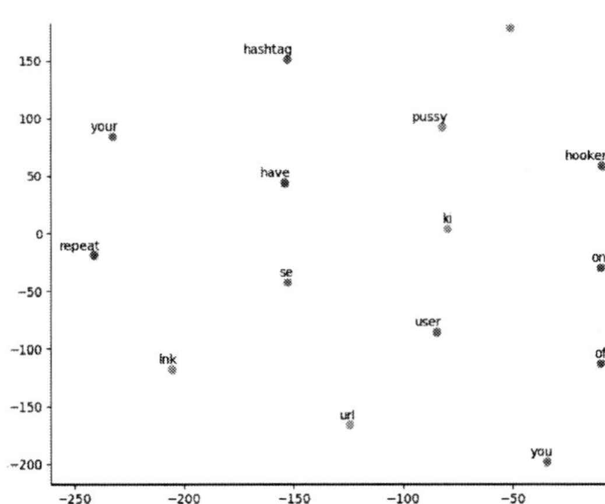

Figure 2: T-SNE plot of the HOT dataset

Multilingual Index (M_i): It is a word-count-based measure that quantifies the inequality of the

	A_1	A_2	A_3
A_1	–	0.76	0.84
A_2	0.76	–	0.88
A_3	0.84	0.88	–

Table 5: Cohen's Kappa for three annotators A_1, A_2 and A_3

language tags distribution in a corpus of at least two languages (Barnett et al., 2000). Let k be the total number of languages and p_j is the total number of words in the language j over the total number of words in the corpus. The value of M_i ranges between 0 and 1 where, a value of 0 corresponds to a monolingual corpus and 1 corresponds to a corpus with equal number of tokens from each language. Equation 1 depicts the M_i which is approximately equal to 0.601, indicating that a majority of words are in Hinglish.

Integration Index (I_i): Integration Index is the approximate probability that any given token in the corpus is a switch point (Guzmán et al., 2017). This metric quantifies the frequency of code-switching in a corpus. Given a corpus composed of tokens tagged by language $\{l_j\}$, i ranges from 1 to $n-1$, where n the size of the corpus. $S(l_i, l_j) = 1$ if $l_i = l_j$ and 0 otherwise in Equation 2. The value of I_i computed is approximateedly 0.079 portraying a high frequency of code-switching points.

$$M_i = \frac{1 - \sum p^2{}_j}{(k-1)\sum p^2{}_j} \qquad (1)$$

$$I_i = \frac{1}{n-1} \sum_{1<=i<j-1<=n-1} S(l_i, l_j) \qquad (2)$$

4.2 Implementation Details

4.2.1 Baseline

Several baseline models were experimented such as Support Vector Machine (SVM) and Random Forests (RF). The supervised models were trained using k-fold cross-validation with 10 splits (k=10) each. The hyper-parameters for Random Forest classifier were fine tuned and the results were found to be optimal when n_estimators, max_depth and max_features were fixed at 1000, 15 and log2, respectively. Other parameters for the SVM classifiers were initialized to default values. Inspired by Badjatiya et al. (2017) and Mathur et al. (2018a), various features were extracted from preprocessed tweets to be used as input to the baseline models such as (i) Character n-grams, (ii) Bag of

Words Vector (BoWV) and (iii) TF-IDF count vector and the results have been summarized in Table 6.

4.2.2 Transfer Learning

The number of trainable and static layers were toyed with to get the best combination giving suitable results. For the classification task, both CNN and LSTM models are trained using 10-fold cross validation to identify the best hyper-parameter settings as presented below:

- **CNN**: Convolutional 1D layer (filter size=15, kernel size=3) $\rightarrow$ Convolutional 1D (filter size=12, kernel size=3) $\rightarrow$ Convolutional 1D (filter size=10, kernel size=3) $\rightarrow$ Dropout (0.2) $\rightarrow$ Flatten Layer $\rightarrow$ Dense Layer (64 units, activation = 'relu') $\rightarrow$ Dense Layer (3 units, activation = 'softmax')

- **LSTM** : LSTM layer(h=64, dropout=0.25, recurrent dropout=0.3) $\rightarrow$ Dense (64 units, activation = 'relu') $\rightarrow$ Dense (3 units, activation = 'sigmoid')

The final layer of both CNN and LSTM models is the compile layer with categorical cross-entropy as the loss function, *Adam* as the optimizer, learning rate kept at 0.001 and L2 regularization with strength of 1E-6. The CNN and LSTM models were tested using three flavors of word embeddings : (i) Glove, (ii) Twitter word2vec and (iii) FastText separately. The dimensions of input word embeddings were kept constant at 200 as for consistency across all embeddings. The hyper parameters were chosen by grid search by running the experiments over a wide range. The batch size was experimented from size 8 to 128. Similarly, the number of epochs were limited at point were the model training loss plateaued by exploring different values from 10 to 50 in intervals of 5. The epochs and batch size were fixed to 20 and 64 respectively so as to maintain consistency in performance evaluation in each case without compromising on the optimality of the results corresponding to each configuration as summarized in Table 7.

4.2.3 MIMCT Model

Distinct word embedding representation are generated from each participant embedding layer that are concatenated along with secondary features

Feature	Char N-grams		BoWV		TF-IDF	
Classifier	SVM	RF	SVM	RF	SVM	RF
Precision	0.679	0.565	0.688	0.579	**0.721**	0.655
Recall	0.708	0.587	**0.731**	0.664	0.724	0.678
F1-Score	0.688	0.574	0.703	0.639	**0.723**	0.666

Table 6: Baseline results for non-offensive, abusive, hate-inducing tweet classification on HOT

and fed to the MIMCT model as independent inputs to both CNN and LSTM channels. The features after passing through both the channels are merged and passed to the Max-pooling 1D layer. The resultant vector is reshaped and fed into a final softmax layer to perform tertiary classification. The architecture of CNN channel comprises of three successive Convolutional-1D layers with filter size chosen as 20, 15 and 10 respectively. This is followed by a dropout layer of value 0.25 and flatten layer. This is immediately followed by a single dense layer of 3 units with *softmax* activation. The LSTM channel is simply a layered structure comprising of a LSTM layer (128 units and dropout value of 0.2) and a dense layer (3 units and *softmax* activation). The MIMCT model uses *Adam* optimizer (Kingma and Ba, 2014) along with L2 regularization to prevent overfitting in the model. MIMCT was initially trained on the EOT dataset and the complete model is re-trained on the HOT dataset so as to benefit from the transfer of learnt features in the last stage. The model hyper-parameters were experimentally selected by trying out a large number of combinations through grid search.

4.3 Results and Discussion

Table 6 clearly show that SVM model supplemented with TF-IDF features gives peak performance in terms of F1-score and precision when compared to other configurations of baseline supervised classifiers. The general inference that can be drawn at this stage is that the SVM classifier outperforms Random Forest. Another useful observation is that TF-IDF is the most effective feature for semantically representing Hinglish text and gives better performance than both Bag of Words Vector and Character N-grams on respective classifiers. These observations are in agreement with the results presented by Badjatiya et al. (2017) who also used supervised classification for offensive tweet classification in English.

Table 7 shows results (in terms of F1-score, precision, and recall) for the classification task

Embedding	Glove						Twitter Word2vec						FastText					
Model	CNN			LSTM			CNN			LSTM			CNN			LSTM		
Data	EOT	HOT	TFL	EOT	HOT	TFL	EOT	HOT	TFL	EOT	HOT	TFL	EOT	HOT	TFL	EOT	HOT	TFL
Precision	0.843	0.734	0.789	0.819	0.753	0.802	0.856	0.762	0.793	0.821	0.756	0.810	0.800	0.730	0.758	0.799	0.746	**0.823**
Recall	0.841	0.804	0.820	0.834	0.764	0.819	0.861	0.811	0.817	0.835	0.779	**0.846**	0.820	0.805	0.827	0.807	0.677	0.838
F1-Score	0.841	0.755	0.801	0.816	0.752	0.813	0.857	0.799	0.815	0.835	0.765	**0.830**	0.811	0.772	0.793	0.800	0.755	0.823

Table 7: Results for non-offensive, abusive, hate-inducing tweet classification on EOT, HOT and the HOT dataset with transfer learning (TFL) for Glove, Twitter Word2vec and FastText embeddings

of transfer learning on CNN and LSTM models. Macro metrics are preferred in experimentation evaluation as the class imbalance is not severe enough to skew the outcomes. Training and testing the same models from scratch on HOT without transfer learning reports a sharp downfall in performance of CNN and LSTM, which is quite expected as the Hinglish tweets in the HOT dataset suffer from syntactic degradation after transliteration and translation. But following the transfer learning methodology, the model performances on HOT improve significantly strengthening the argument that there was a positive transfer of features from English to Hinglish tweet data. A relative comparison between several configurations of CNN and LSTM with corresponding word embeddings reflects that LSTM's are slightly better in each case relative to the corresponding CNN models and the Twitter word2vec outperforms its contemporary embeddings in most cases.

Lastly, the observation of the MIMCT model gives us useful insights to examine the effects of using multiple inputs. While the combination of Twitter word2vec (Tw) and FastText (Ft) shows superior performance than other embedding combinations, the addition of sentiment score has little affect on the overall classification performance. In contrast, the usage of profanity vector and LIWC features boosts the metric values and the best classifier performance is recorded when all the secondary features are used together in conjugation with Twitter word2vec and FastText embeddings. MIMCT shows significant performance improvement over the baselines presented in our work to emerge as the current state of the art in the task of Hinglish offensive tweet detection. MIMCT model (Tw + Ft + SS + PV + LIWC) out performs SVM supplemented with TF-IDF features and the Twitter-LSTM transfer learning model by 0.166 and 0.165 F1 points, respectively.

4.4 Error Analysis

Some categories of error that occur in MIMCT:

MIMCT Features	Precision	Recall	F1
Glove (Gl)	0.819	0.849	0.805
Twitter Word2vec (Tw)	0.867	0.810	0.852
FastText (Ft)	0.860	0.777	0.831
(Gl) + (Tw)	0.859	0.745	0.844
(Tw) + (Ft)	**0.861**	**0.854**	**0.857**
(Gl) + (Ft)	0.800	0.850	0.812
(Gl) + (Tw) + (Ft)	0.819	0.795	0.804
(Tw) + (Ft) + [SS]	0.782	0.902	0.858
(Tw) + (Ft) + [LIWC]	0.793	0.925	0.885
(Tw) + (Ft) + [PV]	0.618	0.890	0.888
(Tw) + (Ft) + [SS + PV]	0.759	0.904	0.886
(Tw) + (Ft) + [SS + LIWC]	0.732	0.865	0.889
(Tw) + (Ft) + [PV + LIWC]	**0.851**	0.905	0.893
(Tw) + (Ft) + [SS + PV + LIWC]	0.816	**0.928**	**0.895**

Table 8: Results of the MIMCT model with various input features HOT compared to previous baseline. Primary inputs are enclosed within parentheses, e.g., (Tw), and secondary inputs are enclosed within square brackets, e.g. [LIWC].

1. **Creative word morphing**: Human annotators as well as the classifier misidentified the tweet 'chal bhaag m*mdi', which translates in English as 'go run m*mdi', as non-offensive instead of hate-inducing. Here 'm*mdi' is an indigenous way of referring to a particular minority that has been morphed to escape possible identification.

2. **Indirect hate**: The tweet 'Bas kar ch*tiye m***rsa educated' was correctly identified by our annotators as hate-inducing but the classifier identified it as abusive. This is because pre-processing of this tweet as 'Limit it m*ther f*cking religious school educated' leads to lose in its contextual reference to customs and traditions of a particular community.

3. **Uncommon Hinglish words**: The work in its present form dos not deal with uncommon and unknown Hinglish words. These may arise due to spelling variations, homonyms, grammatical incorrectness, mixing of foreign language, influence of regional dialect or negligence due to subjective nature of the

transliteration process.

4. **Analysis of code-mixed words**: It has been shown in previous research (Singh, 1985) that bilingual languages tend to be biased in favour of code-mixing of certain words at specific locations in text. Contextual investigation in this direction can be a useful to eliminate the subjective problem of Hinglish to English transliteration in future work.

5. **Possible overfitting on homogenous data**: The data usually present on the social media portals tend to be noisy and often repetetive in content. The skew in the class balance of dataset coupled with training on deep layered model may lead to overfitting of the data and may possibly induce large variation between expected and real-world results. We suspect this might be inherent in present experiments and can be overcome by extracting data from heterogenous sources to model a real-life scenario.

5   Conclusion and Future Work

We introduced a novel HOT dataset for multiclass labeling of offensive textual tweets in Hindi-English code switched language. The tweets in Hinglish language are transformed into semantically analogous English text followed by experimental validation of transfer learning for classifying cross-linguistic tweets. We propose the MIMCT model that uses multiple embeddings and secondary semantic features in a CNN-LSTM parallel channel architecture to outperform the baselines and naive transfer learning models. Finally, a brief analysis of the HOT dataset and its associated errors in classification has been provided. Possible future enhancements include applying feature selection methods to choose the most prominent features amongst those presented similar to the work done by (Sawhney et al., 2018b,c), extending MIMCT to other code-switched and code-mixed languages and exploring GRU-based models. Also, stacked ensemble of shallow convolutional neural networks can be explored for Twitter data as shown by Mahata et al. (2018a).

References

Stefano Baccianella, Andrea Esuli, and Fabrizio Sebastiani. 2010. Sentiwordnet 3.0: an enhanced lexical resource for sentiment analysis and opinion mining. In *LREC*, volume 10, pages 2200–2204.

Pinkesh Badjatiya, Shashank Gupta, Manish Gupta, and Vasudeva Varma. 2017. Deep learning for hate speech detection in tweets. In *Proceedings of the 26th International Conference on World Wide Web Companion*, pages 759–760. International World Wide Web Conferences Steering Committee.

Kalika Bali, Jatin Sharma, Monojit Choudhury, and Yogarshi Vyas. 2014. ” i am borrowing ya mixing?” an analysis of english-hindi code mixing in facebook. In *Proceedings of the First Workshop on Computational Approaches to Code Switching*, pages 116–126.

Ruthanna Barnett, Eva Codó, Eva Eppler, Montse Forcadell, Penelope Gardner-Chloros, Roeland van Hout, Melissa Moyer, Maria Carme Torras, Maria Teresa Turell, Mark Sebba, et al. 2000. The lides coding manual: A document for preparing and analyzing language interaction data version 1.1–july 1999. *International Journal of Bilingualism*, 4(2):131–271.

Yoshua Bengio. 2012. Deep learning of representations for unsupervised and transfer learning. In *Proceedings of ICML Workshop on Unsupervised and Transfer Learning*, pages 17–36.

Hemant K Bhargava, Michael Bieber, and Steven O Kimbrough. 1988. Oona, max and the wywwywi principle: generalized hypertext and model management in a symbolic programming environment. In *ICIS*, page 23.

Tej K Bhatia and William C Ritchie. 2008. The bilingual mind and linguistic creativity. *Journal of Creative Communications*, 3(1):5–21.

Piotr Bojanowski, Edouard Grave, Armand Joulin, and Tomas Mikolov. 2016. Enriching word vectors with subword information. corr abs/1607.04606.

Thomas Davidson, Dana Warmsley, Michael Macy, and Ingmar Weber. 2017. Automated hate speech detection and the problem of offensive language. *arXiv preprint arXiv:1703.04009*.

Björn Gambäck and Utpal Kumar Sikdar. 2017. Using convolutional neural networks to classify hatespeech. In *Proceedings of the First Workshop on Abusive Language Online*, pages 85–90.

Fréderic Godin, Baptist Vandersmissen, Wesley De Neve, and Rik Van de Walle. 2015. Multimedia lab @ acl wnut ner shared task: Named entity recognition for twitter microposts using distributed word representations. In *Proceedings of the Workshop on Noisy User-generated Text*, pages 146–153.

Brian J Grim and Alan Cooperman. 2014. Religious hostilities reach six-year high. *Pew Research Center, January*, 14.

Gualberto Guzmán, Joseph Ricard, Jacqueline Serigos, Barbara E Bullock, and Almeida Jacqueline Toribio. 2017. Metrics for modeling code-switching across corpora. *Proc. Interspeech 2017*, pages 67–71.

Timothy Jay and Kristin Janschewitz. 2008. The pragmatics of swearing. *Journal of Politeness Research. Language, Behaviour, Culture*, 4(2):267–288.

Aditya Joshi, Ameya Prabhu, Manish Shrivastava, and Vasudeva Varma. 2016. Towards sub-word level compositions for sentiment analysis of hindi-english code mixed text. In *Proceedings of COLING 2016, the 26th International Conference on Computational Linguistics: Technical Papers*, pages 2482–2491.

Mitesh M Khapra, Ananthakrishnan Ramanathan, Anoop Kunchukuttan, Karthik Visweswariah, and Pushpak Bhattacharyya. 2014. When transliteration met crowdsourcing: An empirical study of transliteration via crowdsourcing using efficient, non-redundant and fair quality control. In *LREC*, pages 196–202.

Diederik P Kingma and Jimmy Ba. 2014. Adam: A method for stochastic optimization. *arXiv preprint arXiv:1412.6980*.

Laurens van der Maaten and Geoffrey Hinton. 2008. Visualizing data using t-sne. *Journal of machine learning research*, 9(Nov):2579–2605.

Debanjan Mahata, Jasper Friedrichs, Rajiv Ratn Shah, and Jing Jiang. 2018a. Did you take the pill?-detecting personal intake of medicine from twitter. *arXiv preprint arXiv:1808.02082*.

Debanjan Mahata, Jasper Friedrichs, Rajiv Ratn Shah, et al. 2018b. # phramacovigilance-exploring deep learning techniques for identifying mentions of medication intake from twitter. *arXiv preprint arXiv:1805.06375*.

Puneet Mathur, Meghna Ayyar, Sahil Chopra, Simra Shahid, Laiba Mehnaz, and Rajiv Shah. 2018a. Identification of emergency blood donation request on twitter. In *Proceedings of the Third Workshop On Social Media Mining for Health Applications*.

Puneet Mathur, Rajiv Shah, Ramit Sawhney, and Debanjan Mahata. 2018b. Detecting offensive tweets in hindi-english code-switched language. In *Proceedings of the Sixth International Workshop on Natural Language Processing for Social Media*, pages 18–26.

Hamdy Mubarak, Kareem Darwish, and Walid Magdy. 2017. Abusive language detection on arabic social media. In *Proceedings of the First Workshop on Abusive Language Online*, pages 52–56.

Sinno Jialin Pan and Qiang Yang. 2010. A survey on transfer learning. *IEEE Transactions on knowledge and data engineering*, 22(10):1345–1359.

Weike Pan, Erheng Zhong, and Qiang Yang. 2012. Transfer learning for text mining. In *Mining Text Data*, pages 223–257. Springer.

Ji Ho Park and Pascale Fung. 2017. One-step and two-step classification for abusive language detection on twitter. *arXiv preprint arXiv:1706.01206*.

James W Pennebaker, Roger J Booth, and Martha E Francis. 2007. Liwc2007: Linguistic inquiry and word count. *Austin, Texas: liwc. net*.

Jeffrey Pennington, Richard Socher, and Christopher Manning. 2014. Glove: Global vectors for word representation. In *Proceedings of the 2014 conference on empirical methods in natural language processing (EMNLP)*, pages 1532–1543.

Kumar Ravi and Vadlamani Ravi. 2016. Sentiment classification of hinglish text. In *Recent Advances in Information Technology (RAIT), 2016 3rd International Conference on*, pages 641–645. IEEE.

Sahil Rizwan. 2016. This Reddit Thread On The Best Indian Gaalis Will Increase Your Vocabulary, If Nothing Else. `https://www.buzzfeed.com/sahilrizwan/speak-no-evil?utm_term=.kgPxblYyl#.suP6XO4VO`. [Online; accessed 19-May-2018].

Björn Ross, Michael Rist, Guillermo Carbonell, Benjamin Cabrera, Nils Kurowsky, and Michael Wojatzki. 2017. Measuring the reliability of hate speech annotations: The case of the european refugee crisis. *arXiv preprint arXiv:1701.08118*.

Koustav Rudra, Shruti Rijhwani, Rafiya Begum, Kalika Bali, Monojit Choudhury, and Niloy Ganguly. 2016. Understanding language preference for expression of opinion and sentiment: What do hindi-english speakers do on twitter? In *Proceedings of the 2016 Conference on Empirical Methods in Natural Language Processing*, pages 1131–1141.

Ramit Sawhney, Prachi Manchanda, Raj Singh, and Swati Aggarwal. 2018a. A computational approach to feature extraction for identification of suicidal ideation in tweets. In *Proceedings of ACL 2018, Student Research Workshop*, pages 91–98.

Ramit Sawhney, Puneet Mathur, and Ravi Shankar. 2018b. A firefly algorithm based wrapper-penalty feature selection method for cancer diagnosis. In *International Conference on Computational Science and Its Applications*, pages 438–449. Springer.

Ramit Sawhney, Ravi Shankar, and Roopal Jain. 2018c. A comparative study of transfer functions in binary evolutionary algorithms for single objective optimization. In *International Symposium on Distributed Computing and Artificial Intelligence*, pages 27–35. Springer.

Rajendra Singh. 1985. Grammatical constraints on code-mixing: evidence from hindi-english. *Canadian Journal of Linguistics/Revue canadienne de linguistique*, 30(1):33–45.

Quan-Hoang Vo, Huy-Tien Nguyen, Bac Le, and
Minh-Le Nguyen. 2017. Multi-channel lstm-cnn
model for vietnamese sentiment analysis. In *Knowledge and Systems Engineering (KSE), 2017 9th International Conference on*, pages 24–29. IEEE.

Decipherment for Adversarial Offensive Language Detection

Zhelun Wu, Nishant Kambhatla, Anoop Sarkar
School of Computing Science
Simon Fraser University
Burnaby, BC , Canada
{zhelunw,nkambhat,anoop}@sfu.ca

Abstract

Automated filters are commonly used by on-line services to stop users from sending age-inappropriate, bullying messages, or asking others to expose personal information. Previous work has focused on rules or classifiers to detect and filter offensive messages, but these are vulnerable to cleverly disguised plaintext and unseen expressions especially in an adversarial setting where the users can repeatedly try to bypass the filter. In this paper, we model the disguised messages as if they are produced by encrypting the original message using an invented cipher. We apply automatic decipherment techniques to decode the disguised malicious text, which can be then filtered using rules or classifiers. We provide experimental results on three different datasets and show that decipherment is an effective tool for this task.

1 Introduction

Under-aged social media users and users of chat rooms associated with software like video games are routinely exposed to offensive language including sexting, profanities, age-inappropriate languages, cyber-bullying, and requests for personal identifying information. A common approach is to have a filter to block such messages. Filters are either rule-based (Razavi et al., 2010) or machine learning classifiers (Yin et al., 2009; Warner and Hirschberg, 2012; Williams and Burnap, 2015). However, users wishing to bypass such filters can subtly transform messages in novel ways which can be hard to detect.

Since malicious users and spammers can change their attacks to avoid being filtered, an approach to offensive text detection that takes into account this adversarial relationship is what can deal with real-world abusive language detection better. Techniques like spelling correction have been used to correct misspelled words in user generated content (Kobus et al., 2008), but in an adversarial setting it is easy to defeat a spelling correction system trained on predictable errors. Context based normalization methods have been proposed to convert erroneous user generated text from social media to standard text (Choudhury et al., 2007; Schulz et al., 2016). We, however, treat this problem as follows: we model malicious users trying to bypass a filtering system as having invented a new cipher, and our goal is to decipher their encrypted messages back to plaintext. We use a large space of possible ciphers that could be invented by those seeking to bypass a filter.

This paper addresses the problem of finding and filtering offensive messages as a special case of decipherment. In decipherment, a message in *plaintext* (original text) is converted into *ciphertext* (encrypted text). Encryption disguises the content of the original *plaintext* to a *ciphertext* so that it cannot be filtered out or blocked. Decryption or decipherment is the process of recovering the *plaintext* from the *ciphertext*. We treat disguised inappropriate content as ciphertext, and the actual intended content as the plaintext. Then we apply decipherment to recover more recognizable plaintext from the ciphertext and apply filters on the plaintext. Conceivably these users may create very complex unbreakable ciphers which cannot be deciphered by our system, but in such cases the ciphers are likely to also be unreadable by other humans who are the intended audience. We do not see many examples of this in our real-world chat messages.

We use Expectation Maximization (Dempster et al., 1977) and Hidden Markov Models (HMM, Rabiner (1989)) for our unsupervised decipherment method (Knight et al., 2006). We use an efficient beam search decoding algorithm to decipher ciphertext into the most likely plaintext. We also compare against supervised noisy channel models

Proceedings of the Second Workshop on Abusive Language Online (ALW2), pages 149–159
Brussels, Belgium, October 31, 2018. ©2018 Association for Computational Linguistics

and a state-of-art spelling correction system (Aspell). We discover that our method is immune to many previously unobserved types of changes made by users to disguise the original message.

2 Decipherment for Offensive Language Detection

The goal of decipherment is to uncover the hidden plaintext sequence $p_1...p_n$, given a disguised ciphertext sequence $c_1...c_n$. We assume that all corrupted forms of offensive language are originally explicit plaintext encrypted using letter substitution, insertion, or deletion.

2.1 NULL Insertion

A user can hide plaintext by inserting additional letters, or making substitutions and deletions in the plaintext:

Offensive text :you are a B*n@n@ee

Intended Plaintext :you are a bunny

we lowercase the texts and substitute the special symbols and punctuation marks inside the words with NULL, and then map NULL to any letter or NULL. Thus, the corrupted word B*n@n@ee is changed to

b<NULL>n<NULL>n<NULL>ee

When dealing with insertion of symbols, we treat it as an injective decipherment problem and solve it by adding NULL symbols in the ciphertext so that the decipherment model could map candidate letters. We compare two methods: 1) Inserting the NULL in a random position of the corrupted offensive key words; 2) Using a character-level n-gram model to segment the ciphertext adapting the technique for unsupervised word segmentation Ando and Lee (2003) in order to find where to insert NULL symbols.

The character-level n-gram model is trained on an unsegmented corpus (spaces removed between words). At each position k, we determine whether to insert a NULL symbol or not by calculating an n-gram score using Eqns (1) and (2).

$$v_n(k) = \frac{1}{2(n-1)} \sum_{d \in \{L,R\}} \sum_{j=1}^{n-1} I_>(c(s_d^n), c(t_d^n))$$
$$(1)$$

$$v_N(k) = \frac{1}{N} \sum_{n \in N} v_n(k) \qquad (2)$$

where n is the n-gram order, and s are n-grams that straddle the potential NULL position k to the left L and right R and t are n-grams that are on either side of position k also on the left L and right R and $c()$ is the n-gram frequency. For a sequence A B C D W X Y Z, for $n = 4$ and position $k = 4$ between D and W, Eqn (1) for a particular n compares the frequency of the s type n-grams that straddle position $k = 4$ (so, in this case frequency of B C D W, C D W X, D W X Y against the frequency of the t type n-grams on either side: A B C D and W X Y Z. Eqn (2) then takes the average for each n-gram order (for n=1,2,3,4). The position k that has a score from Eqn (2) higher than a threshold value is chosen as the position for NULL insertion.

2.2 Decipherment Model

A decipherment model maximizes the probability of a substitution map that converts the ciphertext sequence c to plaintext sequence p (Eqn 3).

$$P(c) = \sum_e P(p) \cdot P(c \mid p) \qquad (3)$$

where $P(.)$ is a character-level language model of the plaintext source trained using a monolingual corpus. We model $P(c \mid p)$ as the emission probability of a Hidden Markov Model (Knight et al., 2006) with cipher characters c as observations and plaintext characters p as the hidden states of the HMM. We train this using unsupervised learning using the Forward-Backward algorithm (Rabiner, 1989).

We propose our own initialization algorithm (Algorithm 1), based on the assumption that the previous trained table can help us to reach better local optima with fewer iterations compared to uniform initialization with random perturbations.

With the learned posterior distribution and language model score we use beam search to obtain the best plaintext (Forney Jr, 1973; Nuhn et al., 2013). Beam search combines breadth-first search and child pruning reducing the search space for each partial hypothesis of the decipherment.

Algorithm 1 Initialization with previous trained table

1: Given a set of cipher text sentences with size of d, a plain text with vocabulary size v and plain text trigram model b
2: Randomly initialize the $s(c \mid e)$ substitution table and normalize
3: **for** $i = 1 \ldots d$ **do**
4:    preprocess the i-th cipher text sequence by removing repeated characters and lower case the text
5:    insert `NULL` based on techniques in Sec. 2.1
6:    **if** $i \neq 1$ **then**
7:       initialize $s(c \mid e)$ using the $(i-1)$th trained table $s(c \mid e)$
8:    apply Forward-Backward algorithm to learn parameters $s(c \mid e)$

---

3 Data

3.1 Wiktionary

We created an offensive language dataset from English Wiktionary data. We use Wiktionary labels for vulgar, derogatory, etc. and selected example sentences for words tagged with such labels. From the entire English Wiktionary data , using this method, we extracted 2298 offensive sentences and 152,770 non-offensive sentences. This data is organized as $\{$`key word : example sentence`$\}$ as in a dictionary. With the duplicates removed, for each `key word`, the corresponding sentences were split into a 3:1 ratio as training and testing data.

We used 1,532 sentences offensive training set data and sampled 1,532 non-offensive sentences as a balanced dataset for training an offensive sentence classifier. We split 716 offensive testing sentences into 4 parts in sequence. The first three parts we set as test sets A, B and C and the latter part as development set. Every set has 179 sentences. The three test sets are taken from the same larger corpus to measure the variance in performance of the decipherment powered classification technique.

The Wiktionary dataset is used to train our language model. The offensive sentences had fewer instances than the non-offensive counterparts. To offset any loss in information, the offensive sentences were duplicated until they were as many in number as the non-offensive sentences, resulting in a balanced training set of 155,251 tokens.

3.2 Other data

Language Model: For the character models we used a combination of Wiktionary and the European Parliament Proceedings Parallel Corpus 1996-2011 (Koehn, 2005). 100K English sentences were sampled from the German-English EuroParl Corpus to give us a 2.7M token English plaintext corpus.

Spelling Correction: We use the English Gigaword corpus (Graff et al., 2003) to train the language model for the noisy channel spelling correction module. The preprocessed corpus has 7.4M lowercase English word tokens. For spelling correction, the Linux system dictionary with 479,829 English words in lower case is used. We used 3,393,741 pairs of human disguised words and original plain text words from the rule-based filtering system to train the error model.

3.3 Real World Chat Messages

We obtained 4,713,970 unfiltered, unlabelled chat messages from a provider of filtering services for chat rooms aimed at under-aged users. The data was provided by *Two Hat Security* which provides human powered chat room monitoring and filtering. Two Hat combines artificial intelligence with human expertise to classify chat room discussions and images on a scale of risk, taking user profiles and context into account. We pre-processed the chat messages to produce a cleaner version of the original message using tokenization rules.

We used 4,700,000 chat messages provided to us by Two Hat Security as a training set to train a letter based language model. To build a more comprehensive language model, this language model was interpolated with the ones trained on Wiktionary and Europarl datasets.

We also collect a separate set of 500 plaintext chat messages flagged as offensive by the filtering system to use as a development set. For the test set, we sampled 500 chat messages from 265,626 chat messages which were identified as offensive using a rule-based filtering system that uses lists of offensive words. These messages were marked inoffensive and cleared for posting in an older version of the same rule-based filtering system (two years older). We use this data to evaluate our decipherment system: can we match the performance improvement of two years of rule development?

Over two years new rules were added to account for user behaviour of trying to bypass the rule-based filtering system. Can decipherment discover these patterns automatically?

4 Experimental Setup

4.1 Language Model

Character Language Model: We used the SRILM toolkit (Stolcke et al., 2002) to train a character language model (LM) from Wiktionary and Europarl data. We trained two LMs and interpolated them using a mixture model. The interpolation weights were tuned on the development set. We used `py-srilm-interpolator` (Kiso, 2012) for the mixture model.

Word Language Model: We trained a word trigram language model on English Gigaword data.

4.2 Encipherment

The sentences in the test set are encrypted using different techniques: the Caesar 1:1 substitution cipher, the Leet simple substitution cipher[1] and replacing the offensive keywords with real human-disguised versions of curse words obtained from the rule-based filtering system. This was done to mimic the way people disguise their messages online.

4.3 Decipherment

HMM: For the HMM based decipherment, we run 100 random restarts (Berg-Kirkpatrick and Klein, 2013), running the EM algorithm to convergence 100 times, to find the initialization that leads to the local optima with highest likelihood.

Spelling Correction: We use settings for the noisy channel model based spelling correction as stated in Norvig (2009): $p_{spell\_error} = 0.05$, and $\lambda = 1$. The maximum edit distance limit is set to 3, and the error model is trained on the real chat messages we collected. The error model trained on pairs of misspelled words and the correctly spelled English words from the Linux system dictionary.

4.4 Evaluation

We evaluate our approach in terms of the classifier accuracy and the risk level from the rule-based filtering system for the real chat messages. We are using a simple logistic regression classifer from the LibShortText toolkit (Yu et al., 2013) to train

a classifier to classifies offensive and normal sentences. After training the classifier, we classify the original test sentences without any encryption.

We do not use a very sophisticated classifier because the goal of classification here is not to correctly classify offensive messages, but rather, to measure how well the decipherment method can recover the original messages containing offensive text back from the encrypted messages. We compare the classification accuracy between the original and deciphered messages. If the classification accuracy gap between the original and deciphered messages is small, the decipherment approach can recover the original user-intended messages from encrypted messages.

Tuning: We have a set of 179 sentences as the development set which is used for tuning the classifier and other hyper-parameters. After tuning, we were able to achieve the highest classification accuracy of 86%.

5 Experiments and Results

On the test sets A, B and C (see Sec. 3.1), in both our experiments on Caesar ciphers and Leet code, we first measure the number of offensive instances that were correctly classified by our logistic regression classifier. Then, the same classifier is run on the encrypted versions of these messages. The first two columns in the Table 1 and Table ?? show the classification accuracy obtained in those settings.

In our experiments, we apply Spelling Correction and our Decipherment techniques on the encrypted messages separately and finally use our classifier to determine the number of offensive instances that were correctly classified in decrypted text. The objective here is to measure how well either of the techniques is able to recover the originally intended message from the encrypted version of the message, simulating a real online user's behaviour of disguising an offensive text to beat a rule-based filter. In other words, we aim at decreasing the gap between the classification accuracies on a test set and its encrypted form.

5.1 Decipherment of Caesar Ciphers

Caesar cipher is a simple substitution cipher in which each plaintext token is 'shifted' a certain number of places down the alphabet. We encrypted three test sets A, B, C with Caesar cipher encryption by shifting 3 letters to the right.

---

[1] https://en.wikipedia.org/wiki/Leet

Test Set	Original text	Caesar cipher encrypted text	Noisy Channel Spelling Correction	Deciphering per line	Deciphering whole set
A	86% (154/179)	4% (8/179)	28% (51/179)	55% (99/179)	86% (154/179)
B	86% (154/179)	3% (7/179)	22% (41/179)	51% (92/179)	86% (154/179)
C	84% (152/179)	5% (10/179)	22% (41/179)	58% (104/179)	84% (152/179)

Table 1: Classification Accuracy of Spelling Correction and Decipherment Results in Caesar Cipher Encrypted Text

After being encrypted with a Caesar cipher, all the letters in the original messages are replaced, making the text unreadable. Applying spelling correction on such text sequences is almost futile as the text does not contain lexically correct words. HMM based decipherment approach, however, is capable of handling such obfuscated text sequences by design. We apply both the methods on three separate test sets A,B and C that built from the Wiktionary dataset (see Sec. 3.1).

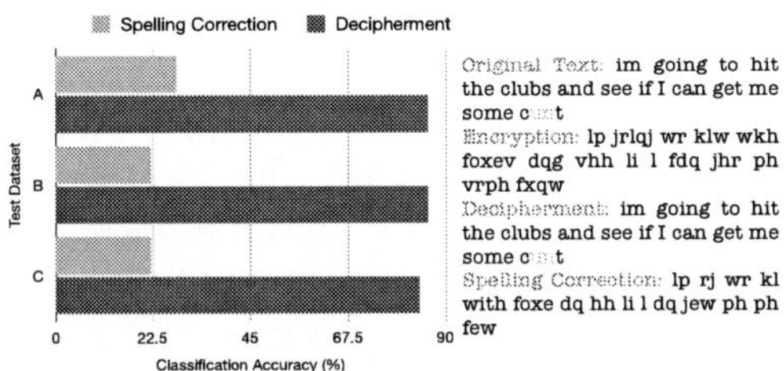

Figure 1: Decipherment vs. Spelling Correction approaches on Caesar cipher encrypted offensive messages. (Example from Test set A.)

The classification accuracies in Table 1 show that the HMM decipherment approach outperforms our other baselines.

With 100 random restarts on EM during the decipherment of the Caesar cipher encrypted dataset A, our system reports a mean loglikelihood of -27923 and a standard deviation of 23. The Figure 2 shows every loglikelihood value in 100 random restarts. As the Caesar cipher is relatively easy to decipher, the loglikelihood does not vary greatly. The highest loglikelihood yields a classification accuracy of 86% (154/179), which is the same as the original plain text classification accuracy. The decipherment process seems to recover the whole message that was encrypted by the Caesar cipher.

5.2 Decipherment of Leet Substitution

Leet is a quasi-encryption method which makes use of modified spellings and verbiage primarily used by the Internet community for many pho-

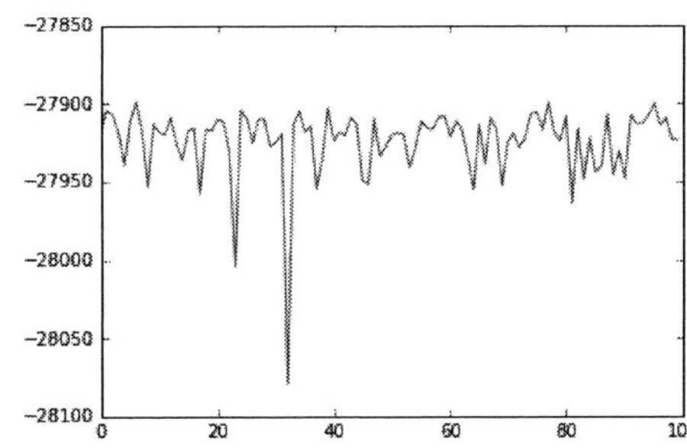

Figure 2: 100 Random Restarts Loglikelihood in Caesar Cipher Decipherment

netic languages. For the Leet substitution cipher, we referred to the KoreLogic's Leet rules (Kore Logic Security, 2012) which tagged as "#KoreLogicRulesL33t" . We used John the Ripper password cracker (Solar Designer and Community, 2013) to apply the KoreLogic Leet rules encrypting our test sets.

Encrypting a text with a Leet substitution does not change all the letters in the original messages. A spelling correction, therefore, performs better on such text sequences compared to the ones enciphered with a Caesar cipher. So the noisy channel spelling correction is able to recover the original form of some of the corrupted messages. HMM based decipherment approach, however, still manages to outperform spelling correction. For decipherment of Leet ciphers, we employ beam search to decode the final results having obtained the posterior probabilities from EM training. We apply both the methods on the test sets A,B and C.

Table 1 shows that the noisy channel spelling correction method is able to obtain an average classification accuracy of 65 out of the 179 encrypted messages. For HMM based decipherment techniques, however, we record higher accuracy, as before. With a beam width of 5, when applied to the whole set instead of a per-sentence basis, the resulting messages are flagged at an average of 82% across the three test sets. The *deciphered*

Test Set	Original Text	Leet Encryption Set	Noisy Channel Spelling Correction	Deciphering per line	Deciphering whole set
A	86% (154/179)	59% (107/179)	68% (122/179)	56% (102/179)	82% (147/179)
B	86% (154/179)	64% (115/179)	60% (108/179)	62% (112/179)	82% (148/179)
C	84% (152/179)	62% (112/179)	65% (117/179)	67% (121/179)	81% (146/179)

Table 2: Classification Accuracy of Spelling Correction and Decipherment Results in Leet Substitution Cipher with Beam Search Width of 5

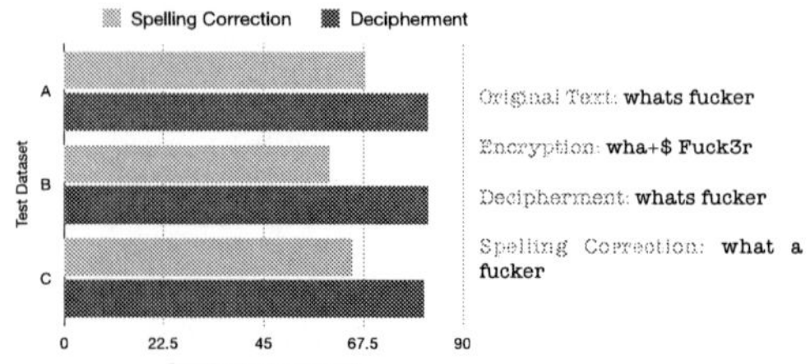

Figure 3: Decipherment vs. Spelling Correction approaches on Leet cipher encrypted offensive messages. (Example from Test set A.)

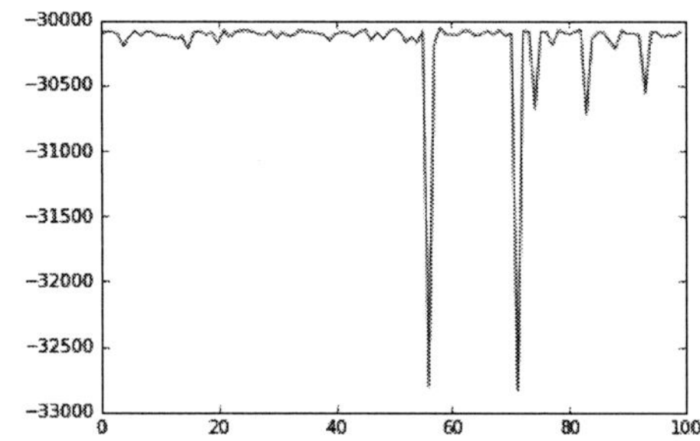

Figure 4: 100 Random Restarts Loglikelihood in Leet Substitution Cipher Decipherment

On performing 100 random restarts on EM during the decipherment of the Caesar cipher encrypted test dataset A, our system records an average loglikelihood of -30183 and a standard deviation of 390. Figure 4 shows every loglikelihood value in 100 random restarts. The high deviation in the loglikelihood shows that a Leet substitution is harder to solve than a Caesar cipher.

5.3 Decipherment of Real Chat Offensive Words Substitution Dataset

In each of the offensive test sets A, B and C, the offensive keywords in the messages are substituted with real human corrupted words obtained from real-word chat messages. These chats are transformed versions of these offensive words that are matched using a hand-written rule-based system. We used enciphered offensive words collected from real chat messages and the corresponding plain text for this task.

Original Text: hes really bitchy in the morning
Encryption: hes really bitchyou in the morning
Decipherment: hes really bitchy in the morning
Spelling Correction: hes really bitchy in the morning

Since this quasi-encryption is based on real chat messages, it closely mimics the inventive ways users employ to disguise their messages to bypass the filter system, which can involve both insertion and deletion.

It is then imperative that we handle insertion, deletion and substitution in the disguised words to recover the original plain text words. In the insertion case, for example, if the original word `hello` is disguised as `helo`, a NULL symbol is inserted inside the disguised word `helo` to decipher. The ideal position to insert the NULL symbol is `he<NULL>lo` but it is not known during training. To circumvent this, we experiment with two techniques: (1) to insert NULL at random before the beginning of the EM training, and (2) to insert the NULL using the method in Sec. 2.1.

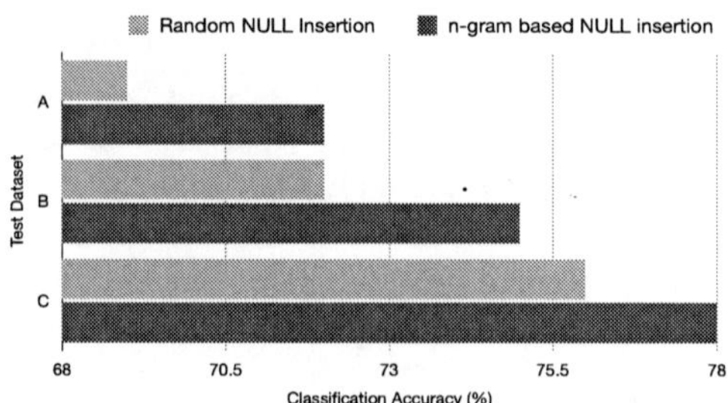

Figure 5: Random vs. n-gram count based NULL insertions.

This insertion techniques uses the word-

Test Set	Wiktionary Encrypted Set	Noisy Channel Spelling Correction	Aspell Spelling Correction	NULL Insertion	Decipherment
A	64% (116/179)	72% (130/179)	77% (138/179)	Random	69% (124/179)
				n-gram Count Based	72% (129/179)
B	72% (129/179)	76% (137/179)	73% (131/179)	Random	72% (130/179)
				n-gram Count Based	75% (136/179)
C	75% (136/179)	77% (138/179)	77% (138/179)	Random	76% (137/179)
				n-gram Count Based	78% (140/179)

Table 3: Classification Accuracy of Spelling Correction and Decipherment Results in Real Chat Offensive Words Substitution Wiktionary Dataset

level language model 4.1 to learn the n-gram counts.From Table 3 and Figure 7, the n-gram count based insertion decipherment has a higher classification accuracy than the random insertion NULL decipherment. An advantage of this type of HMM decipherment method is that it tends to not change the words that are already correct since these words have the highest language model score. Rather, it changes the words that are corrupted or misspelled. Irrespective of the type of encryption, the HMM decipherment approach always deciphers the messages which fit with the language model we trained.

We conducted an additional experiment to test with the Aspell program. Table 3 shows that deciphered messages obtain better accuracies than Aspell on test sets B and C while on test set A, it is about 5% less accurate. Note that the noisy channel model was trained on data obtained from a hand-tuned filtering system that was domain specific and created specifically for these chat messages. What we find in our results is that the decipherment system can match this domain expertise using unsupervised learning without any domain specific knowledge.

Figure 6 shows every loglikelihood value in 100 random restarts on test-set B. The mean of loglikelihood is -41444.7 and the standard deviation was 115.53. The greater diversity among the real chat offensive words renders the decipherment much harder than controlled synthetic-scenarios.

5.4 Decipherment of Real Offensive Chat Messages

We use two versions of a rule-based offensive language filtering system to evaluate our decipherment approach. The first version of the filter sys-

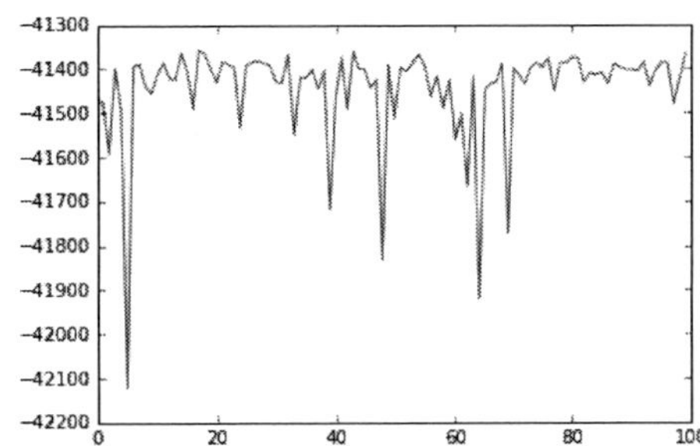

Figure 6: 100 Random Restarts Loglikelihood in Decipherment of Real Chat Offensive Words Substitution on Test Set B

tem was two years old and the second version of the filter system has benefited from daily updates from humans monitoring the chat room. The question we want to ask in this evaluation is if our decipherment system can replicate the human effort of two years of rule development in this filtering system.

We use a test set of 500 offensive messages sampled from the set of chat room messages which were *not* flagged as offensive by the first (older) version of the filter system but which *were* flagged as offensive by the second version of the filter system. This allows us to evaluate how many of those offensive messages can be identified using decipherment.

Before deciphering these messages, we preprocessed the text to remove repeated characters such that only two sequential repeated characters remain. For example, the text `heeeellllooo` is preprocessed to `heelloo`. Further, all the special symbols were replaced with `<NULL>`.

The preprocessed test-set is then deciphered with the HMM based decipherment technique. The deciphered messages are then passed back into the first version of the filtering system. This lets us check if deciphering the user-disguised message into a simpler plaintext message allows the two year old filter to catch it as offensive. The above example shows that decipherment can handle substitutions and insertions.

The two year old rule-based filter was able to successfully flag **51.6%** of the deciphered messages as offensive text. Thus, the decipherment approach is able to transform about half of the corrupted messages into a readable form so that the filter system without the benefit of two years of development can recognize them as offensive. This shows that decipherment can lead to much faster development of filtering systems for offensive language.

6 Discussion

We observe that HMM decipherment trained on the whole set is particularly able to recover most encrypted letters (cipher text) into their original letters (plain text). When we decipher each line

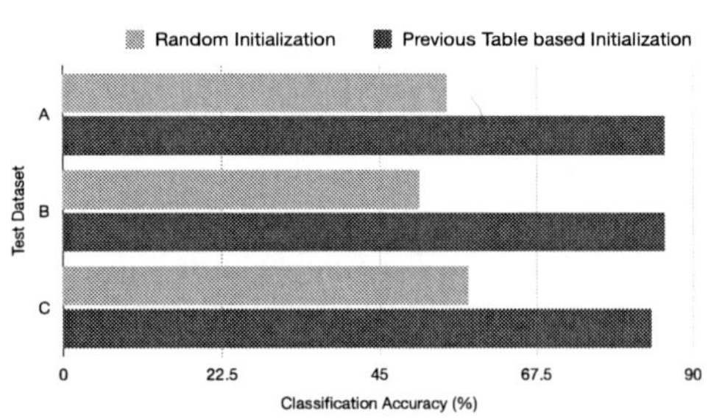

Figure 7: Decipherment per line vs on whole set.

of messages individually, the EM training does not observe enough data to learn the posterior probabilities. In contrast, the substitution table trained by previous messages being passed into next message initialization table will not lose the information learned from the previous messages. Therefore, the results of whole set decipherment are better than per line decipherment.

As Tables (1 2, 3) show, HMM decipherment training can recover most of the words in our test sets compared to the original message classification accuracy of each set. From the results shown in Table 1 and Table 2, no matter what encryption of substitution cipher was used, be it Caesar cipher or Leet substitution cipher, the HMM decipherment with language model could always recover the original messages.

7 Related Work

For detecting offensive languages, rule-based filtering systems and machine learning techniques are widely used. Razavi et al. (2010) leveraged a variety of statistical models and rule-based patterns and applied multi-level classification for flame detection. Chen et al. (2012) introduced a Lexical Syntactic Feature (LSF) architecture to detect offensive content and identify potential offensive users in social media. Kansara and Shekokar (2015) proposed a framework that detects bullying texts and images in using feature extraction and classifiers. Djuric et al. (2015) leveraged word embedding representations (Mikolov et al., 2013) to improve machine learning based classifiers. Nobata et al. (2016) unified predefined linguistic elements and word embeddings to train a regression model. Su et al. (2017) presented a system to detect and rephrase profane words written in Chinese. samghabadi2017detecting

Recently, deep learning methods have been employed for abusive language detection. Zhang et al. (2018) presented an algorithm for detecting hate speech using a combination of Convolutional Neural Networks (CNN) and Gated Recurrent Unit (GRU). Gambäck and Sikdar (2017) used four CNNs to classify tweets to one of four predefined categories. Park and Fung (2017) adopted a two-step approach with two classifiers. The first step performs classification on abusive language and the second step classifies a text into types of sexist and racist abusive language given that the language is abusive. Three CNN-based models have been used for classification: Char-CNN, WordCNN and HybridCNN. Badjatiya et al. (2017) used an LSTM model with features extracted by character n-grams for hate speech detection. As malicious users can change their ways of transforming text to avoid being filtered, an approach such as ours which takes into account the adversarial relationship between the chat room user and the offensive language filter is likely to perform better at filtering.

Previous work on decipherment are often based on noisy-channel frameworks. Knight and Yamada (1999) proposed to use EM algorithm to estimate the mapping distribution over the sound to characters, then generated the plaintext using Viterbi algorithm (Forney Jr, 1973). The learning objective is to maximize the probability of the mapping ciphertext phoneme-tokens to plaintext characters. Further, Knight et al. (2006) studied using EM for unsupervised learning of the substitution maps for 1:1 letter substitution ciphers. Ravi and Knight (2011) proposed to regard foreign language as ciphertext and English as plaintext, converting a translation problem into one of word substitution decipherment. They employed iterative EM approach and a Bayesian learning approach to build the translation mechanism using monolingual data.

We use the EM based decipherment technique to convert user-disguised offensive text into a filter-recognizable plaintext.

8 Conclusion

The HMM decipherment can decipher disguised text based on the language model regardless of the encryption type. The decipherment approach we proposed can cover more disguised cases than spelling correction methods. However, due to the limitation of edit distance and lack of traning data, the noisy channel spelling correction has its limitations and cannot handle high edit distance case. Large edit distances are common in real chat messages, and thus the decipherment approach has its advantages. The difference between the decipherment with traditional spelling correction methods like Aspell is that decipherment method only needs a language model to decipher cipher text, and does not need a dictionary to refer to. The language model has the advantage that we can train a domain specific language model to decipher specific topic messages as real chat messages usually have some sort of topics or domain, such as sports, news and so on. The future work is that we can try different language messages to decipher, as long as we can have the corresponding language model.

Acknowledgments

We would like to thank the anonymous reviewers for their helpful remarks. The research was also partially supported by the Natural Sciences and Engineering Research Council of Canada grants NSERC RGPIN-2018-06437 and RGPAS-2018-522574 and a Department of National Defence (DND) and NSERC grant DGDND-2018-00025 to the third author. We would also like to thank Ken Dwyer and Michael Harris from the Two Hat Security Company who collected and organized the real-world chat data for us. Thanks also to the Two Hat CEO, Chris Priebe, who supported this research and also provided an internship to the first author where he worked on spelling correction for chats.

References

Rie Kubota Ando and Lillian Lee. 2003. Mostly-unsupervised statistical segmentation of japanese kanji sequences. *Natural Language Engineering*, 9(2):127–149.

Pinkesh Badjatiya, Shashank Gupta, Manish Gupta, and Vasudeva Varma. 2017. Deep learning for hate speech detection in tweets. In *Proceedings of the 26th International Conference on World Wide Web Companion*, pages 759–760. International World Wide Web Conferences Steering Committee.

Taylor Berg-Kirkpatrick and Dan Klein. 2013. Decipherment with a million random restarts. In *EMNLP*, pages 874–878.

Ying Chen, Yilu Zhou, Sencun Zhu, and Heng Xu. 2012. Detecting offensive language in social media to protect adolescent online safety. In *Privacy, Security, Risk and Trust (PASSAT), 2012 International Conference on and 2012 International Confernece on Social Computing (SocialCom)*, pages 71–80. IEEE.

Monojit Choudhury, Rahul Saraf, Vijit Jain, Animesh Mukherjee, Sudeshna Sarkar, and Anupam Basu. 2007. Investigation and modeling of the structure of texting language. *International Journal of Document Analysis and Recognition (IJDAR)*, 10(3-4):157–174.

Arthur P Dempster, Nan M Laird, and Donald B Rubin. 1977. *Maximum likelihood from incomplete data via the EM algorithm*. Journal of the royal statistical society. Series B (methodological), page 1-38.

Nemanja Djuric, Jing Zhou, Robin Morris, Mihajlo Grbovic, Vladan Radosavljevic, and Narayan Bhamidipati. 2015. Hate speech detection with comment embeddings. In *Proceedings of the 24th international conference on world wide web*, pages 29–30. ACM.

G David Forney Jr. 1973. The viterbi algorithm. *Proceedings of the IEEE*, 61(3):268–278.

Björn Gambäck and Utpal Kumar Sikdar. 2017. Using convolutional neural networks to classify hate-speech. In *Proceedings of the First Workshop on Abusive Language Online*, pages 85–90.

David Graff, Junbo Kong, Ke Chen, and Kazuaki Maeda. 2003. English gigaword. *Linguistic Data Consortium, Philadelphia*.

Krishna B Kansara and Narendra M Shekokar. 2015. A framework for cyberbullying detection in social network. *International Journal of Current Engineering and Technology*, 5.

Tetsuo Kiso. 2012. A python wrapper for determining interpolation weights with srilm. https://github.com/tetsuok/py-srilm-interpolator.

Kevin Knight, Anish Nair, Nishit Rathod, and Kenji Yamada. 2006. Unsupervised analysis for decipherment problems. In *Proceedings of the COLING/ACL on Main conference poster sessions*, pages 499–506. Association for Computational Linguistics.

Kevin Knight and Kenji Yamada. 1999. A computational approach to deciphering unknown scripts. In *ACL Workshop on Unsupervised Learning in Natural Language Processing*, pages 37–44. 1.

Catherine Kobus, François Yvon, and Géraldine Damnati. 2008. Normalizing sms: are two metaphors better than one? In *Proceedings of the 22nd International Conference on Computational Linguistics-Volume 1*, pages 441–448. Association for Computational Linguistics.

Philipp Koehn. 2005. Europarl: A parallel corpus for statistical machine translation. In *MT summit*, volume 5, pages 79–86.

Kore Logic Security. 2012. Kore logic custom rules. http://contest-2010.korelogic.com/rules.txt.

Tomas Mikolov, Ilya Sutskever, Kai Chen, Greg S Corrado, and Jeff Dean. 2013. Distributed representations of words and phrases and their compositionality. In *Advances in neural information processing systems*, pages 3111–3119.

Chikashi Nobata, Joel Tetreault, Achint Thomas, Yashar Mehdad, and Yi Chang. 2016. Abusive language detection in online user content. In *Proceedings of the 25th international conference on world wide web*, pages 145–153. International World Wide Web Conferences Steering Committee.

Peter Norvig. 2009. Natural language corpus data. *Beautiful Data*, pages 219–242.

Malte Nuhn, Julian Schamper, and Hermann Ney. 2013. Beam search for solving substitution ciphers. In *Citeseer*.

Ji Ho Park and Pascale Fung. 2017. One-step and two-step classification for abusive language detection on twitter. In *Proceedings of the First Workshop on Abusive Language Online*, pages 41–45.

Lawrence R Rabiner. 1989. A tutorial on hidden markov models and selected applications in speech recognition. *Proceedings of the IEEE*, 77(2):257–286.

Sujith Ravi and Kevin Knight. 2011. Deciphering foreign language. In *Proceedings of the 49th Annual Meeting of the Association for Computational Linguistics: Human Language Technologies-Volume 1*, pages 12–21. Association for Computational Linguistics.

Amir H Razavi, Diana Inkpen, Sasha Uritsky, and Stan Matwin. 2010. Offensive language detection using multi-level classification. In *Canadian Conference on Artificial Intelligence*, pages 16–27. Springer.

Sarah Schulz, Guy De Pauw, Orphée De Clercq, Bart Desmet, Veronique Hoste, Walter Daelemans, and Lieve Macken. 2016. Multimodular text normalization of dutch user-generated content. *ACM Transactions on Intelligent Systems and Technology (TIST)*, 7(4):61.

Solar Designer and Community. 2013. John the ripper password cracker. http://www.openwall.com/john.

Andreas Stolcke et al. 2002. Srilm-an extensible language modeling toolkit. In *Interspeech*.

Hui-Po Su, Zhen-Jie Huang, Hao-Tsung Chang, and Chuan-Jie Lin. 2017. Rephrasing profanity in chinese text. In *Proceedings of the First Workshop on Abusive Language Online*, pages 18–24.

William Warner and Julia Hirschberg. 2012. Detecting hate speech on the world wide web. In *Proceedings of the Second Workshop on Language in Social Media*, pages 19–26. Association for Computational Linguistics.

Matthew L Williams and Pete Burnap. 2015. Cyberhate on social media in the aftermath of woolwich: A case study in computational criminology and big data. *British Journal of Criminology*, 56(2):211–238.

Dawei Yin, Zhenzhen Xue, Liangjie Hong, Brian D Davison, April Kontostathis, and Lynne Edwards. 2009. Detection of harassment on web 2.0. In *Proceedings of the Content Analysis in the WEBb*, pages 1–7.

H Yu, C Ho, Y Juan, and C Lin. 2013. Libshorttext: A library for short-text classification and analysis. Technical report, University of Texas at Austin and National Taiwan University.

Ziqi Zhang, David Robinson, and Jonathan Tepper. 2018. Detecting hate speech on twitter using a convolution-gru based deep neural network. In *European Semantic Web Conference*, pages 745–760. Springer.

The Linguistic Ideologies of Deep Abusive Language Classification

Michael Castelle
Centre for Interdisciplinary Methodologies
University of Warwick
`M.Castelle.1@warwick.ac.uk`

Abstract

This paper brings together theories from sociolinguistics and linguistic anthropology to critically evaluate the so-called "language ideologies"—the set of beliefs and ways of speaking about language—in the practices of abusive language classification in modern machine learning-based NLP. This argument is made at both a conceptual and empirical level, as we review approaches to abusive language from different fields, and use two neural network methods to analyze three datasets developed for abusive language classification tasks (drawn from Wikipedia, Facebook, and Stack-Overflow). By evaluating and comparing these results, we argue for the importance of incorporating theories of pragmatics and metapragmatics into both the design of classification tasks as well as in ML architectures.

1 Introduction

Some problems lend themselves more easily to A.I. solutions than others. So, hate speech is one of the hardest, because determining if something is hate speech is very linguistically nuanced. Right?... I'm optimistic that over a five- to 10-year period, we will have A.I. tools that can get into some of the nuances, the linguistic nuances of different types of content to be more accurate in flagging things for our systems.

(Excerpt from testimony to the U.S. Senate and Judiciary and Commerce, Science and Transportation Committees by Mark Zuckerberg, April 10th, 2018)

The term *nuance*, as used in the above quote from Mark Zuckerberg's testimony to the U.S. Senate, appears to imply that, like the successes of convolutional neural networks in computer vision, the classification (or "flagging") of (textual) hate speech should be considered a matter of advanced pattern recognition, of recognizing the right 'shade' or 'color' of a given sentence in isolation. This view of linguistic action is in contrast with a tradition of speech-act theory (Austin, 1962; Searle, 1969) in which the meaning of an utterance is not solely determined by lexical or syntactic structure but by its *social context* and *performative effects*. In studies of hate speech following these latter perspectives, such as those of Butler (1997), words are seen not just as arbitrary lexemes but something capable of actively causing violence to one or more addressees.

Butler, in her account of hate speech, optimistically saw a 'gap' between a speech act and its effects (Butler, 1997)—comparable to Austin's distinction between the *illocutionary* (the addressee's intention) and *perlocutionary* (the outcome of the utterance)—which she uses to argue against legal regulation of hate speech and instead for the possibility of 'restaging' and 'resignifying' such speech on the part of the addressee. Schwartzman (2002), however, contended that Butler's account was fundamentally missing an awareness of existing social structures of power, and that if any successful 'resignification' (as in the "taking back" of slurs) occurs it is due to an active and political response against oppression.

The question remains: is detecting hate speech a matter of sufficiently advanced pattern recognition a matter of building the right distributed architecture on a large enough data set of "hateful" vs. "non-hateful" expressions? Or is it necessary for any such automated classification to be integrated with long-term ethnographic and contextual immersion in the communities, however problematic, in which said expressions emerge (Sinders and Martinez, 2018)? To what extent should

Proceedings of the Second Workshop on Abusive Language Online (ALW2), pages 160–170
Brussels, Belgium, October 31, 2018. ©2018 Association for Computational Linguistics

we expect researchers to attempt to integrate the sociocultural complexities of contemporary online communication into their "A.I. tools", and to what extent should we expect success or failure from those tools?

This article assesses the current potential for, and limitations of, machine learning methodologies—both in terms of how the 'gold standard' datasets are normally constructed and how neural networks are applied—for abusive language detection in natural language text. We will, through our own experiments, explore the specific conflicts between the research culture of achieving "state-of-the-art" scores (Manning, 2015) with (relatively) black-boxed architectures and theories of the pragmatics (and metapragmatics) of linguistic abuse in practice.

2 The Language Ideologies of NLP

With its 1950s intellectual origins in a) naïve, word-by-word machine translation and b) Chomsky's conception of language as generated by a machinic automata, the field of natural language processing (NLP) inherited what we refer to as a *language ideology* (Woolard and Schieffelin, 1994), a set of beliefs and ways of speaking about 'language'.[1] Fundamental to the Chomskyan language ideology, for example, is the purported existence of an innate language faculty which is held to explain the purported lack of training data for humans (the so-called "poverty of the stimulus") (Pereira, 2000). This faculty is conceived as the locus of a *generative grammar* which can in theory enumerate all possible valid sentences.

Other disciplines of human communication, however, developed alternative perspectives which embed language in a more complex sociocultural environment. The field of *sociolinguistics* (Labov, 1972) considered quantitative measurements of language variation (such as dialects and creoles) not as a matter of syntactic validity but as intrinsically related to social differentiation and class structure; and *linguistic anthropology* (Duranti, 1997) simultaneously drew from the semiotic and structuralist traditions of Peirce and Jakobson, emphasizing acts of reflexive, sociocultural en-

textualization and contextualization (Bauman and Briggs, 1990) inherent to any communicative situation.

From the perspective of these latter fields, the study of 'natural language' by computer scientists (so named to distinguish itself from formal logic and 'artificial' programming languages devised in early AI research) would be seen as largely focused on *entextualized* utterances (such as written sentences or recorded speech) and the uncovering (or 'processing') of their hidden symbolic patterns and structures. The introduction of *statistical* approaches to NLP (Charniak, 1996) laid the groundwork for the eventual incorporation of a machine learning methodology which uses of a *corpus* of data composed of training inputs with labeled outputs. Today's neural network models in NLP are strongly dependent on this arguably *behaviorist* (i.e. stimulus-response) ideology of language, one in which syntax and semantics can be durably encoded through the presentation and re-presentation of vectorized 'stimuli' (which, through backpropagation, modifies the model's parameters based on the distance of the 'response' vector from the true values).

The study of abusive language in NLP, then, represents a profitable collision between two potentially compatible language ideologies — one a "statistical NLP" ideology which claims the potential to efficiently and intelligently discretize and classify the contextually dense and multimodal miasma of real-time communication; and the other, to be described in the next section, which seeks to carve out and eliminate impurities and danger (e.g., abusive language) in search of a 'safe', non-'toxic', and yet highly scalable environment.

3 Abusive Language Ideologies

So, if *language ideologies* are a set of beliefs and ways of speaking about 'language', then *abusive language ideologies* are a set of beliefs and ways of speaking about what it means for 'language' to be 'abusive'. As a review of the literature on this topic immediately indicates, there are a variety of theories regarding the nature of hate speech, abusive language, cyberbullying, etc.; in this section we will characterize the main positions, especially in their potential relation to NLP methodologies.

---

[1]The term 'ideology' as it used here is not intended as a pejorative; following Woolard (1998), we see ideology as "derived from, rooted in, reflective of, or responsive to the experience or interests of a particular social position" but not necessarily "in the service of the struggle to acquire or maintain power" (although it may also be that.)

3.1 Politeness

The study of online antagonism was preceded by much research in the linguistic field of pragmatics on *politeness* such as Brown and Levinson (1987), who isolated the concept of politeness as a set of interactional strategies to preserve 'face', a concept from Goffman (1967) reflecting the ideal self-image of the addresser or addressee in each communicative situation. This approach took into account the four cooperative 'maxims' of Grice (1975), which are implicit interactional norms in which speakers strive to be informative, unambiguous, brief, and orderly—norms which, we suggest, are potentially relevant to understanding online Q&A platforms like StackOverflow. Culpeper (1996) showed how a focus on *impoliteness* brought the importance of interactional context to the fore, in contrast to a focus on surface form in the work of Brown and Levinson; but later work on gender difference and politeness argued that impoliteness itself is only something classified as such by those in dominant positions of power (Mills, 2003). The linguistic study of politeness thus helpfully charts a development from the study of lexical and syntactic structure to interactional pragmatics to considerations of power relations within and among communities of practice.

3.2 Hate Speech

The concept of hate speech (and the debates surrounding its definition, legal and otherwise) is itself predicated on precisely a (conscious or unconscious) philosophical dispute about whether language can be segregated from action; the "fighting words" doctrine in U.S. law (Chaplinsky vs. New Hampshire, 1942), for example, was a legal intervention that (in a single instance) outlawed speech acts capable of provoking violent action (i.e. based on their perlocutionary force). From such an Austinian perspective, to be a free speech absolutist is to consider speech merely as locution and not illocution or perlocution (Hornsby and Langton, 1998); NLP methodology, which typically takes as input a set of text-artifacts segregated from their original communicative situation and consequences, could also be said to (implicitly) take this position of considering speech solely as locution (even if researchers commonly appreciate that their data was drawn from a past existence in richer contexts). For example, the work of Warner

and Hirschberg (2012) acknowledges the limits of their decontextualized comment dataset, but argues that hate speech can still be distinguished through the recognition of stereotyped expressions about social groups.

The most comprehensive philosophical attempt to give meaning to the concept of hate speech is by Alexander Brown. In his two recent articles (Brown (2017a), Brown (2017b)), he explains that the term 'hate speech' likely emerged from a 1988 conference paper at Hofstra (Matsuda, 1989), and came to take on significant value for legal scholars before becoming integrated into a more popular discourse. Matsuda's intervention represents a *performative ideology* of language; if words are action, and some words are violent action, then hate speech can be regulated without violating a constitutional free speech principle. However, Brown comes to a somewhat negative conclusion regarding the possibility of coming to a coherent universal definition of the concept of hate speech; while it can be summarized as "a rough but nevertheless serviceable term to describe... the expressive dimensions of identity-based envy, hostility, conflict, mistrust and oppression", more fine-grained enclosures are never sufficient, and he argues that the meaning of 'hate speech' is closer to the 'family resemblances' concept of Wittgenstein (1953), who argues that terms like 'game' (and—implicitly—'language') can only denote an ever-shifting family of related practices irreducable to a precise definition.

It is thereby unsurprising that NLP's methodological detachment from the speech situation (itself embedded in other sociocultural contexts which do not become part of the training data), along with the fundamental indeterminacy of the 'hate speech' category, makes the reliability of 'coding' for hate speech a significant challenge (Ross et al., 2017). In their survey of hate speech detection in NLP, Schmidt and Wiegand (2017) mention this time-consuming dependency on hand-labeled data; but they also point out the many strategic ways that NLP researchers have proposed (if not always attempted) to overcome the decontextualized limitations and problems of definition of their data, and we will report similar findings below.

3.3 Abusive Language

Despite his critical conclusions, Brown argues that the term 'hate speech' is still, for now, effective; it "is used because it is useful, and it will remain useful so long as it can be used to do more than merely signal disapproval. If [that was] all it did... [it] would soon fall out of fashion or be replaced by newer, cooler bits of language that did the same thing but in more interesting ways" (Brown, 2017a). One such current variant term is *abusive language*, which appears in some of the earliest literature on antagonistic Internet communication (Spertus, 1997) but has in the past years taken on a greater prominence.

In part, the potentially milder connotations of the 'abusive language' term reflects a shifting from seeing online abuse as occurring on behalf of identity-based communities to occurring towards social groups in general, where those social groups might be something like "new users of StackOverflow". So for example, Nobata et al. (2016) uses the concept of abusive language to include hate speech, derogatory language, and profanity together. In their work on personal attacks in Wikipedia talk pages, Wulczyn et al. (2016) adopts the rhetoric of 'toxic' behavior, a term which metaphorically transposes affective concepts (such as *hate*) to one of environmental contamination and taboo (Douglas, 1966; Nagle, 2009); this represents a subtle move away from an otherwise dominant *personalist ideology* in which meaning emerges from the beliefs or intentions of the speaker (Hill, 2008).

Recognizing the overall lack of consensus on the boundaries of abusive language, Waseem et al. (2017) proposes a twofold typology: (1) whether language is "directed towards a specific individual or entity" or "directed towards a generalized group" and (2) whether the content is 'explicit' or 'implicit'. The resulting four axes, then, are each analyzed for the methodological approaches needed. *Directed* abuse can be detected with attention to proper nouns and entities like usernames; *Generalized* abuse may be associated with lexical patterns based on the targeted groups; *Explicit* abuse also often involves specific keywords and *Implicit* abuse the most difficult category, where more advanced semantic approaches such as word embeddings can fail in a complex polysemous and creative environment.

The view that indirectness and implicitness in text-artifacts can be eventually 'captured' by machine learning models is related to the performative ideology of speech-act theory, which has been criticized for its overemphasis on so-called *explicit* performatives (such as "I now pronounce you man and wife") over (far more common) implicit performative utterances which depend on contextual cues (Gumperz, 1982; Lempert, 2012). As Asif Agha puts it, "an indirect speech act is just a name for the way in which a denotational text diagrams an interactional text without describing it" (Agha, 2007, p. 100). This diagramming instead often happens through forms of pragmatic and metapragmatic *reflexivity* which may be difficult to recognize through analyzing the utterance detached from its interactional context, as is often the case for NLP datasets.

That researchers see indirect and implicit speech as a significant challenge, however, is in part due to our methodological embeddedness in a *referentialist ideology* which typically holds that the meaning of words are stable (as realized, for example, by static embedding vectors), and that the purpose of language is to communicate information. Jane Hill explains how the combination of referentialist and performative ideologies typifies conventional approaches to racism:

> Stereotypes and slurs are visible as racist to most people because they are made salient by referentialist and performative linguistic ideologies respectively. But other kinds of talk and text that are not visible, so called covert racist discourse, may be just as important in reproducing the culturally shared ideas that underpin racism. Indeed, they may be even more important, because they do their work while passing unnoticed. (Hill, 2008)

We argue that it will be essential for NLP researchers to recognize how our tools and techniques may, in part, be material embodiments of these ideologies, but also how one might partially escape those ideologies without abandoning the use of tools and techniques entirely. One positive example of this is from Saleem et al. (2017), which argues that supervised labeling based on keywords is problematic, but also that one can improve performance by training on language from specific *speech communities* (Gumperz, 1968).

In the second part of this paper, we apply basic deep NLP methods to building predictive models for abusive language on three different datasets. Through qualitative reflection on the data, training process, and results, we articulate the specific limitations of common methods, as well as the future directions, of deep learning methodology for addressing concerns about abusive language.

4   Experiments

The nascent research cluster around NLP and abusive language constitutes not just a 'speech community' but a *language community*, i.e., "an organization of people by their orientation to structural (formal) norms for denotational coding (whether explicit or implicit)" (Silverstein, 1996). The combination of linguistic ideologies described above is fully realized in the conventional experimental architecture of the *shared task*, in which multiple teams of researchers independently attempt to build systems with good classificatory performance by determining the true denotational meaning of utterances which, most commonly, have been excised from their interactional context.

For example, the tasks addressing abusive language typically have as their goal the determination of whether stand-alone utterances should be considered rude, offensive, or abusive. Training data is provided in the form of utterance-label pairs, where the label may be a binary value (i.e. abusive or not) or multi-class (for different categorical and/or ordinal levels of offensiveness). In order to explore these kinds of tasks directly, in this paper we chose to experiment with 3 datasets: the Kaggle Toxic Comment Classification Challenge[2], the shared task in the 1st Workshop on Trolling, Aggression and Cyberbullying (TRAC1)[3], and the StackOverflow dataset from the 2nd EMNLP Abusive Language Workshop.[4]

4.1   Data Description

The Kaggle Toxic Comment Classification dataset provides decontextualized Wikipedia "talk page" comments, each paired with multi-class labels on toxic behavior, judged by human raters; we emphasize that the dataset is *decontextualized* to indicate that additional information about each dis-

cursive interaction is not provided (but for a depiction of the organizational structure of their production, one may consult Geiger (2017)'s "ethnography of infrastructure" of Wikipedia). The labels of toxicity include 'toxic', 'severe toxic', 'obscene', 'threat', 'insult' and 'identity hate'. Because the other datasets we examine classify differing but related categories, it was necessary to combine these into one 'offensive' category to make comparisons across datasets possible (a common methodological decontextualization which elides available difference even at the level of the 'clean' dataset). 10.2% of the resulting dataset had an 'offensive' label. We split the data into training (150,571 observations), validation (6,000 observations) and holdout sets (3,000 observations).

The TRAC1 shared task dataset contains 15,000 stand-alone Facebook posts and comments in both Hindi and English unicode, each paired with human-rated multi-class labels, distinguishing "Overtly Aggressive", "Covertly Aggressive" and "Not Aggressive". There are separate English and Hindi subsets, and we used the English portion, which still contains significant amounts of Hindi-English code-switching (Verma, 1976). Again for comparison, it was necessary to group the first two categories together; in the resulting dataset, 58% of the comments are considered aggressive. We split the dataset into training (11,999 observations) and validation (3,001 observations) sets, and used the provided test set as our holdout set (601 observations).

The StackOverflow dataset is yet another collection of decontextualized comments, some of which are flagged by the users to be "Not Constructive or off topic", "Obsolete", "Other" (not the same as unflagged), "Rude or offensive", or "Too chatty". Notably, however, these flags are *provided by the site's users*; when a comment is flagged as "Rude or offensive", it is reportedly dynamically *removed from the website*, which makes this dataset's semantics different from the previous ones which were—as far as we can tell—labeled *post hoc* by independent raters. Instead, the StackOverflow data is a textual archive of *speech acts about speech acts*, or of *metapragmatic* utterances (Silverstein, 1993). They are traces of in-the-moment judgments that may have acted to spontaneously eliminate the judged utterance from a discourse.

The total number of flagged comments is

---

[2]https://www.kaggle.com/c/jigsaw-toxic-comment-classification-challenge
[3]https://sites.google.com/view/trac1/home
[4]https://sites.google.com/view/alw2018/resources/stackoverflow-dataset

525,085, of which 57,841 are "Rude or offensive" (and thus were dynamically removed as per the above). In addition, there are 15 million comments that are not flagged to be undesirable in any way. We joined a sample of 1 million of the unflagged comments and the flagged comments, but considered only the flag "Rude or offensive" (the rest are grouped with unflagged). We used this dataset, which has 3.8% comments flagged as "Rude or offensive", for training and testing. We split this dataset into training (1,516,085), validation (6,000) and holdout (3,000) sets.

Out of the three datasets, both StackOverflow and Kaggle have a significant class imbalance, which is more significant for the StackOverflow set (3.8% offensive) than Kaggle (10.2% offensive).

4.2 Methods and Results

While some earlier research in the classification of abusive language used feature-based classification techniques such as support vector machines (Warner and Hirschberg, 2012), we were interested in evaluating deep learning methods comparable to work such as Founta et al. (2018). We implemented two neural network architectures widely used in text classification: a convolutional neural network (CNN) and a recurrent neural network using Bidirectional Gated Recurrent Units (RNN Bi-GRU).

CNN Model Convolutional neural networks (CNNs), originally popularized in the context of computer vision for recognition tasks (Le Cun et al., 1990), can be applied to sequences of word embeddings in a similar manner to how they are applied to bitmap images, and have been shown to perform well in some abusive language detection tasks (Park and Fung, 2017). Although CNNs are unlikely to capture longer-term sequential relations in the manner of the recurrent neural networks discussed below, they can plausibly capture local patterns of features, and offensive speech can often be detected by local features such as swear words/phrases and racial slurs.

We implemented a vanilla CNN using Keras (Chollet et al., 2015). The input is tokenized into words, and converted into 300-dimensional word embedding vectors using 1 million word vectors trained on Wikipedia using the Fasttext classifier (Joulin et al., 2016).[5] We set a maximum length

---

[5]https://fasttext.cc/docs/en/english-vectors.html

of 100 tokens per input, and a vocabulary size of 30,000. The input layer is then fed into 2 convolutional layers (of kernel size 1*5) each followed by a max-pooling layer. This is followed by 2 dense layers (dimensions 128 and 64) and finally the output layer. We trained the model using the Adagrad optimizer (Duchi et al., 2011), using a batch size of 512 and 10 maximum epochs with early stopping.

RNN Model Recurrent neural networks are widely used in NLP tasks (e.g. Pavlopoulos et al. (2017)) because they are good at capturing longer-term sequential patterns in text. We used the RNN variant known as Bidirectional GRU (Chung et al., 2014; Cho et al., 2014); GRUs are recurrent units with both an update gate and a reset gate that aim to solve the "vanishing gradient" problem of vanilla RNN units.

We implemented the Bi-GRU model using Keras. The input layer is the same word embedding layer as the CNN model, which is fed into a 80-unit Bi-GRU layer, followed by a pooling layer concatenating features from an average and a max-pooling operation. This is then fed into the final output dense layer. We trained the model using the Adam optimizer (Kingma and Ba, 2014) and a dropout rate of 0.2, using a batch size of 512 and a maximum of 10 epochs with early stopping.

4.3 Results

Model	Offensive		Normal		F_1 (micro)
	Prec	Recall	Prec	Recall	
Kaggle Toxic (327 offensive, 2673 normal)					
CNN	.74	.76	.97	.97	.86
GRU	**.83**	**.76**	.97	.98	.89
TRAC1 Trolling (354 offensive, 247 normal)					
CNN	.77	73	.64	.70	.71
GRU	.75	.85	.73	.59	.73
StackOverflow (114 offensive, 2886 normal)					
CNN	.56	.19	.97	.99	.68
GRU	**.59**	**.22**	.97	.99	.69

Table 1: Results on test sets of three data sources using two architectures. The numbers next to the data sources shows the size of each class in the test set. Hyperparameters were manually tuned using the validation sets. We calculated the micro-averaged F1 score because of the varied class imbalance in the datasets.

Our results show that the two architectures performed similarly, but there were large differences across the three datasets (see Table 1). The Kaggle dataset has the best results in terms of micro-averaged F1 score, with very high precision and recall for the "normal" class and around 0.8 precision and recall for the "offensive" class. The TRAC1 dataset had a lower micro-averaged F1 score, but the performance on the two classes are more balanced than the Kaggle model. The StackOverflow dataset has the lowest micro-averaged F1 and the most unbalanced results between the two classes: high precision and recall for the non-offensive class, low precision and even lower recall (0.2) for the "offensive" class.

We argue that the large differences among the three datasets using the same architectures cannot be explained by differences in class imbalance; both Kaggle and StackOverflow have heavy class imbalance, yet the Kaggle model did much better on the offensive class (results highlighted in bold in Table1). Why, then, did the models perform so poorly on detecting offensive comments on Stack-Overflow?[6] Looking at the model predictions, we found that the predictions given by the GRU and the CNN models are highly correlated (Chi-squared = 1009.9, p < 2.2e-16).[7] The mediocre precision on the "offensive class" is mainly caused by the fact that StackOverflow users don't always flag offensive comments, i.e., most of the false positives (where positive is a classification of 'offensive') should arguably be true positives. There are 23 comments that are predicted to be offensive by both models but don't receive an 'offensive' flag in the data. Out of the 23, two comments are indeed not (overtly or covertly) 'offensive': "`close(f)`-> `f.close()`"; "fuck bro !!! how the fuck didnt i see that , jesus !! thankssssss !!!!!!". Among the rest, most are overtly offensive but not flagged, e.g. "dude can you answer the question or not? if not stop wasting my time"; "teach him instead of being a dick.". A few can be considered offensive in particular contexts or by certain users, e.g. "jesus christ! what're you doing?"; "don't. migrate. crap."; "no shit sherlock". This implies that the models would have had a higher precision if the gold standard was provided by annotators who judge every comment in the dataset. In this case, the pragmatic context of labeling matters.

The even lower recall, on the other hand, reveals a genuine limitation of the models and of the dataset. Again, the two models agree highly. Out of the 355 comments that are flagged as "offensive" by StackOverflow users, the majority (75%) are considered not offensive by both models (i.e. they are false negatives). 22 comments (6%) are identified as offensive by only one model, and only 52 comments (15%) are correctly labeled as offensive by both models. Why is the recall so low? To investigate, we sampled 100 of the false negatives and asked three human raters to determine whether these comments are offensive. Only 11 were considered offensive by at least two out of three raters even though they are flagged as "rude or offensive" by StackOverflow users. Here are some examples of comments flagged as offensive but *not* considered offensive by a majority of raters:

- *please post *code,* not screenshots.*

- *did not get you? where in the query that you have provided should i add this?*

- *the phrase is "want to."*

- *no testing!!!! i would prefer no coding*

- *you sir, deserve an unlimited amount of up-votes for that comment*

While these comments' lexical 'surface' content is unlikely to be considered offensive by our classifier, they can potentially be considered offensive in their pragmatic implicatures (Levinson, 1983), which can only be recovered or enriched given the context of the interaction and/or the broader context of conventions and norms in the StackOverflow forum.

Such context-dependent offensive comments appear to account for the majority of the false negatives in the StackOverflow results; this pattern is much less obvious in the Kaggle results. Unlike the StackOverflow dataset, the Kaggle dataset was constructed by showing annotators stand-alone comments. Therefore, the interactional context of those comments was not overtly considered during the rating, although it is likely that raters would sometimes imagine or "accommodate" context (Tian and Breheny, 2016). An analysis of the false negatives show that while a few comments likely require contextual enrichment (i.e., in the

---

[6]In this section we focus on predictions of offensive comments in the StackOverflow dataset, and compare it with results of Kaggle. Because of the heavy presence of Hindi and English code switching in the TRAC1 data, we did not perform an error analysis for this dataset. For in-depth discussions, please see the TRAC1 proceedings at https://sites.google.com/view/trac1/accepted-papers.

[7]We looked at predictions of both the validation set and the holdout set in order to have more samples to form a better understanding of the models.

referentialist ideology, they are "implicitly" offensive), the majority of the errors are due to unconventional ways of spelling, a known problem already being tackled by previous researchers who convincingly argue for character-level as opposed to word-level approaches (Mehdad and Tetreault, 2016).

To sum up, we saw that neural network models with different architectures (CNN and Bi-GRU) performed similarly and have the potential of reliable abusive/offensive language detection when the offensiveness is signaled and/or classified via expressions in the text-artifact itself (supported by the Kaggle results). However, when the offensiveness is marked in a context-dependent way, current neural network methods perform poorly; this is not necessarily because neural networks cannot be used to model context, but because the available datasets on abusive language detection do not provide this context. This is manifested in the poor performance of neural models on the Stack-Overflow data: the context-dependency of offensiveness results in low recall, and the inconsistency of user-generated flagging results in low precision. Because the flags are provided by users who have seen the entire interaction, many comments are considered offensive in context but not offensive when standing alone. By contrast, Kaggle and TRAC1 are labeled by independent annotators who did not participate or observe the full interaction.

5   Conclusions and Future Directions

In this paper, we have attempted to provide a quantitative justification for a qualitative perspective: namely, that theories of pragmatics (such as the primacy of context in the dynamic construction of meaning (Levinson, 1983)) and of metapragmatics (e.g. the fundamental reflexivity of interactional speech at various semiotic levels (Agha, 2007)) should take on a greater role in the classification of abusive language in NLP research.

Our experiments using common neural network architectures on text classification show promising performance when the offensiveness/ abusiveness is signalled within a single utterance, but give poor performance when the offensiveness require contextual enrichment. This is a limitation of popular abusive language detection tasks. For future work, we would propose to investigate the modeling of not just stand-alone utterances and their labels, but

the affective and interactional dynamics of online communication.

In the case of StackOverflow, we suggest that a serious approach to tackling the problem of abusive language on the site would likely want to take advantage of the site's periodic data dumps, which provide millions of user questions, answers, votes, and favorites (Anderson et al., 2012). However, the dynamic removal of flagged material from the site poses some serious methodological issues, and the question of how to incorporate this vast relational data into neural network classifier architectures is another challenge, which we speculate will involve embeddings of networks of interactions as in Hamilton et al. (2018).

Finally, as a longer-term goal for the study of abusive language in online communities, we believe that it is quite promising that some researchers have implicitly or explicitly moved towards the notion of a *speech community*, in which actors in different social spaces may possess differing norms for appropriate behavior (Saleem et al., 2017). However, we argue that it will ultimately be necessary to attend to those theorists emphasizing so-called *communities of practice* (Holmes and Meyerhoff, 1999), a perspective which brings to the fore the embodiment of communities in *practical action* (of which language is only a part); to consider the role of conflict as well as consensus; to see identity as more than just a static set of categories; and to more seriously take into account the participants' understanding of their own practices (Bucholtz, 1999).

6   Acknowledgments

Many thanks to Ye Tian and Ioannis Douratsos for their assistance and suggestions; thanks also to Ana-Maria Popescu and Gideon Mann for their remarks. We would also like to thank the anonymous reviewers for their comments, critiques, and suggestions. Any opinions, findings, conclusions, or recommendations expressed here are those of the authors and do not necessarily reflect the view of their institutions.

References

Asif Agha. 2007. *Language and Social Relations*, 1 edition edition. Cambridge University Press, Cambridge ; New York.

Ashton Anderson, Daniel Huttenlocher, Jon Kleinberg, and Jure Leskovec. 2012. Discovering Value from Community Activity on Focused Question Answering Sites: A Case Study of Stack Overflow. In *Proceedings of the 18th ACM SIGKDD International Conference on Knowledge Discovery and Data Mining*, KDD '12, pages 850–858, New York, NY, USA. ACM.

J.L. Austin. 1962. *How to Do Things with Words*. Oxford University Press.

Richard Bauman and Charles L. Briggs. 1990. Poetics and Performance as Critical Perspectives on Language and Social Life. *Annual Review of Anthropology*, 19:59–88.

Alexander Brown. 2017a. What is hate speech? Part 1: The Myth of Hate. *Law and Philosophy*, 36(4):419–468.

Alexander Brown. 2017b. What is Hate Speech? Part 2: Family Resemblances. *Law and Philosophy*, 36(5):561–613.

Penelope Brown and Stephen C. Levinson. 1987. *Politeness: Some Universals in Language Usage*. Cambridge University Press.

Mary Bucholtz. 1999. "Why Be Normal?": Language and Identity Practices in a Community of Nerd Girls. *Language in Society*, 28(2):203–223.

Judith Butler. 1997. *Excitable Speech: A Politics of the Performative*. Routledge, New York.

Chaplinsky vs. New Hampshire. 1942. 315 U.S. 568.

Eugene Charniak. 1996. *Statistical Language Learning*. A Bradford Book, Cambridge, Mass.

Kyunghyun Cho, Bart Van Merriënboer, Dzmitry Bahdanau, and Yoshua Bengio. 2014. On the properties of neural machine translation: Encoder-decoder approaches. *arXiv preprint arXiv:1409.1259*.

François Chollet et al. 2015. Keras. https://keras.io.

Junyoung Chung, Caglar Gulcehre, KyungHyun Cho, and Yoshua Bengio. 2014. Empirical evaluation of gated recurrent neural networks on sequence modeling. *arXiv preprint arXiv:1412.3555*.

Jonathan Culpeper. 1996. Towards an anatomy of impoliteness. *Journal of Pragmatics*, 25(3):349–367.

Mary Douglas. 1966. *Purity and Danger: An Analysis of the Concepts of Pollution and Taboo*. Routledge, London.

John Duchi, Elad Hazan, and Yoram Singer. 2011. Adaptive subgradient methods for online learning and stochastic optimization. *Journal of Machine Learning Research*, 12(Jul):2121–2159.

Alessandro Duranti. 1997. *Linguistic Anthropology*. Cambridge University Press, New York.

Antigoni-Maria Founta, Despoina Chatzakou, Nicolas Kourtellis, Jeremy Blackburn, Athena Vakali, and Ilias Leontiadis. 2018. A Unified Deep Learning Architecture for Abuse Detection. *arXiv:1802.00385 [cs]*. ArXiv: 1802.00385.

R. Stuart Geiger. 2017. Beyond opening up the black box: Investigating the role of algorithmic systems in Wikipedian organizational culture. *Big Data & Society*, 4(2):2053951717730735.

Erving Goffman. 1967. *Interaction Ritual: Essays on Face to Face Behaviour*. Penguin, Harmondsworth.

Paul Grice. 1975. Logic and Conversation. In P. Cole and N.L. Morgan, editors, *Syntax and Semantics, vol. 3: Speech Acts*, pages 41–58. Academic Press, New York.

John Gumperz. 1968. The Speech Community. In *International Encyclopedia of the Social Sciences*, pages 381–386. Macmillan, New York.

John J. Gumperz. 1982. *Discourse Strategies*. Cambridge University Press, Cambridge.

William L. Hamilton, Payal Bajaj, Marinka Zitnik, Dan Jurafsky, and Jure Leskovec. 2018. Querying Complex Networks in Vector Space. *arXiv:1806.01445 [cs, stat]*. ArXiv: 1806.01445.

Jane H. Hill. 2008. *The Everyday Language of White Racism*, 1 edition edition. Wiley-Blackwell, Chichester, U.K. ; Malden, MA.

Janet Holmes and Miriam Meyerhoff. 1999. The Community of Practice: Theories and Methodologies in Language and Gender Research. *Language in Society*, 28(2):173–183.

Jennifer Hornsby and Rae Langton. 1998. Free Speech and Illocution. *Legal Theory*, 4(1):21–37.

Armand Joulin, Edouard Grave, Piotr Bojanowski, and Tomas Mikolov. 2016. Bag of Tricks for Efficient Text Classification. *arXiv:1607.01759 [cs]*. ArXiv: 1607.01759.

Diederik P Kingma and Jimmy Ba. 2014. Adam: A method for stochastic optimization. *arXiv preprint arXiv:1412.6980*.

William Labov. 1972. *Sociolinguistic Patterns*. University of Pennsylvania Press, Philadelphia.

Y. Le Cun, B. Boser, J. S. Denker, R. E. Howard, W. Habbard, L. D. Jackel, and D. Henderson. 1990. Advances in Neural Information Processing Systems 2. pages 396–404. Morgan Kaufmann Publishers Inc., San Francisco, CA, USA.

Michael Lempert. 2012. Implicitness. In Christina Bratt Paulston, Scott F. Kiesling, and Elizabeth S. Rangel, editors, *The Handbook of Intercultural Discourse and Communication*. John Wiley & Sons.

Stephen C. Levinson. 1983. *Pragmatics*. Cambridge University Press, Cambridge Cambridgeshire ; New York.

Christopher D. Manning. 2015. Computational Linguistics and Deep Learning. *Computational Linguistics*, 41(4):701–707.

Mari J. Matsuda. 1989. Public Response to Racist Speech: Considering the Victim's Story. *Michigan Law Review*, 87(8):2320–2381.

Yashar Mehdad and Joel Tetreault. 2016. Do Characters Abuse More Than Words? *Proceedings of the 17th Annual Meeting of the Special Interest Group on Discourse and Dialogue*, pages 299–303.

Sara Mills. 2003. *Gender and Politeness*. Cambridge University Press, Cambridge ; New York.

John Copeland Nagle. 2009. The Idea of Pollution. *UC Davis Law Review*, 43(1):1–78.

Chikashi Nobata, Joel Tetreault, Achint Thomas, Yashar Mehdad, and Yi Chang. 2016. Abusive Language Detection in Online User Content. In *Proceedings of the 25th International Conference on World Wide Web*, WWW '16, pages 145–153, Republic and Canton of Geneva, Switzerland. International World Wide Web Conferences Steering Committee.

Ji Ho Park and Pascale Fung. 2017. One-step and two-step classification for abusive language detection on twitter. *arXiv preprint arXiv:1706.01206*.

John Pavlopoulos, Prodromos Malakasiotis, and Ion Androutsopoulos. 2017. Deep learning for user comment moderation. *arXiv preprint arXiv:1705.09993*.

Fernando Pereira. 2000. Formal grammar and information theory: together again? *Philosophical Transactions of the Royal Society of London A: Mathematical, Physical and Engineering Sciences*, 358(1769):1239–1253.

Björn Ross, Michael Rist, Guillermo Carbonell, Benjamin Cabrera, Nils Kurowsky, and Michael Wojatzki. 2017. Measuring the Reliability of Hate Speech Annotations: The Case of the European Refugee Crisis. *arXiv:1701.08118 [cs]*. ArXiv: 1701.08118.

Haji Mohammad Saleem, Kelly P. Dillon, Susan Benesch, and Derek Ruths. 2017. A Web of Hate: Tackling Hateful Speech in Online Social Spaces.

Anna Schmidt and Michael Wiegand. 2017. A Survey on Hate Speech Detection using Natural Language Processing. *Proceedings of the Fifth International Workshop on Natural Language Processing for Social Media*, pages 1–10.

Lisa H. Schwartzman. 2002. Hate Speech, Illocution, and Social Context: A Critique of Judith Butler. *Journal of Social Philosophy*, 33(3):421–441.

John Searle. 1969. *Speech Acts: An Essay in the Philosophy of Language*. Cambridge University Press.

Michael Silverstein. 1993. Metapragmatic Discourse and Metapragmatic Function. In John Lucy, editor, *Reflexive Language: Reported Speech and Metapragmatics*, pages 33–58. Cambridge University Press, Cambridge.

Michael Silverstein. 1996. Encountering Language and Languages of Encounter in North American Ethnohistory. *Journal of Linguistic Anthropology*, 6(2):126–144.

Caroline Sinders and Freddy Martinez. 2018. Online Monitoring of the Alt-Right. The Circle of HOPE, New York City, 27th July 2018.

Ellen Spertus. 1997. Smokey: Automatic Recognition of Hostile Messages. In *Proceedings of the Fourteenth National Conference on Artificial Intelligence and Ninth Conference on Innovative Applications of Artificial Intelligence*, AAAI'97/IAAI'97, pages 1058–1065, Providence, Rhode Island. AAAI Press.

Ye Tian and Richard Breheny. 2016. Dynamic pragmatic view of negation processing. In *Negation and polarity: Experimental perspectives*, pages 21–43. Springer.

S. K. Verma. 1976. Code-switching: Hindi-English. *Lingua*, 38(2):153–165.

William Warner and Julia Hirschberg. 2012. Detecting Hate Speech on the World Wide Web. In *Proceedings of the Second Workshop on Language in Social Media*, LSM '12, pages 19–26, Stroudsburg, PA, USA. Association for Computational Linguistics.

Zeerak Waseem, Thomas Davidson, Dana Warmsley, and Ingmar Weber. 2017. Understanding abuse: A typology of abusive language detection subtasks. *CoRR*, abs/1705.09899.

Ludwig Wittgenstein. 1953. *Philosophical investigations*. Macmillan Publishing Company.

Kathryn A. Woolard. 1998. Introduction: Language Ideology as a Field of Inquiry. In Bambi B. Schieffelin, Kathryn A. Woolard, and Paul V. Kroskrity, editors, *Language Ideologies: Practice and Theory*, pages 3–32. Oxford University Press, U.S.A., New York.

Kathryn A. Woolard and Bambi B. Schieffelin. 1994. Language Ideology. *Annual Review of Anthropology*, 23(1):55–82.

Ellery Wulczyn, Nithum Thain, and Lucas Dixon. 2016. Ex Machina: Personal Attacks Seen at Scale. *arXiv:1610.08914 [cs]*. ArXiv: 1610.08914.